119185

SO-CAU-086

LIFE Pacific College
Alumni Library
1100 West Covina Blvd.
San Dimas, CA 91773

THE MYSTERIES
OF THE KINGDOM

THE MYSTERIES
OF THE KINGDOM
An Exposition of the Parables

Herman C. Hanko
Professor of New Testament, Theological School
of the Protestant Reformed Churches

REFORMED FREE PUBLISHING ASSOCIATION
Grand Rapids, Michigan

Copyright© 1975 by Herman C. Hanko. All rights reserved. No part of this book may be used or reprinted in any form without permission from the publisher, except in the case of brief quotations used in connection with a critical article or review. For information address: The Reformed Free Publishing Association, Box 2006, Grand Rapids, Michigan 49501. Distributed to the book trade by Kregel Publications.

Library of Congress Catalog Card No. 75-13930
ISBN 0-916206-00-9

Printed in the United States of America

L.I.F.E. College Library
1100 Glendale Blvd.
Los Angeles, Calif. 90026

TABLE OF CONTENTS

Preface vii
1. "Why . . . Parables?" 1
2. The Parable of the Different Soils 13
3. The Antithesis in the Church 25
4. The Growth of the Kingdom 35
5. The Worth of the Kingdom 45
6. The Gathering of the Kingdom 55
7. The Evidence of Forgiveness 65
8. Loving as Neighbor 73
9. The Certainty of Prayer's Answer 83
10. What Life Consists In 93
11. The Sovereign Purpose of God's Forbearance 103
12. The Exaltation of the Humble 115
13. That My House May Be Full 127
14. The Seeking Shepherd 137
15. The Returning Sinner 147
16. God's Readiness to Receive His Wayward Children 157
17. The Church's Joy in the Sinner's Repentance 167
18. Making Friends of Unrighteous Mammon 175
19. "Son, Remember . . ." 185
20. The Sufficiency of the Gospel 193
21. An Incentive Not to Faint 201
22. Self-Righteousness and Its Condemnation 211
23. The Reward of Sovereign Grace 221
24. Our Calling While the Lord Tarries 233
25. The Exaltation of the Cornerstone 245
26. The Victory of the Gospel 255
27. The Wedding Robe of Righteousness 265
28. Watching unto Christ's Coming 275
29. Faithful Labor in the Kingdom 285
30. The Final Judgment 295

022613

L.I.F.E. College Library
1100 Glendale Blvd.
Los Angeles, Calif. 90026

062013

TABLE OF CONTENTS

Preface

I first was attracted to the parables of our Lord while preaching a series of sermons on them in the congregation of Hope Protestant Reformed Church. Since that time this interest has continued to grow. There were additional opportunities to restudy them in connection with various society meetings; there were other occasions to ponder their truths in Seminary.

What never ceased to be a reason for interest in them was their obvious simplicity on the one hand, and their amazing profundity on the other. They were meant to be simple because, as the Lord Himself explained, they were used by Christ as a method of instruction in order to make the mysteries of the kingdom as clear as possible. In this respect they accomplished their purpose, for even Jesus' enemies who heard many of them and against whom many of them were spoken, never failed to understand the point Jesus was making. But their profundity remains a magnet drawing the student of Scripture back to them again and again to search their depths of meaning. The more one studies them, the more the conviction grows that there remain depths of truths still uncovered.

But there are other reasons why the parables remain attractive. For one thing, they all discuss the kingdom of heaven. A great deal has been written about the kingdom in recent years, and a large number of scholarly books concerning the kingdom have been published. Yet rarely do those who discuss the kingdom pay close attention to the parables. This is strange, for in them Jesus talks about the mysteries of the kingdom in the clearest possible way. A study of the parables is essential to an understanding of the kingdom, and such a study will reveal much of what Scripture teaches and thus guard against erroneous ideas.

Further, the attractiveness of the parables is enhanced by their practical character. They do not deal abstractly with "a theology of the kingdom," but treat the whole question of the kingdom from the very practical viewpoint of the calling of the citizens of the kingdom.

A study of the parables will therefore yield an abundance of fruit in the lives of those citizens of the kingdom whose eyes have been opened to see its mysteries and whose ears have been opened to hear its truths.

It is our prayer that this study may, under the blessing of God, inspire others to pursue the knowledge of the mysteries of the kingdom beyond what we have said, and to call many to faithful lives in the kingdom until our King returns.

1

"Why . . . Parables?"

And the disciples came, and said unto him, Why speakest thou unto them in parables?

He answered and said unto them, Because it is given unto you to know the mysteries of the kingdom of heaven, but to them it is not given.

For whosoever hath, to him shall be given, and he shall have more abundance: but whosoever hath not, from him shall be taken away even that he hath.

Therefore speak I to them in parables: because they seeing see not; and hearing they hear not, neither do they understand.

And in them is fulfilled the prophecy of Esaias, which saith, By hearing ye shall hear, and shall not understand; and seeing ye shall see, and shall not perceive:

For this people's heart is waxed gross, and their ears are dull of hearing, and their eyes they have closed; lest at any time they should see with their eyes, and hear with their ears, and should understand with their heart, and should be converted, and I should heal them.

But blessed are your eyes, for they see: and your ears, for they hear.

For verily I say unto you, That many prophets and righteous men have desired to see those things which ye see, and have not seen them; and to hear those things which ye hear, and have not heard them.

—Matthew 13:10-17

The Setting

It was during the time when Jesus was making His second circuit of Galilee that He began to make use of parables as a method of instruction. This, in itself, is of significance. It had not been too long before this time that Jesus' Galilean ministry had come to a climax at the time of the feeding of the five thousand. Jesus had fed a large multitude of people in the wilderness with but a few loaves and fishes. The response of the people was instantaneous. They wanted to make Jesus their king and were prepared to do this by force if necessary. Their reasons were obvious. They saw in Jesus an earthly king who would be able to provide them with an abundance of material things. They wanted bread, but for their stomachs. When Jesus made it clear that He would never be an earthly king, that He Himself was the Bread of Life, they all forsook Him and followed Him no more. They wanted nothing of such a king (see John 6).

Thus this miracle had brought Jesus' Galilean ministry to a climax, and soon that work would be over.

This must not be construed in any way as a failure on the part of the Lord to accomplish the work for which He was sent. We read in Matthew 11 that Jesus pronounced most solemn curses upon the inhabitants of Chorazin, Bethsaida, and Capernaum for their rejection of Christ. But at the same time Jesus prayed: "I thank thee, O Father, Lord of heaven and earth, because thou hast hid these things from the wise and prudent, and hast revealed them unto babes. Even so, Father: for so it seemed good in thy sight. All things are delivered unto me of my Father: and no man knoweth the Son, but the Father; neither knoweth any man the Father, save the Son, and he to whomsoever the Son will reveal him" (vv. 25-27).

It is in this situation that the Lord turned to parables as a method of instruction. The inhabitants of Galilee had essentially forsaken Him and rejected Him as their Messiah. His work there must now be brought to its conclusion. Parables are the means which the Lord uses to bring His work to an end.

This purpose is specifically defined in the text quoted at the beginning of this chapter. The scene is described in verses 1 and 2. Jesus left the house where He was staying and went to the shore of the beautiful Sea of Galilee. There large multitudes came together so that He went into a ship to address the multitudes from this podium. As He began His instruction, He turned to parables as a means to teach them. Apparently the disciples were somewhat puzzled by this method of instruction, and at the first available opportunity they quizzed Him on this matter: "Why speakest thou unto them in parables?" The answer which Jesus gives explains in detail His purpose in making use of this method of instruction.

The Nature of a Parable

Before we turn specifically to a discussion of these verses we should ask the question: What precisely is a parable?

I recall clearly the days in grade school when our teacher offered to us a definition of a parable. The definition was not original with her; it was a generally accepted definition: "An earthly story with a heavenly meaning." The idea of this definition was, no doubt, that a parable is a tale of some sort, fictitious in the sense that it was not a narration of an actual happening which was being reported— although the event described could be common enough; and it was used in a way that gave it a spiritual sense.

There is an element of truth in this definition. But there are several deficiencies. In the first place, a parable is not always a story. Jesus only briefly calls attention a little later in Matthew 13 to the fact that the kingdom of heaven is like a dragnet, or a pearl of great price. These brief comparisons can hardly be called stories. In the second place, the definition does not really touch upon the basic character of a parable. A parable is not simply an earthly story with a heavenly meaning; rather, a parable implies a profound connection between the things which belong to this earthly creation and the things which belong to the mysteries of the kingdom of heaven. The former can be used to illustrate and make clear the latter because of this connection.

It is for this reason that a parable must be distinguished from other types of comparisons in Scripture. A parable is not a fable. A fable is a story with a kind of moral to it, and is usually an example of some purely earthly insight into some human relationship. Nor is a parable an allegory. An allegory is a lengthened metaphor or an extended comparison between two things with some obvious similarities. Fables are rare in Scripture. Allegories are nonexistent. The "allegory" which Paul uses in Galatians 4:21-27 is not strictly speaking an allegory in the common sense of that term.

There are also various similes and metaphors which are used frequently in both the Old Testament and the New. These too must be distinguished from parables. They are figures of speech which enrich and enliven the language of Scripture and make clearer various ideas which Scripture teaches. In this class also belong the more extended metaphors that Jesus often uses to describe Himself and His work in relation to His people. Jesus speaks of Himself as the Bread of Life, the Water of Life, the Vine, the Good Shepherd, and so forth. Although these figures of speech come very close to parables, they must be distinguished from parables. While they probably find their basis in a common truth, they are not in the strictest sense of the word parables.

A parable is intended to illustrate and describe a particular truth. It is a method of instruction. It is used by Jesus to illustrate and clarify heavenly realities—particular truths concerning the kingdom of heaven. These illustrations are taken from this earthly creation: from the world of our experience, from history and events, from facts and truths in the world about us. By means of these earthly illustrations, the things of the kingdom of heaven are made clear.

If you give any thought to this, the question immediately arises: How is it possible to illustrate heavenly truths by means of earthly examples? Is not the heavenly spiritual, and thus essentially different from the earthly—from the world of our daily experience? How then can spiritual realities be explained by means of material and earthly illustrations?

The answer to this question lies in the nature of the relation between the heavenly and the earthly. In the heart and mind of God the heavenly is always first. In God's purpose and will to glorify Himself, He determined to realize His glory through the heavenly and spiritual creation. This creation is the end of all things. It shall be realized when Christ comes again to make all things new in the new heavens and the new earth.

Thus, when God created the earthly, He created it as a figure and pattern of the heavenly. Although there is an essential difference between the heavenly and earthly creations, there is, nevertheless, in this earthly a reflection of the heavenly creation. This was already true in Paradise; for when God formed the worlds, He did so with a view to the realization of His full purpose in Christ in the redemption of all things. When God placed our first parents in the beautiful garden of Eden, this was already patterned after the tabernacle and the temple. The country of Eden was comparable to the Outer Court; the garden itself in the east of Eden corresponded to the Holy Place; and the tree of life where God met with Adam in the cool of the day was the pattern of the Most Holy Place where God dwelt in the midst of His people. This temple in turn was the type of the perfect fellowship of God and His people in Christ, for Christ is the true temple of God.

Adam, of course, could not see that as long as he stood in a state of rectitude. But after the Fall this becomes clear. The present creation was formed through the Word of God, the same Word of God which became flesh and dwelt among us. And if the earthly world was created by this Word of God, it stands to reason that this pattern of the heavenly in the earthly creation was easily discernible to the Lord. Walking through the midst of His own world, He could see parables on every hand. He could see heavenly and spiritual truths portrayed in the sower who went out to sow his seed, in the barren fig tree, in the dragnet being pulled through the sea in quest of fish. He called attention to the fact that events such as marriage and death, the hiring and paying of laborers, and the wedding feast of a king's son were all so many pictures of spiritual truths.

Thus parables are not simply isolated illustrations which Jesus invents on the spur of the moment to make clear some point that is difficult to understand. "All these things," Jesus says in Mark, "are done [better: "happen, take place,"] in parables."

Already this earthly bears the image of the heavenly. Presently it will be changed into the heavenly. To the child of God—the one who has ears to hear and eyes to see—the creation speaks in an eloquent language of the spiritual and heavenly truths which he loves and confesses.

The General Purpose of Parables

Thus, in general, the purpose of parables is revelation: they are intended to reveal the mysteries of the kingdom of heaven. Repeatedly Jesus tells us that it is the kingdom of heaven which is like all these things taking place about us. God is revealing the kingdom of heaven to us. He is making known the kingdom of heaven.

We do not intend at this point to enter into a lengthy discussion of the idea and character of the kingdom of heaven. It will have to be sufficient to point out a few essential truths. The kingdom of heaven is a royal commonwealth in which God is the sovereign King and His elect people are the subjects. As subjects of this kingdom, the people of God bow in absolute submission to their heavenly and eternal King, acknowledge Him as sovereign in their lives, find their delight in doing His will, and make their lives conformable to His glory. However, this commonwealth is of a kind in which God and His people also dwell together in covenant fellowship, for God is the Friend of His people and they are His friend-servants.

This kingdom is established in the blood of the cross of Christ, for it is a kingdom in which the righteousness of the cross is the chief characteristic. It is a kingdom with riches that, while they are heavenly and spiritual, are wealth beyond compare; for they are the treasures of everlasting salvation in Christ in the new heavens and the new earth. It is a kingdom established, therefore, over against the kingdom of darkness which Satan sought to establish through the temptation of our first parents. And the elect enter this kingdom only by a work of sovereign and irresistible grace whereby they are called efficaciously out of the kingdom of darkness into the kingdom of God's dear Son.

Of this kingdom there was a picture and type in the Old Dispensational commonwealth of Israel with its throne of David, its temple, its sacrifices, and its feasts. It is a kingdom realized in the blood of the cross of Calvary and through the resurrection and exaltation of Christ into heaven. It is accomplished through the outpouring of the Spirit on Pentecost, but awaits its full perfection in the day of the return of Christ when the kingdoms of this world become the kingdom of our God and of His Christ.

This kingdom is emphatically a kingdom of heaven. Often this is denied today. In one way or another, it is maintained that this kingdom has some kind of earthly realization. Some say that the old kingdom of David will be restored on earthly Mount Zion. Others speak of the hope that this world, through political, economic, and moral development will gradually develop into the kingdom of Christ. But these are all mistakes. The kingdom is *of heaven*. Its origin is heavenly; it is spiritual and heavenly in character; its final realization will be in the glory of heaven. The kingdom is not here now nor ever will be. You cannot find it anywhere. It comes not by observation.

There is indeed a certain manifestation of the kingdom of heaven in this world. This is because God's people are made citizens of the kingdom of heaven while they live here below. Christ sets up His throne within their hearts. And they must walk as citizens of the kingdom of heaven even while they are in the world. Hence, in the walk of the people of God there is a certain earthly manifestation of this heavenly and spiritual kingdom.

It is because the kingdom of heaven is spiritual that Christ speaks of the *mysteries* of the kingdom. Now "mystery" does not mean here what we commonly think of by that term. It is not something in-explicable, a problem difficult to solve, a situation which defies analysis and comprehension. This is never what Scripture means by "mystery." Scripture uses the term to refer to those things of God's purpose and counsel which are hidden. By virtue of the fact that the kingdom of heaven is spiritual, the things of the kingdom are hidden. That is, these things are not apparent to our earthly and natural senses. They are not the object of empirical observation. They cannot be investigated through the use of scientific tools. They are not even the objects of our perception. They are hidden in the mind and heart of God, in His counsel and will, and in the heaven where He dwells.

Besides, these mysteries are the wonders of sovereign grace. They are the truths which God has determined to reveal, the works which He has purposed to perform on behalf of the salvation of His people in Christ. They are wonderful works, far too wonderful for any man to invent them. They surpass our imagination and stagger our comprehension. They are beyond anything man could ever con-ceive. They are too wonderful even to be comprehended after we know about them.

Hence, these mysteries can only be known through revelation. Man has not the power or ability to uncover these mysteries. They must be made known by God Himself. God must reveal them and speak of them. He must reveal them, however, in such a way that we, with earthly perception, can understand and know them. He must reveal them so that we, who can form no conception of the spiritual, can nevertheless know the things of the kingdom which remain hidden mysteries until it pleases the Most High to make them known. Thus the kingdom of heaven is itself a mystery—a part of the whole of the mystery of God. All the realities of this kingdom are so many mysteries. The cross by which the kingdom of heaven is established is a mystery, as well as Christ's birth and resurrection. The work of regeneration and conversion whereby God brings His people through the door of the kingdom is also such "a supernatural work, most powerful, and at the same time most delightful, astonish-ing, mysterious, and ineffable" (Canons, III & IV, 12). But no less when this kingdom finally comes in power and glory will it come mysteriously and wondrously out of heaven.

Yet to see and know these mysteries requires revelation. And this revelation has both an objective and subjective aspect to it. God must make these mysteries objectively known through His Word. But He must also make these mysteries subjectively known. That is, He must give the spiritual and subjective power whereby it is possible to know the mysteries of the kingdom of heaven.

It is this which Jesus speaks of particularly.

The Negative Purpose of Parables

It is evident from the text that in the revelation of the mysteries of the kingdom, God is sovereign. God sovereignly reveals these mysteries to whom He will and He sovereignly hides them from whom He will. This is the point which Jesus so forcibly makes and which is given as the reason why Jesus speaks in parables.

When Jesus, by the shore of the beautiful Sea of Galilee, spoke the parable of the sower who went forth to sow, it was immediately evident to the disciples that Jesus was not simply telling a little story for purposes of entertainment. They sensed immediately that there must be more to the whole matter than this. But the purpose Jesus had in mind escaped them. And so they came to the Lord with the question: "Why speakest thou unto them in parables?"

If we carefully investigate the reasons which Jesus Himself gives, then we learn that the first reason is to make the truths of the kingdom of heaven as clear as possible for the unbelieving and carnal element in His audience. There were many in the number of those who were listening (as there were many in the nation of Israel) who were wicked and apostate Israelites who rejected the Messiah. But Jesus does not simply refer to them with respect to their terrible sin of rejecting Christ; He looks also behind this rejection to the Father's purpose and counsel. And He looks at the counsel of His Father as He is called to carry that counsel out in His earthly ministry.

It might seem as if Jesus intends to put man first when we read in Matthew: "Therefore speak I to them in parables, *because* they seeing see not; and hearing they hear not, neither do they understand." But there is more to the matter than this. If we consult the similar passage in Mark we read: "And he said unto them, Unto you it is given to know the mystery of the kingdom of God: but unto them that are without, all these things are done in parables: That [we must read here: "In order that," or, "for the purpose that"] seeing they may see, and not perceive; and hearing they may hear, and not understand; lest at any time they should be converted, and their sins should be forgiven them." This is also the thrust of the passage in Isaiah from which the Lord quotes. In Isaiah 6 the Lord had said: "Whom shall I send, and who will go for us? Then said I, Here am I; send me." Upon this answer of Isaiah, the Lord gives Isaiah his commission: "Go, and tell this people, Hear ye indeed, but understand not; and see ye indeed, but perceive not. Make the heart of this people fat, and make their ears heavy, and shut their eyes; lest they see with their eyes, and hear with their ears, and understand with their heart, and convert, and be healed. Then said I, Lord, how long? And he answered, Until the cities be wasted. . . ." (vv. 8-11).

Obviously, therefore, Christ is inquiring into the will of God Who is always sovereign and always first. And the question is not simply why Jesus speaks in parables to people, but why Jesus speaks in parables in the name of His Father and to accomplish God's purpose.

The wicked and unbelieving in Israel must see as clearly as possible the mysteries of the kingdom of heaven. They must not only see and hear all that Jesus has to say about these mysteries, but they must see very clearly so that there can be no mistake about the meaning. In this way the mysteries of the kingdom of heaven will be so clearly set forth that there is never any possibility of misunderstanding.

This is accomplished through parables. Those who maintain that the parables of Jesus give the impression of being enigmatic statements, fail completely to understand Jesus' words and the purpose for parables. Jesus is not deliberately choosing a strange and foreign method of instruction which enables Him to speak in riddles so that only those who are given some special kind of ability to penetrate these riddles understand what He is saying. Jesus does not purposely hide the mysteries of the kingdom from His audience by enigmatic sayings so that He can preserve the true mysteries for an elite inner circle who possess some secret key to knowledge. Quite the contrary is true. The parables make clear the mysteries of the kingdom. They make these mysteries so clear that there is no possibility of misunderstanding. This is true on the one hand because they illustrate those mysteries by things from this world which every man can see and know and understand. These truths are not communicated in some heavenly language incapable of being understood by men. They are revealed through the means of earthly and sometimes very homely illustrations. The earthly is a pattern of the heavenly. Jesus points this out.

In the second place, this instruction through parables is as clear as possible because these illustrations are constantly before the eyes of men. They cannot hear these parables without remembering them. They stick in the mind. They hear Jesus point out that a sower sowing his seed is a picture of some aspect of the kingdom; and from henceforth, every time they see such a sower they will be reminded of the particular truth which is illustrated. It is there all the time, concretely and vividly displayed before their minds. There is no escape from it.

That this was true is evident from the fact that oftentimes the wicked Pharisees understood the meaning of Jesus' parables even before the disciples did. While the Twelve were debating in their minds what the Lord could mean, the Pharisees had already grasped the truth Jesus was illustrating. (For an example of this, see Luke 16:14, 15.)

But we have not yet answered the question completely. Why must these mysteries of the kingdom be so clearly set forth so that even the ungodly can understand them?

The answer lies in the first place in the fact that the wicked must never be able to plead ignorance when they are condemned. This was true of the Jews in Galilee in Jesus' day. They had heard the beautiful Sermon on the Mount. They had seen many wonderful signs and listened carefully to Jesus' preaching. They had seen with their own eyes the miracle of the loaves. But they had clearly shown they did not want a Messiah Who would save from sin. And so they left Him to follow Him no more. But now, before the Lord leaves Galilee, He must teach yet in parables so that they will understand clearly the things of the kingdom. For, when they are condemned for their rejection of Christ, they must never be able to say, "The mysteries of the kingdom of heaven, being spiritual, were beyond our comprehension. We had no opportunity to know really what they meant." For if this was their plea, they could no doubt escape their judgment. But now, because Jesus taught in parables, this excuse becomes impossible. They will be judged righteously when they are condemned, and God will be justified.

But there is more. Just exactly in the way of making the mysteries of the kingdom clear, the Lord also sovereignly hardens the wicked in their sin. The sovereign decree of reprobation is sovereignly accomplished in the way of sin and greater sin. And the sovereign hardening of the sinner is brought about through these parables. This is always the effect of the gospel, and it was no less true of the parables of the Lord.

This is the force of the emphatic statement in Mark: "But unto them that are without, all these things are done in parables: [in order] that seeing they may see, and not perceive; and hearing they may hear and not understand." This is the force of the prophecy of Isaiah. Isaiah must preach until Judah is hardened. This is God's will and this purpose must be accomplished. And this the Lord Himself emphasizes. Jesus tells His disciples that *it is given* to them to know the mysteries of the kingdom of heaven, but to the others *it is not given*. Hearing indeed they hear, but do not understand; and seeing indeed they see, but do not perceive. The wicked are not given the eyes and ears of faith to receive the gospel.

That parables accomplish this is not difficult to see. The wicked heart of man always reacts to the truth of the kingdom of heaven in anger and hatred. And the more clearly that truth is revealed, the more is his bitter hatred revealed. As that Word of God becomes more evident, the reaction of the wicked against it becomes stronger and stronger. When Christ was on earth, the Jews increased in hatred and malice until they could not tolerate His presence anymore. And finally they nailed Him to the cross. But in this way God causes all the horror of the sinful heart of man to be completely exposed so that sin may appear as terrible as it really is. It is as a man with very weak eyes who lives in a darkened room for many years. If he should suddenly come out into the brilliant light of day and look up into the sun, he would be immediately struck blind. So also do the wicked who have a natural perception of the truth become spiritually blinded as they look into the brilliant sunlight of the truth of God.

This is always true of God's Word. Wherever that truth is proclaimed through the preaching of the gospel, there is this negative effect. Christ thanked His Father that God had hidden these things from the wise and prudent. Paul wrote to the Corinthians that the preaching of Christ crucified was always a stumbling block to the Jews and foolishness to the Greeks (I Cor. 1:23). And Paul writes in II Corinthians 2:15, 16: "For we are unto God a sweet savour of Christ, in them that are saved, and in them that perish: To the one we are the savour of death unto death; and to the other the savour of life unto life. And who is sufficient for these things?"

It is not superfluous to remind those who preach the gospel about this fundamental truth. Although they may be called of God to be ministers of the gospel, they must never forget that on the pulpit they are really nothing. It is not what they do that is important —other than the fact that they are solemnly called to preach the whole of the Scriptures. God's purpose must be accomplished and His cause justified. Besides, although it is the heartbreaking experience of all those who preach to see many leave the truth, this is to be expected, for this is the purpose of the gospel. The gospel saves, but it also hardens. It brings to glory, but it also condemns. It is the Rock of Ages, but it is also a stone of stumbling. And when this takes place the true servant of God stands aside that the purpose of God may be accomplished.

The Positive Fruit of Parables

Although Jesus does not say very much about the positive fruit of parables, He nevertheless alludes to it in several different ways. In verse 11 Jesus says: "Because it is given unto you to know the mysteries of the kingdom of heaven." In verse 12 He refers to this same positive fruit when He says: "For whosoever hath, to him shall be given, and he shall have more abundance." And in verse 16 we read: "But blessed are your eyes, for they see: and your ears, for they hear."

The emplasis again quite obviously falls upon the sovereign work of God. To His people God gives the Spirit of Christ. That Spirit banishes the power of sin, calls the Saints irresistibly out of darkness into light, gives them eyes to see and ears to hear the mysteries of the kingdom. The blindness of sin is destroyed and the dreadful power of rebellion against God and hatred of His Word is conquered by the grace of the Spirit. And so they are able to receive the mysteries of the kingdom of heaven.

Although it is true that these mysteries are spiritual and heavenly, and although it is true that we cannot with our natural senses perceive them, they are nevertheless given to us. Paul writes of this in that beautiful passage in I Corinthians 2:7-16: "But we speak the wisdom of God in a mystery, even the hidden wisdom, which God ordained before the world unto our glory: Which none of the princes of this world knew: for had they known it, they would not have crucified the Lord of glory. But as it is written, Eye hath not seen, nor ear heard, neither have entered into the heart of man, the things which God hath prepared for them that love him. But God hath revealed them unto us by his Spirit: for the Spirit searcheth all things, yea, the deep things of God. For what man knoweth the things of a man, save the spirit of man which is in him? even so the things of God knoweth no man, but the Spirit of God. Now we have received, not the spirit of the world, but the spirit which is of God; that we might know the things that are freely given to us of God. Which things also we speak, not in the words which man's wisdom teacheth, but which the Holy Ghost teacheth; comparing spiritual things with spiritual. But the natural man receiveth not the things of the Spirit of God: for they are foolishness unto him: neither can he know them, because they are spiritually discerned. But he that is spiritual judgeth all things, yet he himself is judged of no man. For who hath known the mind of the Lord, that he may instruct him? But we have the mind of Christ."

This is the wonder of revelation. God speaks to us of the incomparable mystery of heaven. And He speaks in a way that we can understand through the enlightening of the Spirit. But to assist us in the feebleness of our understanding the Lord gives us parables. The earthly is the pattern of the heavenly. There is a reflection of the heavenly all about us. It is true that we do not see as clearly as some day we shall see, for we see through a mirror darkly. Some day we shall see face to face. Nevertheless, we see and know enough to catch the breathtaking beauty and glory of the heavenly treasures which are for us through the cross of Jesus Christ. The parables of our Lord illustrate these truths to us. And we have only to gaze about us in the world of our God to see the truth of the kingdom demonstrated before our eyes.

The Old Dispensational saints were not able to see these things. There were many prophets and righteous men who longed to see what we see. But all they could see were the types and shadows—the pictures on the wall. They saw the figures, the dim outlines of these truths. And they longed to see more. They died in faith, not having received the promises, but having seen them afar off. They were persuaded of them, however, and confessed that they were pilgrims and strangers in the earth. But we see these things in the light of the gospel. We see them through the Spirit of our exalted Lord. We see them in all their clarity and beauty.

And this is all a gift of grace, and of grace alone.

2

The Parable of the Different Soils

Behold, a sower went forth to sow;
And when he sowed, some seeds fell by the way side, and the fowls
came and devoured them up:
Some fell upon stony places, where they had not much earth: and
forthwith they sprung up, because they had no deepness of earth:
And when the sun was up, they were scorched; and because they had
no root, they withered away.
And some fell among thorns; and the thorns sprung up, and choked
them:
But other fell into good ground, and brought forth fruit, some an
hundredfold, some sixtyfold, some thirtyfold.
Who hath ears to hear, let him hear.
Hear ye therefore the parable of the sower.
When any one heareth the word of the kingdom, and understandeth it
not, then cometh the wicked one, and catcheth away that which was
sown in his heart. This is he which received seed by the way side.
But he that received the seed into stony places, the same is he that
heareth the word, and anon with joy receiveth it;
Yet hath he not root in himself, but dureth for a while: for when
tribulation or persecution ariseth because of the word, by and by he is
offended.
He also that received seed among the thorns is he that heareth the
word; and the care of this world, and the deceitfulness of riches, choke
the word, and he becometh unfruitful.
But he that received seed into the good ground is he that heareth the
word, and understandeth it; which also beareth fruit, and bringeth
forth, some an hundredfold, some sixty, some thirty.

—Matthew 13:3-9, 18-23

This is one of two parables for which Jesus Himself gives the
interpretation. There is, no doubt, good reason for this. By giving
the interpretation of two of the first parables He taught, the Lord
lays down for us the principles of interpretation we must follow as
we seek to understand, by means of His parables, the mysteries of
the kingdom of heaven. It is true that the Lord does not give these
principles of interpretation in the way that they might be found in a
book on "Hermeneutics"; rather, He gives us these principles by
interpreting the parable for us—and for His disciples. But inherent
in that interpretation are to be found the principles we must follow.

It is evident, then, that one important principle (which dominates all the others) is to ascertain from the parable the specific "mystery" of the kingdom which Jesus is elucidating. It is clear that in the parable we are now discussing this main point is: the reaction to the preaching of the Word in the hearts and lives of those who hear.

Once this main point of the parable is determined, the rest follows rather easily. It is evident, on the one hand, that not every detail of the parable must be pressed so far that some particular meaning is found in it. Many of these details are only a part of the story itself. If one persists in pressing them to some final meaning, one can conceivably come up with some very strange interpretations which are foreign to and detract from the main point the Lord is making. Hence, on the other hand, only those details which relate to and make clear the main point are to be given a place in the interpretation of the parable. This is precisely what the Lord Himself does.

If we examine closely our Lord's interpretation of the parable of the different soils, we discover that He speaks of the preaching of the Word and the reaction to that preaching on the part of those who hear. There are really only two possible reactions: those who hear either bear fruit in their lives, or they do not. And whether they do or do not depends on the condition of their hearts. Hence, there are really only two kinds of soil: there is bad soil and there is good soil. But each of these two kinds of soil is divided into three "sub-kinds." The bad soil is divided into hard soil, rocky soil, and weedy soil. The good soil, on the other hand is divided into soil which bears fruit a hundredfold, sixtyfold, and thirtyfold.

While, generally speaking, it is true that the bad soil represents those hearers who are not regenerated by the Spirit of Christ, and the good soil represents those hearers whose hearts have been prepared by the sovereign operations of the Holy Spirit, nevertheless, the people of God, though regenerated and converted, sometimes reveal the marks of what we may call "bad-soil hearers." This is because of the fact that they still manifest in their lives the works of darkness.

All this makes this parable a very practical one. The admonition of the Lord at the end of this parable is certainly important: "He who hath ears, let him hear."

If we contrast, therefore, the "bad-soil hearers" with the "good-soil hearers" we may best get at the meaning of the parable by discussing, in turn, "Hard- and Soft-Soil Hearers," "Shallow- and Deep-Soil Hearers," and "Thorny- and Clean-Soil Hearers."

The Sower, The Seed, The Field

The picture which the parable brings to mind is one of the sowing of seed as it took place in the days when the Lord was on earth. The farms of the Hebrews were plotted out in relatively small fields, each of which was surrounded by a hard path. This hard path was used to bring the cultivating tools into the field and for walking from one field to the other to do the necessary work. When, in the fall of the year, after the early rains, the soil had been prepared for sowing, the farmer tied an open pouch to his belt which he filled with seed. Walking over his cultivated land, he dipped his hand into the pouch and took out a handful of seed which was then broadcast over the soil.

Jesus Himself tells us that the seed is the Word of God. The seed represents, however, the Word of God as that Word is preached in the gospel and by the Church in her ordained ministry. This figure is not at all uncommon in Scripture. Peter writes in I Peter 1:23-25: "Being born again, not of corruptible seed, but of incorruptible, by the word of God, which liveth and abideth forever. For all flesh is as grass, and all the glory of man as the flower of grass. The grass withereth, and the flower thereof falleth away: But the word of the Lord endureth for ever. And this is the word which by the gospel is preached unto you."

This seed of the Word of God is a living seed. All seed has within it the principle of life. Yet that very seed will not come to life and grow and bring forth fruit until it is planted in soil which is prepared for it. So it is with the Word of God. That Word of God is living and powerful. It is such because it is the Word of God Himself which He speaks. The fact that this Word is brought by the Church through the means of her ordained ministry does not alter this essential truth.

This is why the Sower in the parable is Christ. That Word, though preached by men, is proclaimed in the service of Christ and by Christ Himself. That Word of the gospel has no power in itself. It derives its power from the fact that Christ proclaims it through His servants and brings that Word into the hearts of His people through the operation of the Spirit. Jesus, in speaking of this same truth, tells the Pharisees: "But he that entereth in by the door is the shepherd of the sheep. To him the porter openeth; and the sheep hear his voice; and he calleth his own sheep by name, and leadeth them out. And when he putteth forth his own sheep, he goeth before them, and the sheep follow him: for they know his voice" (John 10:2-5). And again: "And other sheep I have, which are not of this fold: them also I must bring, and they shall hear my voice; and there shall be one fold, and one shepherd" (v. 16).

Not only does Jesus Himself preach the Word, but He determines where that Word shall be preached. Even as the farmer determines where his seed shall be sowed, so the Lord determines where the seed of His Word shall be planted. This was true of the apostles when they began the work of the extension of the gospel (cf. e.g., Acts 8:26; 10:19, 20; 16:6-10). This general principle is incorporated into our Confessions in the statement in Canons, II, 5: "This promise . . . ought to be declared and published to all nations, and to all persons promiscuously and without distinction, to whom God out of his good pleasure sends the gospel."

In general, the field is the world. It is in this present world that the gospel is preached. This means, on the one hand, that the field is the world from the viewpoint of the historical manifestation of the kingdom of heaven. For the Word of the gospel is preached in the historical line of the covenant. And we know from Scripture that not all those who are born in the line of the covenant are elect seed; there are Esaus in the covenant as well as Jacobs. But, on the other hand, it means also that the field is the world from the viewpoint of the mission task of the Church. Christ Himself gave the command: "Go ye into all the world and preach the gospel."

Nevertheless, from a more particular point of view, the field is representative of the hearts of those who hear the preaching. Many come under the preaching of the Word. They hear that preaching and know what is being said through the preaching. That seed of the preaching even enters into their hearts. The preaching of the Word is not only for the elect. God wills that the reprobate hear that preaching as well. The Word must be scattered promiscuously.

We know from other parts of Scripture that God always sovereignly accomplishes His purpose through the preaching, for His Word never returns to Him void. But the emphasis in the parable is slightly different. The heart of man is the heart of a rational and moral creature. And as a rational and moral creature, man is responsible to God for all he does. He is also responsible for what he does with the preaching. He must give an account of it. Those who hear the preaching bear a greater responsibility even than those who do not. For it will be more tolerable in the day of judgment for Chorazin and Bethsaida than for Tyre and Sidon.

Nevertheless, the seed of the Word will bear fruit only in those whose hearts have been first prepared by the operations of the Spirit. The farmer cannot expect that the seed which he sows will bring forth fruit if he does not first of all carefully prepare the soil. A dead man who lies in a coffin cannot profit from the preaching of the Word though it be proclaimed to him in the loudest possible voice. No more can a man who is spiritually dead in trespasses and sins hear and understand the Word of the kingdom and bring forth fruit, unless his heart has first been made ready by the Spirit of Christ. That Spirit must first come to dwell within him to call him sovereignly out of darkness into light, to give him ears to hear, to raise him from spiritual death into spiritual life. Only then will the soil of the heart be prepared for the seed. "The natural man receiveth not the things of the Spirit of God: for they are foolishness unto him: neither can he know them, because they are spiritually discerned" (I Cor. 2:14).

On the other hand, we must remind ourselves that also the people of God many times give evidence of being bad-soil hearers. Upon them too rests the responsibility of how they hear the Word of God. In fact, one gets the impression that the words of this parable are addressed by Jesus especially to the people of God. After all, it is to those who already have ears to hear that Jesus says: "Let him hear!"

Hard- and Soft-Soil Hearers

The first class of hearers is described in the parable by means of the seed which fell upon the paths that surround the fields. Since the ground here is hard packed and the seed cannot penetrate the soil, the flocks of birds which followed the sower on his course through the field, swooped down on these seeds and ate them almost as soon as they touched the ground.

In the interpretation of this parable, the Lord describes these hearers in Mark and Luke as those who indeed hear the Word; but Satan comes and takes the Word away from them. Matthew adds that they hear the Word of the kingdom, but they do not understand it.

It is apparent from this, in the first place, that this kind of hearer, without a heart prepared for the Word of the kingdom, is indeed one who hears the preaching. And the idea undoubtedly is that, from a certain natural point of view, he indeed hears what is being said in the preaching. Not only does he hear this with his ears, as something of a drone, but he even knows what is being said.

However, the text adds that he does not understand the preaching. It is doubtful whether this refers to mere intellectual understanding. The fact of the matter is that, inasmuch as these hearers do actually hear, they also understand what is being said from a natural point of view. The trouble is not that the minister speaks in a language unintelligible to them or that he preaches sermons "too deep" for them. In this case, the trouble would lie with the preacher or the preaching; whereas Jesus clearly means to lay upon the hearers the responsibility for their reaction to the preaching.

Nor is the inability to understand the preaching only a spiritual fault. It is that too. But this is a sin which is characteristic of all the "bad-soiler hearers." Apparently what Jesus refers to here is the kind of people who really have no interest in the preaching. They are interested in many different things that are part of this present world. They are interested in their jobs, how to earn their daily bread, how to get ahead in the world, perhaps how to gain the pleasures of life for themselves; but they have no real interest in the Word. And they have no interest in the Word because they have no spiritual and personal interest in the kingdom of heaven. Hence, although they hear what the minister is saying and even understand from a purely intellectual point of view the propositions which the minister sets forth, they are quite uninterested in the truths of the gospel which are being proclaimed.

And so Satan comes and takes away that Word as quickly as it is preached. Jesus does not mean to absolve these hearers from responsibility by putting the blame on Satan for taking away the Word. These hearers are themselves responsible before God for letting Satan come into their hearts to take that Word away. And they are responsible because they have no interest in things of God, but only in things of the world. Thus Satan has ready access into their hearts to pluck that Word out of their minds as quickly as it comes there. The Word, quite literally, goes in one ear and out the other.

You are able to find these hearers in any audience where the Word is preached. They are, fundamentally, bored with the preaching. They can scarcely endure forty to fifty minutes of the preaching of the Word. And their boredom with the preaching gives ample opportunity for the devil to come and snatch that Word away. If you should ask them what the sermon was about immediately after church, they would be very hard pressed to tell you. The Word is gone almost before the closing notes of the doxology are played.

The result is that, while the Word is preached, their minds easily wander into other channels of thought. Or, perhaps, in their boredom, they gradually doze off into sleep. But they are always quick to criticize the preaching as being too deep for them to understand; or too doctrinal for them so that they have nothing to take with them into their everyday life. That this is all an excuse to cover their own spiritual disinterest is plain from the fact that, when pressed a bit to give account of what the subject of the sermon was, they cannot even remember the text. Because they are interested only in entertainment, they soon drift off to a church where their senses are stimulated by something other than the lively preaching of the Word.

But it is quite different with those whose hearts have been prepared by the Holy Spirit. The Lord tells us that some seed falls on good ground, and that some of this good ground is more fertile than other ground. The result is that some bear fruit a hundredfold, some sixty, and some thirty. Evidently there are two separate ideas here. On the one hand, there is a difference among the people of God themselves. There are some people of God in whom the Word brings forth abundant fruit; but there are other people of God in whom the Word does not bring forth great amounts. No doubt the amount of fruit which is brought forth is directly proportionate to the spiritual condition of the hearers. Some people of God are very spiritual; some are spiritually weak. Some eagerly hear the Word of the preaching and apply it by grace to their lives. Others hear with less eagerness and lack a measure of wisdom to make the Word a lamp to their feet and a light upon their path.

On the other hand, the various spiritual conditions which Jesus describes can also be applied to the same child of God at different times in his life. There are also different kinds of reasons why our spiritual receptivity differs at one time from another when we go to church on the Lord's Day. Some differences in spiritual receptivity are due simply to the physical and intellectual development of a child of God from childhood, through youth, to adulthood. But even from a spiritual point of view, we are not always equally receptive to the Word. There are times when the eagerness to hear the Word and the spiritual power to receive it are very strong. This may, for example, be in times of deep distress and trouble. But there are also times when our faith is weak, when our spiritual receptivity is at a low ebb, and when it is very easy to permit Satan to snatch some of the seed from our hearts. There are Lord's Days when the fruit is one hundredfold. But there are also Sabbaths when the fruit is a relatively meager thirtyfold. How important it is then that we see to it that we have ears to hear.

But in contrast to the hard-soil hearers, the people of God are soft-soil hearers. They, because their hearts are prepared by the Holy Spirit, recognize the great need for the preaching in their lives. When Sunday comes and it is time to go up to the Lord's house, they go with eagerness and a certain impatience because they reach out to the Word as a means of grace. When they hear the preaching, they find that the truth of the Scriptures is reflected in their own consciousness so that the Word speaks to them personally. The truth of the knowledge of God fills them with joy in Him who loves them. When they are admonished and chastened, they see their sins and repent of them and resolve, by grace, to walk in a new and holy way. The Word brings forth abundant fruit in repentance and sorrow for sin and in a delight in God's commandments.

Rocky- and Fertile-Soil Hearers

The second type of bad soil into which the seed falls is described by the Lord as rocklike soil. By this description the Lord evidently does not refer to soil which has in it a great deal of gravel or many stones. Such soil can often produce large crops. Rather, the Lord refers to soil such as can be found in some parts of our own country, which is a rather thin layer of soil over a solid rock or hardpan base. This also was common enough in mountainous Palestine.

This type of soil is first very warm and moist because the rock underneath it holds the heat and rain. The result is that the seed which is sown in it springs up quickly. The trouble is that the tender plant never develops a very extensive root system. There is no place for the roots to go. This spells future trouble. When the hot and dry season comes, the soil quickly dries out and the plant is scorched and withered by the sun. The roots cannot sink deeply in the soil to get moisture where the sun has not dried the ground.

There are certain hearers who strikingly resemble this type of seed. Quite often these people tend to be of an emotional temperament, easily affected and moved by a dramatic and forceful speaker.

They hear the gospel—in many instances for the first time—and it seems to them to be very beautiful. They are moved to weep or to sing and cry "Hallelujah." They seem to be converted, just as the soil seemed, at first glance, to be good soil. You can often find this type of person at revivals or large crusade meetings. They hear one message and rush forward to make their "faith" known.

But they too are bad-soil hearers. Their hearts are not really prepared for the Word. They are without any genuine faith to lay hold upon the Word. Therefore, they are "for a time." Presently persecution and affliction come because of the Word. This always happens. The devil knows, perhaps even better than many church members, that the Word of God is the power whereby God accomplishes His purpose in the salvation of His Church. In his fierce and unrelenting wrath against the cause of God, he always seeks to destroy the Church and drive her from the Word. And so he brings upon the Church suffering. This suffering is not always as severe as in times of terrible persecution. There are times when the Church seems to have relative peace and quietness. But even then the people of God who are faithful are often denied their jobs because of their refusal to join a worldly labor union. They are mocked and ostracized because of their confession and walk. They are also derided for their faithfulness to the Scriptures. But there are also times when Satan brings the full fury of persecution upon God's people. This happened in the days of the Roman Empire in the time of the early Church. This happened in some places in Europe after the Reformation. This is happening even in our own time in Communist countries.

This persecution is comparable to the heat of the sun in the parable. The fiery heat of persecution comes upon these people, and they are offended by the Church and by the preaching. The Word of God becomes a rock over which they stumble. And so, suddenly their seeming faith and enthusiasm wither under persecution's scorching heat. Soon they deny the Church, forsake the truth, and will have nothing of the preaching. They had no root.

How different it is with the fertile-soil hearers. The seed of the Word of God sinks deep roots within their hearts. And these roots are in Christ, for Christ dwells within their hearts, and from Christ they draw their strength and life. And so, even when persecution comes because of the Word, they bear fruit.

Their reaction to the Word is not only emotional. It is that, of course; but their reaction is not the superficial emotional reaction which comes from mere feeling. They hear the Word of God as it conveys to them the knowledge of God in Christ, Whom to know is eternal life. With enlightened minds, they understand the Word. With softened wills, they turn to that Word to receive it. They know and understand and love the truth. Thus, their emotional reaction to the Word of God is not a hasty reaction of joy. This is never the case. Always the first reaction of a fertile-soil hearer is a deep sorrow for sin. And this is not only true the very first time one who is regenerated comes into contact with the preaching. This is also true every time the child of God hears the Word of God proclaimed. He cries out: Woe is me. He smites upon his breast and does not dare to lift up his eyes toward heaven, but cries: O God, be merciful to me, the sinner. It is precisely this sorrow for sin which brings him running to the cross. There he finds again the joy of forgiveness and the hope of his salvation. His fruit is the fruit of true sorrow for sin and true joy in the cross.

Then, when persecution comes, he does not wither away. Persecution with its flaming heat and scorching power has the effect of driving the roots of the Word more deeply into Christ. He does not deny his faith for the sake of his job. He is not embarrassed by his faith because of the mockery and hatred of the world. He does not turn his back on his faith out of fear of persecution. Persecution has exactly the opposite effect. It teaches him to sink his roots more deeply into Christ his savior. Out of Christ he draws his sustaining life and power. Out of the overflowing fountain of Christ's strength he lives in the world in faithfulness no matter what the ungodly may do to him.

This is the fruit which he brings forth.

The Thorny- and Clean-Soil Hearers

There is yet another kind of soil. This soil, too, seems at first glance to be good soil. In itself it does not differ from the soil where the crops flourish. But the trouble is that in this soil there are other seeds—the seeds of thorns and thistles. They even have the advantage over the good seed, for they were there first and thus have a head start. The result is that the weeds start to grow before the good seed; and, although the good seed may evidence a bit of growth, the thorns and thistles soon choke them and they never come to maturity.

These thorns, according to Jesus, are three things: the anxieties of the age, the deceitfulness of riches, and (according to Mark), desire for other things, or (according to Luke) the pleasures of life. These three have their own distinctive meaning, but are closely related to each other. "The anxieties of the age" refers to those things about this present life which bring anxiety. In general, the reference is to all those things about the direction of the world which cause men to worry. People may worry about the prospect of war, about labor unrest, about racial turmoil and rioting. They may worry about corruption in high places of government. They may worry about whether their sons will have to go to battle. But always their worry is directly related to their own personal well-being. Will there be sufficient food for the world's population? and particularly for me and my family? Will there be a shortage of energy so that my home will be cold and so that I will have to endure the hardships of fuel rationing? And so, particularly, they are concerned chiefly about what they shall eat and what they shall drink and wherewithal they shall be clothed.

The deceitfulness of riches is also a thorn in their hearts. The expression is very forceful one. The idea of the Lord is that riches always deceive. They deceive because they seem to promise happiness and security and freedom from care and anxiety. So subtle is this deception that almost everyone is persuaded of it—even often the people of God. It is not true, of course. The rich are no happier and no more secure than the poor. They all worry; they all fret; they all are fearful; they all know that sickness and suffering cannot be resisted by wealth and that death cannot be defeated by piles of money. Nevertheless, this is the deceit of riches: if only one has enough, one will have no problems in life.

It is clear to see that this stands connected with the anxieties of the age. The deceit of riches is exactly that men are persuaded to think that wealth will deliver from anxiety. And so this very wealth becomes an object of lust and covetousness. They all strive for it. It is the one goal of all men. It is behind much of their conduct and the explanation for a great deal of what they do.

So it is also with the pleasures of life. The life which is referred to here in Luke is life from a natural point of view. There is one word in Scripture for *life* from which we get our English word *biology*. There is another word for *life* which refers to the life unique to man and is the word used to describe eternal life that the believer has in Christ. The first word is the one used in Luke. There are, in the lives of these hearers, the pleasures of life. That is, these hearers seek the pleasures of life. This is their main interest. In fact, this is really the controlling principle of the whole of their life. They are worldly-minded. They want only to enjoy life to the full, and their whole life is devoted to the pursuit of these pleasures. John, in his first epistle, speaks of these pleasures when he talks about the lust of the flesh and the lust of the eyes and the pride of life (I John 2:16).

And this too stands related to the other thorns. Because this is the controlling principle of their life, they are easily deceived by the false promises of riches. And they fret and are filled with anxiety when anything in the history of the world seems a threat to this.

All these thorns grow steadily in their heart. It stands to reason that there is really no room for the seed of the Word to grow. It is true that they hear the Word and even understand it. They may sometimes consider it and discuss it. They may go so far as to promise amendment of life when their worldliness is called to their attention. But these thorns choked the Word. This happens already in church. They sit in church, but their minds are on their business, their work, their problems in making ends meet. They are easily distracted to meditate upon life's pleasures here below, and they even get their minds involved in dreams of what they would do if only they had large amounts of money. The result is that the Word is choked and bears no fruit.

The clean-soil hearers are quite different. We must be clear on this. It is certainly true that the people of God also are distracted often by the anxieties of the age and the deceitfulness of riches. All we have said about these fundamentally unbelieving hearers is also true of the people of God at various times in their lives. This is why the earnest admonition comes to us: He that hath an ear to hear, let him hear.

Nevertheless, basically and fundamentally the believer's heart has been prepared carefully by the Holy Spirit. The soil has been so carefully prepared that the weeds are taken out. There is room for the seed of the Word to grow and flourish and presently to bring forth fruit.

The people of God too are oppressed sometimes with the anxieties of this age. But they have learned to escape these cares by casting all their cares upon God. They know He cares for them. They are not deceived by riches, for they have made a spiritual evaluation of the riches of the world in the light of the Scriptures. They can therefore put these riches in their right perspective. They know that the riches of the kingdom of heaven are infinitely greater than all the treasures of the world. They know that these earthly "things" are only means to help them walk their pilgrimage here below. They are people who do not find their pleasures in life as such. Their pleasure is in the things of God. They delight in His Word. They set their affections on things above. They seek first the kingdom of God and His righteousness. And so these thorns do not choke the Word.

Hence, when this Word bears fruit in their lives, it bears the fruit of a holy and sanctified walk. It bears the fruit of an antithetical walk in obedience to the will of their Christ.

There are many hearers of the Word who are unbelieving hearers. The judgment is the greater for having heard the Word.

But this Word of Christ comes to all God's people. We must be careful how we hear. We bear responsibility for our hearing. We must hear with a hearing mixed with faith, that we may take that Word of God into our hearts and lives and walk as citizens of the kingdom of heaven.

3

The Antithesis in the Church

Another parable put he forth unto them, saying, The kingdom of heaven is likened unto a man which sowed good seed in his field: But while men slept, his enemy came and sowed tares among the wheat, and went his way.

But when the blade was sprung up, and brought forth fruit, then appeared the tares also.

So the servants of the householder came and said unto him, Sir, didst not thou sow good seed in thy field? from whence then hath it tares? He said unto them, An enemy hath done this. The servants said unto him, Wilt thou then that we go and gather them up?

But he said, Nay; lest while ye gather up the tares, ye root up also the wheat with them.

Let both grow together until the harvest: and in the time of harvest I will say to the reapers, Gather ye together first the tares, and bind them in bundles to burn them: but gather the wheat into my barn. Then Jesus sent the multitude away, and went into the house: and his disciples came unto him, saying, Declare unto us the parable of the tares of the field.

He answered and said unto them, He that soweth the good seed is the Son of man;

The field is the world; the good seed are the children of the kingdom; but the tares are the children of the wicked one;

The enemy that sowed them is the devil; the harvest is the end of the world; and the reapers are the angels.

As therefore the tares are gathered and burned in the fire; so shall it be in the end of this world.

The Son of man shall send forth his angels, and they shall gather out of his kingdom all things that offend, and them which do iniquity; And shall cast them into a furnace of fire: there shall be wailing and gnashing of teeth.

Then shall the righteous shine forth as the sun in the kingdom of their Father. Who hath ears to hear, let him hear.

—Matthew 13:24-30, 36-43

The most striking feature of this parable is the extensive contrast which Jesus uses. He contrasts the wheat and the tares, the householder and the enemy, the fruit of the wheat and of the tares, and the final end of both—the fire and the granary.

In the explanation of the parable, Jesus makes clear that He has in mind the contrast between the children of the kingdom and the children of the wicked one. But because the children of the kingdom and the children of the wicked one are permitted to live in close proximity to each other until the end of the world, the parable stresses the reason for this. Why is this allowed to continue? The answer to this question forms the main point of Jesus' instruction.

There is, however, another point in this connection. Jesus is not discussing this fact merely to relate what ought to be obvious to all. He is not giving an explanation for the presence of wicked men in the kingdom merely for the purpose of passing out some general information on the subject. His purpose is quite practical. The words of the parable are intended to be for the encouragement and comfort of the people of God. The presence of the children of the evil one is a reason for considerable distress and suffering for God's people throughout history. But the Lord makes clear that God has His purpose in this—a purpose which is wise and good. If God's people understand this, they will not be dismayed by this fact, but will understand that it must be this way for God's purpose to be realized.

The Meaning of the Field and the Seed

In His explanation of the parable, Jesus says: "The field is the world."

Some who have overlooked this fact have argued that the field is a reference to the Church, or, more particularly, to a local congregation. They have pointed out that every congregation has hypocrites in it. And they have used the parable in support of the argument that Jesus forbids the excommunication of anyone from the congregation. Always, so it is said, the congregation must continue to labor in love with those who are not faithful members of the Church. Never must anyone in the Church be cut off from the fellowship of the people of God.

Apart from the fact that the Scriptures emphatically point out that Christian discipline, including excommunication, is a mark of the true Church, Jesus' own words point out the error of this interpretation: "The field is the world."

Others take this expression in the most literal way and insist that the references of the Lord is to the whole creation. They then explain that the parable means simply to teach that there are in the world good people and bad people. They point out that this has always been true and that it always will be true. They explain the parable to mean that every effort to root out the wicked from the creation is impossible and forbidden; we must simply recognize the fact that this is the way it will be, and we must accept this fact.

There are objections against this view. In the first place, one senses immediately that if this were the only meaning of the parable, there would be little point in Jesus' efforts to expound on this. It is so obviously a fact and so clearly something that is true that there is no reason to belabor the obvious in such an extensive way. In the second place, there is no reason for the express command in the parable to refrain from rooting out the tares. If the whole world is intended, and the children of the wicked one are all the wicked people in the world, it is obvious, on the face of it, that it is impossible to take all the wicked out of the world. The idea would never enter the mind of anyone. In the third place, the parable is spoken particularly for the comfort of the people of God. It must therefore deal with a problem of more pressing importance than the mere fact that there will always be wicked people in the world.

The reference of the Lord must therefore be to the historical manifestation and development of the kingdom of heaven. Jesus is speaking of the kingdom of heaven in the parable: "The kingdom of heaven is likened unto. . . ." As that kingdom of heaven comes to manifestation in history, it includes the whole of what is sometimes called nominal Christendom. All that ever was the Church, all that still calls itself Church—even though it has become apostate—belongs, in the widest sense of the word, to this historical development of the kingdom of heaven.

Jesus speaks of the fact that the field is the world because as long as the kingdom comes to manifestation in the world, there are tares among the wheat. Within nominal Christendom are to be found the children of the kingdom. But alongside of and growing in the same field as the wheat are also to be found the tares who are the children of the evil one. The contrast and the antithesis is to be found here. There is no antithesis as such between Christianity and paganism; there is contrast and antithesis between the true Church of God and false Christianity. It is here that the problem arises, and it is to this problem that the Lord addresses Himself in the words of this parable.

Thus the good seed are the children of the kingdom. They are those who are eternally elected by God to be children of the kingdom. In Matthew 25:34, these children of the kingdom are addressed by the Lord with the words: "come, ye blessed of my Father, inherit the kingdom prepared for you from the foundation of the world." Not only is the kingdom itself prepared from the foundation of the world, but the Lord expressly states that it is prepared for *His own* from the world's foundation.

These are called sovereignly by God to be citizens of the kingdom. Paul speaks in Colossians 1:13 of the fact that we are delivered from the power of darkness, and translated into the kingdom of His dear Son by God our Father. These children of the kingdom manifest themselves as such in the world by walking as citizens of the kingdom. They serve the Lord Christ, walk in obedience to His will, and look forward to the day when they will inherit the kingdom in glory. They are planted by Christ; for Christ alone gathers, defends, and preserves His Church. He rules sovereignly in His kingdom. He is the Lord of the kingdom. He creates the kingdom's citizens. It is His kingdom and His alone.

The tares, on the other hand, are the children of the evil one. The word *tares* designates a kind of plant, rather common in Palestine, which looked exactly like a wheat plant during the time of its germination and growth. Only when the plant headed out did the difference become evident. The kernel of the tares was black and was useless as a food for man or animal. These tares depict the children of Satan. No doubt, the expression denotes their spiritual origin. Jesus speaks of the wicked Pharisees as belonging to their father the devil. This is apparently also the idea here. From a spiritual and ethical viewpoint, these wicked ones belong to the devil, they are part of his kingdom, and they can trace their spiritual origin to him. They are not simply unbelievers; they are reprobate.

The Relation between the Two Seeds

According to the parable, the tares are planted over the wheat. The devil does this. It was not such an uncommon thing in Eastern lands that something similar to this would happen. After a man had sowed his field with good seed, an enemy would come and spread throughout his field the seed of weeds. And it was particularly dastardly if this enemy sowed tares, because the two could not be distinguished until both ripened.

This evil deed, according to the parable, was done at night. The point is not that the Church is unwatchful. Rather Jesus means to say that the devil does his work stealthily. He never comes with blasts on a trumpet announcing his presence. The wicked are put within the Church undetected.

It is for this reason also that they are, at first, indistinguishable from the good seed. Perhaps they are born within the Church to begin with. This often happens. We know from Scripture and experience that not all those who are born from believing parents are children of the kingdom. There are Esaus born within covenant lines. But they do not immediately reveal themselves. They are born within the Church. They receive the sign of baptism. They are brought up in a godly home and given covenant instruction in the home and Church and school. They perhaps even make confession of faith within the Church and partake, along with God's people, of the sacrament of the Lord's Supper.

Or it is possible that they come into the Church from outside. There are various reasons why they may come. Perhaps they marry someone from the Church. Perhaps they are outwardly attracted to the Church for various reasons. So they make an outward pretense of agreeing with the confession of the Church; and they seem, for a time, to be part of the Church. Such was the case with Simon who joined the Church when he heard the preaching of Philip, but who tried to buy the gift of the Holy Spirit with money (Acts 8:13-24).

Whatever may be the reason, these are tares sown in the wheat-field by Satan. They are not immediately distinguishable from the children of the kingdom. It is only in the process of time that their true nature is revealed. For a time they act just like the true believers. They confess the truth, use the language of Scripture, walk in conformity with the principles of Scripture. But when they begin to manifest themselves, their true character is exposed. They introduce into the Church false doctrines. They are responsible for a spirit of carnality and worldy-mindedness. They begin to complain about the preaching and the strictures of Scripture required of one who is a disciple of the Lord.

In the gradual process of time they develop into modernists and liberals. While all the time claiming to represent true Christianity, they take the Church down the path of false doctrine and apostasy. They become a false Christianity, and, in fact, develop in time into Antichrist. The apostle John speaks of this very thing in his first epistle when he writes: "Little children, it is the last time: and as ye have heard that antichrist shall come, even now are there many antichrists; whereby we know that it is the last time. They went out from us, but they were not of us; for if they had been of us, they would no doubt have continued with us: but they went out, that they might be made manifest that they were not all of us" (vv. 18, 19).

The Problem This Presents

It is obvious that this presents a problem to the Church.

The Lord pictures this very graphically in the parable. As the plants began to head out, the servants noticed that there were tares sowed in the wheat. The servants are deeply disturbed by this. They come to the master with the questions: "Sir, didst not thou sow good seed in thy field? from whence then hath it tares?" And, after the master explains, they ask: "Wilt thou then that we go and gather them up?"

It is irrelevant to the parable who these servants are. The Lord makes no effort to explain that aspect of the parable in the interpretation which He gives. The point is rather that the servants are afraid that the tares will hurt the wheat. This is not at all surprising. The presence of carnal seed within the Church is a source of constant worry to the people of God. These children of the kingdom notice that there is a considerable amount of carnal seed in the Church. And they are afraid that the carnal seed do harm to the cause of Christ. They see the wicked in the majority. They see apparent evidence of the harm these wicked do. Even in Jesus' day the ungodly Pharisees were in control and the saints could plaintively sing: "In Thy heritage the heathen / now, Oh God, triumphant stand. . . ." They see that the wicked apparently lead many astray through heresy, worldliness, and spiritual indifference. They see the cause of God reduced to very small numbers time and again. They see even persecution rising in which those who profess to be of the Church persecute those who hold fast to the commandments of Jesus. This happened repeatedly in the Old Testament. It happened in the days of Jesus. The history of the New Testament Church is replete with similar examples. It is a constant source of worry to those who are concerned for the cause of Christ.

The answer seems to be to pluck them up and get rid of them. There are some who advocate this course of action even today. They have fond dreams of a gradual development of the kingdom here upon earth. They look forward to a day when the children of the kingdom will be in the majority, when all the institutions and structures of life will be made subservient to the cause of Christ. They look forward to the kingdom of Christ being realized on this earth. Then will come the time for all the tares to be plucked up and the kingdom to be purified. But Jesus holds forth no such promise.

He expressly forbids the servants to pluck up the tares: "Nay; lest while ye gather up the tares, ye root up also the wheat with them. Let both grow together until the harvest."

What may be the reason for this? Quite obviously, the Lord is emphasizing that there is a good reason why the tares must remain in the field; that, in fact, to pluck up the tares prematurely will be harmful for the wheat.

We may be certain that the reason is not that there is always some hope that the tares will become wheat. The reason is not that there is always a chance that the wicked in the Church who are children of the devil will be converted. The Lord is not discussing this. He has set up an absolute antithesis between the children of the kingdom and the children of the wicked one. It never happens in nature that tares become wheat; it doesn't happen in the Church either. The Lord knows those who are His.

Nor does this nullify the need for the exercise of the keys of the kingdom. It is the Church's solemn responsibility to cut off from her membership those who manifest themselves as tares.

Rather, the Lord is speaking of the obvious fact that throughout the history of the Church there is always the true Church and the false Church; and that these exist side by side. They cannot be separated from each other in the world. The devil sows his seed wherever the good seed is found. Where Christ is preached, there also Antichrist will raise his voice. Where the kingdom of heaven comes to manifestation, there will Satan try to bring about the kingdom of hell. Where the godly live in the world, there will also the ungodly be found. It has never been any different. It will never be any different on this side of the coming of Christ.

But the Lord has His purpose in this. He Himself has determined that such it will be.

What are the reasons for this?

In general, first of all, there are two remarks which we must make. The first of these is that there is implied here a word of comfort to the Church. The people of God may be dismayed and fearful about this fact, but, by implication, the Lord assures the Church that the tares cannot harm the wheat. It may seem this way sometimes. The Church may think that the ungodly rule in God's heritage. They may echo the words of Isaiah in chapter 1:8, 9: "And the daughter of Zion is left as a cottage in a vineyard, as a lodge in a garden of cucumbers, as a besieged city. Except the Lord of hosts had left unto us a very small remnant, we should have been as Sodom, and we should have been like unto Gomorrah." They may conclude that the wicked overcome and triumph and that the cause of God goes down to defeat. They may see bastions falling into the hands of the carnal seed and denomination after denomination go the way of apostasy until there seems to be none left to hold fast the faith. They may conclude that the presence of the children of the wicked one has destroyed God's cause. But Jesus assures us that this can never be the case. The tares can never really harm the Church. God always takes care of His Church and always gives her the victory. The gates of hell cannot prevail against her. "Nevertheless the foundation of God standeth sure, having this seal, The Lord knoweth them that are his. And, Let every one that nameth the name of Christ depart from iniquity" (II Tim. 2:19).

In the second place, in general, there are positive reasons why the tares must remain. They serve a good purpose. They are necessary for the well-being of the Church. Their absence would be harmful to the cause of Christ. This idea is surely in keeping with the general truth of Scripture that God makes all things work together for the good of His people (see Rom. 8:28). And this is the principle here.

It is possible to demonstrate this also.

In the first place, the very presence of such wicked seed makes it necessary for the people of God to be on their guard always. They are called to live an antithetical life in the midst of the world. They are called to serve their heavenly King by a rejection of that which is evil and by seeking the kingdom of God by fighting against all that which is of sin. They know that they cannot fall asleep even for a moment. They know that if they are not always in readiness, the enemy will overcome them. The cause of Christ must be maintained, and it is maintained only by constant and unceasing vigilance.

In the second place, the wicked seed serves the welfare of the Church because it inspires the Church to search out the riches of the Word of God. Heresy arises in the Church. The faithful are called to defend the truth over against such heresy. But this very calling prompts them to turn with renewed zeal to the Scriptures, for there is the truth in all its purity. Such it has always been in the world. Never has the Church developed the truth of the Scriptures in the ivory towers of theological speculation or in the cozy quietness of the theologians' rooms. The truth has been hammered out on the battlefield of faith. It has been developed by forcefully opposing all attacks against that very Word which the Church loves and cherishes. It has been forged in the heat of battle. It is a truth which has become so rich and pure because of all the attacks made against it. Anyone acquainted with the history of the Church will know that this is true.

In the third place, the presence of both provides time for both seeds to ripen. The wheat seed ripens into the man of God who is thoroughly furnished unto every good work. It is true that this ripening takes place only through the way of struggle, war, suffering, and watchfulness. But God uses these things as means to prepare His people for glory. On the other hand, the wicked also develop. They reveal themselves as truly of the kingdom of darkness. They increase in wickedness until they become ripe for judgment. But it is their very nearness to the children of the kingdom that brings about this development in sin. For the presence of the Church is the immediate occasion for their greatest sins. It was the presence of Christ in Palestine which served to expose the hypocrisy of the wicked Jews. If Christ had not come, they perhaps could have maintained their hypocrisy and left the impression that they were pious and holy. But their basic hatred of God was roused to expression by Christ; and they became ripe for judgment when they crucified Him. But this is the way it always is. The presence of the Church serves to uncover the basic evil which lurks in the hearts of those who hate God and His cause, but who hide their hatred under a cloak of piety. The manifestation of their sin is especially in their persecution of the cause of God. In this way they become ripe for judgment. This too is God's purpose.

The Separation at the Harvest

The harvest is the end of the world.

This is the end of the world in the absolute sense. Jesus knows only of this end, not the many "ends" of which pre-millennialism speaks. It is that moment when God's purpose, according to His counsel, is realized: for all that He has determined to do has been accomplished. Creation and history are brought to their *telos*, their purpose, their goal. Then all things are ready. The wicked have filled the cup of iniquity and the filling of this cup has made them ripe for judgment. The Church is ripe for her final salvation, and all things are ready for Christ to return.

Many times in Scripture the angels are given a place in the final coming of Christ. In Revelation 14:15-20 we read: "And another angel came out of the temple, crying with a loud voice to him that sat on the cloud, Thrust in thy sickle, and reap: for the time is come for thee to reap; for the harvest of the earth is ripe. And he that sat on the cloud thrust in his sickle on the earth; and the earth was reaped. And another angel came out of the temple which is in heaven, he also having a sharp sickle. And another angel came out from the altar, which had power over fire; and cried with a loud cry to him that had the sharp sickle, saying, Thrust in they sharp sickle, and gather the clusters of the vine of the earth; for her grapes are fully ripe. And the angel thrust in his sickle into the earth, and gathered the vine of the earth, and cast it into the great winepress of the wrath of God. And the winepress was trodden without the city, and blood came out of the winepress, even unto the horse bridles, by the space of a thousand and six hundred furlongs."

In this parable the angels are pictured as gathering out of the kingdom all the things which offend and them who do iniquity. The first description is impersonal: "the *things* which offend." Evidently the reference is to all those evils and temptations which the wicked placed in the way of the people of God in an effort to cause them to stumble and fall into sin. This was constantly the trial of God's people on the earth. The wicked held before them the allurements and enticements of those things which are forbidden by God's law. The wicked attempted to lead the faithful into the ways of worldliness and apostasy. And the evil ones in this world held the threat and reality of persecution over the righteous in an effort to persuade them to abandon their path of faithfulness to the kingdom. But now all these things are taken away forever.

And the wicked themselves are cast into the furnace of fire, there to be burned. They are sentenced to the indescribable torments of God's eternal wrath. This is the just judgment of Almighty God upon them for their terrible sins which they have committed. They shall be separated for eternity from the righteous and punished in hell.

But the righteous shall shine forth as the sun in the kingdom of their Father. These children of the kingdom are not righteous in themselves. They have not made themselves righteous by their own works. They are children of the kingdom because they are made righteous in the blood of the cross of Christ their Savior. As that blood of Christ was shed in order to establish the kingdom of righteousness, so is the righteousness of the citizens of the kingdom a righteousness which comes to them through the cross of Christ alone.

Their glory awaits them in the kingdom of the Father.

In that kingdom they shall rule with Christ as princes and princesses. They shall inherit the kingdom prepared for them from the foundation of the world. In that kingdom they shall shine as the sun in glory. This is because they shall be perfected in glory. Everything that is of sin and of this earth shall be taken away. They shall become fully members of the body of Christ. And the glory of God which is so bright that, before it, the angels hide their faces, shall shine through Christ and through them as members of Christ's body so that they themselves, in body and soul, become the instruments of the revelation of that great glory of their God Who has saved them.

Then all their suffering on this earth shall be rewarded in heaven. Then shall they see that, though on the earth they suffered at the hands of the wicked and were often threatened with extinction, God preserved His cause through Christ and never allowed the wicked to overcome them. In fact, God used their sufferings and trials in the world to prepare them for their final glory with Him. All that happened on earth was but the means, under the hand of a sovereign God, to realize the kingdom of heaven. And all that happened to them was but the means to give them a place in that great and everlasting kingdom.

Who hath ears to hear, let him hear. What must he hear? He must hear the word of Christ that it is the will of God that the wicked are always very near the righteous as long as the world continues. He must hear that, because of this, the way of the righteous is often hard and filled with suffering so that the righteous ponder often whether the presence of the wicked will not send the cause of God down to defeat. He must hear the voice of Christ assure him that the gates of hell cannot prevail against the Church. In fact, he must hear the reassuring word of Christ that it is necessary, according to the purpose of God, that the wicked always be present. And he must hear Christ say that the righteous have the calling to maintain the antithesis; for if they are faithful—faithful unto death so that no one takes their crown—there awaits them in glory a place in the kingdom of Christ where they will shine forth as the sun.

4

The Growth of the Kingdom

Another parable put he forth unto them, saying, The kingdom of heaven is like to a grain of mustard seed, which a man took, and sowed in his field:
Which indeed is the least of all seeds: but when it is grown, it is the greatest among herbs, and becometh a tree, so that the birds of the air come and lodge in the branches thereof.
Another parable spake he unto them; The kingdom of heaven is like unto leaven, which a woman took, and hid in three measures of meal, till the whole was leavened.

—Matthew 13:31-33

These two parables, which form the basis for our discussion in this chapter, must not be separated from the parables which precede them. When they are considered apart from the parables of the different kinds of soil and of the tares, those who interpret them are inclined to let their imaginations wander, with the result that they are led to miss the point of Jesus' teaching. These two parables are related to the parables which precede them because they were all taught by Jesus at about the same time. But the relation is also inherent in the thought. In the parable of the different kinds of soil, we learned that the seed of the preaching of the Word does not always fall on the same kind of heart; thus there are different reactions to the preaching of the gospel. In the parable of the tares the Lord taught us that the wicked must remain in the historical manifestation of the kingdom until the very end of time. In the parable of the mustard seed we are told that the kingdom, although inconspicuous in its beginning, eventually grows to a large herb. And in the parable of the leaven, the Lord points us to the truth that the inward working of the power of the kingdom, though hidden, nevertheless permeates all of that in which it is hid.

Thus, if we were to carry on the method of explanation which Jesus Himself used in the two previous parables, we could conclude that the field is the world—that is, the historical manifestation of the kingdom of Christ in the world. The seed and the leaven are both the Word of God. The herb tree is the Church of Jesus Christ as it represents the kingdom of Christ. The thoroughly leavened dough

is the perfected Church, or, taken individually, the perfected believer.

There is also a relationship of purpose between these two parables
and the parables which precede them. In the first parable, the Lord
instructed His disciples (and us) as to the reason why all do not
believe the gospel. In the parable of the tares, the Lord explained
why the wicked had to remain in close proximity to the Church. And
at the same time He comforted His Church with the assurance that
the tares can never hurt the wheat. In these two parables the Lord
admonishes us that we must never be discouraged by nor scoff at the
small beginning and invisible working of the power of the kingdom
of heaven. This, no doubt, the disciples were very much inclined to
do. They envisioned a kingdom of considerable power and glory
with the whole of Palestine and the nation of the Jews restored to the
glory of Solomon's kingdom, with Christ on Mount Zion seated on
David's throne, and with the disciples themselves as high officers in
that kingdom. But the trouble was that most of the Jews never
believed in Jesus. In fact, enmity against Him was on the increase so
that His life was even endangered. The kingdom seemed not only to
be very far away, but it seemed to be impossible of realization. Often
these disciples were impatient and were tempted to take matters into
their own hands before it became too late.

But now the Lord shows them (and us) that, although this kingdom may have a very inconspicuous beginning, and although it may
work invisibly, it nevertheless has a very mighty growth and a very
marvelous end. This fact the Church must remember, lest it be
tempted to adopt the earth-shaking efforts of sinful men to establish
the kingdom.

The Insignificant Beginning of the Kingdom

Before we enter into the parable in detail and attempt to expound
its positive meaning, it is well to discuss a few interpretations that
have been put forth by other expositors of Scripture. These interpretations are interesting, because they reveal some obvious mis-
conceptions concerning the nature of the kingdom which are very
common today.

One interpretation of these parables emphasizes that the kingdom of God will grow historically until at last it fills the whole earth.
There are several variations of this interpretation, but basically they
are the same. This is the interpretation which is given by post-millennialism. Whether it be of the conservative kind or the post-millennialism of liberalism and modernism, the idea is basically the
same. The kingdom is then pictured as having a very small beginning in Jesus and His disciples. In fact, after Jesus' ministry on earth
had come to an end, there were only 120 members of the New
Dispensational Church. But, although that was a very small beginning, from the day of Pentecost on, the kingdom grows mightily. It

marches on from victory to victory: first in Palestine and Syria, then in Asia Minor and Greece, then on into Europe and America, and finally to the ends of the earth. It advances in numbers and strength, gathers force and momentum, attains ever greater triumphs, until the knowledge of God fills the whole earth. The extreme of this view, current in all modernism, teaches that the spirit of Christianity, in its triumphal march through the world, grows until, through social and political evolution and revolution, it permeates every area of life. It changes the home and the school, the shop and society in general, the state and the area of international politics, until all becomes subservient to the cause of Christ. Gradually all things are subjected to Him Who is Lord over all, until the kingdoms of this world become the kingdom of our Lord and of His Christ, and the kingdom of heaven is realized here upon earth.

It is startling indeed to learn how thoroughly this idea has penetrated the thinking of the Church. Whether deliberately or mistakenly, today's Church is always intent on trying to make this world a better place to live. It cannot rest, it seems, until all men have come to the knowledge of the truth, until every area of life has been touched by Christian thought, until Christ is recognized as Lord in every nook and cranny of this vast globe.

Yet this view is as false as it is dangerous.

In the parables immediately preceding this one, Jesus taught the opposite. The seed of the Word does not always fall on good soil. And this is exactly the purpose of the sovereign Sower. Furthermore, there are always, to the very end, tares in the midst of the wheat, which, while they cannot harm the wheat, will remain until the judgment. Nor is this view in keeping with the idea of the seed. The seed is not the early Church which is the seed of the Church of today, but it is rather, the preaching of the gospel.

In addition to this, Scripture gives quite another view of the kingdom of God. The Word tells us that the kingdom of God will not, on this earth, grow larger and larger and larger, but that it will continuously decrease in size. There is a continual falling away from the faith, with a terrible apostasy foretold just before the end. Before the Lord comes back, there is hardly any kingdom left here below. The world is not gradually Christianized, but it develops instead in false religion and false culture. It develops in worldly philosophy and human progress. It develops, under the prod of Satan, until it becomes the kingdom of the Antichrist, and until it is permeated with the spirit of hatred and rebellion against God.

It is well to bear this in mind; for it is to be feared that many who exert every effort to make this world a Christian place in which to live are in danger of identifying their efforts, not with the efforts of Christ, but with the efforts of Antichrist to realize the kingdom of darkness. Then, when it is too late, they will find themselves working for his cause and promoting his ends. Lured by the siren songs of post-millennialism, they are attracted to a cause which is opposed to God and to His Christ.

There is another interpretation of these parables which identifies the mustard seed and especially the leaven with false doctrine. This is a favorite interpretation of those who are addicted to pre-millennialism. The woman then becomes the false church, especially the Roman Catholic Church. The leaven is then false doctrine. The world will presently be thoroughly permeated with the leaven of corruption. While there is an element of truth to such a view, it will hardly serve as an explanation for the parables, for the Lord Himself quite expressly says: "The kingdom of heaven is like a mustard seed . . .; the kingdom of heaven is like leaven. . . ." It is impossible to imagine how the kingdom of heaven is like false doctrine or spiritual corruption.

Positively then, we must maintain that the seed which is mentioned here is the seed of the Word of God. It is safe to maintain this, for this is not only in harmony with the parable which Jesus already taught, but it is also in harmony with the rest of Scripture where seed is more than once compared with the Word (cf., e.g., I Peter 1:23-25). But then it must be understood once again that the seed is first of all Jesus Christ Himself Who is the Word become flesh; and second, that this seed is the Word of the gospel which Christ Himself preaches concerning Himself in and through His Church.

As such, this living Word of the gospel is the spiritual power of the kingdom of heaven. This kingdom is not earthly and will never be found or realized on this earth. It is from above; it is heavenly and spiritual. Its power, therefore, is not the earthly power of human might and force, but the spiritual power of the Word of the gospel of Jesus Christ and the operation of the Spriit Who brings that Word to its determined purpose. Christ is exalted in heaven. All authority is given to Him alone so that He reigns supreme over all the works of the Father. But He reigns in order that the kingdom of God may be realized. And this realization of the kingdom Christ accomplishes by His own power and might through His Word which He brings and through the spiritual power of that Word in the hearts of His people.

It is true that this spiritual power of the kingdom has a seemingly insignificant beginning. This seemingly innocuous beginning is emphasized especially in contrast to the ambitions and efforts of men. The disciples worked without tiring for an earthly kingdom in which their Master and Lord would reign over the whole of Jewry, acknowledged as David's Son, and head of a very glorious kingdom. To attain this end they were prepared to do anything within their power. They were prepared to persuade Jesus and the people to acknowledge each other mutually. They were even prepared to take up the sword should this prove to be necessary.

In reality, little has changed through the ages. Also today men make mighty and forceable beginnings to realize their dreams and ambitions and to bring utopia and heaven here on earth. To arrive at their cherished goals, they form mighty organizations such as a League of Nations or a United Nations. To realize their ambitions they are prepared to resort to the awesome power of weapons and armies. They make use of human might and power, wisdom and ingenuity. They make frantic attacks on the frontiers of science and medicine. They make huge strides in the areas of culture. And this is all done to make life pleasant and agreeable, to banish sickness and pain, suffering and dying, grief and distress, so that heaven may come on earth and earth will have no need of God's heaven. Every part of society must be brought under the rule of Christ, and every effort must be expended to realize this goal.

The battle cry is the false doctrine of the general fatherhood of God and the common brotherhood of man. And the Church is prepared at any given time to attain the realization of this remarkable dream. Distrustful of the Word and not content to rely upon the power of the preaching of the Word, the Church is even prompted to replace the preaching of the Word with various forms of entertainment and new experiments in liturgy, in order that crowds may be attracted to the church services made enjoyable and pleasing for all.

How insignificant and despised then is the little seed of the Word of the gospel which is dropped here and there by the Sovereign Sower. It was this way already when Christ was on earth. He was born in a cattle stall where almost no one noticed His birth. He preached only about three and a half years of a lifetime of thirty-three years. He went about doing miracles and preaching the gospel of the kingdom, but He gained only a few converts; and these were the lowly and despised, the uneducated and unlearned. Publicans and harlots were His companions, while the high and the mighty, the rulers and princes despised Him. At last He suffered a cruel and painful death on the cross and was cast out from the midst of His own nation. And when all was done there were only 120 common folk which composed the church He left behind.

But so it has always been. The cross of a hated and despised, a condemned and apparently defeated man is always the stone of stumbling and the rock of offense. For always the gospel is preached here and there by a little handful of men dedicated to its proclamation. Is this sufficient to bring about the kingdom? Especially when apparently the powers of darkness grow stronger and when the cause of Christ repeatedly appears to go down to defeat? The gospel does not grow more powerful according to men's standards. It is repeatedly corrupted and polluted and changed into a lie. Gradually the voice of the gospel dies down until it is barely heard. So it was just before the dawn of the Reformation. So it will be at the end of time. And along with it the Church remains small. Shall this small seed establish the kingdom?

The Invisible Growth of the Kingdom

What the Lord points out concerning the beginnings of the kingdom of God is equally true of its growth.

We find this described especially in the figure of leaven. Leaven was a small lump of sour dough which was put into a large measure of other dough. The sour dough, through the process of fermentation, gradually worked its way through the entire mass until the whole was leavened. The woman who put this lump of leaven into her dough was, of course, unable to see the leaven work. It was possible therefore that she would come to the conclusion that her attempts to bake bread would result in failure. But this was not the case; for, although she could not see the working of the yeast, she was perfectly confident that, given time, the yeast would affect every particle of the bread. Trusting that what she expected would happen, she waited patiently for the desired result.

The leaven refers to the same thing as the mustard seed: the invisible power of the kingdom of heaven. This power is the preaching of the gospel of that kingdom as that preaching is applied to the hearts of the elect by the sovereign operation of the Holy Spirit.

Here, however, the emphasis falls on the fact that the working of the spiritual power of the kingdom is not only small in its beginning, but is invisible in its power and accomplishments. For that reason, the meal (three measures was about the normal amount for baking, since many loaves would be baked at one time) represents the elect child of God considered individually, and the whole elect Church of Christ taken in its entirety.

And so the meaning of Jesus is clear. Even as the world attempts to establish the kingdom through mighty forces and startling beginnings, it also attempts to do this with great external show and outward ostentation. The attempts of men are always external and visible. To bring about the kingdom one must clean up the world, make laws to enforce lawlessness, conquer disease with powerful drugs and medicines, regenerate society with social tools, legislation, and charitable gifts, curb delinquency, enforce the peace with the sword, and so on.

Impatient to realize the kingdom, and, for that matter, not really caring for the kingdom of God, the world resorts to might and ingenuity. The future of man lies in the test tube of a scientist, in the machinery of the lab of a physicist, in the hidden power of the atom. But these external and visible efforts are always doomed to failure. Even history makes mockery of all the best attempts of man. A hollow laugh echoes down the corridors of time, hangs heavy over battlefields, shatters the silence of the graveyard, reverberates through the filled prisons and riot torn streets.

Scripture tells us that laws cannot bring righteousness unless the law of God is written invisibly on the heart. One disease, though conquered, simply moves over to the left to make room for another.

The cemeteries of the world express silent agreement with the ancient Psalmist of Israel that a man's life span is threescore years and ten, or perhaps fourscore years if strength is great. There is no conquering of disease except the disease of sin be conquered by the Great Physician. Peace imposed by the sword is no peace, and a thousand battlefields echo the sad cry: "there is no peace for the wicked, saith my God." There is peace, but only at the foot of Calvary. How futile these efforts of men, external and visible, are to bring about the kingdom.

What then shall bring about the kingdom?

There is only one power: the silent, small, seemingly insignificant, oft-despised power of the gospel of Jesus Christ. We must believe this. This gospel, by the power of the Holy Ghost, works from within. Quietly, invisibly, yet powerfully and effectively it works its way through the whole man—through the whole Church—until the whole is not only affected but purified and made new. Mysterious, other-worldly, yet powerful—such is the working of leaven. Can one see it? Not at all. But trust and wait; it will surely do its work. Either the gospel is the power of that kingdom, or there is nothing that can bring the kingdom to realization.

The Marvelous End of the Kingdom

So often the Church is lacking in faith. It is unwilling to wait. The preaching of the gospel seems so insignificant and so feeble in comparison with the mighty efforts of men. The Church, weary with unbelief, ceases to drop the small seeds of the Word into the soil, and prefers to join the mighty efforts of the world. How easy it is to resort to force and power to gain our ends!

Or, to turn to the figure of the leaven, the process by which the whole is leavened takes time; and the Church becomes impatient. It cannot wait for the leaven of the Word of God to do its work. It seems so often as if the Word of God accomplishes nothing. The powers of darkness grow stronger and evil becomes more universal and more terrible as time goes on. This is not only true in the world at large, but it seems often to be true in the lives of the people of God. So often we become despondent and discouraged with the slow progress of sanctification in our lives and in the lives of our fellow saints. The temptation is to become impatient with the Word of God and to doubt whether that Word will accomplish its end. Is it perhaps not better, after all, to substitute something else for the little mustard seed or the slow and invisibly working leaven? Yet glorious results do occur. Mighty things are accomplished through this preaching of the gospel.

Many commentators have wondered why Jesus did not use the figure of a mighty oak tree or a cedar in His parable. After all, while the mustard plant grows quite large, it still remains an herb. Travelers to the East inform us that sometimes the mustard plant can grow so high that a horse and rider can pass safely under its branches; or, on occasion, a man can climb into it. Nevertheless, it remains an herb and never becomes a large tree. Why then does not Jesus use the figure of a lofty cedar or a graceful elm or a sturdy oak to describe the growth of the kingdom?

All these speculations are but efforts to fashion the kingdom of heaven after our own imagination. Even when the kingdom of heaven is full grown here on earth, it remains an herb. The mustard bush correctly represents the figure. Even at maturity, the kingdom of God looks small and insignificant if measured according to the standards of this world. It never becomes universal. It never becomes so large that it encompasses all the earth. It is always, in the eyes of men, an herb.

But nevertheless a great kingdom is established. The preaching of the gospel establishes this kingdom throughout all the ages of this world's history. It establishes the only kingdom in which can be found righteousness, peace, love, holiness, and the solution to all the evils and troubles that afflict this poor world. It establishes a kingdom that is many times more blessed than all the fondest dreams of men. What the world longs for it never attains, for it longs for these things apart from God. What the gospel brings in establishing the kingdom is all this and much more; it brings the forgiveness of sins, true peace with God, the righteousness of the cross of Calvary, the holiness of a sanctified walk, the blessing of fellowship with the Most High. As small as it may appear in the eyes of men, you need only ask a citizen of that kingdom if he is rich and blessed, and he will assure you that the kingdom to which he belongs is incomparably great.

And so it is also with the leaven. It takes time for the preaching of the gospel to work. We must be patient and trust its power. What the gospel brings with its leavening power is far greater than anything which can be found in the world. The gospel penetrates into every part of the life of the elect child of God. It is true that the process of leavening is never finished in this life. The child of God always carries with him the body of this death, and he must struggle daily with the many weaknesses of his flesh. Nevertheless consider what once he was. He was a filthy and repulsive sinner, with stinking sores, clothed in rags, lying in his blood, filled with sin, and stained and weighted with guilt. But the gospel, which works invisibly and silently, mysteriously and from within, permeates the whole of his life. It regenerates and sanctifies. Working from the heart, it floods the soul. It enlightens the mind and renews the will. It makes of a sinner a saint; of a guilt ridden object of wrath, a beautiful disciple who walks in the light of God's love. It takes away all that is old and makes a new creature conformed to the image of Christ. It sanctifies the whole Church of Christ so that the Church can show forth the praises of its God.

It is for this reason that we must always put our trust in that Word.

We must continue to drop the seed and put the leaven of God's Word in the Church. If the fruits seem meager, the beginning small, the working of the Word invisible, especially over against the mighty power and force of the world, we must not be tempted to substitute something else for the seed, but rather trust in the mighty power of the gospel.

Yet this is not the end. Even though the seed of the mustard grows to an herb here in this age, it shall presently become a mighty tree in the kingdom of Jesus Christ. The gospel will have reached its final triumph and victory when the kingdom of God is taken to glory and is established forever in heaven. Then the kingdom will be universal in the strictest sense of the word. It will embrace the new heavens and the new earth. Through the power of the exalted Christ, all the wicked kingdoms of this world shall be destroyed and the kingdom of Christ shall be established forever. The perfected saints of God shall enter into God's everlasting kingdom clothed in the righteousness and holiness of the garments of Christ. There we will all be gathered without spot or wrinkle in the assembly of the elect in life eternal. And all of this is brought about by the Word of the kingdom.

Let us then put our trust in that Word of God. It alone will have the victory.

5

The Worth of the Kingdom

Again, the kingdom of heaven is like unto treasure hid in a field; the which when a man hath found, he hideth, and for joy thereof goeth and selleth all that he hath, and buyeth that field.
Again, the kingdom of heaven is like unto a merchant man, seeking goodly pearls:
Who, when he had found one pearl of great price, went and sold all that he had, and bought it.

—Matthew 13:44-46

These two parables, like the two we discussed in the previous chapter, ought to be treated together because they form a unity. Both parables speak of something which is very precious and valuable. The one speaks of a treasure in the field, while the other speaks of the one pearl which is so very costly because there is none like it in all the world. They both speak of the cost involved in obtaining these treasures, and both times the cost is all that a man has. But in spite of this high cost, both men are more than willing to pay in order to obtain the treasure they have found.

The differences between the parables we are now going to examine are of such a kind that the two complement each other. The differences are not of essential importance; rather they are differences which make the two parables taken together a complete whole. The first parable emphasizes the treasure itself: "the kingdom is like unto a treasure hid in a field. . . ." The second parable lays emphasis more on the costliness of obtaining the treasure. The Lord does not say: "The kingdom of heaven is like unto one pearl of great price"; rather the Lord says: "The kingdom of heaven is like unto a merchant man. . . ." Lest the differences between the parables be an occasion for misinterpreting the meaning of the Lord, it is well to bear this difference in mind.

This parable, too, had application to the disciples of Christ and to their calling as apostles. As a matter of fact these parables were spoken privately to the disciples and evidently meant exclusively for them, at least in the first place. The reason for this is not difficult to see. On the one hand, the disciples not only had a very earthly and

carnal idea of the kingdom which Christ had come to establish, but
they also clung tenaciously to this idea since thay anticipated for
themselves a rather high position in the kingdom to which the Lord
would appoint them. In fact they often quarreled about who was the
greatest, at one point even making an effort to settle the dispute as to
who would be vice-president in the realm over which Christ would
rule. They were therefore not at all concerned about or even capable
of facing the question what the kingdom of heaven would *demand* of
them; they could only worry about what *benefits* would accrue to
them as the favored of the Lord.

On the other hand, these same disciples would be given the calling
of bringing the gospel to the ends of the earth, of being the means
whereby the Lord would gather His Church from all nations and
tribes and tongues. A very great price would be asked of them in
fulfilling this high calling; they would, in fact, be asked to pay the
ultimate price of their life. It is with this in His mind that the Lord
begins to instruct them in the true character of the kingdom of
heaven and of its spiritual work.

Yet this mistake of the disciples is by no means foreign to us. How
often is it not true that we take a place in the kingdom and participate in its activities for personal profit? But the Lord points out that
to obtain the treasures of the kingdom it is necessary to make total
sacrifice.

The Incomparable Treasure of the Kingdom

In attempting to discover the meaning of Christ in these two
parables, we ought not to be unduly preoccupied with aspects of the
parables that are irrelevant to the main point of the Lord. Commentators are often not only absorbed in these details, but are led from
the main teaching of the parables by an unnatural preoccupation
with them. As is so often true of our attempts to explain these
parables, we must be sure that we understand the main point which
the Lord intends to teach. Having done this, the rest of the pieces of
the puzzle will fit nicely into place; while it will also become obvious
that not every detail of the parable must be pressed into service with
some specific meaning attached to it.

One of these points is the element in the first parable which speaks
of a peasant stumbling onto the hidden treasure unawares while
evidently plowing the field that belongs to his master. Comparable
to this, the merchant finds the one pearl while in search of goodly
pearls. This is often interpreted to mean that all men truly seek the
riches of the kingdom of heaven. There is, so it is claimed, in all men
a desire for God, a thirsting after the true religion, an anxious quest
for peace with the Most High. Yet unexpectedly and in places
unanticipated they stumble on this treasure, either right in the field
which they are plowing or in the marketplace they are visiting.

Apart from the fact that this is not the point which Jesus is making here, this whole view is obviously contrary to Scripture. Scripture does not teach that all men desire God and anxiously search for the riches of the kingdom. Rather Scripture makes plain again and again that wicked men know where these riches are, know that there is a God and that He must be served. But if men are not saved by the power of grace, they rebel against God and deliberately and consciously turn to every form of idolatry. (See, e.g., Rom. 1:18-32.)

Others are troubled by the moral question involved in hiding the treasure that a man found in another's field in order to obtain that field at its cost, without divulging the added worth of the field. Again, apart from the fact that it was a well-known ancient law that the finder of a treasure was its legitimate owner no matter where the treasure was found, this is beside the point as far as the teaching of the Lord is concerned. For this reason too it is idle to ask why the man did not simply take the treasure as his own without purchasing the field.

Turning now to the parable proper, three points are necessary to understand the meaning of the Lord's teaching here.

In the first place, the Lord makes a considerable point of it that both men find a treasure of incomparable worth. The peasant finds a buried treasure of a large number of gold coins; the merchant finds the one pearl of great price. This incomparably valuable treasure is especially emphasized by the pearl. Pearls were considered of greater value to the ancients than to us, although even now a pearl is very costly. Then, however, they were more to be desired than any precious stone or even gold or silver. Besides, this pearl was one by itself. It stood in a class all alone. There was no other pearl like it in all the world. It was *the one pearl.*

In the second place, both men form an opinion of the worth of what they find. The peasant who comes upon a treasure hidden in the field not only immediately hides it again, but sells all that he has to buy the field with great joy. The merchant who spends his time traveling to many countries and roaming many marketplaces immediately sees the value of this one pearl. There were no doubt other people who had seen it; but, either it did not strike them as being particularly desirable, or, upon inquiry, they thought the price was too high. But this merchant is an expert in his field. He is able to tell a faulty or imperfect pearl from a faultless one. He is able to ascertain the worth of any one pearl by looking at it. Of this one pearl also he forms a mental appraisal while his heart beats wildly within him. Both the peasant and the merchant, therefore, are willing to give all that they have in order to obtain what they have found. No cost is too high to pay for this treasure. Even though the cost is everything, they are undaunted.

In the third place, through the sale of everything they own, they are also able to obtain their mutual treasures. It is not as if the last minute the deal falls through because someone else beats them to its purchase. It is not as if they fail after having sold all. No, making the supreme sacrifice, their treasure also comes into their possession.

What is this treasure for which a man is willing to give all that he has?

We will be safe by concluding that the field in which the treasure is hid is once again the kingdom of heaven. This was true of the previous parables which the Lord taught; we are safe in concluding that is true also of this one. By way of analogy, therefore, we may also safely assume that the marketplace in which the merchant locates the pearl is also the kingdom of God.

It must be remembered, however, that this kingdom is manifested on this earth in the Church. It is true that this kingdom is heavenly and spiritual; it is not of the earth and will not be realized here upon earth. It is likewise true that there was an old dispensational picture of this kingdom of heaven in the kingdom of David and Solomon. But this was nevertheless type and shadow, not the reality. But God determined to manifest this kingdom in this world in the Church of Christ. It stands spiritually over against the kingdom of Satan and the wicked kingdoms of the world. It is the kingdom in which Christ rules by His Word and Spirit, through the power of His own shed blood, establishing His throne in the hearts of His people and swaying the scepter of His power in their lives. Only when Christ finally returns will this kingdom be fully perfected. Then this earthly will become heavenly, and the kingdom will be fully realized.

The treasure is to be found therefore in the Church. Yet, the Church must not be considered merely as a society of people or as a human organization. The Church is established and gathered and instituted by the Lord Himself. By the Church is meant, therefore, the Church of Christ as it engages in its one work and calling, the preaching of the gospel. No other work is the Church called to do. It is not a social organization, a political pressure group, a lobbying agency, a business establishment, or an agency for solving the world's ills. It is the body of Christ called to no other task than the ministry of the gospel. How often this is forgotten today!

From this it follows that the treasure can be found only where the gospel is preached. Not the human philosophy and wisdom of men bring the treasures of the kingdom; nor does a social gospel carry with it the riches of heaven. Only the Church entrusted with and making use of the faithful and true ministry of the gospel is the repository of the riches of which this parable speaks.

These riches are first of all *one*. The merchant finds one pearl. There is one great treasure of the kingdom of heaven. If we search Scripture to determine what this treasure is, we may safely conclude that this treasure is the incomparably rich and glorious pearl of fellowship and communion with the Most High God through Jesus Christ His Son. Of this great, wonderful blessing the Church has always sung. For it the Church has longed and prayed. To have it is to have the greatest blessing a man can possess. To lack it is to be driven from God's presence until one perishes in everlasting perdition. The ancient Psalmist of Israel sang in a certain place: "One thing have I desired of the Lord, that will I seek after; that I may dwell in the house of the Lord all the days of my life, to behold the beauty of the Lord, and to enquire in his temple" (Ps. 27:4). This is the blessing of covenant fellowship with God; the blessing of communion and friendship with the Most High through Jesus Christ; the blessing of dwelling with God in one tabernacle in perfect joy forever.

Yet this one blessing is so rich that it has many blessings implied in it. It has innumerable nuggets of choicest blessings that are part of the whole. Just as the treasure in the field was composed of many parts, so is the one blessing of salvation rich and varied in its many facets.

There are, in the first place, all the blessings of salvation which we often refer to as the *ordo salutis*. These are the treasures of regeneration, faith, conversion, justification, sanctification, preservation, glorification. These in themselves principally include all that the people of God receive as heirs of the kingdom of heaven.

There are, in the second place, countless blessings such as the knowledge of God Whom to know is eternal life, the peace that passes all understanding, the forgiveness of sins in the blood of the cross, the right to everlasting adoption as children by our heavenly Father, the happiness of God's favor and love, the constant and abiding experience of God's goodness and mercy, the strength and courage to bear the heavy burdens of life and to fight the good fight of faith.

There are, in the third place, blessings which are ours in our labors for the cause of Christ, such as the promise of salvation for us and our children in the line of the covenant, the communion of the saints in the assembly of the elect, the privilege of witnessing for the Name of Christ and His cause in the midst of a world of sin and evil.

How rich and varied, how beautiful and glorious are the many blessings which are ours through the cross of our Lord. How great is the treasure which we find in the Church of Jesus Christ. And all of these things are only the beginnings of the fullness of salvation which we shall receive in glory: the blessing of everlasting life, of the inheritance of a new heavens and a new earth, of ruling with Christ in the kingdom of God. Shall our ears ever become dull of hearing the age-old-gospel of our salvation? Shall our hearts ever be sated with the loveliness of the treasure which is ours? Shall our mouth ever be silenced from proclaiming the riches of grace in praise to God?

These great and costly treasures, so incomparably wonderful, are beyond description. They are so magnificent and altogether lovely that they cannot be weighed in the same scales with any other riches that men give. They stand alone and in a class by themselves. Shall the forgiveness of sins be valued in terms of dollars and cents? Shall peace with God be compared with gold and silver? Shall the blessings of salvation for us and for our children in God's covenant be measured on the same scale as houses and lands? Could ever fame and earthly glory be valued in comparable terms with everlasting life?

Greater than all of life's treasures, far surpassing them all, standing in a class apart are these glorious riches of the kingdom of heaven. That they stand apart is due to the fact, in the first place, that they are heavenly and spiritual. They are not of this earth nor part of the material creation. They have a heavenly color and spiritual substance, in addition to a value that transcends mere earthly things. In the second place, they are everlasting. Incorruptible and undefiled, enduring when all earth's treasures are destroyed, never exhausted or depleted, never tarnished or faded, they ever satisfy from now until forever.

Yet the worth of this treasure can only be ascertained by grace. This also is emphasized by the two parables. The peasant who found a treasure buried in a field hurried to cover it up again until he could purchase the field for himself and make the treasure and the field his own. He saw the worth of what he had found, and determined that he would surely obtain it. so it was also with the merchant. He was a man skilled in his trade. He could recognize imperfect and faulty pearls as well as imitations. He could accurately and swiftly assess the value of any pearl by its size and shape, its clarity and luster. Thus we find him traveling the marketplaces of the ancient world in search of *good* pearls. But when his trained eyes fell upon the one pearl of great price, he could immediately see that it was the best. Incomparably large and beautiful as it may have been, he could see at a glance its value and worth.

But so it is also with the spiritual treasures of the kingdom. There are those who see these treasures but are not able to ascertain or assess their worth. A child does not know the value of money and will use a hidden treasure as a plaything. A novice does not know the value of a pearl and will probably overlook the pearl of great price or consider its price as not worth the cost. There are those who cannot and do not and will not properly evaluate heavenly treasures. On the contrary, when these see the treasures of the kingdom of heaven, they scorn and despise them and mock those who esteem them. To these untrained eyes and sin-darkened minds the treasures of the kingdom of heaven are worthless.

Why is it that there are those who see the value of these treasures of God? The answer lies first of all in the fact that their minds and hearts have been enlightened by grace. God has saved them from sin and already begun the work which makes them heirs of these treasures. They are delivered from the darkness and vanity of depravity, turned away from evil and the things of this present world, placed in abiding and unbreakable contact with heavenly things. They are cleansed in the blood of the cross and are able to assess the value of things earthly and heavenly with faith and understanding of Scripture, with spiritual insight and heavenly wisdom. They are able to become experts in the field of evaluation because the eyes of their understanding are opened.

In the second place this is also true because they have the experience of these good things in their lives. They not only know that one of the treasures of the kingdom of heaven is the forgiveness of sins, but they know that *their* sins are forgiven and they taste the blessed wealth of this great treasure. They do not simply become aware of the fact that numbered among heavenly riches is the blessing of God's favor, but they experience this in their life. They know what they mean when they sing with the sweet Psalmist of Israel: "The loving kindness of my God is more than life to me." This the wicked do not have. They live out their lives under the heavy hand of God's anger and curse. They never have the least experience of the riches of the kingdom. And so they despise the heavenly treasures. The worth of these treasures can only be determined by the people of God to whom is already given by grace part of this treasure. No one else will ever consider these treasures of any worth.

The Treasures of the Kingdom Worth Total Sacrifice

Because the wicked are unable to determine the worth of the treasures of the kingdom, they pass over them without doing anything to obtain them. They stumble over the treasure in the field and with a superior grin go their way. They see the pearl of the greatest price and with callous disregard pass it over. They want nothing of the riches of the kingdom because they despise these riches. And it must never be forgotten that the cause of this, in the deepest sense of the word, lies in their bitter rebellion and hatred against God and Christ. They are unable to assess the work of the kingdom, but they are unwilling as well. They hate Christ and crucify Him. They despise God because they love themselves and are intent on stealing God's glory for themselves. And so, when their path crosses the path of one who highly esteems the treasures of the kingdom, they mock and ridicule and shake their heads in hypocritical wonder. They are intent only in gaining from life what they can. They eat and drink and are merry, for they know that tomorrow they will die. And lest death come before their wicked souls are sated with sin, they pursue pleasure and lust with unnatural devotion and desperate concentration.

And yet there is something of this sin left also in believers—I would almost say that there is much of this sin left. It was this way with the disciples. They too had been guilty of these things. They were especially interested in the kingdom of heaven because, seeing it as an earthly kingdom, they envisioned for themselves positions of honor and power in that kingdom. They were part of the kingdom to see what they could get out of it for themselves.

And yet it is so often like this with us. We seek the kingdom and assume a place in it for personal reasons. What benefits will accrue to us? How can our cause be furthered in this kingdom venture? What will we gain for ourselves by taking a place in the kingdom? These are the dominating questions of our life. And so, while piously claiming to seek the kingdom of heaven, we at the same time are intent on satisfying our personal desires. And when we are disillusioned and bitter because the benefits we had anticipated failed to materialize, we are tempted to disassociate ourselves from any part in the kingdom.

And these things we do because we underestimate the worth of the spiritual treasures of that kingdom. We fail to fight against the carnal and deadly lusts and pride of our flesh. We are swept away unresistingly by the tidal waves of materialism and secularism.

But the kingdom of heaven demands total sacrifice. Both the peasant and the merchant, Jesus tells us, sold all that they had to buy the treasure. There was, of course, a difference. The peasant probably did not have very much, while the merchant was very wealthy and possessed many goodly pearls. But the point is that regardless of how much they had, they sold everything they possessed. The cost was everything. The price was all they owned. I recall reading about a famous criminal lawyer who would defend certain clients for this same price. When asked what the cost would be, he invariably responded, "everything you have." And when a shocked client would protest, he would say: "If you die for your crime, everything you have means nothing. If I save you from death, is not life worth everything?" The demanded price for the treasure of the kingdom is total.

And it ought to be noticed that each in his own way did not consider the price too high to pay. With joy in his heart the peasant went and sold all that he had. And there was no reluctance or quibbling about the price on the part of the merchant. He saw the one great and valuable pearl. He knew the cost was not too much. He paid it with eagerness and joy to obtain what he longed for. Yet the Lord also emphasizes that, by this total sacrifice, each obtained the treasure. It did not happen that they set their hearts upon it, that they sold everything they had, and then, at the last moment, they were frustrated in their attempt to obtain the treasure. No, total sacrifice also guaranteed that the treasure was theirs.

So it is in the kingdom of heaven. This is the mystery—the irony, if you will—of the kingdom of heaven. Total sacrifice brings incomparable riches. He that would save his life must surely lose it. But he that loses his life shall find it. He that would be lord of all must first become a servant. And indeed, if he does not become a servant, he shall never be lord. He that would gain the world must give up the world. For how shall he obtain the world without sacrificing the world? It is the proud that shall be abased and brought low. But it is the humble that shall be exalted. To obtain the treasures of the kingdom it is necessary to sacrifice all. And only in this way shall they ever be attained.

This is not to say that by means of sacrificing all, we earn for ourselves the treasures of the kingdom. It is not our work that gains for us the treasures which God has in store for His people. Not what our hands have done shall save our guilty souls. Indeed, we are already a part of that kingdom before we can recognize the value of its treasures. The principle is that all that we have and all that we are—all that we receive from God—must be totally and completely dedicated to God's service and the welfare of His cause and covenant. If anything stands in the way, we must discard it immediately. If our eye offend us we must pluck it out, for it is better to go to glory with one eye than with both eyes to be cast into everlasting hell. To follow Jesus demands that we forsake husband and wife, parents and children, should this be necessary in the pursuit of heavenly treasures, for the claims of the kingdom are total and absolute.

Are we rich and possess much of this world's goods? If these things stand in the way, go and sell all that thou hast and give to the poor; and thou shalt find treasure in heaven. Do we seek ourselves and magnify our own personal interests? The test of true discipleship is: deny thyself and take up thy cross and follow Jesus. Is our job, our wealth, our home, our daily bread demanded of us? Seek ye first the kingdom of God and His righteousness and all these things will be added unto you.

Does the ultimate price of life itself have to be paid in order to obtain this treasure? Remember: he that would gain his life must first lose it. There were those who loved not their lives unto death in order that they might attain the reward of the people of God. There was a Moses of old who by faith "when he was come to years, refused to be called the son of Pharaoh's daughter; Choosing rather to suffer affliction with the people of God, than to enjoy the pleasures of sin for a season; Esteeming the reproach of Christ greater riches than the treasures in Egypt: for he had respect unto the recompense of the reward" (Heb. 11:24-26). There were other saints "Who through faith subdued kingdoms, wrought righteousness, obtained promises, stopped the mouths of lions, Quenched the violence of fire, escaped the edge of the sword, out of weakness were made strong, waxed valiant in fight, turned to flight the armies of the aliens. Women received their dead raised to life again: and others were tortured, not accepting deliverance; that they might obtain a better resurrection: And others had trial of cruel mockings and scourgings, yea, moreover of bonds and imprisonment: They were stoned, they were sawn asunder, were tempted, were slain with the sword: they wandered about in sheepskins and goatskins; being destitute, afflicted, tormented; (Of whom the world was not worthy:) they wandered in deserts, and in mountains, and in dens and caves of the earth. And these all, having obtained a good report through faith, received not the promise: God having provided some better thing for us, that they without us should not be made perfect" (Heb. 11:33-40). Did not even the apostle say: "But what things were gain to me those I counted loss for the excellency of the knowledge of Christ Jesus my Lord: for whom I have suffered the loss of all things, and do count them but dung, that I may win Christ, and be found in him" (Phil. 3:7-9a).

How total and complete are the demands of the kingdom! And yet how glorious is the treasure that is attained through this way. All that a man has. Nothing less will ever do. But the eternal riches of the kingdom are ours through this way of sacrifice.

And yet it must be remembered, that while this is indeed a calling, it is also a glorious privilege. There must be no reluctance or need of force to sacrifice all things for the kingdom. For the joy that is his, a man must go and sell all that he has to obtain the treasure. This means that the holy compulsion must come from within. It must be the fruit of grace and the Spirit of Christ. It can only be the power of salvation within us that moves us to sacrifice all to obtain the treasure. The joy springs from a profound realization of the privilege that is ours to sacrifice all on behalf of the cause of our God. A treasure so exceedingly great is surely worth the loss of all things.

6

The Gathering of the Kingdom

Again, the kingdom of heaven is like unto a net, that was cast into the sea, and gathered of every kind:
Which, when it was full, they drew to shore, and sat down, and gathered the good into vessels, but cast the bad away.
So shall it be at the end of the world: the angels shall come forth, and sever the wicked from among the just,
And shall cast them into the furnace of fire: there shall be wailing and gnashing of teeth.

—Matthew 13:47–50

Many commentators have observed that there is a very striking parallel between this parable and the parable of the tares in the field. Both, it is true, speak of the close proximity of good and bad people in the historical manifestation of the kingdom of heaven. And this similarity has led many to identify these two parables. While it is evident that there is such similarity, there is nevertheless an important difference. In the parable of the tares in the field the emphasis falls on the fact that the devil plants evil men close to the saints of God after the kingdom is established. Therefore that parable looks at the presence of the wicked within the historical manifestation of the kingdom from the viewpoint of the devil's purpose. In this parable, however, the dragnet sweeps both good and bad fish before it as it is dragged through the seas of time. Hence emphasis in this parable falls on the gathering of the sons of the kingdom and the inevitable presence of wicked men in the kingdom. God gathers His own even though there are wicked present; and the very manner in which God gathers His Church makes it inevitable that wicked men will be present.

This parable, too, was spoken for the benefit of the disciples—for their instruction and against the background of their wrong conception of the nature of the kingdom. The disciples did not only envision an earthly kingdom made up of Jews, nor did they only think of this kingdom in terms of their own personal gain as high officials in it; they also thought of the kingdom as limited solely to the Jewish people. The matter of gathering the sons of the kingdom was therefore comparatively simple: be born a Jew. This fact of birth would surely guarantee a place in the kingdom. And if one was born a

Gentile, he could become a Jew through the rite of circumcision and the adoption of the Mosaic legislation which had come down from Mount Sinai in ancient times.

And so in this parable the Lord points out that the kingdom is to be universal in the broadest sense of the word. This implies, in the first place, that it is surely not enough to be born a Jew. God gathers His Church by His Word and Spirit from every nation on earth. In the second place, in both Israel and the kingdom throughout the entire New Dispensation there would always be apostate seed—bad fish—which could not and would not be taken out of the kingdom until the very end. Not all Jews would be saved. Nor, when the gospel went to all parts of the world, would all Gentiles be saved. The kingdom, though universal, would remain a kingdom peopled by a remnant according to the election of grace.

And this is true because the citizens of the kingdom are gathered in the line of continued generations. This was true in the Old Dispensation; it is no less true in the New.

The Various Elements of the Parable

The parable which Jesus told His disciples in the comparative solitude of the home where He had retired for the evening contained elements that were surely familiar to them. Jesus had called several of His disciples away from their fishing nets by the shores of the beautiful Sea of Galilee, where they had plied their trade for many years. And so they had often been engaged in doing what Jesus describes here.

But in contrast, this familiar figure is applied by the Lord to the spiritual realities of the kingdom of heaven. No doubt the disciples had never given a thought to the fact that, while engaged in their daily obligations, they were portraying a spiritual truth in which they would someday have a vital part.

The net of which the Lord speaks was not a small net that was thrown by hand into the lake to be immediately retrieved. Nor was it a net that was used by anglers who fished with worm and hook, but would take recourse to a net if the fish was too large for their pole. The net that Jesus referred to was a large net sometimes as long as half a mile, made with floats on the top and weights on the bottom so that it would hang perpendicularly in the water. It was customarily used for fishing in shallow water. Yet it was used where schools of fish would collect for food. The net would be placed a certain distance from the land in a straight line by two or more boats. The ends would then be brought together as the net was dragged closer to the shore so that the fish would be caught in it and could easily be brought up to the shore, where the bad ones would be cast out and the good ones preserved.

Thus the point of the parable is that the fishermen would, of course, fish for good fish only. They were not interested in the bad ones. They were intent on catching fish which they themselves could eat or which could be sold in the markets. Yet, the very nature of the method used in fishing made it inevitable that also worthless and inedible fish would be trapped in the net. These latter fish were not the purpose of dragging the net through the waters. They were in the net, outwardly at least, and treated as good fish only until the net was finally drawn to the shore where they could be eliminated.

Thus the meaning of the Lord is comparatively clear. By the sea the Lord refers to the whole world. And the point which Jesus wishes to make first of all is the fact that the citizens of the kingdom will be gathered not only from Jewry within the confines of Palestine, but will be gathered from every nation and tribe and tongue. This fact is further emphasized in the parable when it is mentioned that all kinds of fish were caught. There was not merely one species of fish but many varieties which were gathered into the net. And the good and the bad fish are not distinguished by their species, but by their worth, no matter what their species may have been. It is true that in the past the kingdom had been established exclusively in Canaan with the Jews as its only citizens, but now this was all to be changed. Pentecost would presently come and the Church would break out of the narrow confines of national Israel to spread over the whole earth, becoming universal in the strictest sense of the word.

The net refers to the kingdom as to its external operation, development, and manifestation. Within the net the fish are caught. They are brought into the kingdom through the action of the net which is pulled through the seas of the world. This external operation and development and manifestation of the kingdom are especially the preaching of the gospel. The spiritual activity of the kingdom is the preaching of the gospel by the Church, by means of which the kingdom is gathered.

The good fish which are caught in the net are therefore the elect citizens of the kingdom. They are the ones ordained by God from all eternity to inhabit the kingdom of glory. They are the redeemed ones ransomed by the blood of the Lamb. They are the ones destined to inherit the kingdom of heaven according to the promise of God. The bad fish are the reprobate seed who are born in the covenant and kingdom, but who will, at the end, be cast out. The shore is the dawn of eternity when history comes to an end and when all appear before Christ. The ones who make separation are the angels, who are the ministering spirits of God and who labor night and day on behalf of the cause of God's people.

The Net as the Preaching

Bearing all these things in mind, we can now turn our attention more specifically to the parable.

First of all, our attention must be briefly focused on the preaching of the gospel. This would hardly be necessary were it not for the fact that the true idea of the gospel is so often distorted in our colorless and indifferent age. It is true, that the emphasis in the parable does not fall as such on the preaching. The emphasis is not on *how* the citizens of the kingdom are gathered; the emphasis falls rather on the gathering itself. We must, nevertheless, make some remarks about the gospel as the power whereby the citizens of the kingdom are gathered.

The gospel is the spiritual and sovereign power of the kingdom. The gospel is the Word of God which is revealed in Jesus Christ. Because He is the Word of God par excellence, He is also the One Who alone can preach the gospel. This gospel He preaches through the Church which He calls into being.

The implications of this are of considerable importance. It is because Christ preaches His own gospel that the gospel can never be characterized as an offer of salvation, as an indication of God's love for all men, or as an invitation to be accepted or rejected at will. That is not a characterization, but a caricature. Christ is not a powerless agent of the almighty Word of God Who brings a word so weak that it is dependent on man's will for its ultimate effect. This is no gospel at all. The gospel is the *power* of God unto salvation (Rom. 1:16). It is therefore the sovereign and irresistible and efficacious instrument in the hands of the exalted Christ through which He accomplishes all the Father's purpose. The gospel is the means of accomplishing election as well as reprobation. Men may sap the gospel of its strength by making it an offer, but this does not alter the fact that men sin by doing this and that Christ continues to preach His own gospel in spite of the efforts of men to destroy it.

For this reason, too, the gospel—as to its contents—is always in complete harmony with Scripture; for Scripture is the written record of the Word of God. The central and all-pervasive message of that Word is the sovereign grace of God revealed in the cross of Calvary for the salvation of the elect. No other message but that ever should be preached.

Besides, it ought to be noticed that the net is not dragged through the whole sea and that not all the fish in the sea are caught in it. This does not mean to negate the fact that the gospel is not preached in every nation on the earth, for such is certainly the case. But it does mean to say that not all men who ever lived or who ever will live hear the gospel preached. Nor is this according to the purpose of God. God causes His gospel to be preached where it pleases Him and where He, in His good pleasure, directs it. Those who are intent on seeing to it that every man hears the gospel have already failed and will fail in the future, for this is not God's purpose.

The gospel is nevertheless general in its proclamation. It is not general in the sense that it comes to all men, but it is general in the sense that it comes to both elect and reprobate. Yet, in spite of the fact that it is general in its proclamation, it is very particular in its contents. It does not speak of the universal love of God and a desire on God's part for all to be saved. It speaks rather of the particular salvation of a particular cross and a limited atonement that will be applied to a particular people according to God's particular good pleasure. It is considerably limited both in its contents and in its operation.

This gospel is the external operation and development, the external manifestation of the power of the kingdom. We must not conceive of this kingdom as being limited to one particular congregation. Nor is the kingdom even one individual denomination. The reference is the catholic Church of Jesus Christ which exists in all the world. And in its broadest sense, it includes all that goes under the name of historical Christendom. The kingdom is revealed in a broad sense and develops in a wide sphere. In this external development and visible manifestation, it includes not only the true people of God but also the apostate seed of God's covenant. Where the gospel is preached, the kingdom is founded and established. In fact, because the gospel is preached, this kingdom comes to external manifestation. The purpose is always nothing else but to gather the true sons of the kingdom out of the world of sin and death. This is always accomplished, for Christ controls the gospel and preaches it sovereignly and efficaciously. But it is true that in the gathering of the sons of the kingdom many bad men are also brought in. And these are treated not only as the true sons of the kingdom, but they will exist in that external kingdom to the very end.

The Church Gathered in Continued Generations

Why does it happen that there are also carnal seed within the kingdom? The parable of the tares looked at this problem from the viewpoint of the devil's purpose in his efforts to destroy the Church. The Lord, in this parable, looks at this problem from the viewpoint of the gathering of the Church. The problem of the presence of the wicked within the historical manifestation of the kingdom must be explained by the fact that not individuals are gathered into the kingdom, but generations.

There is one serious mistake which many make today in their efforts to preach the gospel and in their work of gathering the Church. This is a serious mistake because it fails to take into account a fundamental truth concerning the work of God. The gathering of the citizens of the kingdom is viewed individualistically. Men look at the gathering of the Church from the viewpoint of individuals, and consider individuals alone in isolation from their forebears and from their children. But God never works in this way. God always works organically and deals with men in their connections with each other. This truth has many implications, only a few of which can be pointed out now. But if this fundamental truth is forgotten, the most serious consequences result.

First and foremost among these implications is the fact that God always saves His people in the line of continued generations. This was already true in the Old Dispensation. It is easy to trace this covenant line from father to son. The line began in Adam. It is true that Adam fell, and it must never be forgotten that the entire human race fell in Adam. The whole organism of the human race perished in him when he was disobedient. It is the fundamental mistake of all Arminianism, which by its very nature is individualistic, to forget this. Nevertheless, immediately after the Fall, God spoke to Adam and Eve of the seed of the woman and of the seed of the serpent which would rage long and bitter warfare throughout all history. And while it is true that this seed of the woman was centrally Christ, nevertheless in Christ the seed included all the elect who would be saved in the line of the generations of the woman. Thus in the Old Dispensation the covenant line can easily be traced from Adam to Seth to Enoch to Methuselah to Noah to Abraham to Isaac to Jacob and the twelve patriarchs; and more narrowly, to Judah to David to Solomon to Mary to Christ.

But this is no less true in the New Dispensation. It is not only a fact that the gospel follows a definite course from Jerusalem to Judea to Samaria to Syria to Asia Minor to Greece to Italy to Europe to America; it is also a fact that in this steady and sure progress of the gospel, there were not simply individuals picked out here and there, but generations were saved. Households were baptized and brought into the Church. Families were gathered into the covenant. Believers and their seed were made citizens of the kingdom of heaven. Not individuals were saved, but believing parents and their posterity. This truth was not only revealed repeatedly in the Old Dispensation when God spoke of establishing His covenant with Abraham and his seed, but the apostle Peter picks up this same refrain in his Pentecost sermon when he says: "For the promise is unto you, and to your children, and to all that are afar off, even as many as the Lord our God shall call" (Acts 2:39).

But it is for this precise reason that there are not only good fish caught in the net, but also bad ones. This does not mean that certain people come into the Church from without because they are attracted by the gospel outwardly although they are not really true believers. This happens too, no doubt. There are always people of the stripe of Ananias and Sapphira. But this is by no means the real reason. It is inevitable that bad fish are found in the net. This cannot possibly be avoided. The reason why this cannot be avoided is because, within the lines of believers and their seed, there is always reprobate seed. They are not all Israel that are of Israel. (See Rom. 9:6.) This was already true in the Old Dispensation. There were always unbelievers born in the historical dispensation of the kingdom. Isaac was born there, but also Ishmael. Isaac and Rebekah had two sons, one of whom was Jacob, but the other was Esau. And among the twelve tribes by no means were all saved. In fact, more often than not, the wicked seed of the covenant was in the majority, while the true people of God were the remnant, the hut in the garden of cucumbers. (See Isa. 1:8)

Nor is it any different in the New Dispensation. All that are born in the line of the covenant from believing parents are not the true seed of the covenant. There are always the apostate seed, the unbelievers, the hypocrites, the wicked within the historical manifestation of the kingdom. The line of election and reprobation cuts right through the historical line of the covenant.

But again it must be remembered that God deals organically with people. Not only are individuals reprobated, not only do individuals fall away, but generations apostatize. Not with individuals as individuals, but with generations, and with individuals only in their relation to their generations does God accomplish His purpose. Not only is this true in election, but in reprobation as well. God visits the iniquity of the fathers upon the children unto the third and fourth generation of them that hate Him. Generations apostatize and forsake the truth. This is a fundamental premise of all the activity of the Church also in her missionary work. From these apostate generations a remnant may be saved, but it always remains a remnant. Israel as a nation forsook Christ and was forsaken of God. A remnant, however, was saved, and will be saved throughout the New Dispensation. Not only individuals, but nations reject the gospel. And although the Church is surely gathered from them, as nations, organically considered, these nations are forsaken of God. To them God never returns.

We may compare the line of the covenant as a mighty river that flows through the river bed of history. This river bed represents the historical realization of God's everlasting covenant of grace. Into the river which flows in the river bed new streams constantly empty. These represent new covenant lines, new generations which are brought by the preaching of the gospel into the covenant. But as the river rushes through the ages of history, much water from that river is expelled. Some of it is absorbed by the soil surrounding the river. Some of it is taken up by the heat of the sun. Some of it is caught in swirling eddies along the riverbanks. Some of it is splashed from the river as the river hits rocks and stones. This water which is lost from the river bed represents the generations which are, through history, excluded from the covenant. But even though there is much water in the river which never reaches the destination of the river at its mouth, the river nevertheless is God's covenant and the historical manifestation of the kingdom of heaven.

Thus in the net of the kingdom are to be found many bad fish. The result of this is twofold. On the one hand, while the net is being dragged through the seas of history, all the fish caught by it are treated the same. The same is true in the historical dispensation of the kingdom of God. In the Old Dispensation the wicked seed as well as the true seed of the covenent were separated from the world and the surrounding nations. They were separated physically and geographically. And in this respect, they shared many things. They shared a common law, temple, priesthood, sacrifice, king, and a promised land. So it is also in the New Dispensation. All the children of the historical manifestation of the kingdom and covenant are separated from the world by the water of baptism. Hence they share a common preaching, common sacraments, covenant instruction, covenant schools, the calling to fight the battle of faith, the hope of everlasting reward.

But this does not mean that all are true seed of Abraham and children of the promise. There is much bad seed. There are apostate generations. There are worthless fish. It is nevertheless God's purpose that this be so, for God has willed it. It shall remain this way unto the end.

In the second place, the result of this is that the antithesis is always the sharpest within the kingdom. This was also true in the Old Dispensation. So often the wicked seemed triumphant in God's heritage. They corrupted the temple, led the people to worship idols, forsook the law, and caused Israel to be conformed to the nations surrounding her. This happens also in the New Dispensation. The apostate element in the Church corrupt the truth; they lead the Church into heresy and false doctrine; they advocate world conformity; they subject to their own sinful purposes the causes of the kingdom; the Christian schools, the mission program of the Church, the sacraments, the calling of believers.

But they do this within the kingdom. They do not become less bad because they are in the kingdom. On the contrary, their sin appears the more terrible because they operate in the sphere of God's covenant. They are not permitted to remain within the net in the hopes that perhaps someday they will become good fish. This is nonsense. But they are left in the covenant so that the antithesis may be clearly revealed in all its implications.

It is only at the end that final separation takes place.

The Separation of the End of the Age

The end of which the parable speaks is the end of the age. This end is not an arbitrary end or an end among many ends, as some like to speak of it. It is the final and absolute end of the age from the viewpoint of God's purpose. God's purpose is fully accomplished as He determined that purpose from before the foundation of the world. And that means that all God determined to do has been done. All the elect ordained by God have been brought into the kingdom, so that not one is missing. The wicked have developed in sin also within the historical kingdom, until they have filled the cup of iniquity and have become ripe for judgment. The end is therefore that point in time when history comes to its close. Beyond that point history cannot and will not go. It is the final end of all that was begun in Paradise. There is, from God's point of view, no possibility of history continuing. It cannot go on; therefore all things come to an abrupt halt. Just as in a battle between two nations, the end of the battle is not arbitrarily decided upon. The end comes only when the purpose and goal of warfare is achieved. Victory has been gained. The triumph over the enemy has come. Then the battle is over.

For this reason too it is an end marked by the salvation of the true believers. They were hunted and persecuted until there were only a few left to mention the name of God. The truth of the gospel is no longer heard. The witnesses are dead and their bodies lie on the streets of apostate Jerusalem. (See Rev. 11:1-10.) The place of God's dwelling here on earth has been trampled under foot by the wicked. The apostate seed of the covenant have gained the ascendency. All is now subjected to the power and dominion of Antichrist. Not Christ reigns in the world, but Antichrist. And his kingdom is universal.

But God has achieved His purpose. The net of the kingdom is brought to the shore of eternity.

The angels make final separation. And so it should be. The angels are ministering spirits of God who are sent to do His will. They are the defenders of God's people, the champions of the cause of Christ. They are always vitally interested in the affairs of the kingdom and work for the well-being of the elect. How often did they not appear to the hard-pressed saints of the Old Dispensation with words of comfort and good cheer? They were singing in the silent night of the incarnate One on Ephratah's hills. They were present in the garden to comfort the Lord as he writhed beneath the crushing anticipation of the cross. They were the first to preach the glorious gospel of the resurrection on that early Sunday morning in Joseph's garden. They were the ones to point the disciples away from the ascending Lord to the coming of Christ upon the clouds of heaven. They were present with the Church to care for her and to watch over her in the years of her infancy. It is more than fitting that now also they will come to bring about the final salvation of the Church.

They will separate the good from the bad. When on the shores of eternity, the net is finally opened, the people of God are taken into the everlasting kingdom of their Father, while the wicked are cast into the furnace of fire where is only weeping and gnashing of teeth. On earth the two developed side by side. This shall happen no more. On earth both were, of necessity, treated the same. This is finished at last. On earth the people of God had to fight for the cause of Christ, for there were wicked subjects in the kingdom. Now their spiritual swords are changed into palms of victory. On earth the true children of the covenant were reproached and killed all the day long. Now they wear the crown of life and enter into the glory of their Lord. The wicked are killed all the day long in eternal death.

They no longer can stand at the side of the righteous. They no longer can be part of the historical manifestation of the kingdom. The final separation has come on heaven's shores, a separation that will last forever.

Thus, for a time, in this world, it is the portion of the righteous to suffer, for the presence of the carnal seed is a never ending source of grief and trial. But the people of God must be of good cheer, for presently the Lord will come again. Now the wicked may stand in God's heritage, but it will be only for a short time. They must indeed become even stronger than they are now. But he that is born of God overcometh the world. And the victory which overcometh the world is our faith. Lift up your heads, for your redemption draweth nigh.

7

The Evidence of Forgiveness

Therefore is the kingdom of heaven likened unto a certain king, which would take account of his servants.

And when he had begun to reckon, one was brought unto him, which owed him ten thousand talents.

But forasmuch as he had not to pay, his lord commanded him to be sold, and his wife, and children, and all that he had, and payment to be made.

The servant therefore fell down, and worshipped him, saying, Lord, have patience with me, and I will pay thee all.

Then the lord of that servant was moved with compassion, and loosed him, and forgave him the debt.

But the same servant went out, and found one of his fellowservants, which owed him an hundred pence: and he laid hands on him, and took him by the throat, saying, Pay me that thou owest.

And his fellowservant fell down at his feet, and besought him, saying, Have patience with me, and I will pay thee all.

And he would not: but went and cast him into prison, till he should pay the debt.

So when his fellowservants saw what was done, they were very sorry, and came and told unto their lord all that was done.

Then his lord, after that he had called him, said unto him, O thou wicked servant, I forgave thee all that debt, because thou desiredst me:

Shouldest not thou also have had compassion on thy fellowservant, even as I had pity on thee?

And his lord was wroth, and delivered him to the tormentors, till he should pay all that was due unto him.

So likewise shall my heavenly Father do also unto you, if ye from your hearts forgive not every one his brother their trespasses.

—Matthew 18:23-35

This parable had a specific occasion. Peter came to the Lord with the question: "Lord, how oft shall my brother sin against me, and I forgive him? till seven times?" This question of Peter was, in turn, prompted by Jesus' teaching that within the Church a man must do all in his power to save his brother who falls into sin. In verses 15-17 of this chapter Jesus had said: "Moreover if thy brother shall trespass against thee, go and tell him his fault between thee and him alone: if he shall hear thee, thou hast gained thy brother. But if he will not hear thee, then take with thee one or two more, that in the mouth of two or three witnesses every word may be established. And if he neglect to hear them, tell it unto the church: but if he neglect to hear the church, let him be unto thee as an heathen man and a publican." Peter had correctly seen that to follow the injunctions of the Lord in these verses involves forgiving our brother—and forgiving our brother even before we go to him. Peter wondered how often this had to be done.

When Peter suggested forgiving his brother seven times, he thought he was being extraordinarily generous. The rabbis taught that this forgiveness must be extended three times. In a spurt of generosity, Peter more than doubled this amount and increased the number to seven.

This forms the background for the teaching of the parable. Jesus first of all answers Peter's question. We must forgive our brother, not seven times, but seventy times seven. That is, there is no limit to the number of times we forgive our brother. This is a fundamental principle of the kingdom of heaven: forgiveness is without end. We must always forgive our brother, and we must do this from the heart. This is proper conduct within the kingdom of heaven because we are forgiven by God, and our forgiveness of our brother is evidence of the forgiveness we receive from God.

God's Forgiveness of Our Sins

The king of whom Jesus speaks in the parable is evidently a very powerful king who rules over many provinces. He had appointed satraps or governors to rule over his many provinces. These men ruled in his name and exercised authority on behalf of their king. They were responsible for the collection of taxes from the people which would be turned over to the royal treasury.

One servant had been unfaithful and had used the money he collected for himself. He had done this a long time, and the result was that he owed the king 10,000 talents. This huge sum came to about $15,000,000 in our money.

We ought to notice how the tremendous size of the debt is emphasized in the parable. It was too great even to be imagined and far too large ever to be paid back.

When the king decided to make a reckoning with his servants, the unfaithfulness of this man came to light. The king decided to punish the servant. The type of punishment was in complete harmony with the law in that time. The property of the man, his wife, and children were all to be sold, as well as the man himself. Because he was unable to pay the debt, the man himself and all his property belonged rightfully to the king. In this way the king could recover at least a fraction of what was due him. This was fair and equitable and in conformity with justice. It was not an evidence of cruelty or arbitrary despotism. It was the only course of action left open to a righteous king.

But the servant pleaded for mercy. He pleaded with the king that his sentence be not executed upon him immediately. He promised, if given time, to pay the whole debt, although this was obviously impossible.

The king was moved by this request of the servant. The Lord tells us that he was merciful to the servant. The king took pity on him in his wretchedness and was eager to make his servant happy again. The result was that he not only heeded the request of the servant, but went far beyond the request and simply forgave the debt. It was canceled and would never have to be paid again.

In this very powerful way the Lord teaches us a lesson in the mercy of our God. We owe to God a tremendous debt. We too are servants in God's kingdom. To us is committed the calling of using all things which are ours to God's glory and in His service. The things over which we are placed are never ours; they belong to the King. We are given responsibility for them to use them for the King's benefit. This is a daily debt we owe God. This is rooted in the fact that He is the Creator and we are His creatures.

But we never pay the debt, not even for a moment. We use all the things in God's world for ourselves. And, in using them for ourselves, we use them to sin against God. Thus we steal from God. And, in stealing from God, we accumulate a vast debt.

The debt is absolutely unpayable. There are several reasons for this. In the first place, we constantly face the same obligations to love God and serve Him. These obligations are present every moment of our life. We never can pay off on a back debt, therefore, because we are always confronted with current debts which need to be paid. If we owe the grocery store $1,000 because we have not paid our bills there for several months, we cannot expect that we will pay that back debt by suddenly beginning to pay current bills. If we owe God our complete devotion and service every moment, we cannot pay back debts even if we could pay current bills. The Lord Jesus said: "So likewise ye, when ye shall have done all those things which are commanded you, say, We are unprofitable servants: we have done that which was our duty to do" (Luke 17:10).

In the second place, this debt is unpayable because it is far too large. Even one sin which we commit makes us worthy of eternal hell. It is impossible, therefore, to pay for even one sin, to pay back even a small fraction of the debt we owe. The payment of the vast debt we accumulate is far too great to be paid.

In the third place, we are sinners who not only cannot pay our back debts, but who cannot even pay current bills. Daily we increase our debt. Our sins rise up against us prevailing day by day. The result is that we deserve only to be sold without mercy into the slavery of sin and death and hell. Every day this reckoning with Jehovah comes; every day the same thing is true: our debt grows greater.

But God forgives the debt of His people. This is the fundamental character of the kingdom of heaven. It is a kingdom in which God the eternal King forgives His people and gives to them the righteousness of the cross of Christ.

This forgiveness is, from the viewpoint of God's counsel, eternal. When Balaam was asked by Balak, king of Moab, to curse Israel, God changed his cursings into blessings. He was forced to say, among many other things: "He hath not beheld iniquity in Jacob, neither hath he seen perverseness in Israel: the Lord his God is with him, and the shout of a king is among them" (Num. 23:21). The idea is that God *never* sees iniquity in His people.

This is possible only because God sees His people as those who belong to Christ. Their forgiveness was historically realized on the cross of Christ. Christ assumed responsibility for the debt which His people owed to God, taking upon Himself the payment of that debt. He did this because the punishment of eternal hell was endured by Him when He suffered and died. Though each sin we commit deserves eternal hell, and though the number of the people of God is very great, Christ paid back all that debt when He endured the horrors of hell on the cross. And He paid the debt because, while He suffered the anguish and torments of hell, He still loved God, served Him and glorified His Father. When the dark and dreadful waves of God's fierce wrath swept over His soul, He still loved God with a perfect heart. And thus He paid the debt for all God's people. It is paid so completely that not one small particle of that debt remains to be paid.

This is all the manifestation of God's mercy. God's mercy is His attitude of longing toward His people. He desires earnestly to save them from their terrible misery and to make them happy and blessed. But God's mercy is not a mere feeling or desire; it is God's living will. And so, the cross is the highest manifestation of the mercy of God. God gave His own Son to the death of the cross. God did not consider even this price too great to pay, for His mercy is great and beyond our comprehension.

This forgiveness becomes our forgiveness in the way of confession of sin. We become conscious of this great blessing when we carry the burden of our sin and guilt to Calvary and confess at the foot of the cross our own unworthiness. We find the assurance of forgiveness when we, by faith, lay hold on Christ and His perfect sacrifice. Then we actually come to know that this great debt is taken away.

The Evidence of this Forgiveness

This great forgiveness of God must be manifested in our lives.

This truth is sharply set forth in the parable, in the confrontation of the forgiven debtor with a fellow servant who owed him money.

But there are striking differences between the way in which he treated his fellow servant and the way his king treated him. In the first place, he was now dealing with a fellow servant, a man equal to him. He was not superior in any way to his fellow servant and had no claim upon him because of superiority of position and authority. But in contrast he was a servant to his king. He owed his king obedience and honor; his fellow servant owed him nothing.

In the second place, although the servant owed his king an amount comparable to $15,000,000, his fellow servant was indebted to him in the amount of 100 pence, a total of about $15. The Lord deliberately accentuates the vast differences in the size of the debt.

In the third place, the king originally called simply for a reckoning. But the servant gave no opportunity to his fellow servant to make any explanation. He roughly grabbed his fellow servant by the neck and began to choke him.

Finally, although his fellow servant also asked for a little time to pay and, strikingly, used almost the same words which the servant himself used in talking to his lord, the servant would have none of it. He demanded immediate payment or just punishment. His total lack of mercy is most astounding.

The whole matter was sorrowfully reported to the king. And the king, in anger, reminded the wretched servant of the mercy he had received, of his own obligation to show mercy, and of the punishment which was now his due.

And so, in this way, the Lord describes an important aspect of the relations which ought to exist between those who belong to the kingdom and those who are members together of the Church of Christ.

When we sin, this sin is committed not only against God, it is also often against our fellow saints. We offend our fellow saints by our sins, do harm to them, and put ourselves in debt to them by the sins we commit.

Yet, there are important differences. When we sin against God, we sin against our Creator and Sustainer who holds our life in His hands. We sin against the Most High Majesty of God and we rob Him of the glory which is His due. But when we sin against one another, we sin against our equals. We are together creatures and together we are sinners. We stand on the same level before God. The debt that is incurred at the hands of our fellow saints is accordingly not nearly as great. It is about $15 as over against $15,000,000. The debt incurred by our sins is insignificantly small in comparison with what we owe God.

Nevertheless, it is always true that in the Church we stand in debt to one another. No saint is perfect as long as he lives in this world. All our sins, in one way or another, are sins that affect our relationships with our fellow saints. And we must live in this consciousness that we continually put ourselves in debt to those with whom we live. Or, to put it in the form in which the parable brings this to our attention, our fellow saints put themselves continually in debt to us by their sins.

Hence, the point of the parable is clear. If we experience the forgiveness of God for the sins which we commit against Him, we will surely forgive our fellow saints also. This follows in the nature of the case. If we know our sins, we are overwhelmed with the consciousness of the staggering debt we owe to God. But when we experience the wonder that God has forgiven us, then this can only fill us with awe and thanksgiving. It is of the Lord's mercies that we are not consumed. And this mercy is completely undeserving. God does not need to forgive us. He is under no obligation to forgive our debt. We have, in no way, made ourselves worthy of forgiveness. If God would refuse to cancel our debt, and if He would punish us forever in hell, we could raise not one word of complaint. We would receive what is justly our due. How can we ever be grateful enough for such a great wonder?

It stands to reason then that to forgive our brother is relatively easy. On the one hand, it is surely an obligation on our part. But on the other hand, it is inevitable. If we experience God's forgiving mercy and understand even a little of the astonishing wonder of it, then there is no problem at all in forgiving our brother. Then we do not forgive him three times, or, in generosity, seven times; but there cannot possibly be any end to such forgiveness. God forgives us again and again. How can we do anything less? We confess our sins and yet commit the same sins over again. This happens not once or twice, but throughout our lifetime. Yet God is ever faithful and merciful to forgive. He never, so to speak, wearies of forgiving us.

But the opposite is also true. We may perhaps refuse to forgive our fellow saints. If we do this, it is only evidence of the fact that we are not forgiven ourselves. After all, the debtor was not really forgiven. Jesus describes him in the parable as forgiven for the purpose of making the point. But the debtor went to hell.

There is, therefore, a kind of reciprocal relation of which the Lord speaks in this parable: "So likewise shall my heavenly Father do also unto you, if ye from your hearts forgive not every one his brother their trespasses."

We are under solemn obligation to forgive one another. It is true, of course, that we cannot truly forgive our brother unless he gives evidence of repentance for his sins. But there are two remarks which must be made in this connection. In the first place, if our brother sins against us we must go to him and, with a spirit of humility and love, bring him to repentance. This is the Lord's teaching in verses 15-18 of this chapter. We may not sit back with a haughty spirit and wait for him to come. In the second place, we must already forgive our brother in our hearts before we go to him. God also deals thus with us. Our forgiveness is an objective fact in the cross of Christ and in the mind and heart of God. We experience that forgiveness in the way of confession of sin. So also must we reflect this when we go to our brother. We must forgive him in our hearts, for only then can we truly seek his repentance. And when the sin is removed, then the relationships of love and communion are again restored.

But we often find it difficult to forgive our brother. We harbor thoughts of superiority and condescension, and set up ourselves as the only standard of virtue. We may even forgive outwardly and verbally, but not from the heart. We may say: "I will forgive, but I will never forget."

It would be a terrible thing if God would deal so with us. Living in the consciousness of His great forgiving mercy, we must forgive from the heart. We must forgive wholly, sincerely, forgettingly, thankfully. We must forgive knowing that we go together to the foot of the cross and that we both stand daily in need of forgiveness from God. We can never send anyone to Calvary; we must go with them to cry out together for the forgiveness our Savior earned for us in His death. In this way we forgive again and again—as God does to us. We forgive because we always look first at ourselves and the wonder of the cross of Christ. Then we can surely pray as the Lord teaches us: "Forgive us our debts as we forgive our debtors."

And so the relation is reciprocal. If we fail to forgive our brother, it is only because we have not been forgiven by God. And when we fail we shall never experience forgiveness ourselves. We cannot hold grudges against our brother, refuse to forgive him, and then expect God to forgive us. This is making a hollow mockery of God and His mercy. God will cast us into the place of torment if we from our hearts forgive not every one his brother their trespasses.

Therefore, only in the way of forgiving our brothers will we experience the blessed peace of forgiveness. Experiencing this forgiveness, we will sing: "Blessed is he whose transgression is forgiven, whose sin is covered. Blessed is the man unto whom the Lord imputeth not iniquity, and in whose spirit there is no guile" (Ps. 32:1, 2). And forgiving one another, we will live in the rich blessedness of the communion of saints who together have salvation in the cross of Jesus Christ.

8

Loving as Neighbor

And Jesus answering said, A certain man went down from Jerusalem to Jericho, and fell among thieves, which stripped him of his raiment, and wounded him, and departed, leaving him half dead.
And by chance there came down a certain priest that way: and when he saw him, he passed by on the other side.
And likewise a Levite, when he was at the place, came and looked on him, and passed by on the other side.
But a certain Samaritan, as he journeyed, came where he was: and when he saw him, he had compassion on him,
And went to him, and bound up his wounds, pouring in oil and wine, and set him on his own beast, and brought him to an inn, and took care of him,
And on the morrow then he departed, he took out two pence, and gave them to the host, and said unto him, Take care of him; and what-soever thou spendest more, when I come again, I will repay thee.
Which now of these three, thinkest thou, was neighbour unto him that fell among the thieves?
And he said, He that shewed mercy on him. Then said Jesus unto him, Go, and do thou likewise.

—Luke 10:30-37

This parable was taught by Jesus in direct response to a question presented to Him by a lawyer: "Who is my neighbour?" The correct understanding of this parable, therefore, is dependent upon an understanding of the circumstances and occasion for it.

It was especially after the transfiguration that the Jews increased their efforts to find some reason to condemn Jesus. They attempted to try to catch Him in His words so that they might find something in His teaching contrary to the law of Moses or the prophets. To this end, they asked Him questions which they hoped would lead Him to make a mistake of some kind, on the basis of which they could pass sentence against Him. The lawyer spoken of in the context, made such an attempt. "What is necessary to inherit eternal life?" is the seemingly innocent question he asked. The lawyer was fully aware of the fact that Jesus often interpreted Moses' law; and because this interpretation seemed to the legalistic Pharisees to be a denial of Moses, the lawyer now thought also that Jesus would say something contrary to Moses. But he fell into his own well-prepared trap. Jesus turned to the law immediately and said: "What does the law say? You ought to know since you are a student of the law. What do you read there?"

The lawyer answered by quoting Deuteronomy 6:5 and Leviticus 19:18: "Love God and your neighbor." This was exactly right. The everlasting requirement of the law is: love—love God and love your neighbor. This never changes throughout all time. He who loves shall surely live. The way to life is the road of love. Therefore: "Do this and thou shalt live."

But with this answer of the Lord, the lawyer was embarrassed. He had tried to trap Jesus in His words, but had only succeeded in leaving the impression of his own ignorance. Besides, it seemed as if these words of Jesus implied that he did not do this, something which he felt in his heart was true. And so he attempted to justify himself. He wanted to know who his neighbor was. As was the case with so many of the self-righteous Jews, he loved only those whom he chose to love: his own select circle of friends, those whom he esteemed worthy of his love. He was at bottom selfish, doing good to those who did good to him. So now he attempted to justify his own conduct by asking who, after all, was his neighbor.

But Jesus' answer is penetrating and surprising. Indeed, the way to eternal life is the way of love. But Jesus turns the question of the lawyer about. If one walks the way of love, he must not ask who his neighbor is. He must ask instead, to whom am I neighbor? This is the question of love. If this question is answered, the question of who my neighbor is, will be answered of itself.

Who One's Neighbor Is

The parable which Jesus tells in answer to the question of this lawyer reads almost like a tale of some gifted storyteller. Yet it is not only entirely true to life, but vividly and dramatically illustrates this all-important question of spiritual relationships in the kingdom of heaven.

A certain man was traveling the road from Jerusalem to Jericho. No doubt the man is purposely left anonymous by Jesus, for it is exactly the point of the parable that it doesn't make any difference who this man is. Most likely we may assume that he was a Jew; at least, if this is the case, the startling contrast between the reactions of the priest and Levite on the one hand and the Samaritan on the other is more sharply drawn. The road over which he traveled was a road that led from Jerusalem, which was about 2,600 feet above sea level, to Jericho, which was about 1,300 feet below sea level. This drop of almost four thousand feet was accomplished in about seventeen miles. Consequently, the road was rough and rocky and steep and lonely. On each side were high boulders offering good protection to the bandits that lurked in the desolate mountains to prey upon the traveler. Sharp twists and turns winding down the steep descent made it difficult for the traveler to see beyond a few feet ahead of him. No wonder then that it was a common thing for the wild and lawless brigands of the day to concentrate on the Jericho road to attack the solitary traveler going from Jerusalem to Jericho or returning again to the Holy City.

So also this anonymous man was attacked by bandits who stripped him of his clothing in order to take from him everything he possessed. When he resisted them, they beat him and wounded him severely so that without assistance he would soon die. They made off to the caves and tunnels of the back mountains to divide their loot and make plans for their next attack.

It happened by coincidence that along this same road passed a priest. And soon after the priest, a Levite. Whether they were returning from Jerusalem to Jericho after having finished their service of God in the temple, or whether they were going to Jerusalem to take up their work for a time again, makes no real difference. We are told that there was a large colony of priests and Levites in Jericho, and it ought not to surprise us that there was a rather steady flow of traffic down this lonely road. However that may be, the point is that these men were busily engaged in the ministry of the law of God in the temple. This was their calling and purpose in life. This was the distinct privilege of those who belonged to the priesthood and the tribe of Levi. Besides, it was the calling of the priesthood to show mercy, for they were the means of revealing the mercy of God to His people. In the service of the law in the temple, they brought the sacrifices for sin, which some day God Himself would bring. They taught the people the mercy of God in their ministrations of the law; at least, this was what they were supposed to do. The trouble was that while they served the law outwardly they hated the law inwardly and cared not at all for its eternal principle of love.

This lack of love became evident on the Jericho road. For when, each at his own time, they came to the wounded and bleeding man, they cast only a brief and indifferent look in his direction, then passed by on the far side of the road. No doubt, they had their reasons which they used to justify themselves. And as they pursued their journey, these reasons sprang readily to their minds. The man was really beyond help already. Nothing they could do would save him, for he was obviously on the point of death. Besides, if they were on their way to the temple, they might become ceremonially defiled. He appeared to be one of their brethren, but who could be sure? After all, if he was a Gentile and they became defiled by touching him, would not God be angry that they had spoiled their opportunity to serve in the temple? Perhaps even the bandits might still be lurking in the road behind them. There was the real possibility that at any moment they might spring out and rob them on their way to the temple. Those accursed bandits had no respect for the high office of the priesthood. To jeopardize one's own life at this point would be tempting God. And who knows how long it would take to care for this man? After all, the King's business requires haste. A late arrival at the temple could never be justified. And so on and on came the excuses.

But along this same road came a Samaritan. It must have shocked Jesus' listeners when they heard Him bring a Samaritan into the narrative. We who view the entire account in retrospect, can scarcely appreciate the bitter hatred that existed between the Jews and the Samaritans. There was a mutual and deadly hatred that bordered on insanity. The Jews cursed the Samaritans in their synagogues, prayed that the Samaritans might have no part in the resurrection and no place in heaven, rejoiced when a Samaritan died, and refused them as proselytes into the Jewish nation and as travelers in their country. On their part, the Samaritans set up a rival temple, priesthood, and worship of God, scattered human bones in the temple at Jerusalem to defile it, and sometimes even went so far as to murder Jewish travelers.

But this Samaritan was different. Passing along the Jericho road and seeing this poor man beaten and wounded and dying, he was filled with compassion for him. Without considering the risk to his own person and without giving a thought to the urgency of his own business, he bent over the man to help him. Cleaning and anointing his bleeding wounds with wine and oil, he bound them up with his own clothing. Then, putting the man upon his donkey, he led him to the nearest village where he was cared for in an inn. But even this obvious and immediate help did not seem to be enough to the Samaritan, for, although his business now required urgent haste, he remained with the man to care for him that night. It was only in the morning that he finally left. But first he gave careful instructions to the inn keeper to care for the needs of the man until he should return. The Samaritan himself would assume financial responsibility for his care.

So the difference between these men becomes painfully obvious. The priest and the Levite, in justifying themselves and their own conduct, were really justifying evil. They had no love in their hearts—not only for their own neighbor, but not even for their own brother. They could not therefore love God or inherit eternal life. They loved only themselves, and to that love they devoted their life.

The Samaritan, on the other hand, meets one who is, from a natural point of view, his bitterest enemy. But he had a love in his heart which the priest and the Levite lacked, a love for God and a love for his neighbor. And with this love he fulfilled the law.

And so the question is, who then is my neighbor? The answer of Jesus is: your neighbor is the one who needs your help when your path crosses his in the journey of life. He is not necessarily the starving man on yonder side of the ocean—it is comparatively easy to send him a bushel of wheat to hush his hungry cries. Nor is your neighbor your friend and bosom pal who walks laughingly at your side down the road of life. There is no problem with loving him. Your neighbor is the one who lies on your path ahead of you. You will probably have to make a detour in your life's path to avoid him. But he is in need of your help. He is your neighbor.

And yet this is not the real question. When Jesus is finished with the parable He does not ask the lawyer: "Now then, who is your neighbor?" Rather Jesus turns the question around: "Which now of these three, thinkest thou, was neighbour unto him that fell among thieves?" Not, who is my neighbor? But, whose neighbor am I? Not, where can I find my neighbor? But rather, to whom must I be neighbor? That is the all-important question: "Am I living as a neighbor? Do I love as a neighbor should always love?" And the painful and accusing part of this penetrating question is exactly that if we ask this question we will not have to ask the question: who is my neighbor? The answer to that will follow of itself. It will prove to be irrelevant. It will be a question that, because of the nature of it, no longer needs to be answered. But, on the contrary, if you go through life asking the question, "who is my neighbor?" you will never find him. That is the strange yet accusing paradox of Jesus' words.

What Loving Our Neighbor Involves

It is from the perspective of this question that also the true love of God which leads to life everlasting becomes evident.

Jesus points out that this love is rooted in compassion. The Samaritan was moved with compassion for the wounded man. Genuine compassion is a powerful force in one's life. Compassion is literally suffering with someone else. It obliterates completely every other thought but the thought of helping. Compassion never thinks of friend or foe, of danger, of trouble, of the need for haste. And that is because compassion makes one forget all about himself and think only of the needs of one whom he sees suffering. It is such a compassion that is the fountain and source of love.

Then love also reveals itself by giving. Giving is always the highest revelation of love. This is true also in God. "For God so loved the world that he gave . . ." (John 3:16). "Herein is love, not that we loved God, but that he loved us, and sent his son to be the propitiation for our sins" (I John 4:10). Our love must always be a reflection of God's love because our love is rooted in God's love for us. The love which is the fulfillment of the law is a love that always gives. Love gives of oneself, of one's comfort and ease and time and patience. Love gives whatever is needed. The Samaritan was in the same position as was the priest. He too could have argued about the urgency of his business, about the miserable Jew lying on the road who ought not to detain him. Better anyway that there be one less Jew in the world. He could also have reasoned about the dangers of lurking brigands. But compassion does none of these things. Love binds up and soothes the wounds of life. Love helps until it is no longer within one's power to help. Love forgets all about oneself, and thinks only of the other.

This love is the fulfillment of the law. All the other command-ments of the law can be resolved in the one word *love*. Without love there is not one of the commandments that can possibly be kept. By loving God and our neighbor, we keep the law and fulfill it. This love is love for God first of all. The one, all-embracing commandment of the law is: love the Lord thy God with all thy heart and mind and soul and strength. This is the law. This is its fulfillment. It must never be argued that, after all, there are two commandments to the law: love God and love thy neighbor. For even the love which we must show to our neighbor is rooted in the love of God. If we love God we will love our neighbor. Hating our neighbor, we cannot love God. Loving our neighbor, we reveal the love of God that is in our hearts.

This love of God that is revealed in love for our neighbor is the love of which the text speaks. This love comes to its finest and fullest expression in the fellowship of the saints in the Church of Jesus Christ. There the love of God reigns in the hearts of all God's people. There love is perfectly revealed as the bond of Christian fellowship. There love is revealed in sacrifice and giving of oneself. Forgetting oneself—one's own personal comfort and need, we help those who are one with us in the faith. We help them to the end. This love is also revealed in all life's relationships. It is revealed in the relation of husband and wife, of parents and children, of friends and compan-ions. Always the love we have for one another must be love for God.

But the question remains: whose neighbor am I? Do I love only those who love me? This is indeed my calling. But is it enough? Does my calling begin and end in loving those who love me? Sinners do the same. In His Sermon on the Mount, Jesus says: "Ye have heard that it hath been said, thou shalt love thy neighbor, and hate thine enemy. But I say unto you love your enemies, bless them that curse you, do good to them that hate you, and pray for them which despitefully use you, and persecute you; that ye may be the children of your Father which is in heaven: for he maketh his sun to rise on the evil and on the good, and sendeth rain on the just and on the unjust. For if ye love them which love you, what reward have ye? do not even the publicans the same? And if ye salute your brethren only, what do ye more than others? do not even the publicans so? Be ye therefore perfect even as your Father which is in heaven is perfect" (Matt. 5:43-48).

Whose neighbor am I?

When the love of God fills our hearts and floods our souls it is a love that is revealed to all who cross our path and need our help. There are those that hate and despise the people of God. They hate God and they hate His cause. They speak evilly of the saints and do all manner of wickedness against the Church of Jesus Christ. They live in unbelief and wickedness. They transgress God's commandments. They despise all that is holy and trample under foot the Word of the Almighty. Am I neighbor to them?

The calling of God's people is surely to hate those who hate God. David sings of this in Psalm 139: "Do not I hate them, O Lord, that hate thee? and am not I grieved with those that rise up against thee?" (v. 21). This is the calling of God's people because it is impossible that the child of God loves those who hate God. And this hatred of those who hate God must be revealed by keeping them outside our fellowship. We can have no communion with them. We must condemn their sin and point them to the path of righteousness. We may not take them into our house nor go into their home to commune with them. The perfect fellowship of love is impossible between God and Satan, between the people of God and the people of the world. For what fellowship hath light with darkness, what concord hath Christ with Belial? (See II Cor. 6:14-18.) In fact, the man who professes to love God and still loves the world and seeks fellowship with the world shows clearly that he does not love God at all. The apostle John writes in I John 2:15: "Love not the world, neither the things that are in the world. If any man love the world, the love of the Father is not in him."

But this does not alter the truth of the parable. Although we must surely hate those who hate God, this hate is after all a manifestation of love. God loves Himself. And in loving Himself He hates all the workers of iniquity. Should He deny Himself and love those who hate Him, He could no longer love Himself. The Scriptures know of no universal love of God. But so it is also with the Christian. Loving God, the Christian hates the world. And the love of God fills him with hatred for the world.

Nevertheless, he must love as well. He loves those who hate him and despitefully use him. He does not love them with the love of perfect fellowship and communion, for this is not his calling. He reveals the love of God in having compassion on them when they are in trouble. He is moved by their suffering. He does not ask, are you friend or foe? Are you Christian or unbeliever? Do you deny or confess the truth? And he does not use the answer to these questions to determine whether or not such a man is his neighbor. This is precisely the point of the whole parable. Not, who is my neighbor; but whose neighbor am I? He is neighbor to those who are in need. And he reveals the love of God without asking questions first or justifying himself. He comes to the rescue of such a suffering one completely forgetful of himself. He binds their wounds and alleviates their suffering. He is moved with compassion by their pain and cries and does all that he can to help them down the pathway of life. It is in this way that he reveals the love of God that shines so brightly in his heart and in his life.

This is the fulfillment of the law. This is the life of citizens of the kingdom of heaven.

Loving Our Neighbor as a Principle of the Kingdom

But it must be clearly understood that this love is not of ourselves. It is of our nature as fallen men to hate. We hate God and we hate our neighbor. If love is the essential perfection of the law, hate is its essential violation. Lost in sin and corrupted in nature, we can only hate.

It is because of this that the parable which Jesus teaches is not a mere lesson in human philanthropy. There are those who would have it such. They see the moral lesson of Jesus and are overwhelmed with the simplicity of Jesus' teaching. And a mere moral lesson of the parable becomes, in their way of thinking, a basis for a kind of social gospel. Give to the poor, help the suffering, aid the dying, and heaven shall be yours. But they fail to see that this is more than a mere lesson of social significance. It is a principle of the kingdom of heaven. Love for our fellow man must be rooted in love for God. If we help those who need our help without any sacrifice on our part, if we love in order that we may reap the harvest of the praise of men, we still walk the way of sin.

After all, the question was: "What must I do to inherit life eternal?" How is love the way to life?

God loves His people with an eternal love. When we were yet sinners, God revealed His love toward us in sending His own on to the bitter and shameful death of the cross in order that when Christ became a reproach for us, we might be covered with His precious blood. God's love is the eternal and unchangeable fountain of all the blessings which He bestows upon us. He loves His people when they hate Him. He loves them when as yet they had no love in their hearts. He loves them because He loves Himself; He loves them for His own Name's sake. And He loves them through the cross of Christ; and, therefore, He loved them while they were yet sinners. He loves them through Christ because He Himself has taken away all their sins in the blood of the cross.

The greatest revelation of the love of God is the perfect giving of His Son. He loved His people so much that the beloved Son of His own heart was not too great a gift to give to save us. The love of God comes to His people only through Jesus Christ.

To put it a little differently, when we could not keep the law of love, Christ kept it for us. He loved God perfectly. He loved God all His life long, but He loved God also on the tree of the cross when the billows of God's wrath were poured out on Him. He loved God to the end, but for us. The apostle John in his own unique way puts it this way: "Now before the feast of the passover, when Jesus knew that his hour was come that he should depart out of this world unto the Father, having loved his own which were in the world, he loved them unto the end" (John 13:1). Christ fulfills the law of love for us and for all His elect people, but He also pours forth this love within our hearts. He sheds abroad the love of God within us.

It is only because of this that we can love. Christ fulfills the law of love within us so that we are caught up in the stream of God's love. Our hearts are tuurned from hatred to the love of God. We love God because He first loved us, and we love God by the power of the love of God in Christ for us.

By the power of that love we have eternal love. Indeed, as this love was merited for us on the cross, so also was the eternal life which we shall inherit merited for us. We have not this life of ourselves, we have it out of the fountain of God's grace and love. To love is indeed to have life—life eternal. But the life which is eternal is given us graciously, for the perfect love of the law of God is given to us as a mighty stream that pours forth from the fountain of God's own love. Hence we have the spiritual power to love our neighbor. But this love for our neighbor is always fundamentally love for God. We love our neighbor for God's sake. And, loving our neighbor for God's sake, we manifest to him the love of God. That is, we love him and help him in his need, but make it very clear to him that this is for God's sake. He himself therefore stands before the solemn obligation to love the Lord his God with all his heart.

Who then is my neighbor? Of course, anyone—anyone at all—that needs my help. But let us not persist in asking this question. It is not the question that needs asking. The question is: whose neighbor am I? That is the question that will surely lead us to the course of Christian love. For I am neighbor to everyone who needs me every moment when my life touches his and when our pathway in life crosses. And in loving my neighbor I reveal the love of God that is within my heart.

"Which now of these three thinkest thou, was neighbor unto him that fell among thieves? And he said, he that showed mercy on him. Then said Jesus unto him, go, and do thou likewise."

9

The Certainty of Prayer's Answer

*And he said unto them, Which of you shall have a friend, and shall
go unto him at midnight, and say unto him, Friend, lend me three
loaves;*

*For a friend of mine in his journey is come to me, and I have nothing
to set before him?*

*And he from within shall answer and say, Trouble me not: the door is
now shut, and my children are with me in bed; I cannot rise and give
thee.*

*I say unto you, Though he will not rise and give him, because he is his
friend, yet because of his importunity he will rise and give him as
many as he needeth.*

*And I say unto you, Ask, and it shall be given you; seek, and ye shall
find; knock, and it shall be opened unto you.*

*For every one that asketh receiveth; and he that seeketh findeth; and
to him that knocketh it shall be opened.*

—Luke 11:5-10

One of the main characteristics, if not the most important characteristic, of the citizens of the kingdom of Jesus Christ is that they pray. This lies in the nature of the case. The great blessing of citizenship in the kingdom of heaven is that the citizens live in covenant fellowship with their Father in heaven. And it is especially through prayer that these citizens, while on this earth, enter into this fellowship. It is by the power of God's grace alone that they walk as citizens of that kingdom in the midst of the world. But since that grace comes only from God, it is but natural that the child of God, deeply conscious of his dependence on the Most High, seeks that fountain of all grace in prayer.

It is therefore no wonder that the disciples came to Jesus with the request: "Lord, teach us to pray, as John also taught his disciples" (v. 1). The Lord Himself spent much time in prayer. In fact, there were whole nights that the Lord would forget sleep and spend the quiet hours of a Galilean night in prayer to His Father. The disciples must have felt very keenly that if their Master Who was perfect was in need of prayer, how much were not they?

In answer to their request, the Lord gave to His disciples—and to the Church of all ages—the spiritual model of all true prayer: "Our Father which art in heaven, hallowed be thy name. . . ." But along with this perfect prayer, the Lord also turned to a parable to teach those whom He loved throughout all time the true character of prayer.

The main idea of this parable is the absolute certainty of prayer's answer. This is evident from the Lord's own application: "Ask, and it shall be given you; seek, and ye shall find; knock, and it shall be opened unto you" (v. 9).

In teaching us that no prayer of the child of God would go unanswered, the Lord also encourages us to persevere in prayer. This encouragement we need. So often we forget to pray. Our prayers are, on the whole, few and far between. No doubt, when finally we arrive in glory, we will discover more clearly than we know now how few our prayers really were. Furthermore, so often when our prayers are not immediately answered, we become discouraged and stop praying. We need, then, the promise of the Lord that when we persevere in prayer the Lord will surely give us all that we ask.

Why We Must Pray

In some respects, this parable is somewhat strange. It soon becomes evident to any serious student of this passage of Scripture that the Lord does not mean to draw an absolute analogy between the elements of the parable and the reality of prayer. This is surely impossible. In fact, the key words of the parable are found in its application: "*How much more. . . .*" If certain things are true in earthly relationships, *how much more* are they not true in heavenly relationships. If, according to the parable, this is how a neighbor acts toward a friend, how much more is it not true that our heavenly Father is willing to answer the prayers of His elect children.

A man received a visitor in the hollow of the night. The visitor had come a long way and had entered the house of his friend hungry and weary from traveling. But the friend had nothing in the house to feed his guest. This was not really so strange in the East. The people there lived in a hot climate and had no means of refrigeration. The result was that in many cases people would buy sufficient only for the needs of the day at the beginning of the day, so that by night there was nothing left in the house to eat. In spite of this, when a friend came, even though it was night, he must be cared for and his needs supplied. He could not be put to bed hungry and could not be asked to wait till the morning for something to eat.

There was only one thing to do. The host went to his neighbor and knocked on his door to arouse him from sleep in order that he might obtain some bread. But the neighbor was not in any mood to get up in the hollow of the night and wake his family while searching for a light and for bread. And so he answered: "Trouble me not: the door is now shut, and my children are with me in bed; I cannot rise and give thee." This was a flat refusal that could not possibly be misunderstood.

But this did not discourage the host. He continued to pound on the door and lay before his neighbor his important needs. He would not be turned away. He persisted with vehemence and growing insistence. And, at last, when the neighbor's patience was exhausted, the neighbor came to the door to give the man what he asked. He did not do this because the man was his friend, but because the shamelessness of his persistence in knocking at such an hour.

There are several points in the parable which must be clearly defined. In the first place, it is evident that the man who came knocking at midnight came to ask for what he truly needed. He did not make a vain or silly request. He did not trouble his neighbor with nonessentials. He needed bread, for he was under the solemn obligation to feed the traveler who came into his home.

In the second place, the knocking friend did not ask for help for any other reason than his desire to care for the needs of the traveler who sought shelter and food beneath his roof. He had love for this traveler who came seeking his hospitality. It was not a carnal desire or a longing for personal gain that prompted him to seek the help of his neighbor; it was rather his deep reluctance to send the traveler whom he loved to bed hungry. He did not therefore disturb the rest and peace of his neighbor out of malice or bitterness. He was moved only by love.

In the third place, he came to his neighbor when he could obtain bread nowhere else. It was midnight. The stores and marketplaces were closed. And, while it was indeed true that his request would inconvenience his neighbor, he had nowhere else to go. It was necessary that his neighbor hear him and give him what he asked.

All these elements must be applied to the relationship between God and His people which is expressed in prayer. Evidently Jesus means to convey to us the idea that the relationship between God and His people is a relationship of Father and son. This becomes clear from the words which are appended to this parable: "If a son shall ask bread of any of you that is a father, will he give him a stone? or if he ask a fish, will he for a fish give him a serpent? Or if he shall ask an egg, will he offer him a scorpion?" (vv. 11,12). The relation between God and His people is a Father-son relationship. And it is precisely this relationship which also explains the need for prayer.

God is the Father of His people; His people are His children. This truth is not rooted, as the modernists like to say, in the fact of creation. It is wrong to speak of a general fatherhood of God and a universal brotherhood of man. It is true that God created all men, and, creating them in His own image, He made them also His children. But they sinned against Him and fell away from the high estate in which they once lived. They denied God and their Father and refused to serve Him. They chose instead the devil as their guide and model. The result is that they now bear the image of their father the devil, whose works also they do. (See John 8:44.) On the contrary, the Father-son relationship which exists between God and His people is rooted in Jesus Christ. Jesus Christ is the Son of God, and it is only through Him that the elect people of God are restored to sonship. Their sonship is rooted in the cross of Christ, through which God legally adopts them to be His sons and heirs. And this sonship is actually accomplished through the wonder of regeneration, by which the people of God are born again unto a new life through the resurrection life of Jesus Christ.

In this Father-son relationship, our heavenly Father loves us and assumes all responsibility for our care. And we, on the other hand, know that all that we need comes only from Him. We do not pray to our Father and bring Him our needs in order to tell Him what our needs are. Our Father in heaven knows what we have need of before we ask Him. (See Matt. 6:8.) Besides, He knows much better than we what our needs are, for He Himself has first of all created these needs.

For this same reason we do not come in prayer to the throne of grace in order to try to impose our will upon the will of our heavenly Father. This can never be done. We cannot change the will of God. His will is eternal and unchangeable. Our prayers do not change things with God. If this is the meaning of the motto "Prayer changes things," it is a motto that ought never to be found on the lips of the child of God. Whatever we ask for in prayer and receive from our heavenly Father, He has already determined to give us through the way of prayer. We may be humbly thankful that this is the case. I would certainly never dare to pray again if I had any reason to suppose that my prayers would change the mind of the Almighty. This indeed would be a terrible thing. Our Father knows what is best for us. We never know, for we are little children.

The reason for prayer is something quite different. Because God is our Father and we are His children, God wants us to pray in order that we may ask Him for the things we need. He wants us to ask Him for these things because it is in this way that we learn to seek all things from His hand as a son seeks all things from the hand of his father. In this way we learn to trust in Him alone and to commit our way with contentment to the higher knowledge and wisdom of our heavenly Father. Prayer is the deepest expression of the relationship of Father and son which exists by grace between God and His people.

For What We Must Pray

The question remains: what is it for which we must ask?

Negatively speaking, we must not ask for earthly things such as material riches, prosperity, the worldly things that our carnal flesh so often craves. Jesus Himself emphasizes this when in verse 13 He says: "If ye then, being evil, know how to give good gifts unto your children: how much more shall your heavenly Father give the *Holy Spirit* to them that ask him?" This does not mean that we must not ask for our daily bread from God. The Lord Himself teaches us to do this. But we must be sure that we ask only for the needs of one day; and we must be sure that we ask only for bread, not butter on our bread. In the second place, we do not always know what we ought to ask for. There are many details of our earthly life and pilgrimage which our Father has hid from us. When we are sick we do not know whether it is the Lord's will to make us better again; or if He wills to make us better, just when health will be restored. When we walk down life's pathway we do not know what troubles, what problems we shall have to face from one moment to the next. There are any number of details which the Lord does not reveal. But in respect to all these things, we must pray, "Thy will be done." Or, as James expresses it, we must learn to say: "If the Lord will, we shall live, and do this, or that" (James 4:15). If we learn to pray, "Thy will be done," our Father in heaven will also surely hear us and give us His answer to this petition. At the same time, it is also our calling to cast all our cares upon God (see I Peter 5:7), bring to Him all the things that trouble our deepest hearts, and pour out to Him our sorrows and griefs. But always this must be done in the humble submission to His will which He, Who is infinitely wiser than we, demands.

Positively, we need the Holy Spirit. This means that we need the spiritual blessings and spiritual strength which only the Holy Spirit can bring to us. All the blessings of salvation are earned for us in the cross of Jesus Christ. They are like a stream of salvation and grace which we need in our pilgrimage from here to glory. These blessings are applied to our hearts through the operation of the Holy Spirit within us. Specifically, this means that we need grace to enter into the kingdom of heaven each day through repentance and sorrow for sin. We need grace to walk within that kingdom fighting the good fight of faith against sin and temptation. We need grace to persevere in faithfulness in the midst of suffering, sorrow, distress, trouble, persecution, and in carrying all the heavy burdens which our Father is pleased to place on us. We need the grace of the Holy Spirit to represent God's cause and God's covenant in the midst of a world of sin and evil. We need the grace of the Spirit to seek God's kingdom and His righteousness; to bring up our children in the fear of His Name which is the beginning of all wisdom; to be faithful in searching His Word that we may study to show ourselves approved unto

God. And each saint needs this grace according to his own unique calling in his place in the battle lines of faith, with the individual position and station and circumstances of life which the Father has given him. This is an essential need. This is basic to all our needs. This we have need of beyond anything else. It is this need of the Holy Spirit which brings us in prayer to the throne of grace.

The Need for Encouragement

To seek this need from our heavenly Father requires much encouragement. In the first place, this is true because sometimes we hardly dare to pray. So, no doubt, it was also in the parable. It was midnight when the traveler came to his friend's house. It was a tremendous inconvenience for this friend's neighbor to get up from his bed in the hollow of the night, unlock the door, wake his children with stumbling about, and get bread for him who knocked. It took a lot of courage based on the hope that his neighbor would respond in love for this man to come to his neighbor at such an hour asking bread.

It is also this way with our prayers. We are indeed children of God, but we are yet very wicked. We do not walk as children of our Father in heaven. Often we prefer to manifest ourselves in life as children of the world. We, as Peter did, deny our Lord. We often manifest love for the enemies of God and seek their approval. We daily forfeit all right to be blessed by our Father. We come home at night after a day of sinning, and we must seek the grace that we need from Him Whom we have denied. A thousand times we become undeserving and lose any claim to the blessings of our God. It therefore takes a great deal of courage to come to our Father and ask Him to bless us. This courage must be based on the fact that our Father loves us even when we sin because He has forgiven all our sins in the blood of the cross of His own Son.

In the second place, it seems many times as if our Father is not always ready to help us. This was especially true in the parable. The neighbor would not help. He told the man who knocked at his door to cease troubling him. The door was locked; he could not answer it. The children were sleeping; he did not want to waken them with his stumbling about. Not this time. The man at the door had better go home. It was impossible to help. He met his neighbor's demand with a flat refusal. And so the host had to continue to knock. He needed the bread desperately, and, since his neighbor would not permit himself to be inconvenienced, he continued to pound on the door until he prevailed upon his neighbor to help him.

This is often true in our prayers. It seems as if the door of heaven is closed to our prayers and our Father is not willing to help us. We pray for grace to fight against sin, but that grace does not come. We pray for the peace of forgiveness, but heaven is silent. Trouble disturbs our souls and we seek relief from distress, but our Father does not seem to hear our anxious cries. We pray for help in life's problems to find the solution to the difficult choices we must make, but light does not come from above and it seems as if we are told to wander in the darkness and seek our own way. It seems as if our Father in heaven says to us: "Do not trouble me. I cannot help you." Even the Psalmist of Israel knew of this experience. He writes in Psalm 77: "In the day of my trouble I sought the Lord: my sore ran in the night, and ceased not: my soul refused to be comforted. I remembered God, and was troubled: I complained, and my spirit was overwhelmed. . . . I call to remembrance my song in the night: I commune with mine own heart: and my spirit made diligent search. Will the Lord cast off for ever? and will he be favourable no more? Is his mercy clean gone for ever? doth his promise fail for evermore? Hath God forgotten to be gracious? hath he in anger shut up his tender mercies?" (vv. 2, 3, 6-9).

We may well ask the question why this happens. And the answer is not difficult to find. It is, in the first place, entirely possible that the reason lies in us. We may not ask in faith, but instead we perhaps ask doubting that we will receive that for which we ask. And he that doubteth is like the wave of the sea driven by the wind and tossed. (See James 1:6-8.) Or perhaps we are not sufficiently sincere in our request; and we wonder secretly whether we really desire strength for the battle, or whether we prefer the sins for which we are asking forgiveness. But our Father knows our hearts and knows what we really want.

But then again, we may ask from our heavenly Father in all sincerity and honesty, and yet our Father does not hear us. Why is this?

This was also the case in the parable. The man did not immediately receive what he wanted. But this did not prevent him from asking by a continual and insistent knocking on the door. It was at last because of the very shamelessness of the man—that he should come at that hour not only, but that he should continue to pound on the door after being refused—that finally the neighbor gave him the three loaves of bread. And so the Lord means to teach us: do not stop praying when you come to the throne of grace with your petitions, and when it seems as if you are not immediately heard. We have no right to throw up our hands in despair and discouragement as if our Father is not interested in hearing us at all. We must persevere in prayer. We must ask and seek and knock.

This is very important. The Lord tells us to ask. This means that we must come with all our petitions before the throne of grace. And when we come, we must come in the faith that we will be heard.

But if the Lord does not immediately hear us, we must seek. This is a stronger word than "ask" and implies more. By seeking, we put forth effort to be heard. We look for the reason why we have not been heard in ourselves first of all. Perhaps we will find the answer there. And if we do not find it there, we must continue to assail the throne of grace with prayers and supplications to gain what we desire.

And even then perhaps we are not heard. The apostle Paul prayed three times that the thorn in his flesh might be removed. He prayed three times before at last the Lord answered his prayer. And when the Lord answered his prayer He did not remove the thorn from his flesh, but told him: "My grace is sufficient for thee: for my strength is made perfect in weakness" (II Cor. 12:7-9).

So we must knock. If we find the door of heaven closed and it seems as if the Lord does not answer by giving us entrance into His sanctuary, we must continue to knock. We must persevere in knocking on the door of God's dwelling place. We must be like Jacob, who would not let the angel go until he blessed him. Because Jacob persevered, the Lord changed his name to Israel, for he had wrestled with God and had prevailed. (See Gen. 32:26,28.) The same thing was true of the Syrophoenician woman. She sought the Lord to heal her daughter. How easy it would have been for her to be discouraged and disappointed if she had ceased her pleading when the Lord seemingly rebuked her for her request. The Lord said to her in answer to her plea: "It is not meet to take the children's bread, and to cast it to the dogs." This was a flat refusal. But the woman, by faith, persevered: "Truth, Lord: yet the dogs eat of the crumbs which fall from their master's table." And her prayer was answered. We must persevere in prayer. We must ask. We must seek. We must knock.

The Certainty of Being Heard

The Lord assures us that in this way we will certainly be heard. If, after all this perseverance, we would have no guarantee that we would be heard, there would be no incentive to continue in prayer. But this is not the case. We have the certain promise of Christ that the Lord will answer us.

This certainty is first of all expressed in the contrast of the parable which Jesus makes by the words "how much more." The man who had retired for the night did not want to answer his neighbor's knocking. He would surely not have come to the door if the man had retired after his first request. Even when finally he answered, he did not do this out of love. He saw that giving his neighbor bread was the only way to rid himself of the man. The man was going to disturb his whole night, probably wake his children, and keep knocking till he answered. "How much more will not your heavenly Father. . . ." God is not at last overcome with our shamelessness. He loves us with an eternal love that is rooted in His own purpose to glorify Himself. He has promised to bless us through Jesus Christ. The proof is in the cross. How much more then shall not He give us His Holy Spirit?

It was a severe imposition on the goodwill of the neighbor to come at midnight asking bread. But how much more shall not our heavenly Father. . . . We never impose on Him, for He Who watches over Israel never slumbers nor sleeps. (See Ps. 121:4.) Can God's people ever impose on the Most High? He delights in their prayers. They are a continual sacrifice before Him. How much more then will He not surely hear us when we pray!

The example Jesus appends to this parable makes this very strong. Even an earthly father gives his son bread and an egg and fish when he is asked for these things. But an earthly father is evil. He does this only out of natural love. He does this imperfectly and insincerely. How much more your heavenly Father. . . . Will our Father in heaven mock us when we seek His Spirit from Him? Will He give us stones for bread, serpents for eggs, scorpions for fish? If an earthly father would not do this, how much more will not our heavenly Father give us all that we ask? He knows all our needs. He delights in us when we seek the throne of His grace to have these needs satisfied. He will surely give us all that we ask.

This answer to prayer is certain for several reasons. First of all, God will not ignore His own work. We do not and cannot pray of ourselves nor in our own strength. God brings us to Himself in prayer. Only when He inspires prayer within us can we also bow our heads to seek from Him the needs of our life. Our prayers are the fruit of His grace. Will He ignore His own work in us? This is impossible.

Second, Christ prays for us. Our eternal High Priest has entered into the Most Holy Place where God dwells. Christ prays continuously for us before the face of God. When we forget to pray, Christ prays for us. When we pray in sin, these prayers are perfected by our High Priest. When we ask for things we should not be asking for, our High Priest tells our Father not to give us these things; for they will harm us. Will our Father ever ignore the prayers of Christ His own Son?

Third, it is God's eternal will to hear us when we pray. He eternally determines to give us all that we need. We ask for the things which He has purposed to do. We pray for His cause, His kingdom, His covenant. These things He has determined to prosper and bless. Therefore He will surely hear us when we pray because He cannot deny Himself.

How great and marvelous this certainty is! Therefore indeed we may be sure that we shall be heard.

Ask. Ye *shall* receive. Seek. Ye *shall* surely find. Knock. It *shall* certainly be opened to you. This is God's own promise. There is no praying saint who goes unanswered. There is no seeking soul who will not find. There is no one who ever knocks at the door of God's sanctuary who will be turned away. Before God's throne we will surely find peace when our hearts are troubled, strength when life's burdens become heavy, grace for the rigors and trials of the day, wisdom to solve life's problems, faithfulness in the battle, courage to walk even through the valley of the shadow of death. Eternity will reveal that our heavenly Father heard all our prayers and answered them, even if it was in His own way and in His own time.

10

What Life Consists In

And he spake a parable unto them, saying, The ground of a certain rich man brought forth plentifully:
And he thought within himself, saying, What shall I do, because I have no room where to bestow my fruits?
And he said, This will I do: I will pull down my barns, and build greater; and there will I bestow all my fruits and my goods.
And I will say to my soul, Soul, thou hast much goods laid up for many years; take thine ease, eat, drink, and be merry.
But God said unto him, Thou fool, this night thy soul shall be required of thee: then whose shall those things be, which thou hast provided?
So is he that layeth up treasure for himself, and is not rich toward God.
                                                              —Luke 12:16-21

The parable which is recorded for us in this passage of Scripture was spoken by Jesus during His Perean ministry as His earthly ministry neared its end. The context of the parable tells us that Jesus was teaching the throngs of people who followed Him the eternally important principles of the kingdom of heaven. Suddenly, as Jesus was speaking, a man forced himself through the crowd into the presence of Jesus with a question which was nothing less than a harsh interruption. He was, while the Master was concerned with heavenly matters, interested only in earthly things. His demand of the Lord was: "Master, speak to my brother, that he divide the inheritance with me."

How crude and unsuited to the occasion was this rude insertion of earthly things into the sermon of Jesus! The answer of the Lord is therefore pointed and concise. With respect to the legal aspects of the matter, Jesus answers that He is not an earthly judge. There are courts for these things and laws given by God Himself which are just and fair. But with respect to the spiritual aspect of the question, the man must learn to beware of covetousness, for his demand was obviously occasioned by a covetous heart. The man was so filled with his longing for material things that he looked at the Lord through his covetous eyes and was bent on using Christ to satisfy his thirst for money. But covetousness, the Lord says, is always rooted in the fundamental error that a man's life consists in an abundance of earthly things. This is a serious and fatal mistake.

And so the Lord uses the occasion to speak a parable in which a fundamental principle of the kingdom of heaven is defined. To lay up earthly treasures is folly. These treasures cannot give life to a man. A man who seeks them is poor toward God, and the end is hell. Life consists in being rich toward God. The richness of life is not dependent on the amount of one's material possessions, but on fellowship with the Lord. This is a life which is blessed both here and in eternity. For, while earthly treasures cannot be taken through the dark valley of the shadow of death, spiritual treasures can indeed be carried along. The admonition is therefore: "Be rich toward God."

The Parable Itself

In the parable which Jesus speaks, there was a certain rich man whose ground brought forth abundantly. Although his identity is deliberately not mentioned, it is evident that he was already rich before the harvest of which the text speaks. Furthermore, evidently he had acquired his wealth by just and honest means; for his ground brought forth abundantly. He had not become rich at the expense of the poor. He was not an extortioner, or a thief, or a cheat. He was an ourstanding citizen of his community, respected for his honesty and thrift. His sin was not the sin of robbery or murder or ruthlessness in acquiring his material possessions. He had but one sin—the sin of covetousness.

The particular year which is referred to by the parable was an extremely prosperous year for this farmer. Wealthy already, he faced the prospect (pleasant to him) of additional wealth and a greater abundance of the world's goods. But this exceedingly great wealth presented a problem which required some concentrated thought. It was the type of problem which worldly men jokingly and yet seriously speak of as "a problem they wish they had." He had no place to go with his crops; he had insufficient storage room in his barns and granaries to hold the harvest. He recoiled from the idea of letting his crops rot on the ground for he knew this would be wicked. He was obligated to make use of them and preserve them as the fruit of his field.

The solution to the problem soon presented itself. He would tear down the barns and granaries which he had once thought were adequate for his needs, and he would build bigger storehouses sufficient to hold all his goods and treasures. Although this would require a certain outlay of capital, he would have plenty for many

years to come; and even though the future was long, he had sufficient to retire from his labors and live a life of ease. No more would
he have to labor unceasingly in the hot sun. No more would he allow
the rising and setting sun to determine his working day. No more
would there be any need of depriving himself of the good things of
life. His barns and granaries, sufficiently large to provide for many
years, would be his guarantee of a bright and happy future.

What a pleasant picture! How often do not men today live in the
same expectation. Such men consider themselves to be wise. They
provide for their future and old age. They look forward to enjoying
retirement in luxury and ease. The world pronounces them com-
mendable and virtuous citizens. But God calls them fools. And it is
the sentence of God that, in the final analysis, counts.

The folly of this man is evident on the very surface of the parable.
It is already evident in the fact that the whole parable centers about
the man himself. Six different times he says: "I." "What shall I
do? . . . This I will do. . . . I will do this and I will do that." Seven
times he speaks of himself using either "my" or "thou." "My
fruits . . . my goods; soul, thou hast many goods laid in store. . . ."

His foolishness was apparent in that he thought he was lord over
all these things. The goods he had heaped up and even his own soul
belonged to him. And belonging to him, they were to be used
exclusively for his own personal enjoyment. He had many years
stretching out before him; his goods and riches were of lasting value.
He had nothing but a life of pleasure to anticipate when he sent his
reapers away at the end of the harvest.

But his folly became apparent that same night. On the eve of the
harvest, when he was pondering with pleasure the fruits of his
labors, a sentence was sounded in heaven. That night the soul which
he claimed to be his own but which inhabited a very frail body would
be required of him. He faced eternity. Then whose would all these
riches be? He could not take them along, for death permits no
earthly treasures to pass through its domain. He stood in eternity
naked.

The Life of which Jesus Speaks

In what does a man's life consist? How important this question
becomes!

We must not make the mistake of thinking that Jesus refers only to
the life which is to come. The Lord's point is not that there is true life
only beyond the grave. In itself it is true that there is life after death.
But this is not the whole truth. It is not sufficient to ask: "In what
does the life to come consist?" This question surely needs answering,
but it is not the only question. We live in this world. Here we are
called to walk for our threescore years and ten. The question is: "In
what does this life consist?"

This life is our present existence in the midst of the world. It is a life that we must and do live here below. It is a life in which we stand in a certain relationship to the creation about us, to those whom we know and with whom our lives come in contact, whose paths we cross, and the life in which we live in a certain relation to God. It matters not now for the present what this relation to God is; the fact is that it is there. We cannot escape it. Even though we would want to be free from these relationships, we cannot escape them. Here we are destined to live; here we must spend our time.

In what does this life consist? What is its true character, its fundamental meaning, its basic significance? These are the questions that hammer their way into our consciousness. Is this a life which consists in nothing else than the body and the things of the body? Is it a life of eating and drinking and being merry because tomorrow we die? Or is there more to life than this? And if there is, what is it?

But Jesus speaks also of the life to come. Death is not the end of existence. The grave is not annihilation. There is an eternity beyond this life into which we must enter and which we must face after death has taken us from this world. This life to come also has meaning and significance. There too we stand in relation to God. In what does this life consist? And indeed, in what relation does our present life stand to the life to come? Surely they are not two separate lives completely divorced from each other. They are basically the same. They are one life lived by one person who, though he passes through death, continues in another existence beyond death. And these two aspects of life, though radically different because of death, are nevertheless one life that is lived as a whole.

It is striking that both this life and the life to come are considered in the parable not only from the viewpoint of our body, but also from the viewpoint of our soul. The rich fool emphatically addresses his soul. He is, and rightly so, not only concerned with the life of the body, for he realizes full well that he must also consider the life of the soul. He says to himself: "Soul, thou hast much goods. . . ."

Although there is no room in the thinking of those who have accepted the God-denying theory of evolution for the concept of the soul, Scripture teaches that man not only possesses a soul, but that the soul of man is that spiritual and immaterial aspect of his existence which places him in relationship to God. Man stands on a higher plane than the animals because he stands not only in certain relationships with this earthly creation, but he stands also in relationships with the things of heaven and the things of God. His soul is the seat of his mind and will. From the soul issues the life of thinking, willing, desiring, aspiring, hoping, longing, pondering, meditating, and so forth. This stream of life, in the final analysis, is the main lifestream of his whole existence. He lives in the world in bodily relationships as he is directed in the innermost recesses of his soul.

Thus, to ask the question, in what does life consist? is to ask concerning the life of the soul as well as the life of the body. The question not only touches upon our material life in an earthly and physical creation, but it concerns the well-being of our souls. The question implies, therefore, to ask concerning what brings true peace and quietness within. It is to ask concerning true blessedness and joy. It is to inquire into the nature of true happiness and contentment. For this is the life of the soul.

In what then does life consist? What an important question.

In What Man's Life does not Consist

Jesus emphatically states: "A man's life consisteth not in the abundance of the things which he possesses."

This was exactly the answer of the rich fool. This is the answer of many men. Whoever answers the question in this way is a fool as great as the rich man of the parable.

Foolishness is a spiritual fault and moral sin. There are those who consider foolishness to be mere mistaken notions arising out of ignorance and producing unavoidable mistakes. This is not, however, the Scriptural idea of foolishness. Just as true wisdom is a spiritual virtue, a virtue given by grace through the cross of Christ, so foolishness is a moral fault, a sin against God. It arises not out of ignorance, but out of a corrupted and depraved nature. It has its origin not in lack of knowledge, but in rebellion against God. It is deliberate, conscious, willful sin upon which a man sets his heart in bitter enmity against the Lord.

As far as its character is concerned, foolishness is the refusal to evaluate things in the light of true reality. A fool is one who knows the truth but does not want it. He distorts reality according to the sinful imaginations of his own heart. He evaluates all things and estimates their worth, not according to the true nature of things, but according to sinful imagination. On this false and sinful evaluation of things he bases his judgments, and he acts accordingly. The end is always bitterness and despair. A fool knows that reality means that all things will come to an end, for this is what God says. But he hates this, refuses to recognize it, and denies its truth. Instead he claims that all things will last forever. The earth is all that there is. And so he adjusts his life according to it. The result is bound to be disaster. This foolishness is graphically portrayed in the parable.

The fool made a serious and yet deliberate mistake with regard to his earthly possessions: he thought he was lord over them all. He spoke of *his* field, *his* farm, *his* harvest, *his* barns and granaries, *his* soul. In his opinion they all belonged to him. This was a most serious error and is really the root of all covetousness.

In the second place, he thought that these goods he had acquired were lasting. He piled them higher and higher. He hoarded them and saved them until he could hardly look over them. He built bigger and bigger barns and granaries, filling them with the things he had gained for himself. And when he had them all, they were his life. They would last. They could give him all he wanted for body and soul. All he had to do was enjoy them. He faced the bright prospect of having—so he thought in his folly—everything he needed.

In the third place, he thought that these things could satisfy the needs of his soul. In the parable he emphatically addresses his soul: "I will say to my soul, soul, thou hast much goods laid up for many years; take thine ease, eat, drink, and be merry." How foolish he was! He speaks of many years. But he was wrong. That very night his soul was demanded of him. Yet this was not his only mistake. Even if he should have had many years in which to enjoy the things he had acquired, he still faced eternity. This was something quite different. He was a fool in that he persuaded himself that earthly goods are food for the soul. He sought to bring his soul to the cup of earthly pleasure in order that, drinking at the cup of food and wine, his soul might be sated and find its rest. How utterly foolish was this covetous man.

It is, of course, very easy to point a contemptible finger at the rich fool, forgetting all the while that the sin which is condemned in this parable is very real in our own lives. The folly of the rich fool is found not only in the world of wicked men, but is found in much of our life in the world. How often is it not true that we speak of what we have as belonging to us. How often do we not live as if the things of this world will last forever. Our boldness is perhaps not as brazen as the rich fool who speaks loudly of what lives within his own heart. But the life we live and the manifestation of our inmost opinions is identical with the loudly spoken words of this man. Is it not true that, considering all things to be ours, we set our hearts upon the acquisition of more of them? We live indeed as if life consisted in the abundance of things which we possess. We consider success to be weighed in dollars and cents, in insurance policies and retirement benefits, so that the more we have the more content we think we will be. We try to find peace for our souls at the fountain of mammon, and happiness in the worship of houses and lands.

Yet, how foolish this is. The things of the rich man were not his own. Indeed, his fields brought forth abundantly; but whose field was it? Was it not the Lord's—the One Who claims the cattle on a thousand hills as His own? It is true that an abundant harvest was produced. But who gave the rain and sunshine by which the crops flourished? Is it not the sovereign Lord of heaven and earth Who sends rain and sunshine or withholds it? And so, whose harvest really was it? Did not the harvest belong to God? The man stood on God's ground in the midst of God's harvest as a servant of God. His folly consisted in his denial of this, a denial which could not possibly alter the fact. And so it is with all that we have. Perhaps today things do not come to us directly from the soil under our feet, but they are no less given to us from the hand of the sovereign Dispenser of all things. He created all things; to Him alone they belong; He alone possesses the right to distribute them as it seems good to Him. When He gives to a man or takes away from a man, He does so with a prerogative which no man can question.

And because they are God's possessions and come from His hand, we are only servants and stewards in the house of our God to use all things for Him.

Yet this is not all.

What folly it is to seek food for the soul in earthly things! The fool stood in boldest outline as the fool he really was. "Soul, have rest!" But the soul cannot find rest in corn. "Soul, eat and drink!" But the soul cannot eat and drink money and houses. "Soul, be merry!" But the misery of life cannot be drowned in drinking the cup of worldly joy and carnal pleasure.

This is true even in this life. Does life consist finally in peace and quietness, in well-being and joy? It does, but these cherished and longed-for blessings of life cannot be obtained from material things. The soul cannot take them in. Folly is the impulse that leads the fool to this fountain to have the thirst of his soul satisfied.

And yet even this is not all.

"This night shall thy soul be required of thee; then whose shall these things be, which thou hast provided?"

Death comes. From it there is no escape. And passing through the valley of the shadow of death, the accumulation of earthly possessions is of no avail. They are a burden which cannot be carried to the grave. They are treasures which are gone when the scythe of death carries men away. They are of this world, but the grave opens in eternity. And the fool that has accumulated only these earthly and material things—things that cannot be taken with him—stands naked before the throne of the Almighty.

Then comes eternal death. For death alone in bitterest hell awaits the fool who is not rich toward God. Such is the folly of the world.

In What Life does Consist

In what then does life consist? What is the full measure of life both here and now, and also in eternity?

First of all, beware of covetousness. And because the root of all covetousness is really the denial that all things belong to God, the only way to beware of covetousness is to stand firmly grounded on the principle that all things are God's and His alone. We are only stewards in the house of our Father. We have nothing of ourselves, nothing that we can call our own. We do not possess our house and lands. We do not even possess our own life and our soul. Even the breath we breathe and the existence which is ours moment by moment is given to us by Him Who is the sovereign dispenser of all things.

And if this fundamental thought becomes a ruling principle in our lives, then the question which we ask is not: "What shall I do?" This was the question of the rich fool. The question we ask is rather: "What wouldst Thou have me to do?" This is the fundamental principle in life with all that God gives us. How would God have us use the houses and lands, the food and drink, the cars and clothing, the shelter and sunshine which He gives us? This is the question that leads from covetousness. And leading from covetousness, this alone can bring true contentment in all the things that the Lord is pleased either to give us or to take from us. It is only then that we can learn with the apostle Paul to say: "Not that I speak in respect of want: for I have learned, in whatsoever state I am, therewith to be content" (Phil. 4:11). Then alone can we fulfill the admonition of Hebrews 13:5: "Let your conversation be without covetousness; and be content with such things as ye have: for he hath said, I will never leave thee, nor forsake thee."

It is, understanding these things, that our life below becomes a pilgrimage. We walk as those who have here no abiding city. And when we walk in this way, we proceed down the pathway of our pilgrimage in the consciousness that at any time our stewardship may end. God may call us home, for toward that home we are directing our footsteps. Thus the possessions which we have received are but *means* to aid us in our trip to our eternal destination. Using them we must live every moment as those who have been called by God to walk in this life as those who represent His cause and as those who may be called tomorrow to give an account.

This life is also the life of the soul. The soul cannot eat bread nor can it drink wine. We live in a higher relation to God. And this relation is through Jesus Christ our Lord. For we are by nature rebels in God's house, rebels who do nothing but sin. We are restored to fellowship with God only through Jesus Christ and by the power of His cross. We live as stewards in God's house by grace. We live as pilgrims and strangers by the power of faith, and this faith is the gift of God.

But then our souls must be brought to the fountain of living waters. For the bread which is able to nourish our souls is the bread of the Word of God. The water which alone can slake our thirst so that we never thirst again is Jesus Christ our Lord and His Spirit. Our souls must be fed with Christ, with the righteousness and holiness of Christ, with the peace and joy of fellowship with God through Jesus Christ His Son.

This heavenly and spiritual bread comes to us through the Word of God and the preaching of the gospel of salvation. It is at this table of the Lord that we must eat and drink and be merry. It is at the fountain of living waters that we have all we need. For if life is joy and happiness, peace and quietness, well-being and serenity, this can come with the true heavenly bread which God has provided and with which He feeds us. This is true wisdom. Life consists in this.

Then we are rich toward God. There comes a time when our souls are required of us. We leave earthly things behind, for their purpose is ended. We would not want them along anyway on our last journey home, for they were not the riches our hearts were set upon. Gladly and willingly we lay them aside. They have helped in our pilgrim sojourn, but that is now ended and we need them no longer. We enter into eternity, the object of our hope.

The true treasures of God we take along. We do not appear in eternity with nothing. We wear the clothes of the righteousness and holiness of Christ. We carry in our souls the Word of God which endures forever. These treasures we possessed already in this life, but they are treasures which death cannot snatch from our grasp, for we take them through the grave into life everlasting. And these treasures are made perfect and full when at last we meet with our God. With these treasures we dwell in the house of many mansions forever. Such is the wise man who is rich toward God.

11

The Sovereign Purpose of God's Forbearance

He spake also this parable; A certain man had a fig tree planted in his vineyard; and he came and sought fruit thereon, and found none. Then said he unto the dresser of his vineyard, Behold, these three years I come seeking fruit on this fig tree, and find none: cut it down; why cumbereth it the ground?
And he answering said unto him, Lord, let it alone this year also, till I shall dig about it, and dung it:
And if it bear fruit, well: and if not, then after that thou shalt cut it down.

—Luke 13:6-9

The immediate occasion for this parable was the report that came to Jesus in Perea of a terrible atrocity Pilate had perpetrated in the temple in Jerusalem. Pilate had killed some Galileans while they were sacrificing in the temple. The fact that Luke alone mentions this, and then only in passing, while secular historians are silent about the event, shows how common these things were in Judea as it suffered under the yoke of Rome. If there was any reason at all for this evil crime of Pontius Pilate, it is not mentioned in the text. Evidently, while the Galileans were bringing their sacrifices, the soldiers under Pilate's command had rushed into the hallowed court of the temple and had slain the Galileans when they had no opportunity to defend themselves. Their blood had mingled with the blood of the sacrifices they had brought; thus the temple not only, but also the sacrifices had been polluted. One can imagine the horror that arose in the minds of the Jews as the news which was brought to Jesus swept through the excited crowd.

Yet we must not mistake the purpose of the Jews in bringing this report. It is evident from the words of Jesus that more was implied than a mere sketch of some happening, as gruesome as it may have been. The Jews had interpreted the crime as some special judgment that had come upon these Galileans for some sin they had committed. Only some transgression of a most unusual sort could have called forth such a display of divine justice. They made the mistake that we too are often inclined to make—to connect some chastisement which we or others are called to bear with some particular sin in our or their lives.

But there was even more implied in the report. For the Jews (and we so often agree) intended this incident as an occasion for self-congratulation, as if this crime confirmed their own superior piety. It is almost as if the Jews are heard to say: "We are far better than they, for no such calamity has befallen us."

This mistaken and evil conclusion Jesus immediately refutes. Jesus does not deny that these Galileans were sinners. That is not the point at issue. In fact, the entire point would be obscured if these Galileans were righteous. But Jesus does insist that those Galileans who were murdered were no worse than all the other dwellers in Galilee. And in order to bring the point still closer home, for the Jews of Judea were inclined to look down on the Jews from "Galilee of the Gentiles," Jesus refers to another incident that took place right in Jerusalem. In referring to the fall of the tower of Siloam in which eighteen died, Jesus points out that they too were no greater sinners than the rest of those in Jerusalem.

The question then that requires answering is: "Why were not the exempted Jews destroyed with the others if they were equally as wicked?" This question, cutting so sharply into the hearts of the listeners, is answered by Jesus in a twofold way. (1) Even for Israel—Israel who prided itself in its piety—the only way of escape from judgment was the way of repentance. If they did not repent, they would all likewise perish. (2) But God's sovereign purpose with both the wicked and the righteous is always accomplished even when He forbears to come in judgment. It is to this question and to these answers that we must address ourselves in our interpretation of the parable.

The Elements of the Parable

There is no inconsiderable dispute among commentators concerning the interpretation of the various elements in the parable. There is first of all the question of the vineyard. While it is quite likely that the Lord intended no definite analogy between the vineyard and a reality in life, those who maintain that the vineyard is the kingdom of God in the broad and general sense, no doubt, come closest to the truth. This kingdom is the Church in the broadest sense as including all those places where the light of the gospel shines to a greater or lesser degree, where God gathers His Church, where the influences of the gospel are felt; in short, that which is called in our day, "Christian."

Concerning the fig tree there can be no doubt. The fig tree refers to the nation of Israel. It does not refer specifically to any one individual, but to the nation as a whole organically considered as the seed of Abraham. This is evident from other parts of Scripture where Israel is referred to as a tree or a vine. It is also evident from the fact that the cursed fig tree is a symbol of the curse that will come on the nation of Israel for rejecting their Messiah.

The Lord of the vineyard is God Himself Who sovereignly accomplishes His purpose in the vineyard and Who sovereignly deals with the fig tree that He Himself has placed there. The vinedresser is Christ, the Servant of Jehovah, Who is appointed to rule in God's vineyard to accomplish all the purpose of the Father.

Taking these points together, it is evident that the sovereignty of God is the outstanding feature. The kingdom belongs to God, for He has established it and planted it in the midst of the world. This is an act of His own free and sovereign will, for He was not obligated to do this. He chose, in His eternal purpose, to establish His kingdom. He remains therefore the sovereign Proprietor over this vineyard, to do with it as it seems good to Him. In the midst of this vineyard of His kingdom, the sovereign Lord planted the fig tree of the nation of Israel. This nation He chose as His own and separated it from all other nations throughout the ages of time. This also was the sovereign choice of the Most High, for there was nothing in Israel as such which distinguished it from the other nations of the earth and which made it favored above others. God often reminded Israel of this. We read for example, in Deuteronomy 7:7, 8: "The Lord did not set his love upon you, nor choose you, because ye were more in number than any people; for ye were the fewest of all people: But because the Lord loved you, and because he would keep the oath which he had sworn unto your fathers, hath the Lord brought you out with a mighty hand, and redeemed you out of the house of bondmen, from the hand of Pharaoh king of Egypt." God freely chose to do this. Over this vineyard the Lord placed His own Son. Christ is eternally appointed as the Lord of the vineyard, and the King of the kingdom. In this vineyard He is called to do all the will and purpose of God, which finally results in bringing this kingdom to the everlasting glory of heaven.

Yet the parable turns on the barrenness of the fig tree.

The lord of the vineyard came looking for fruit. This is not surprising, for a fig tree was considered one of the most desirable trees in Canaan. It required diligent care and attention to nurse it along the way to maturity. Its fruit was delightful and an especially delicious part of the diet of the Israelite. It was, in fact, a sign of prosperity and peace. It was a peculiar tree in that its fruit began to appear before its leaves. And while the fruit was ripening, the leaves grew large and dense so that, by the time the fruit was ripe, the leaves had completely obscured it. Thus when the leaves were full grown, one could reasonably expect that fruit was to be found within the dense foliage. In this respect also the fig tree was a startling picture of the nation of Israel. On the outside and to all external appearances the nation was a pleasing sight. It gave every evidence of being a fruitful tree. But when one would penetrate through the dense foliage of the tree in search of fruit, to his amazement and dismay there was none, for the tree was barren.

Many times the lord of the vineyard had come looking for fruit. But throughout the years that the tree had lived, it had repeatedly proved to be barren. And so now the command came from the lord to cut it down. There were two reasons for this. On the one hand, it was failing to serve its purpose and was therefore useless. There was no point in keeping it. But on the other hand, inasmuch as it did not bear fruit, it was a threat to the other trees. It cumbered the soil, draining it of its nutrients and keeping these essential minerals from being used by other plants which bore fruit. It robbed the plants surrounding it of sunlight, for its shade was complete. Because it was in its barrenness a threat to the other plants in the vineyard, there was every reason to destroy it.

But the vinedresser asked for one more year in which he would apply once again diligent toil and assiduous care to the barren tree. If, at the end of another year, after care and fertilizing, it still did not bear fruit, then indeed he would agree to its being destroyed. So the reason for preserving it is to see whether it would bear fruit at last. In this the lord of the vineyard evidently concurs.

A Lesson in God's Care for Israel

But this diligent care had indeed been bestowed on Israel as a nation. This was particularly evident from the fact that God had given to Israel the full revelation of His promises. He had taken the nation of Israel from out of all other nations under the heavens. He had chosen Israel as His own peculiar possession to give them the glorious light of His promises. In Egypt, in spite of persecution, He had made of them a great nation. From the bondage of Egypt He had delivered them with a strong arm and a mighty display of power. He had guided them safely through the Red Sea by an astounding miracle while their enemies were destroyed. He had led them to Sinai where He had conferred on them the blessings of His law and His covenant. In the wilderness He had fed them with heavenly manna and given them water out of the rock. At last He had brought them safely into the land flowing with milk and honey, where they could dwell every man under his vine and fig tree. He had given this land to them by driving out their enemies with signs and wonders, fighting their battles for them and leading them on from victory to victory. He had given them David to sit on their throne, and Solomon as ruler of the most glorious kingdom in all the East. He had built for them a temple in the midst of which He Himself had taken up His abode. He sent them prophets to reveal to them the mysteries of His truth. When they were disobedient, He brought them into captivity, but in His memory of David His servant He brought them back again to their own land. And finally, He revealed as never before the glorious wonders of His promises through the coming of His own Son Who was the fulness of all the glory of God.

Scripture repeatedly makes reference to these blessings which God had bestowed on Israel. We read, for example, in Psalm 80:8-11: "Thou hast brought a vine out of Egypt: thou hast cast out the heathen, and planted it. Thou preparedst room before it, and didst cause it to take deep root, and it filled the land. The hills were covered with the shadow of it, and the boughs thereof were like the goodly cedars. She sent out her boughs unto the sea, and her branches unto the river." Again, in Isaiah 5:1-4 we read: "Now will I sing to my well beloved a song of my beloved touching his vineyard. My well beloved hath a vineyard in a very fruitful hill: And he fenced it, and gathered out the stones thereof, and planted it with the choicest vine, and built a tower in the midst of it, and also made a winepress therein: and he looked that it should bring forth grapes, and it brought forth wild grapes. And now, O inhabitants of Jerusalem, and men of Judah, judge, I pray you, betwixt me and my vineyard. What could have been done more to my vineyard, that I have not done in it? wherefore, when I looked that it should bring forth grapes, brought it forth wild grapes?" The apostle Paul refers to this same truth in Romans 9:4,5 where he writes: "Who are Israelites; to whom pertaineth the adoption, and the glory, and the covenants, and the giving of the law, and the service of God, and the promises; Whose are the fathers, and of whom as concerning the flesh Christ came, who is over all, God blessed for ever. Amen."

But what had Israel done all this time? They had departed again and again from the worship of Jehovah their God. They had rebelled at every turn of the way in the wilderness. They had bowed down to a golden calf while the thunder of God reverberated from Sinai. They had refused to enter the land in unbelief because they were convinced that their God could not and would not fight for them. They complained about and rejected the food and water the Lord provided. They turned to idols every opportunity they had, committing all the abominations of the heathen. They committed sins and multiplied transgressions that even the wicked had never considered, so that they became more godless than the heathen. They killed the prophets who came with the Word of God and stoned them whom God sent to them.

On the other hand, although they never returned to idolatry after the captivity, they fell into the more terrible evil of lip service, vain and haughty self-righteousness, empty pride, and hypocritical temple worship. They scorned God and mocked His commandments. They trampled under foot His covenant and destroyed the light of His revelation. They built the graves of the faithless man and adorned the graves of unjust men with praise and flattery. This was Israel's sad history. The brighter the light of the revelation of God shone, the more fully they revealed the corruption of their own godless and depraved hearts.

Yet this is always true of the history of the Church. God sovereignly causes His gospel to shine and the light of His revelation to appear in those places which He chooses. But wherever the light of this gospel shines and the brilliant and glorious sun of His truth blazes forth, there also sin develops with astounding speed and unbelievable horror. Over against the truth, the lie is developed by men who hate the truth. And when there are faithful people of God who confess the truth and walk according to its precepts, the enemies of the truth rise up against the saints in hatred and bitterness to wipe their name from the earth. The closer one comes to the center of this revelation and the nearer he comes to the brightest revelation of the gospel, the worse does sin appear. It is not in heathen lands where the light of the gospel is never seen that the worst sins of men are manifest. It is the civilized nations, influenced outwardly by the gospel, where sin is unveiled in all its horrors. And the additional yet frightening truth is that these are the ones who know better. History is replete with illustrations of this truth. We need only think of the monstrous crimes Rome perpetrated at the time of the Reformation against those who sought and found the truth. We have only to look into the future when Antichrist will sit on the throne of the world, to discover that the monsters of iniquity are those who stand the closest to the revelation of the truth of God.

So it was with the fig tree. Receiving the most diligent care and the tenderest concern, it yet proved to be utterly barren.

A Revelation of God's Just Purpose

Yet the question arises: "Why was the fig tree given another year?" In the occasion for this parable the question must have immediately entered the minds of Jesus' listeners: "Why then are others spared if all are equally wicked?" Why was the fig tree given another year to see whether it would yet bear fruit?

Or to put the question into the entire context: "If Israel had throughout the ages committed these monstrous crimes, why were they given more time? Why were they not immediately destroyed?" In our answer to this question, we must be sure that we consider the teaching of the whole of Scripture. If we do this, then we will notice in the first place that we must consider that the nation of Israel was formed by God as an organism, and it must be considered organically. That Israel was an organism means that it was one nation which came forth from Abraham its father and lived in the unity of this organic relationship. The nation constituted one commonwealth, with one king; it was one country, with one head. It was a separate nation, separated from all other nations, but standing

together in organic connection as a nation. It was created as a
Church. It possessed in common and all the members possessed in
relationship to each other, one temple, one priesthood, one sacrifice, one law, one revelation of God. The people could not be
separated from each other and could not each live their own life. If
this had happened it would only have meant that Israel ceased to
exist as a nation.

This nation of Israel had become barren. This is not to say that
every individual within the nation was wicked. God always,
throughout its entire history, preserved to Himself a remnant according to the election of grace. (See Rom. 11:1-5.) But these few
were indeed a remnant, a minority. In the second place, the throne
of the nation was in the hands of wicked kings. This meant that the
influence of the king was for bad and not for good, so that the nation
followed its king in the paths of wickedness. In the third place, the
entire worship of the nation was corrupted. The priests were godless
men ruled by ambition and desire for personal gain. The temple was
under the control of a corrupt priesthood. The sacrifices were
profaned and it was next to impossible for the faithful to worship
God. The Sanhedrin was composed of rebels and degenerates. The
nation as a whole, considered organically, was faithless and apostate.

Yet this nation is spared for a while. The question is, why? Why
did not God destroy it for all its horrible crimes? Or, to put the
question a little differently, what was God's purpose in not destroying the fig tree of Israel's existence immediately?

Most commentators have a ready answer to this question. They
speak of the fact that this postponement of judgment was a measure
of the grace and mercy of God. And they interpret this to mean that
Israel was given "a last chance," "one more opportunity for repentance." Israel was spared temporarily in order that once more God
might reveal His offer of salvation to them as the way of escape. We
quote one author who is representative of those who teach this view.

> We are too apt to forget that there is a time beyond which God's
> Spirit will not strive, there is a boundary line over which mercy never
> steps.
> At the very point when the forbearance of God seems to end, an
> intercessor appears; Christ comes into view, and pleads for "one year"
> more of probation. "Let it alone this year also; and if it bear fruit, well;
> if not, after that thou shalt cut it down." He does not pray that it
> should never be cut down, but not *now*. Every sinner is at this moment
> under the condemnation of eternal death; and the reason why he is
> not executed is, that Christ pleads, "Let him alone this year also!"
> This, however, is a reprieve, not a pardon; a reprieve for a short
> time, yet long enough to make full trial. During this reprieve God is
> giving him the culture and tillage necessary to fruitfulness; the means
> of grace, the bleeding Savior, the striving Spirit, the ordinances of the
> church. His position is one of extreme peril, and of extreme sol-

icitude: of peril, because the time is short—the isthmus of probation between the land of hope and the world of despair is very narrow, and his feet stand on slippery places; of solicitude, because upon his resolves this year may hinge the destiny on his soul forever (*The Parables Unfolded*, Stevens, pp. 203, 204).

This is a distortion of the truth of Scripture. This is the age-old error of Arminius, who taught that the salvation of man depends upon the freedom of the will. It is a denial of the sovereign dealings of God with men. It is a denial of God's sovereign and determinative decree. It presents man as stronger than God, and God as waiting for the outcome of salvation upon the will of man. Did not God know that Israel would not repent? Of course He did; He is the sovereign Lord. But even more than this, the Lord determined that Israel should not repent. For His counsel stands and He does all His good pleasure.

We must look elsewhere for the solution to this problem.

If we interpret this in the light of the whole of Scripture, the only possible answer to our question is, God preserved Israel as a nation a little longer in order that Israel might fill the cup of iniquity and become ripe for judgment. In becoming ripe for judgment, the justice of God would be perfectly vindicated in rejecting the nation and casting the wicked into hell.

This God accomplished first of all be causing the light of His revelation to shine its brightest. Always there was progress in revelation. From the kernel of that revelation given to our first parents in Paradise, the tree of revelation grew throughout the ages of the Old Dispensation. From the first flicker of this light in the darkness of the night of sin that settled over the world when our parents fell, the light grew brighter and brighter. It increased in intensity through all the means that God used to reveal it in the Old Testament: the history of the nation of Israel itself, the law, the sacrifices, the prophets. Then God sent the Sun of Righteousness, the Dayspring from on High, to shine in all the splendor of His glory. But even in the life of Christ there was progress toward a goal, for the brightest revelation of the promises of God did not shine till Christ died on the cross and rose again from the dead.

With this ever growing light of revelation came the obligation to Israel to repent of her sins. In fact, the brighter this revelation grew, the more insistent came the calling to turn from evil and to return to the living God. This does not mean that Israel could repent without grace. But it does mean that God never relinquished the demands He had placed upon man in Paradise: "Love me!" Israel was given opportunity to repent at every turn. They were given the full revelation of the truth. When they refused to repent, it was not because they did not know the way of repentance. They could never plead ignorance. They could never justify themselves by saying that they had not known that repentance was required of them. Thus, when in their wickedness they refused to repent, the only explanation was the hardness of their hearts and the rebellion of their own transgression.

But this was also God's purpose. For God had determined to destroy Israel. He had determined to bring the gospel to the elect of every nation. Israel stood in the way. It was a fig tree that cumbered the ground. It must be removed so that the other plants and trees in the vineyard could grow. This is evident from the fact that as the light of revelation grew brighter with the passing of the years, the sin of Israel grew proportionately worse. God forbears that sin may appear in its true character. God does not come immediately in judgment in order that the horror of sin may be fully evident. It is possible that for a while the wicked assume as appearance of hypocritical piety. But the light of revelation pierces through the mask of their piety and exposes all the sins of their evil hearts.

The result of it is that Israel at last turns against the Christ of God and nails Him to the accursed tree, thereby committing the crime of the ages. Then all external piety is wiped away and all self-righteouness is swallowed up in sin. Sin has appeared as it really is. Transgression is exposed in the full horror of its terrible character. The Christ hangs despised and mocked by the Church on the accursed tree of the cross. And so, as God reveals the fullest salvation He has prepared for His people, the apostate church stands before that cross and heaps on Christ the mockery of its fullest expression of sin.

This is true throughout the ages. As the gospel increases in brightness and intensity, sin is more clearly exposed. The wicked hate the truth and rebel against it. But always those who have known the way are those who most bitterly despise it. And when at last that gospel is fully revealed, the wicked crucify to themselves the Son of God afresh and put Him to open shame. In this way the cup of iniquity is filled because sin reaches its climax.

And this is all sovereignly determined by God in order that He alone may be vindicated. When the fig tree is at last chopped down, it is done in fullest justice. It has become everlastingly evident that man cannot repent of himself and turn to God. All that he does is increase in sin and multiply his transgression.

But God is revealed as just. He is vindicated in everything He does. As the sovereign Lord of heaven and earth Who rules over all men, He now appears as the righteous judge of all wickedness. And when the wicked are sent to everlasting destruction and beaten with double stripes, they will never be able to raise a complaint against God. They knew the truth but hated it. They saw the Christ but crucified Him. And so they are punished in the justice of God Who is triumphantly vindicated also in their own consciousness. In this way God receives the glory. This is what Isaiah writes in the passage which we quoted above. "And now go to; I will tell you what I will do to my vineyard: I will take away the hedge thereof, and it shall be eaten up; and break down the wall thereof, and it shall be trodden down: and I will lay it waste: it shall not be pruned, nor digged, but there shall come up briars and thorns: I will also command the clouds that they rain no rain upon it. For the vineyard of the Lord of hosts is the house of Israel, and the men of Judah his pleasant plant: and he looked for judgment, but behold oppression; for righteousness, but behold a cry." (See Isaiah 5:5-7.)

The Positive Fruit of God's Forbearance

This does not mean that there is not also a positive purpose in God's forbearance, and this positive purpose is realized in the salvation of the elect.

Always, although the nation of Israel apostatized, God preserved to Himself a remnant according to the election of grace. It is true that this was always a remnant, a "seven thousand that did not bow the knee to Baal." Nevertheless, it was always there. As the church became more and more corrupt and wickedness increased, the elect of Christ, the faithful of God, were preserved by God's power and grace.

These must always be the saved ones. There was this remnant of election in Israel also at the time of Jesus' ministry. This remnant consisted of a Mary and Joseph, a Zacharias and Elisabeth, a Simeon and Anna, a few shepherds on Bethlehem's hills. But they were there throughout Christ's ministry. If the nation of Israel had been destroyed, they could not have been saved. In the inscrutable wisdom and sovereign mercy of the Most High God, judgment did not occur immediately in order that this remnant could be gathered and saved before the end of the nation came.

Thus it always is. Always the world merits judgment. But God does not come now; nor will He come tomorrow in judgment, because there is a remnant that He has chosen which must first be gathered before judgment finally arrives. For the sake of this remnant God restrains as it were His anger and fury against the wicked. Or, to put it a little differently, God not only purposes to reveal the fulness of His wrath and justice in the punishment of the wicked, He also determines to reveal the depths of His mercy and love in the salvation of the Church. And it is only when the full number of the elect are saved that the infinite depths of the mercy and love of God are fully displayed.

Scripture abounds with illustrations of this. Wicked Sodom was spared until Lot was delivered. Wicked Israel was preserved as a nation until the remnant was gathered. The wicked world is not destroyed until the last elect is born and saved. Paul speaks of this in Romans 9:22-24: "What if God, willing to show his wrath, and to make his power known, endured with much longsuffering the vessels of wrath fitted to destruction: And that he might make known the riches of his glory on the vessels of mercy, which he had afore prepared unto glory, Even us, whom he hath called, not of the Jews only, but also of the Gentiles?" Peter also mentions this remarkable truth in II Peter 3:9: "The Lord is not slack concerning his promise, as some men count slackness; but is longsuffering to us-ward, not willing that any should perish, but that all should come to repentance."

And so it is that God saves His Church through the way of repentance. The only escape from judgment is the way of repentance; there is no other way. This was true of Israel, even though it boasted that it was the people of the Lord while it prided itself in its righteousness and in the works of the law. This is always true. There is no road to glory except the road drenched with the tears of repentance. There is no gate to heaven but the gate of a broken spirit and a contrite heart. For repentance is the bitter sorrow for sin and the longing for forgiveness. Repentance is to seek the cross of Christ and the forgiveness of sins in that cross alone. Repentance is to condemn all the works of which we are capable as unworthy of anything but judgment, and to flee speedily to the suffering Savior to find forgiveness in His bleeding body. Repentance is the road to glory because the way of the cross leads home. On the cross of Christ is the salvation of the Church. On Christ the solid rock we stand; all other ground is sinking sand.

But this repentance is God's gift. It cannot come of us. This was true of Israel; this is evident in all time. God works that repentance in the hearts of His people. God breaks the stubborn heart of sin and softens the hard heart of rebellion. God brings tears of sorrow and repentance to our eyes. God takes His people by the hand and leads them to the cross. For as the cross is the revelation of the love of God, so also is the repentance of the sinning elect the fruit of God's love shed abroad within their hearts. It is when the light of the cross shines not only before our eyes but also in our hearts by the power of the Holy Spirit that we say: "In the cross of Christ I glory!"

This repentance is the road to heaven! "Except ye repent, ye shall all likewise perish." In granting repentance to His people, God is fully and triumphantly glorified forever. Not to us must be the glory, but to the sovereign Lord of heaven and earth must be all glory now and forever. Not only in the just punishment of the wicked must this be true, but also in the glorious salvation of the elect.

12

The Exaltation of the Humble

And he put forth a parable to those which were bidden, when he marked how they chose out the chief rooms; saying unto them,
When thou art bidden of any man to a wedding, sit not down in the highest room; lest a more honourable man than thou be bidden of him;
And he that bade thee and him come and say to thee, Give this man place; and thou begin with shame to take the lowest room.
But when thou art bidden, go and sit down in the lowest room; that when he that bade thee cometh, he may say unto thee,
Friend, go up higher: then shalt thou have worship in the presence of them that sit at meat with thee.
For whosoever exalteth himself shall be abased; and he that humbleth himself shall be exalted.

—Luke 14:7-11

Although the point is quite emphatically mentioned in verse 7, many commentators tend to forget that these verses constitute a parable. In their interpretation of these verses, they seem to think that Jesus is discussing nothing more than table manners. Usually in that case the interpretation becomes a sort of "social gospel," which is the kind of gospel preached from so many modern pulpits in our theologically barren times. In that case the humility of which Jesus speaks is nothing more than an outward show of humility—a humility which is an outward cloak in which one appears somewhat humble in the presence of his fellow man. If this is as far as we can go with this parable, we have certainly failed to understand the important word of Christ.

Rather, by this parable Jesus defines a very essential principle of the life of those who are citizens of the kingdom of heaven. Time and again in Scripture this Christian virtue of humility appears as most important in the lives of the people of God. But it is then an inner spiritual grace that is rooted in regeneration. It is a state of heart and mind first of all, and not a mere outward show. It is a humility that must appear as such before the face of God Whose eyes see all that lies within, and Who will surely drive the proud from His presence. Yet this virtue is so completely important that Scripture insists again and again that it is only the humble that will enter into the kingdom of God. The mark of the citizens of the kingdom par excellence is the mark of humility. It is the final and absolute dividing line between those who are within the kingdom and those who remain outside. "For whosoever exalteth himself shall be abased; and he that humbleth himself shall be exalted."

Pride and Humility

Pride and humility are opposites. They are mutually exclusive of each other. Where the one is, the other cannot be.

Jesus was in the house of one of the chief of the Pharisees. There were other guests there, and it seems reasonable from the text to conclude that this Pharisee had not invited Jesus to his house out of a sense of hospitality. Rather, it appears that the motive was to watch Jesus in order to find some basis to condemn Him either in the actions He performed or the words He spoke. Fundamentally, the motive was evil. There was a man present with the dropsy—perhaps deliberately brought to the banquet. And it was the Sabbath day, on which—according to the Pharisees—no man could work. When Jesus ignored their evil intentions and healed the man, they thought they had their ground for condemnation. But Jesus answered their objections and at the same time utilized the occasion to teach a parable which exposed their own sin.

Jesus had often noticed how the Jews always took the chief seats when they were invited to a feast. In those days it was the custom that the table was fashioned so that couches could be placed on the floor around it, so that the guests could recline while eating. There were couches of honor, chief seats in a certain order of rank. Probably the couches of honor were those nearest the host of the banquet and gradually became less honorable as the distance from the host increased. It had become a matter of no little importance to these Pharisees which couch they occupied at any given banquet. So well known was the unspoken struggle between these haughty men for the chiefest of the seats, that the obsession had even carried over to the disciples. You will recall the argument among them as to who was the greatest and who deserved the place of honor as they walked with Jesus to the upper room where Jesus celebrated the last Passover with them.

But when the Pharisees chose the chiefest seats available upon their arrival at a feast, there was behind their action the deeper motive of carnal pride. Each of them thought he was the most noble and honored, hence deserving of the best seat in rank because of his nobility. To attain their goal they often engaged in unseemly conduct, argument, and bitterness among themselves in their struggle to attain the first rank. But all this was merely a manifestation of the haughtiness that lurked in their evil hearts. They could put on a robe of piety when they chose to do so. They could appear before men as being among the spiritually elite, but within them worked the deadly cancer of pride. This pride was deeply rooted in their hearts. It was based on their worthless yet very real opinion of themselves as the holiest of men. They considered that they had earned their own righteousness by keeping every letter of the law.

Pride is the root of all sin. It is not primarily something which distorts our relationships with our fellow men, but it is first of all a sin that is committed against God. This was true already of our first parents in Paradise. When the devil came into the garden with his enticing words, he appealed to Adam and Eve through the temptation of pride: "Ye shall be as gods knowing good and evil." When our first parents listened to the tempter, it was in the hope that they could become as great as God was. This became what they wanted more than anything else. And if the way to becoming as great as God was, was the way of disobedience, pride was so great that they walked that way to gain their end.

This however is the work of all sin in men. And it comes especially to manifestation in this, that the sinner refuses to admit that he is a sinner. The greatest sin of a depraved sinner is that he will not acknowledge that he is a transgressor of God's law. It is this failure to acknowledge his own sin which leads him to all his sins of pride. He claims in his arrogance to have the power of God and to be as great as God. He attempts to drive God out of his world and sets himself up as the king of the creation answerable to no one, a sovereign lord possessing the exclusive right to do in God's world as it seems good to him. He makes what belongs to the living God his own. He steals the honor, the glory, the praise that rightfully belong to the Lord and claims them as his. In pride he becomes a rebel, a haughty and boastful insurrectionist who lives only for himself.

This pride comes also to manifestation in man's relationships with his fellow men. The proud man has the definite opinion that he is better than anyone else. Sometimes he boasts of his riches, sometimes of his talents, sometimes of his holiness and piety, sometimes of his position in the world. He looks down on his fellow men with an inferior and contemptuous glance, assuring himself that there are none who compare with him. He is utterly ruthless in his desire to push himself forward. He is not concerned about what happens to his fellow man in his godless bid for power. He may put on an outward cloak of humility and even seem to have a disinterested concern for the well-being of his fellow man. But this mask of humility is only the worse for its deeper pride; and his seeming concern for the comfort and well-being of his neighbor is but another way devised in his proud heart to attain his ambitions.

The sin of pride is found in an absolute sense in the unbeliever. Pride lied at the root of all his life. He is always moved by this first sin which opened the floodgates of transgression and wickedness upon the world. But this sin is no less present in the people of God. It is true that principally they are saved. They have the life of regeneration within their hearts. They are called out of the kingdom of darkness into the kingdom of Jesus Christ. But they still carry with them on this side of the grave and all the way to the grave their sinful flesh. And in this flesh dwells no good thing. The result of this is that, relatively speaking, this pride is always present in them. In fact, because the new holiness is only a small beginning and is only the principle of complete salvation, the flesh is very strong and the pride that characterizes this flesh is a major factor in their lives.

Humility is precisely the opposite of all this. Humility is fundamentally a virtue in which one stands in a relationship toward God. It is basically the consciousness of God's greatness. It is not, however, simply an awareness of this fact, but a living confession of it. It is not a knowledge of this truth which belongs to the intellect alone, but it is a thankful belief in the awareness that God alone is the high and lofty One. He is absolutely transcendent above all His creation, for He formed it by His own hand. He dwells supremely high and lifted up, far exalted above the heavens and is alone worthy of all praise and glory. He is clothed with majesty and power. There is none like unto Him. Of Him and to Him and through Him are all things; to Him must be glory both now and forever.

The essential corollary of this truth is that we are nothing. Even apart from the fact that we are sinners, we are nothing. All the nations of the earth, says the prophet Isaiah, are as a speck of dust in the balance and as a drop hanging on the outside of a bucket ready to fall unnoticed to the ground. If all the nations that inhabit the globe are less than this, what is each one of us among so many millions in the world? We are only insignificant and puny creatures who depend every moment for all things on the will of the Most High.

And as if this were not enough, we are sinful besides. We have forfeited all right even to that favor which the living God is pleased to show to us. We have deliberately and willingly chosen to walk in our own way of rebellion. We have become transgressors worthy only of eternal death.

Humility as Applied to the Parable

It is this fundamental truth which underlies the parable Jesus expounds. When Jesus advised the Pharisees to take the lowest seat at the feast, He was not simply handing out some advice on social manners. Nor must the motive for taking the lower seat at the feast be a false modesty, for this too is pride. Rather the motive for finding the most humble seat at the banquet must be rooted in the knowledge that we do not even belong at the banquet.

The feast of the parable was a wedding feast. As such it was a picture of covenant fellowship between God and His people. God takes His people into His own house. He gives them a place in the marriage of Christ and His Church. He describes the joy of that fellowship in terms of a feast. This is God's everlasting covenant of grace which He establishes with those whom He has eternally chosen to be His own. Here at this feast we know that we deserve no place at all.

Thus true humility is always the consciousness of sin. Each knows that he is but a wretched sinner. He is overwhelmingly aware of how awful he must appear in the eyes of a Holy God. He says with the apostle Paul: "Of all sinners I am the chief." He knows that he deserves nothing but everlasting punishment, for in him is found no good thing. He is not like the proud Pharisee who thanked God that he is not as other men are; rather he can be found off in a corner by himself, smiting his breast, not daring to lift his eyes to heaven. And the plaintive cry that is wrenched from his heart is: "O God, be merciful to me, a sinner."

When he finds that he has been given a place in the banquet hall of God's covenant, he is amazed that he should be there. He looks about him and notices that many are excluded, and he shall throughout all eternity wonder at the fact that he—no better and far worse than many others—should have been included. And when in his astonishment he inquires into the reason, he finds that that reason could not possibly have been in himself. All his righteousnesses were only filthy rags. All his works made him worthy of hell. All his virtue was only corruption and depravity. He knows only that the reason lies hidden in the eternal mystery of the counsel of God. He knows that not he—as the proud Arminian is wont to say —sought the Lord and reached out for salvation. He is not saved because of anything he did. He forever is filled with wonder that God should show His mercy and grace to him. There is a love and mercy in the heart of God from which salvation flows that he shall never fathom, for he has tasted of a love that came to him undeserved.

It is this inner and profound humility that becomes the basic principle of his relation to his fellow men. He lives knowing that every other saint is better than himself. He does not know what brought them into the house of his Father, but they could not possibly be as bad and undeserving as himself. Not riches, not talents, not honor, not even an office in the church, means anything at all or makes any difference. Every other saint is better than he. It must be so, for no one could be as bad as he.

It is this which leads him and directs him in his life among the saints. Should one of his fellow saints go astray he follows to bring him back, for he knows that he himself will do the same tomorrow and will need the help of him who he now helped. And if he remains faithful in the paths of God's Word, it is not because he has attained to a great level of piety; it is rather because his God holds him by His grace on the path of the truth.

The thanksgiving that floods his soul at the overwhelming consciousness of the depths of God's mercy shown to him is a gratitude that finds its expression in a life of dedicated service to such a great and wonderful God. This humility is not manifested in some false and superficial and carnal modesty which keep him from using the gifts God has given for the well-being of his fellow saints. This, too, would be pride. But instead he possesses an awareness that his chief delight is in the service of his God. It is an unspeakably blessed privilege of grace that he has a place in the house of the Lord.

Nor must this be presented as if it comes automatically, as it were. It is not so that we are one day proud sinners and the next day conversion comes, and from henceforth our lives are lives of humility. Thus it is often presented by those who take a very superficial and essentially proud view of their conversion. Yesterday I was proud, so they say; today I am humble. There is such a thing in the subtle sin of the heart of man as being proud of humility. But the fact is that the struggle against pride is a constant and daily struggle which must be fought throughout life. Our flesh is corrupt. In it dwells all kinds of evil and stinking pride. Against it we must struggle without cessation. It is there in all its vicious rebellion against God. It must be overcome. It is the daily enemy that must be faced and defeated. It rears its ugly head at every turn of the path. Until the grave cleanses us from the last vestiges of sin, it is a continual threat in our lives. It is the real source of the constant and bitter grief of the saints. It is the reason why they fall on their knees in spiritual exhaustion every night to cry for forgiveness. It is the basis for the eager longing of the saints to go to heaven where they will be perfect forever. It inspires the hope to be freed from sin. It drives the pilgrim toward his heavenly city. For it is an enemy, implacable and fierce which torments us all our days.

The Power of Humility is in Christ

This greatest of all gifts, the gift of humility, comes to the people of God only through the power of the cross of Christ. This is possible because Christ humbled Himself. This humility of our Lord Jesus Christ is so deep and so profound that we cannot even imagine it, much less imitate it in our own lives.

He was the Lord of glory. Oh, it is not as if in His humiliation He ceased to be the Lord of glory. He did not empty Himself so that no longer He bore all the majesty of the divine Godhead. No, to deny this is to deny how great His humiliation really was. He was and is and remains God. He dwells eternally in the bosom of the Father. He is all the fulness of the matchless excellency which belongs to God alone. He is, with the Father and the Spirit, Lord and Sovereign over all.

He Who was so great humbled Himself. He became a man. He was born as a baby in the cradle of Bethlehem's manger. He took on Himself the likeness of man, the severe and creaturely limitations of man who is so dependent. Not only that, but He took on Himself the likeness of sinful flesh. He was not a man endowed with supreme power and intelligence as far as His human nature was concerned, nor a man like the first Adam before he fell, but a man in the likeness of sinful flesh. (See Rom. 8:3.) He took upon Himself the utter humility of our sad state.

Even more, He took upon Himself not only our human nature, but He took upon Himself our sin and guilt. He Who was Lord of all became a servant. He bore the heavy burden of our transgression. He was beaten with our stripes. He was wounded for our iniquities. He bore the chastisement of our peace. He was a lamb led to the slaughter. He was hated and despised and suffered the torments of a mocking and wicked world. He was cast out and permitted Himself to be cast out. He was condemned as a common criminal, a hated and despised outcast, a pariah who could not be tolerated in the earth.

Yet He was not only cast out by men, He was cast out by God. Man had no room for Him in the earth, but God has no room for Him in heaven. He was cast out and forsaken of God so that He was thrown into hell. There the fierce billows of God's wrath poured over His soul until He could scarcely understand it. And at last He died—died as men die, although He was the Eternal One. And men laid Him in a grave.

But all this happened to Him because He became a servant. When we say we are worthless we only speak the truth. When Christ made Himself worthless, He was not so, for He was God. He made Himself worthless freely and in obedience. He became a servant of God although He was God. And serving God, He willingly chose to walk the deep way of God's wrath in hell because it was the way of obedience. He was obedient unto death—the death of the cross.

He became a servant to His people. Shall we ever be able to understand it? He created us and still upholds us by the word of His power. He is our Sovereign and Lord. Yet He became our servant. We are less than nothing; He is the living God. Yet He did not hesitate to humble Himself to become our servant. He became our servant because He was made sin for us. He bore our shame and the wrath of God that justly was ours. He was moved in all He did only by love for those whom the Father had given Him. Love us? How can it be? Will eternity be long enough to take all this in with all its wonderful significance?

This truth means two things. It means, in the first place, that He is the power of our humility. Always the humility that characterizes the life of the saints is a humility that is rooted in regeneration. It is a virtue which comes by grace alone. It is worked in us through the power of our Lord Jesus Christ. He, through His humility, gives to us the humility that must be and is principally ours. He works the humility of His own cross within our hearts. Never does this humility come of ourselves. Never ought we to claim that it does, for this claim is the claim of a proud heart. We do not and cannot boast in ourselves. God forbid that we should glory, save in the cross of our Lord Jesus Christ (Gal. 6:14). Christ makes us as He was, insofar as it is possible for the creature to be like the Creator.

In the second place, the meaning of this is that we must take Christ as our example. He is our pattern and His humility is the pattern of our humility. This is emphasized again and again on the pages of Holy Writ. When Jesus came into the upper room with His disciples after they had wickedly been bickering and arguing about who was the greatest, He wrapped a towel about Himself and washed their feet. And when He had washed them all He said to them: "Ye call me master and lord: and ye say well: for so I am. If I then, your Lord and Master, have washed your feet; ye also ought to wash one another's feet. For I have given you an example, that ye should do as I have done to you. Verily, verily, I say unto you, The servant is not greater than his lord; neither he that is sent greater than he that sent him. If ye know these things, happy are ye if ye do them" (John 13:13-17). This truth is taught by Paul in Philippians 2:5-8: Let this mind be in you, which was also in Christ Jesus: Who, being in the form of God, counted not the being on an equality with God a thing to be grasped: (So reads the Reivsed Version which is more correct.) But made himself of no reputation and took upon Him the form of a servant, and was made in the likeness of men: and being found in fashion as a man, he humbled himself, and became obedient unto death, even the death of the cross."

By grace must we walk in the footsteps that Christ walked. And although we will never be able to approximate except in a very small measure the depths of His humility, nevertheless this is our calling. As servants of God, in humility, we also must be servants of one another.

The Reward of the Humble

Our Lord Jesus Christ not only humbled Himself to the lowest possible degree, but because of His humility He was also highly exalted. That same wonderful passage in Philippians 2 which speaks of His humiliation also goes on to describe His exaltation. Connected to the description of His humiliation by the all-important word "wherefore," the apostle goes on to say in verses 9-11: "God also hath highly exalted him, and given him a name which is above every name: That at the the name of Jesus every knee should bow, of things in heaven, and things in earth, and things under the earth; And that every tongue should confess that Jesus Christ is Lord, to the glory of God the Father." Christ's humiliation was deeper than any man's can ever be, but the exaltation which was given Him as a reward for His humiliation was also higher than it is possible for man to attain. He was raised to the right hand of God far above all principalities and powers, crowned with many crowns and made Lord of lords and King of kings.

For this reason we too are exalted in the way of humility. By grace we are the followers of Christ. We walk the path that He walked. And this path, as we follow in the footsteps of our Lord and Master, is not only a path of humility; it is a path that leads to a very high glory.

The opposite is also true. This is the point of the parable. The ones who took a higher seat and sought out the chiefest seats at the feast were shamed before their fellow men. They were taken from the place of honor which they had claimed as their own, for nobler men appeared. Those who had first claimed the chief seats were now sent before the face of their fellow men to the lowest place at the table.

Thus it would be with the proud Pharisees. These claimed the most exalted place in the house of God. They claimed this place for their own in the confidence that they had made themselves worthy of it. But there comes to the wedding feast one more noble than they. Perhaps a harlot, a publican, a sinner—it makes no difference. These are more noble, for they have gained their nobility in the cross of Jesus Christ by faith.

And so the proud are always debased and humbled. This is already true in this life. On the one hand, this may be, in a measure, true of the people of God. The people of God do not always walk in humility. Sometimes pride gains the upper hand. At that point they lose in their consciousness the assurance of the favor of God. Even for them pride goes before a fall. It was this way with Peter. He boasted loudly of his own strength and ability to be faithful. But he stood in his own power, exalting himself above the other disciples and acting as if he alone would follow the Lord. But how he was abased and how great was his fall!

This sometimes becomes necessary also in our lives. We dread this. And so we pray that the Lord will not permit us to become so haughty and vain in our self-conceit that we must be humbled through a difficult trial. Nevertheless, if this happens, the Lord in His compassion always restores those whom He loves. But the wicked are never exalted. They exalt themselves above God and their fellow men. And they are surely debased. Already in this life that becomes a reality. God brings them deeper and deeper into their sin. They sink ever more deeply into the consciousness of His wrath and displeasure.

Yet this is never fully realized in this life. It seems indeed as if the wicked are often exalted. Their final debasement awaits the judgment day. There too they will claim that they have the right to the chiefest seat in the house of God. "Have we not prophesied in thy name? have we not cast out devils in thy name? In thy name have we not done wonderful things?" But the Host at the great supper will say, "Depart from me. I never knew you." And in everlasting disgrace in the sight of all their fellows they will be consigned to everlasting darkness. There shall be weeping and gnashing of teeth.

But the humble are exalted. Thus it was in the parable. They come to the feast in the consciousness that they have no right to be there at all. And so they take the very lowest seat, for even that seat seems too great for them. But when the Host at the supper sees them, He calls them to come up higher, for their place of honor is at His right hand.

This too happens in this life. The humble are exalted. Let it be clearly understood that this humility is of grace alone. This is not abstract theological truth; this is the deepest conviction of those who walk in this humility. They are profoundly aware of the fact that they come through the cross. And so also the reward of their exaltation is a reward of grace, not earned by themselves but given through the cross of Christ. Shall they now claim that reward by their own power? Shall pride destroy all at the last moment? God forbid!

In this life they may not perhaps receive the grace and favor of men. Indeed, if they walk in meekness and humility they will probably be despised and hated. But they are exalted by their God. They are lifted higher and higher in grace and favor. They increase in the knowledge of Him Whom to know is life eternal. They experience more fully the loving-kindness of their God, which is more than life to them.

And yet this is not all. When at last they stand before the judgment seat of the Judge of heaven and earth, they are exalted to the glory of heaven. They cry out even then: "Lord, when have we done anything pleasing in thy sight? When have we fed thee when thou wast hungry and clothed thee when thou wast naked, and warmed thee when thou wast cold? When did we visit thee in prison? We have done nothing good. All our righteousness is as filthy rags." But the Lord wlll say to them: "The way of humility is the way to glory. There is no other way than this. For it is the way of the cross. You confess that all your righteousness is alone in Me. This is the way of exaltation. Inasmuch as ye have done it to the least of My brethren ye have done these things to Me. Ye have washed the feet of the lowliest of My people. Enter thou into the joy of thy Lord."

When at last we arrive with God's people in glory one of the things which perhaps shall surprise us most is exactly the truth that Jesus sets forth in this parable. The lowly and despised here on earth have a special place of exaltation in glory. The exalted ones, the powerful ones, the men of position and honor and fame, here in the world, are the ones, if they enter the kingdom, who even there receive the lower places. But then publicly, before the eyes of all the world, the people of God will be taken into the house of their Father. They sit down with Christ at the right hand of God. There they will enjoy the feast of God's everlasting covenant of grace forever. There they never again boast in anything which they did, for into all eternity they know they deserved nothing. They glory in their God! And in the cross of their Lord!

13

That My House May Be Full

Then said he unto him, A certain man made a great supper, and bade many:
And sent his servant at supper time to say to them that were bidden, Come; for all things are now ready.
And they all with one consent began to make excuse. The first said unto him, I have bought a piece of ground, and I must needs go and see it; I pray thee have me excused.
And another said, I have bought five yoke of oxen, and I go to prove them: I pray thee have me excused.
And another said, I have married a wife, and therefore I cannot come.
So that servant came, and shewed his lord these things. Then the master of the house being angry said to his servant, Go out quickly into the streets and lanes of the city, and bring in hither the poor, and the maimed, and the halt, and the blind.
And the servant said, Lord, it is done as thou hast commanded, and yet there is room.
And the lord said unto the servant, Go out into the highways and hedges, and compel them to come in, that my house may be filled.
For I say unto you, That none of those men which were bidden shall taste of my supper.

—Luke 14:16-24

The parable that is here recorded for us is the second one spoken while Jesus was dining in the house of a certain chief of the Pharisees. As we noticed in the previous chapter, He had been invited there manifestly to give the Pharisees an opportunity to watch Him and to try to find in what He did or said some reason to condemn Him. Jesus had spoken the parable recorded in verses 7-11, in which He had condemned the pride of the arrogant Pharisees and spoken of the exaltation of the humble.

According to verses 12-14 of this chapter, Jesus had continued His instruction, admonishing the guests who were dining with Him that they should not invite their brethren or kinsmen or rich neighbors to share their hospitality. Rather, they should invite the poor, the maimed, the lame, and the blind. Implied in this admonition was also a precept of the kingdom of heaven. The reason why the Pharisees were accustomed to invite their kinsmen and the rich was purely selfish. They gave in order that they might receive an invitation in return. Thus they were acting out of selfish motives; consequently, when the invitation was returned, they "had their reward." But if instead they would invite the poor and the lame and the blind, they could not possibly receive an invitation in return. In extending such invitations, they would simply be acting according to motives of mercy and love—motives which could not be recompensed. Although they would receive no reward by way of a return invitation, their reward would be in the resurrection of the just. This is a precept of the kingdom of heaven because in doing so they would reflect the love and mercy of God. God never calls to His heavenly banquet those who have earned a place there and who justly deserve to come to the feast. God calls the undeserving as an everlasting display of His unrecompensed mercy and grace. And this is also the main point of the parable that follows.

The immediate occasion for the parable is a statement by one of the guests: "Blessed is he that shall eat bread in the kingdom of God." It is difficult to determine the exact point this guest was making. There are some who argue that this guest had an earthly conception of the kingdom of heaven and was speaking out of pride, intending the remark to refer to himself. There are others who maintain that the man, momentarily overcome by the truth of Jesus' statements, uttered a simple statement of fact which had no personal application to himself. Whatever the motive of the guest, Jesus uses the statement to instruct the company concerning those who shall indeed be guests at this heavenly banquet. Jesus teaches that the proud and haughty Pharisees will be excluded from the heavenly banquet, for they thought they had earned their place there. The poor and the blind and the insignificant and the despised are the ones who will find a place there; for this would be a glorious display of God's grace unearned and unrecompensed, given in His mercy and love alone.

The Identity of the Guests

The elements of the parable are rather clear, and commentators are, in general, in agreement with respect to their interpretation. The "certain man" is God Himself. The "great feast" is the final banquet of the perfected kingdom of heaven. This is evident not only from the context, but from other parts of Scripture where the perfection of glory is described as a feast (cf., e. g., Matt. 22:2 ff.; Rev. 19:9). The impression must not be left, however, that Scripture teaches that heaven will be nothing more than a place where we eat

and drink. The idea is rather that the final realization of the kingdom of heaven can be described in terms of a feast because this is
indicative of the perfection of God's covenant which He establishes
with His people through Christ. The figure of a banquet table is
used to express this covenant relation because the fellowship of
eating and drinking is fellowship of intimate communion. Even for a
family, "at the table" is the time of communion and conversation.
There each member of the family has his own place. There the
problems of the family are discussed. There father and mother with
their children unite in prayer and devotion about the Word of God.
There is intimacy and fellowship, laughter and joy, the sharing of
the burdens and cares of life. So it is in the family of God with Jesus
Christ.

The fact that this "certain man" "bade many" is not to be interpreted as the so-called gospel invitation. This is not even true in
actual fact. In another similar parable recorded in Matthew 22, the
call to the supper is sent forth by the king. Now a king does not issue
an invitation and then leave it to the discretion of those called
whether they shall come or stay away. The king issues a royal
command. So also does God. We must beware lest we introduce into
the parable the evil of Arminianism. God does not longingly hope
for all men to come to His feast. He does not issue a mere invitation
and thus permit man to exercise his "free will" in accepting or
rejecting the invitation. Though this is often the interpretation of
this parable and of similar passages in Scripture, this is not the idea
which Jesus meant to teach. The call of God is a royal command. God
commands men to repent. And He does this not because it is His
sovereign intention that all should be saved, but rather because it is
man's obligation before the living God of heaven and earth to do
this. Man must love God. This was true in Paradise, and the fact that
man fell so that he could no longer do it does not negate the truth
that God insists on His rights as the living God. God still demands
that men love Him. And if now, since the Fall, this requires also that
men repent and believe in God, this remains a royal command of
God Himself which is based upon the truth that God cannot deny
His own sovereign claim upon the allegiance of men.

This royal command was ignored. Although in one sense or
another this was true throughout the entire Old Dispensation, we
must understand that Jesus refers in the parable particularly to the
leaders of the Jews. The Scribes and Pharisees, the Sadducees and
Chief Priests—these were the leaders of the people. These were
especially the ones who thought thay they alone, in distinction from
the common people, had a right to attend the supper of the kingdom
of God. They hated and despised the common people and were sure
in their self-righteousness that this scum of the nation would surely
have no place in the kingdom. But when the command to come was
extended to these leaders through the ministry of Christ, they refused. They had all kinds of excuses.

It is evident from the excuses which they offered that their reasons were not legitimate. They were shoddy excuses which revealed that in their hearts they did not want to come at all. Although they professed to have a place in the kingdom of God, they showed by their excuses that they hated that kingdom. The reasons for their refusal were poor attempts to justify their own sin.

The whole ministry of Christ was proof of this. The Pharisees were self-righteous and hypocritical. They claimed a reserved seat at the banquet feast of the kingdom because God owed them such a place. God had no choice but to take them into the feast because of the many favors they had done for God throughout their life. But now, with the coming of Christ, it was evident through the ministry of Jesus that to enter the kingdom required that they renounce their own deeds. To enter the kingdom they had to enter through Christ. And this was the way of humility and faith in the blood of atonement. But this they would never do. Entering this way, they would have to renounce their own works. They would have to admit that they were sinners. And so their real hatred for the kingdom is manifested.

And so the parable speaks of the rejection of these Jews by God from the viewpoint of God's justice.

That the leaders of the Jews had always found excuses not to enter is evident from their entire history. When Christ was born in Bethlehem as the fulfillment of prophecy, they refused to go because they thought a king should be born in Jerusalem. When Christ moved to Nazareth in fulfillment of prophecy, the Jews said that no good thing could possibly come out of Nazareth. This even became proverbial in Israel. When Christ came to preach in His home town and to point to the fact that He was the Anointed of the Lord as the fulfillment of Isaiah 61:1-3, they excused their refusal to hear His words by saying that they knew His father and His mother; and they urged Him sarcastically, "Physician, heal thyself."

In their sin these leaders always took a position of opposition to the kingdom. In Matthew 11:16-19 Jesus points this out. John, Jesus says, came neither eating nor drinking, and they said that he had a devil. The Son of man came eating and drinking, and they complained and whined, "Behold a man gluttonous and a wine bibber, a friend of publicans and sinners." And so Jesus compared them to children sitting in the markets and calling unto their fellows, and saying, "We have piped unto you, and ye have not danced; we have mourned unto you, and ye have not lamented." When Jesus showed His divine power by casting out devils, they answered by accusing Jesus of casting out devils in the name of Beelzebub. Jesus came to seek and to save the lost, but the leaders excused their unbelief by saying that Christ could not be what He claimed to be because He ate with sinners and harlots. The Lord healed the sick and went about doing good, but all the evil leaders could ever do was point out that

He violated the Sabbath and broke the laws of Moses. Finally when they nailed Him to the cross, the hollow ring of their empty excuses echoed over Jerusalem: He is a rebel, a traitor, a temple destroyer, a blasphemer. He saved others, Himself He cannot save. And when He showed with irrefutable proof that He was Christ in His glorious resurrection from the dead, they responded with the lame excuse that the disciples stole the body at night while the guards slept.

Always they had their reasons for not coming to the feast. Always they could find an excuse not to enter the kingdom. Always they were busy in justifying their own unbelief and terrible hatred. And in doing it they showed their deep-seated hatred for the kingdom of heaven which Christ had come to establish.

But the feast must have guests. And when the lord of the feast heard that these men would not come, he, in his fierce anger, sent his servant to the streets and lanes of the city to bring in the poor, the crippled, the blind, the lame. And when they had been gathered so that there were none left in the city to fill the guest hall, there was still room. So the servant was sent outside the city to the highways and hedgerows to bring in the wandering and homeless until at last the house was full.

In the parable the city is a reference to the land of Canaan. From this city the servant was instructed to call the poor and the sick. Who were these people now brought into the feast? In the first place, they were the despised in the circles of Jewry. They were the lowly, the publicans, the sinners, the harlots. They were the common people. In the second place, they were those despised by the haughty Pharisees. These were the ones who, according to the Pharisees, knew not the law and were not considered worthy for a place in the kingdom. They were scorned and mocked, or worse, ignored by those who thought they had first claim to the inheritance of the Jews. In the third place, they were the sinners, the lost. They were not considered as sinners and lost from an objective viewpoint, for this was also true of the Pharisees. But in sharp distinction from the leaders of the Jews, they were those who knew themselves to be lost and who confessed themselves to be sinners. They never considered themselves to have a place at the feet of Jesus. They were the ignorant and uneducated fishermen of Galilee. They were the humble Marys and Marthas. They were the adulteresses "caught in the very act." They were the simple who dared not do anything but weep at Jesus' feet and wipe His feet with their hair. They were the publicans and harlots. But they knew their sins and knew they had no right which would give them a claim to a place at the feast of God. And so, finally, they were the humble and contrite of heart who did not boast of their own righteousness, but who longed for the company of Jesus. And they eagerly sought the kingdom of heaven.

These are the ones who are brought in. The Pharisees with beautiful garments and oiled bodies were rejected; the poor in rags were brought in. The legalists were left out; the sinners were brought to the supper. The ones who prayed on street corners and paid their tithes had no place at the banquet; the ones who smote upon their breasts and paid their penny though it was all they had, found a seat of honor.

And yet the house was not full. So the lord of the supper sent his servant into the highways and hedgerows to bring in those who were outside the city. The reference is to the Gentiles. How the Gentiles were hated by the Pharisees! According to them, the Gentiles had no rights in the inheritance of God. They were unclean, so that any contact with them required elaborate ceremonies of cleansing. They were—even if proselytes—not allowed in the hallowed courts of the temple. They were, after all, not of the seed of Abraham. They were the ill-reputed, the cut-off ones from the inheritance of Abraham, the uncircumcised dogs. Surely they had no place in the kingdom if the Pharisees were doing the calling. But they too must be brought in. They claim no rights to the inheritance. Rather they speak of themselves as dogs satisfied with crumbs that fall from the master's table. They are fully aware that they have nothing which would commend to them a place at the banquet. They know they cannot expect a seat at the table of the Lord. And even then, they are not the kings and rulers, the princes and wise of the world; they are the humble and despised, the wandering and strangers, the ignorant and unlettered, the simple and poor. These must be brought in, "that God's house may be full."

How the Guests are Brought

By what means are these humble and lowly brought to the banquet of the kingdom of heaven?

This is first of all accomplished by the rejection of the Jews as a nation.

In reality the leaders of the Jews wanted no part of that kingdom. They envisioned in their minds' eye a kingdom here on earth. They laid claim to a place in that kingdom because they had carried out the demands of the law with exactitude and had earned this right. They saw themselves in a very elevated and exalted position in that kingdom, a place which God had no choice but to give them. Just as their rich neighbors had to invite them to their homes for supper since they had first invited their rich neighbors, so also God owed them a debt which only a very high position of power and honor could cancel.

But the kingdom of Christ—the true kingdom of heaven—they hated. They hated this kingdom because the light of it exposed their evil hearts. It laid bare the bones of dead men beneath the painted and decorated surface of their lives. It showed them as they really were: rebellious and carnal, hypocrites and godless people who kept the letter of the law but flouted the love of God. They were mercilessly shown for what they really were. The way into the kingdom is the way of the blood of the cross. This way demanded that they renounce all their own works as corrupt in the sight of God, that they forget any claim to a place in that kingdom, that they confess that they have nothing to commend them as worthy of a seat at Christ's banquet table. It demanded of them that they put their trust wholly in the cross of Christ—the Nazarene whom they despised. This they would not do. They excused themselves repeatedly.

But their refusal was simply the background for the display of God's justice. The apostle Paul speaks of this at length in Romans 9, 10. In chapter 9 the apostle shows that the rejection of the Jews as a nation is first of all a matter of sovereign right with God, Who elects and reprobates according to His own good pleasure. In chapter 10 the apostle goes on to explain that in the rejection of the Jews there is the sovereign display of justice. God justly banishes them from the kingdom. None of them shall ever taste of His supper. They never could plead ignorance; they simply rejected the command to believe and repent. Hell will echo and reecho with the despairing cry: "We are here justly. We would not enter in."

But in the sovereign purpose of God they were rejected that room might be made for the others. The amazing wonder of it surpasses the boldest imaginations of men. The Pharisees were rejected to make room for harlots. Scribes were cast out to make room for publicans. Leaders were refused admittance so that crippled and lame might be brought in. The nation of Israel was rejected to make room for the Gentiles. No wonder the apostle exclaims at the end of chapter 11 in his epistle to the Romans: "O the depth of the riches both of the wisdom and knowledge of God! how unsearchable are his judgments, and his ways past finding out!" (v. 33).

Yet there is more. The question remains, how are these poor and blind and halt and maimed brought in? Do they after all come by their own choice?

The parable itself and the rest of Scripture make plain that these are brought into the banquet hall of God's everlasting covenant through the efficacious call of the gospel. The Lord sends out His servant to *compel* them to come in. This means several things.

On the one hand, this is not the compulsion of moral persuasion or overwhelming argumentation. The compulsion is not the force of argument, the arresting of emotions. This is often the meaning imposed upon it in our day of hawking the gospel of Christ as the cheapest article on the market. But this does dishonor to the gospel of Christ and is certainly not "compulsion."

Nor is it "compulsion" which has at times been practiced by the Church in ages past, the compulsion of sword and fire when men were driven into the Church by the threat of torture and death.

Yet it remains compulsion in the strictest sense of the word. Notice that the parable definitely states that not the Pharisees were compelled to come in; the poor were. This surely implies sovereign distinction. God determines who would be compelled to come in. That is,

God calls irresistibly and sovereignly those whom He wills. The Pharisees were indeed placed before the command to come, but they were not compelled to come. The call of the gospel is based on the sovereign decree of election which makes distinction among men. It is based on the sovereign distinction of the cross of Christ, for the cross is planted in the midst of the stream of life and the Christ of Calvary did not die for all men. He died for the elect, for the cross is the manifestation of sovereign election. The call is based on the distinction of the cross.

Besides, the call of the gospel is absolutely irresistible. It is the call of God through Christ which comes into the hearts of the called sinners by the operation of the Holy Spirit and cannot be resisted and frustrated. It always accomplishes its purpose, which is the purpose of the sovereign Lord of heaven and earth. This call is compulsion in the absolute sense of the word. Those who are called will surely come, for they are brought by God.

This does not mean that God calls in such a way that those who are brought are dragged unwillingly into the banquet room of God. God calls in such a way that the hard heart of the sinner is softened, that the will which is opposed to God is now turned to Him. God calls by way of conversion and repentance. God calls in a manner that is powerful to make the sinner willing to come. This is the wonder of salvation and the mystery of the gospel. Those in the highways and byways do not desire to come any more than the Pharisees do. But they are brought through the efficacious gospel which turns them willingly to God and to the cross. Are they the poor in spirit? Are they the meek and lowly, the humble and contrite? Are they the ones who know their sins and see their unworthiness? They are, but the power of the gospel shining in their hearts has made them so. God calls in a voice that cannot be resisted. God calls in a mysterious manner that turns the sinner willingly and eagerly to the banquet hall of the kingdom. God calls in such a way that those who come, come through repentance and confession of sin.

God's house is full, but it is filled by God Himself.

Why God Fills His House with the Poor

The question remains, why must the house of God be filled with such as these?

The text apparently gives the answer to this question when it says: "And the lord said unto the servant, Go out into the highways and hedges, and compel them to come in, that my house may be filled. *For* I say unto you, That none of those men which were bidden shall taste of my supper."

In other words, the meaning of the Lord is that the house if filled with guests in order that there may everlastingly be no room for the self-righteous and proud. When in the judgment day the wicked are faced with the awful consequences of their deeds, they cannot enter in, not only because of their sin but because there is no room. While they were busily engaged in making excuses, the house was filled. And finally they stand before a full house, so that when they begin to plead to enter, they are shown that the guests are all seated in heavenly splendor and there is no room for them. How awful that will be!

Yet, positively speaking, the reason is that all the elect must be saved from both Jews and Gentiles. The whole Church must be brought to glory. A Catholic Church must be saved. Only when the Church is gathered from every nation and tribe and tongue is the full purpose of God accomplished. Then only will the full glory of the grace of God be revealed in all its splendor.

This leads us to the second question, why must the house be filled with the poor and despised?

It is striking that this has always been the way God worked in history. Not the mighty, the rich, the wise, the rulers and leaders of men are called. Always the poor and the despised—the "no-accounts" according to earthly standards—are included in the kingdom. Such it has been from the beginning of time. Such it shall remain until the Lord returns. The apostle Paul expresses it this way in I Corinthians 1:26-28: "For ye see your calling, brethren, how that not many wise men after the flesh, not many mighty, not many noble, are called: But God hath chosen the foolish things of the world to confound the wise; and God hath chosen the weak things of the world to confound the wise; and God hath chosen the weak things of the world to confound the things which are mighty; And base things of the world, and things which are despised, hath God chosen, yea, and things which are not, to bring to nought things that are."

Why is this? Why are not the proud and haughty brought in? Why are the humble and meek gathered about the banquet table of everlasting glory? The answer is given in many places in Scripture. Paul writes, for example, in Ephesians 2:8, 9: "For by grace are ye saved through faith; and that not of yourselves: it is the gift of God: Not of works, lest any man should boast." Or, quoting again from I Corinthians 1, not the mighty and the wise are called, "that no flesh should glory in his presence. But of him are ye in Christ Jesus, who of God is made unto us wisdom, and righteousness, and sanctification, and redemption: That, according as it is written, he that glorieth, let him glory in the Lord" (vv. 29-31).

God calls the weak and despised so that it may be evident that He alone is the God of salvation. He gives grace that is entirely unmerited. He gives to the undeserving. He does not do as the Pharisee who invites in order to receive an invitation in return. He calls the poor and the blind and the halt in order that it may be evident that it is of grace. For He gives a grace that cannot be recompensed and rewarded again. He gives grace to those who deserve it not. And it is in this magnificent and sublime way that all glory is God's forever and ever. He alone is worthy of all praise. He alone will gain this glory for Himself. He alone shall receive it also from that redeemed Church that knows its own unworthiness. He will receive it throughout all eternity.

Let him that glorieth, glory in the Lord!

14
The Seeking Shepherd

And he spake this parable unto them, saying,
What man of you, having an hundred sheep, if he lose one of them,
doth not leave the ninety and nine in the wilderness, and go after that
which is lost, until he find it?
And when he hath found it, he layeth it on his shoulders, rejoicing.
And when he cometh home, he calleth together his friends and
neighbours, saying unto them, Rejoice with me; for I have found my
sheep which was lost.
I say unto you, that likewise joy shall be in heaven over one sinner
that repenteth, more than over ninety and nine just persons, which
need no repentance.

—Luke 15:3-7

The well-known and well-loved trilogy of parables found in Luke 15 has many points in common. They all have as their main theme the recovery of the lost sinner. They emphasize, therefore, similar points. The lost sheep, the lost coin, and the lost son all emphatically point to the truth that the sinner is by nature lost. They all speak of the fact that the Lord Himself brings back such a lost sinner to the safety of the kingdom of heaven. The shepherd goes to find his sheep; the woman sweeps her house until the coin is found; the love of the father follows his son even though he strays far from home. Furthermore, all emphasize that the Lord brings back His lost people through the way of repentance. Although this is mentioned explicitly only in the parable of the lost son, the Lord Himself makes the application in both the parable of the lost sheep and the parable of the lost coin: "There is joy in the presence of the angels of God over one sinner that repenteth." And finally, the joy of the Lord and of His angels is emphasized by the joy of the shepherd in finding his sheep, the joy of the woman in finding the missing coin, and the joy of the father in the return of the son.

Nevertheless, there are also differences of emphasis in the three parables. They each emphasize a particular aspect of the repentance of the lost sinner. The parable of the lost sheep emphasizes the truth of the seeking Shepherd. The parable of the lost coin emphasizes the conscious conversion and repentance of the sinner as he returns to the kingdom and Church once again. The parable of the lost son speaks particularly of the willingness of the heavenly Father to receive His wayward children.

The occasion for these parables is found in the first two verses of the chapter. During Jesus' ministry, particularly the publicans and sinners were attracted to His gospel and eagerly came to hear Him. This was exactly the excuse the Scribes and Pharisees were looking for. The publicans were tax collectors in the hire of Rome. They were often greedy, covetous, extortioners, and guilty of graft. They were despised by the Jews, who considered them traitors to the cause of Israel and the most despicable of sinners. The sinners referred to were the common people of the land who were looked down upon by the leaders of the people because they knew not the law, took no pains to keep it in its details, were the scum of the marketplaces, the adulterers and harlots, the petty thieves and beggars who infested the land. To the self-righteous Pharisees these people had no claim to the promises made to Abraham and no hope of participating in the renewal of the kingdom of Judah. The Scribes and Pharisees alone were worthy to enter the kingdom—or so they thought.

The fact that these people were attracted to Jesus and that He received them and even ate with them was intolerable to the haughty leaders of Israel. To them this was proof enough that Jesus could not possibly be what He claimed to be. He could not be the Messiah because by associating with sinners and eating with them He polluted Himself.

The grumbling of the Pharisees and Scribes became the occasion for these beautiful parables which explain the true nature of Jesus' calling. He points out in the parables that His eating and drinking with publicans and sinners was not the proof of the falsity of His claim to be the Messiah, but was rather precisely the proof that He was the Messiah. He was the Son of man, Who had come to seek and to save those that were lost. And in connection with this, the Lord makes clear that the only way into the kingdom is the way of a broken spirit and a contrite heart. This first parable emphasizes the work of Christ as the seeking Shepherd.

The Sheep Who Is Lost

The parable is simplicity itself. A certain man had one hundred sheep. He cared for them in the grazing pastures of his farm and brought them safely to the fold in the evening. But one evening, as he was leading his sheep into the fold and counting them as they filed past, he noticed that one sheep was missing. This sheep had evidently wandered away in the course of the day and had become separated from the flock.

Three facts immediately enter our minds. In the first place, the sheep had very foolishly wandered away from the safety of the flock and gone its own way. It had refused to follow the voice of the shepherd, and thought instead to make its own way through the pastures in search of food. In the second place, it had become lost in the distance and was unable to find its way back again to the flock or the shepherd. And, although it may have thought it could make its own way apart from the flock, it soon found that it was surrounded by all kinds of dangers. There was not enough grass and water for the sheep to eat. The shepherd had always led it into the greenest pastures, but now it was in danger of starving. Besides, the night had come and there was not the protection of the shepherd or the sheepfold to keep it safe from the wolves that prowled the country-side in search of food. Its life was in danger. Or, should it escape the angry wolves, the dangers of the way were so great that it hardly dared to move. There were pits and ravines, steep slopes and dark canyons, brambles and angry thistles, all of which threatened its life and well-being if it dared to strike out on its own in the dark. It had foolishly walked into the gravest dangers without any hope of escaping. The only prospect for it was death before too many nights had passed. In the third place, therefore, it had put itself in danger from which it could find no way of escape. Left to itself it would surely die.

The sheepfold is a reference to the nation of Israel. The one hundred sheep are the people of that nation. This must be emphasized for a moment, because there are many commentators who dispute this point. They insist that the sheep are all people of God, but that the picture is of one member of the Church who strays away temporarily while the rest are faithful. The commentators who defend this position point to the fact that it often happens in a congregation that one of the members falls into sin while the majority remain faithful.

But this is not the point of the Lord, and if pressed to its conclusion can only lead to the same self-righteousness of the Pharisees which Jesus is condemning. That this is not the point is obvious especially from the statement of Jesus: "I say unto you, that likewise joy shall be in heaven over one sinner that repenteth, more than over ninety and nine just persons, which *need* no repentance." The fact of the matter is that all God's people need repentance. It was precisely the haughty and vain Pharisees who needed no repentance, for they were secure in their own good works. And if it be argued that the Pharisees really needed repentance too although they refused to admit it, we answer that this is precisely the point. Subjectively, before their own consciousness, they had no need of repentance. But in the consciousness of the elect sinner there is precisely this need of repentance, for repentance is a work of God which He performs in the heart and mind of the sinner.

Rather, the ninety-nine are called sheep because outwardly they belonged to the nation of Israel. They were, externally, members of the fold that God chose many years ago in Abraham. They were given that cherished and privileged place above all the other nations of the earth. But in their sin they forsook their shepherds whom God had sent; and now they forsook the only Shepherd, Jesus Christ. They are, therefore, comparable to the Pharisees and scribes who murmured that Jesus received sinners and ate with them. And they are, in the parable, analogous to the elder son who is spoken of in verses 25 and following of this same chapter.

But the lost sheep, though he be but one, is a picture of the elect child of God who is by nature lost in sin and death. The parable means to stress that not only are the people of God by nature lost in the wilderness of sin and death, but even during the entire course of their life, after they are saved, they constantly stray away again and again. This is emphasized in more than one place in Holy Scripture. In Psalm 119:176, the Psalmist confesses and prays: "I have gone astray like a lost sheep; seek thy servant; for I do not forget thy commandments." The prophet Isaiah puts in the mouth of the people of God a similar confession when he writes: "All we like sheep have gone astray; we have turned every one to his own way; and the Lord hath laid on him the iniquity of us all" (53:6). Or again, the apostle Peter mentions this same truth in his first epistle when in chapter 2:25 he says: "For ye were as sheep going astray; but are now returned unto the Shepherd and Bishop of your souls."

The people of God are often called sheep in Scripture. There are probably especially two reasons for this. The word "sheep" seems in Scripture to indicate the sovereign decree of God's election. God's people are sheep because God has from eternity chosen them. They do not have this right to be called sheep because they can claim some special favors or because they have more right than others to this name, for they are not of themselves better than anyone else. God numbered them in His counsel and set His sovereign and eternal seal on them. Besides this, they are the sheep who are purchased as God's peculiar possession by the precious price of the blood of the cross of Calvary. Christ laid down His life for His sheep and bought them with His own blood.

In the second place, Scripture calls God's people sheep because this is an adequate analogy to describe their spiritual condition. Sheep are the most foolish and helpless of all animals. They need constant care and attention. Their inclination is always to wander away from the flock. They cannot find pasture and water for themselves as other animals can. They cannot bear their young without assistance, nor care for them without the help of the shepherd. They will not seek shelter in a storm if they are within twenty feet of shelter. They are in constant danger of killing themselves by all manner of foolish actions.

This is an accurate picture of the child of God as he is by nature. We are all sheep who are lost—lost in the wilderness of sin and hopelessly entangled in the darkness of the night of death. We have forsaken God and His covenant and walked in our own way. And we put ourselves in perpetual spiritual danger. But the emphasis of the parable falls on the fact that the people of God go astray as sheep all their life. As long as we live in this world we continually manifest ourselves as lost sheep. God brings us to His own fold, but we always leave again. This is not simply true of an occasional and individual sinner; this is true of us all. We must not only see this but also confess it in humility before God. If we do not see ourselves reflected in the lost sheep of the parable, we will identify ourselves with the ninety-nine sheep who did not go astray. The result of this will be that we identify ourselves with the Pharisees and scribes who murmured and said of Christ: "This man receiveth sinners and eateth with them."

Foolishly and by our sins we stray from God and refuse to follow the Word of Christ. We go far from the fold and become lost in the wilderness of sin. We think we can find our own way, our own food for our souls, our own shelter in the time of storm. But instead we become lost. We cannot find our way back again, for we are hopelessly entangled in sin and in the darkness of our own foolishness. We place ourselves in all kinds of dangers. We starve spiritually because we forsake or despise the green pastures of the Word of God. We are in danger of being devoured by Satan and his host for we are about to be overcome by the power of sin, and the devil is a roaring lion who goes about seeking whom he may devour. We are helpless, for far from God we are without defense of our own. All about us are the pitfalls and traps of worldliness and carnality into which we easily fall. The Shepherd is not there to guide our feet. We are without the light of His Word to shine on our pathway. We wander about in constant danger of perishing.

This happens again and again. We often forsake God and His truth. This does not simply happen because we flee from the Church outwardly. It happens when our hearts are far from God and from His Word; when week after week we wander aimlessly in the devious pathways of sin. We succumb to the temptations of worldliness and carnal mindedness. Our prayers are empty mouthings. Our works are vain deeds. Our words are idle words. Our lives are filled with sin.

Lost in the darkness of sin and misery, we have only trouble and fear. We huddle alone and afraid in the dark night that settles about us. We are overcome with grief and remorse, with fear and terror. We know not the way back to safety. Or more often, wandering far from the flock and the fold, we are oblivious to the dangers about us; and we refuse to face our precarious position. We blithely go our own way, wandering farther and farther from safety, deliberately

setting our hearts upon sin and priding ourselves in our own sufficiency.

But we are lost. And the danger is great.

The Shepherd Who Seeks Us

That it is the shepherd alone who goes to find his sheep and brings
it back is emphasized very strongly in the parable.

The shepherd forsook the ninety-nine sheep to search for the lost
one. This does not mean that the ninety-nine were safe without him.
The idea is rather that they had no need of him. These are the
self-righteous, who in their own perverted minds had no need of
anyone to feed or lead them. Jesus came to seek and to save those
who are lost. He came not to call the righteous, but sinners to
repentance. This was repeatedly emphasized throughout the ministry of Jesus. On the one hand, it was true that He came unto His own
and His own received Him not. This was their condemnation. But
on the other hand, it was not the purpose of Christ's coming to save
these self-righteous Pharisees. He came to do His Father's will; and it
was His Father's will to hide the things of the kingdom from the wise
and prudent and to reveal them unto babes.

The shepherd is pictured as being filled with anxiety and concern
for the one that is lost. He is filled with love and tender regard for
this sheep which has strayed. He endures the weariness of a sleepless
night, the dangers of rough and rugged country, the pain and
suffering of desperate search, the pangs of hunger and thirst, in
order that this one lost sheep may be restored to the fold.

What a powerful picture this is of the work of Christ for His
people! The Lord went all the way, so to speak, in order to restore
those who are lost. No effort was too great, no danger too frightening, no road too long for Him to save those whom He loved.

He came into the likeness of our sinful flesh from the glory of
heaven. He endured the humility and shame of our life, He Who
knew the blessedness of heaven's glory. He took all our griefs and
sorrows upon Himself. He was steadfast in temptation when He
made all our temptations His own. He bore all our sicknesses and
diseases. He braved the dangers of hateful enemies, their attempts
to kill Him, their scorn and taunts and mockery.

And yet even all this was not enough to save us. He entered into
the night of our sin and guilt. For all our sins were heaped upon
Him. Weary and thirsty, He groaned under the heavy burden of the
wrath of God. He went the long, dark, weary, shameful road to the
cross. He endured every torment. He went far away from God and
willingly bore the burden of God's anger against sin. He entered into
the portals of hell itself because this was required to find and bring
back those who are lost. And at last He paid the ultimate price: He
laid down His life for His sheep. He paid the price of His blood,

willingly and obediently, with tears and groanings. He bore it all until it was utterly gone.

But there is still more. For truly, all of this He did for us. And very really He follows us wherever we wander. He seeks us in the darkness of our night by His Holy Spirit Whom He sends into our hearts. The parable does not mean that our Lord does not know where we are. Rather it pictures to us the infinite patience and love, the earnest mercy by which He always follows us into the weary wastelands of sin to bring us back on the long road home. No matter how far we stray, He follows us with His Spirit and Word.

But the parable is a most remarkable picture of this gracious power of Christ by which we are brought back. He does not come into our hearts suddenly to restore us in a moment to our place in His flock. He gradually leads us back, for the way is sometimes long and hard, and we are desperately tired of sin. Sometimes He finds us longing to return, but even this longing He has already put within our hearts. Sometimes He finds us blissfully enjoying the pleasures of sin, oblivious to the dangers that threaten on every hand. Then He causes us to see the horror of our danger, the foolishness of our wandering, and He works within us the longing to go back with Him. But this way back along which He leads us is the way of gradual turning, of bitter struggle, of earnest prayer to God. The farther we go, the longer the journey back home. The greater the distance, the more rugged the pathway that leads back to the flock.

You may ask, why does the Lord lead us back only in the way of deep and difficult struggle? The answer is not difficult to find. In the first place, He shows us the horror and hopelessness of our sin and guilt. In the second place, He shows us that without Him we can do nothing. We are unable to return of ourselves; we are even unable to 'want to return. Foolishly we take the swift road to destruction—without Him. He alone can bring us back. In the third place, He works within us to show us how good it is in the house of our God and how pleasant it is to be freed from sin's power and the dominion of unrighteousness.

But He does all this in wonderful mercy. He does not come to us with brutal language to whip us as we deserve and drive us with the stick of His fury back to the flock. He does not leave us in our sin into which we wander so often. You must remember that we wander away every day. And it would seem that our Lord would weary of bringing us back. Justly He could say to us that now we have wandered away once too often; accordingly, He will not bring us back again. But this He never does. Always He follows us. Always He restores. And because we are tired of sin, and weary of wandering, and have not the strength or the ability to find our way back by ourselves or walk the long road, He takes us on His own almighty shoulders and restores us gently. He carries us easily over the rough places and leads us around further temptations, holding us tightly by His Spirit within us lest we fall again. At last He brings us into His own home to rest and be refreshed.

Such is the marvelous power and grace of the Lord.

It is no wonder that when the weary night is over and we rest forever in the house of our chief Shepherd, there arises within our hearts a mighty anthem of praise and glory to Him Who has so abundantly loved us. It is because His tender mercies fail not but are new each morning that we are not consumed. It is to the everlasting glory of God that we are brought home to rest in God's arms in perfect peace.

The Joy of the Angels

When all of this happens there is joy in heaven. This joy of which the parable speaks stands in sharp contrast to the murmuring and grumbling of the scribes and Pharisees.

First of all, the shepherd is pictured as rejoicing. We read: "And when he hath found it, he layeth it on his shoulders, rejoicing. And when he cometh home, he calleth together his friends and neighbours, saying unto them, Rejoice with me: for I have found my sheep which was lost."

We may well ask the question, why does Christ rejoice when His lost sheep are restored? Was there ever any doubt about it? Was it as if He rejoices as a mother who receives her child back again from the grave after a very serious illness, while she forgets about her five other children who were all well? There is an element of truth to this. When a father or mother has six children, one of whom is gravely ill, the recovery of the sick child will, for the moment, give the parents more joy than the other five whose lives were never endangered.

But the reason for the joy of Christ is far deeper. In the first place, Christ died for His sheep and shed His blood for them on the tree of the cross. Their return is but the fruit of His grievous suffering and death. In this Christ rejoices. In the second place, Christ loves His sheep as the true Shepherd. In spite of all their sin and foolish wandering, He loves them always. He rejoices in love, restoring them to Himself. In the third place, in bringing them back Christ is doing the will of His heavenly Father. It is the will of God that not one should perish. And in doing the will of His heavenly Father, Christ finds His joy because the will of His Father is His own perfect will. And finally, in the seeking and finding and restoring of those who are lost, Christ is gathering His own Church, His body, His beloved. His glory is only complete in the full salvation of all those who belong to Him.

But Christ also calls the angels to rejoice with Him. They are pictured in the parable as the friends and neighbors. Evidently, therefore, this must be taken literally.

When one sinner is restored, the angels in heaven sing for joy.

How sharply this stands in contrast with the grumbling of the self-righteous Pharisees! And yet, if we think about it, this is really no wonder. The angels are the ministers of God who serve the well-being of the saints and are appointed to minister to the heirs of the promise. Always they took a lively interest in all that happened with respect to the promise of God. They appear to the saints in the Old Dispensation. They sang to the shepherds on Bethlehem's hills. They preached with joy the gospel of the resurrection. They aided the saints in trouble, comforted them in sorrow, and helped them to escape from danger. Their joy is always the final salvation of the Church. Then, when one sinner turns to God in repentance and is rescued from the power of sin and guilt, is there any wonder that the angels lift their hosannas to the highest heavens?

All this joy is based on repentance. The joy is not for the ninety-nine. The text reads literally: "I say unto you, that likewise joy shall be in heaven over one sinner that repenteth, *rather* than [this is the proper translation here] over ninety and nine just persons that need no repentance."

The Pharisees were righteous in their own eyes. They had no need of Christ or of repentance, for they had no sin. There was no need to rejoice over their rescue, for they needed no rescue. But over a lost one there is rejoicing. Such a one may be a lowly and despised sinner. He may be a publican of the baser sort. He may even be scorned and derided—or worse, ignored by self-righteous people. He may be you or I. But Christ found him and brought him home. See, he is on his knees weeping. But the angels are singing beyond the skies.

15

The Returning Sinner

*Either what woman having ten pieces of silver, if she lose one piece,
doth not light a candle, and sweep the house, and seek diligently till
she find it?*
*And when she hath found it, she calleth her friends and her neigh-
bours together, saying, Rejoice with me; for I have found the piece
which I had lost.*
*Likewise, I say unto you, there is joy in the presence of the angels of
God over one sinner that repenteth.*

—Luke 15:8-10

As we noticed in our previous chapter, the occasion for this trilogy
of parables is described in verses 1 and 2 of Luke 15. The Pharisees
were thoroughly disgusted with Jesus because He had received
publicans and sinners and had even eaten with them. From this they
concluded that Jesus could not possibly be the Messiah because, as
the Messiah, He would surely not have fellowship with sinners. Were
not they, the Pharisees, the leaders of the people? Did they not keep
the law and observe the testimonies of God? Were not they the true
Israel? The publicans and sinners were the despised populace who
knew not the law. This very murmuring of the Pharisees was indicative of the fact that they had no need of Christ because they had no
need of the cross. And they had no need of the cross because, before
their own consciousness, they had no sins which needed forgiveness.

In this trilogy of parables Jesus shows that He had come for an
entirely different purpose than they had imagined. He had not
come to pat them on the back and congratulate them on their fine
faithfulness. He had not come to call the righteous, but sinners to
repentance. He had come to seek and to save those who were lost. In
this way He showed that He was indeed the promised Messiah.

We also noticed that although these three parables have many
similarities, they nevertheless emphasize different points. While the

parable of the lost sheep depicts the shepherd as Christ, the Good Shepherd, Who searches for His sheep and restores them again to salvation, the parable of the lost coin depicts the woman as the Church and emphasizes the truth of the return of the sinner. This is evident from the fact that the candle and the broom which the woman uses are specifically brought to our attention in the parable. The parable means therefore to teach us how the returning sinner is restored to the fellowship of Christ and of God.

The Elements of the Parable

In our interpretation of this parable it seems to be of special importance that we pay close attention to its various elements. The various details of the parable must have special significance because, if they do not, the parable has little to say to us. We must not, however, merely speculate concerning what each element of the parable is meant to depict; but we must, also in our interpretation of this parable, permit Scripture to be our guide.

The coin which is lost is called a drachma. This was a coin used in Palestine and approximately equal in value to the Roman denarius. Its worth has been computed at about seventeen cents. While this does not seem to us to be a lot of money, it was in those days the wages of an entire day of labor. There are some who in speculating about the particular reason why the Lord uses a coin in this parable, reason that, because the coin was stamped with the image of a man, the significance is that we have here the picture of a human soul which has been stamped with the image of God. The trouble with this interpretation is that sinful man no longer bears the image of God. As Scripture teaches, that image was lost through sin. Man became an image bearer of Satan rather than of God. The image of God is restored in man only through the operation of the Holy Spirit. The point is rather that the coin represented one-tenth of the savings of the woman and was therefore of great value and importance to her. So it is with the elect sinner who is lost. He may not seem important to men, but he is important to God, to Christ and to the angels, and ought to be important to the Church.

The woman evidently depicts the Church. This figure is commonly employed in Scripture, not only in those passages which speak of the Church as the bride of Christ, but also in Revelation 12 where the Church is consistently called a woman. In connection with the parable, however, the reference is not to the Church as the organism of the body of Christ, but rather to the Church as an institute—as the officially and properly constituted organization which preaches the Word of the gospel in the Name of Christ.

There is some difficulty in connection with the interpretation of the candle and the sweeping. If the Lord intended that we find some significance in these elements of the parable, the candle is probably to be interpreted as the light of the preaching of the gospel. The woman lit the candle and used it in her search of the house. So the Church takes the gospel of Jesus Christ into the world of darkness and sin. This idea is not foreign to Scripture, for David speaks of this very truth when, in Psalm 119:105, he writes: "Thy word is a lamp unto my feet, and a light unto my path." If it is true that the candle is the light of the preaching of the gospel, then it follows that the sweeping with the broom depicts the effect of the preaching in the consciousness of the sinner. Just as the sweeping of the broom by the woman stirs up the dust in the various corners and crannies of the house, so does the preaching of the gospel stir up the dust of sin within the consciousness of the sinner so that he comes to know his own sin and repent of it.

Hence, Christ, Who in the former parable was pictured in His agonizing search for those whom He loves, is here pictured in His search for the lost sinner through the agency of the Church which preaches the gospel. Furthermore, it is through this preaching of the gospel by the Church that Christ brings the sinner to the consciousness of his sin and to conscious repentance so that he is restored. Therefore the point is made that the way of return is always the way of repentance. There is no other way than this. Although this is not specifically mentioned in the first parable, in this parable it comes sharply into focus. This was especially the point which Jesus meant to raise in connection with the grumbling of the proud Pharisees. They had no need of repentance because they had no sin from which to repent. When the gospel of repentance came to them, they looked amazed and asked: "What possibly can this mean? We have committed no sin." To them, in their self-righteous conceit, the word of repentance meant nothing.

Let us turn, then, to the matter of the repentant sinner.

What is repentance according to Scripture?

There are various elements in repentance, all of which are worthy of our attention. In the first place, repentance implies the knowledge of sin. This knowledge of sin is not, however, the mere intellectual knowledge of what sin is. To a greater or a lesser degree all men have an acquaintance with sin. Many could probably write a fine book on the nature and seriousness of sin and provide elucidating and original insights into the subject. Many could speak of the universality of sin and its effects in the broken down mechanism of human life. But none of this, in itself, has anything to do with repentance. Knowledge of sin which is the origin and fountain of repentance is a knowledge of the heart as well as a knowledge of the head. It is above all an overwhelming consciousness of the fact that sin is transgression of God's law and God's will, that it hurts and angers Him, that it is committed against the Most High Majesty of God, and that it must be punished in God's justice with temporal and eternal death.

In the second place, repentance is grief for sin. This stands con-

nected, of course, with the knowledge of sin. Only he who knows
that he has sinned against the living God is also sorrowful for sin. He
is not primarily sorry because sin makes a wreck of his body and soul
and brings devastation and ruin into his life. He is not grieved
because he must suffer the consequences for sin. Rather, he is
grieved because he has provoked God with his awful transgression.
He is overwhelmed with bitter tears and anxious cries because his sin
has been committed against the Lord of heaven and earth. His soul is
wrenched within him, and he lies prostrate in the dust, abhorring
himself and fearing the wrath of God which must surely come upon
him.

In the third place, repentance is longing that sin may be taken
away. The sinner longs for forgiveness. He cries out that his sins may
be removed and that his fear of God's wrath may be taken away. But
more that this, he prays also that his sins may be so completely taken
away that he sins no longer. Although he knows that this will not
happen on this side of the grave, he nevertheless knows that only by
God's grace can sin no longer have dominion over him. And it is
precisely the burden of his sin which makes him long for glory. This
is, as a matter of fact, the most basic reason why he hopes earnestly
for his eternal reward in glory. Not shady meadows and gently
flowing streams under blue skies beckon him to the world beyond
the grave, but the perfect holiness of freedom from sin inspires him
to seek the glory of a home beyond the skies.

Even though all this must of necessity be a rather formal discussion of repentance, we must not permit this to detract from its
importance.

Indeed, it may be said that the sorrow of a sinner in repentance is
the greatest of all good works. It is true that this emphasis is often
lacking in today's preaching. Much more, especially in Arminian
circles, all the emphasis is placed on such things as accepting Christ
as one's personal Savior, surrendering oneself to Christ, permitting
Christ entrance into one's heart, making room for Christ in one's
life. It is striking and of no little significance that seldom in this type
of preaching is sorrow for sin emphasized in the way in which
Scripture emphasizes it. Moreover, it is often also heard in today's
preaching that the life of the believer in good works consists particularly in performing deeds of earth-shaking importance and of
worldwide significance. A Christian's life is measured by how many
souls he has won for Christ, by what he has done in combating the
enemies of poverty, disease, racial discrimination, and warfare, and
what he has accomplished in the area of making this world a better
place to live. This emphasis flows forth from what is commonly
known as a social gospel.

But the Scriptures teach something quite different. The child of
God is rarely busy with such mighty events. They do not hold central
place in his consciousness. He is more deeply conscious of his calling

from God to walk in all God's precepts in the very common and mundane duties of life in which the Lord has placed him. But he is conscious, too, of his great imperfection and of the many sins of which he is guilty. He knows how his daily work is imperfectly done and how his daily calling is imperfectly fulfilled. He is conscious of how often he fails in the little and seemingly insignificant things of life, and of how far he falls short in the small demands God places on him. And so the awareness of sin is of considerable importance in his life.

Indeed, the older one becomes, the more this consciousness of sin grows. In his youth, imperfectly acquainted with sin, he may have great ambitions and high ideals. But with age come soberness and realism. The child of God is aware that sin cleaves to all that he does, that he has only a small beginning of the new obedience, and that even his best works are still corrupted and polluted with sin. Thus repentance becomes more and more important. It is, in the final analysis *the* good work of the Christian. Of what value are earth-shaking events without repentance? What good can come from mighty deeds without sorrow for sin? In the humble and sorrowful cry of the sinner there is greater value than in all else. This confession of sin must be the daily prayer of the believer, indeed, his perpetual consciousness before the face of God. All else fades into unimportance in relation to it. Repentance and repentance alone is the way back from the paths of sin.

Why is repentance of such great importance? In the first place, it is the only way to Christ. All other ways ignore Christ and deny Him because in these ways there is no need of Him. But repentance, arising as it does from the consciousness of sin, confesses that the sinner is hopelessly lost in himself and unable to save himself in any respect. The repenting sinner goes to Christ. And going to Christ, the sinner goes to the cross on which Christ died. For on the cross Christ died for sin. This is the only way to heaven. The road to glory goes over Calvary. The way of the cross leads home. There is no other way than this.

In the second place, repentance is the way to the conscious experience of salvation. It is not God's purpose to save His people in such a way that they are unaware of their own salvation. God saves them so that they know their salvation. But the way to the consciousness of salvation is always the way of confession of sin. The wonder of grace is experienced only in comparison with the horror of sin. The glorious light of salvation is ours only against the background of the blackness of sin and transgression. And in this way the way of repentance is the victory over sin. On this earth this victory does not come through freedom from sin. It does not come in the attainment of perfection. Every day we sin anew. The sins that are forgiven one day we commit again the next day. But the victory over sin is attained through repentance and confession. In this way sin no more has dominion over us. For this is the way that leads to peace with God and rest for our weary souls. When we sin we seek forgiveness in Christ, and repenting we find peace for our hearts in the blood of the cross.

By What Power the Sinner Repents

The question of how the sinner repents is an important one. It arises naturally from the heart of the believer. If he knows that he is lost in sin and unable to save himself, he will wonder how he can even come to sorrow for sin and confession.

The answer to this question was given basically in the parable of the lost sheep. There the Lord taught us that it is the Good Shepherd Who brings us back. And no child of God who knows the depths of his own sin could ever confess anything different. A repentant sinner who knows the depths of his helplessness will also know that he cannot, of his own will, restore his soul. No sinner on his knees is an Arminian. Christ restores the sinner. He went all the way into the suffering and death of the cross to bring us back to Him. He denied Himself, endured every suffering and pain, every heartache and weariness in order that we might be restored. He seeks us by His Word and Spirit. Now He is in heaven and we are yet upon the earth, left behind for a little while. But He restores us nevertheless when we go astray through the power of His Word and by the operation of His Spirit within our hearts.

The parable of the lost coin adds to this teaching of the parable of the lost sheep by explaining that Christ does this through His Church. He brings the sinner to conscious repentance by coming after us with His Word, the Word of His gospel. But this Word is preached through the Church and the Spirit is sent out in connection with the Word to restore the lost sinner.

The Church preaches the gospel of Christ. It preaches the gospel of Christ to the congregation on the Sabbath day; it brings this gospel to the suffering and sick and dying; it comes with this gospel when those who stray are visited; it attends to the diligent instruction of this gospel when the seed of God's covenant are instructed; it comes into the homes of believers to apply this gospel to their own particular and individual needs.

But always the gospel is emphatically the gospel of Christ. This means that the Church never must and never can come with the word of men. It does not come with a story about the natural goodness of man, about how praiseworthy man actually is; it does not come with a general offer of grace which is made to all, or with an invitation which God in His love for all men extends to all. This is not the Word of Christ at all. The Church comes with the age-old and timeless story of the hopelessness of man, of the sovereign love of God in Christ for the elect, of the power of the gospel which is the power of God unto salvation. This is the Word of Christ. This alone the Church preaches. That this gospel is the Word of Christ means that Christ Himself preaches it. The Church carries it to the lost, but Christ preaches. When that gospel is proclaimed, those who listen do indeed hear the Word of Christ as He calls His sheep by name. Christ's voice comes to them, and this voice of Christ they hear. But they hear it because they hear it with their hearts as that Word is applied through the operation of the Holy Spirit which Christ sends forth within them. This is how the sinner is found and brought back in the way of repentance.

Hence the Church is vitally interested in the repentance of the sinner. The point must be clearly understood. Once again, the parable does not refer to but one member of the Church who goes astray while the others remain faithful. Rather, each of us constantly goes astray. We are lost every time we fall into sin and succumb to the enticement of temptation. And each time we are lost exactly because we cannot find the way back by ourselves. This is true not only of the people of the Church to the exclusion of the office bearers who actually preach the gospel. This is true of office bearers too, for they also are sinful men. And the further a sinner strays, the more humanly impossible his return is. Yet this same Church is also engaged diligently in the search for the lost sinner. The Church is vitally concerned with repentance. The Church longs that each member may be brought into the fellowship of the Church and continue in that fellowship through the way of repentance from sin. For this the Church prays and labors night and day. This is the object of the anxious longing of the Church of Christ.

This is done through the Word of God which is a shining light. The light of the Word penetrates the darkest recesses of sin and guilt. When the soul of the sinner is shut in impenetrable darkness through sin and guilt, the light of the Word breaks through. This light of the Word banishes the darkness of the night and causes the light of revelation to penetrate the darkest recesses of the heart and mind.

But it does more. As the broom in the hands of the woman stirs up the dust in the house, so does the preaching stir up the consciousness of sin; and it raises a cloud of the dust of sin in the heart of the sinner that his soul lies naked and open before his eyes. It does all this because it is Christ's Word that calls men sinners and describes the horror of their sin. It is Christ's Word through the Spirit which brings tears of grief and sorrow to the eyes of the sinner and confession of sin to his lips.

But it is also this same Word of Christ that speaks of the wonder of the cross. Through the blackness of the hopelessness of sin shines the wonder of Calvary, brought to the heart on the powerful Words of the gospel. The light of Calvary shines in the blackness of our night. In the cross the sinner sees the love of God, the power of grace, the wonder of salvation. Before his eyes unfolds the mystery of godliness: Christ manifest in the flesh, justified in the Spirit, seen of angels, preached unto the Gentiles, believed on in the world, received up into glory. And when the sinner sees that cross in the Word of Christ, he hides himself beneath the shadow of that cross; for his life depends on it. He falls down in wonder and adoration; he clings to that cross and trusts in it alone. And there at the foot of that cross he finds the peace that passes all understanding.

The Joy of the Church when the Sinner Returns

It is not surprising therefore that the Church rejoices when the sinner is found and is brought back into its fellowship. The Church which carries the burden of the gospel rejoices when that gospel bears its fruit in the conversion and repentance of saints. And surely, the farther one strays from the Church, the greater is the rejoicing when such a one returns.

The way to glory is the way of repentance. But we must remember that all the saints go to heaven together. If one elect child of God is lost, no saint can go to glory. Either all go or none go. The Church is not a mere group of individuals. It is the organic body of Christ. In that Church each saint has his place. The glory of each saint is dependent on the glory of all the others. The body of Christ is completed only when each member is present. And so when one sinner is brought to repentance, the Church sees the coming salvation of all the saints. This is also our own subjective joy. All of us go our sinful ways innumerable times. But when Christ restores through repentance, we see the redeemed Church being gathered, a Church which includes ourselves.

But this same Church also rejoices, for they see in the repentance of the sinner the victory of the gospel. They see the power of the Word of Christ. They see a victory that will continue to the end of the ages when at last all the saints are gathered. They see the final victory of heaven when this victory will be sung to the everlasting praise of God Who sovereignly gathers His Church.

No wonder then that they call upon the angels to sing with them. The angels know of sin. Their ranks, too, were decimated by the apostasy of Satan and his demons. They know that Satan opposes God and does this by trying to conquer the saints. They know that it seemed as if Satan had succeeded when he brought the whole world under sin and bound all men to himself.

But they know, too, of the cross and the resurrection. They sang when Christ was born on the hillsides of Bethlehem and they spoke of the gospel at the door of the empty grave. Now they see the victory of that cross and resurrection when the sinner with tears in his eyes flees to Christ. They see the devil put to flight by the repentance of a saint, and they sing their hosannas before the throne. It has been well said: "The tears of the saints are the wine of the angels." Yet their rejoicing is in the power of the cross. They rejoice with doxologies to God and to Christ, for to God belongs all praise. He alone has accomplished all His purpose.

16

God's Readiness to Receive His Wayward Children

And he said, A certain man had two sons:

And the younger of them said to his father, Father, give me the portion of goods that falleth to me. And he divided unto them his living.

And not many days after the younger son gathered all together, and took his journey into a far country, and there wasted his substance with riotous living.

And when he had spent all, there arose a mighty famine in that land; and he began to be in want.

And he went and joined himself to a citizen of that country; and he sent him into his fields to feed swine.

And he would fain have filled his belly with the husks that the swine did eat; and no man gave unto him.

And when he came to himself, he said, How many hired servants of my father's have bread enough and to spare, and I perish with hunger!

I will arise and go to my father, and will say unto him, Father, I have sinned against heaven, and before thee,

And am no more worthy to be called thy son: make me as one of thy hired servants.

And he arose, and came to his father. But when he was yet a great way off, his father saw him, and had compassion, and ran, and fell on his neck, and kissed him.

And the son said unto him, Father, I have sinned against heaven, and in thy sight, and am no more worthy to be called thy son.

But the father said to his servants, Bring forth the best robe, and put it on him; and put a ring on his hand, and shoes on his feet:

And bring hither the fatted calf, and kill it; and let us eat, and be merry:

For this my son was dead, and is alive again; he was lost, and is found. And they began to be merry.

—Luke 15:11-24

This parable also is part of Jesus' answer to the murmuring of the Pharisees who bitterly resented the fact that He received publicans and sinners. The Pharisees could not understand that these sinners had come to Jesus in repentance, and therefore their resentment was rooted in their own self-righteousness. Hence Jesus is still explaining the truth that He is the One Who has come to seek and to save those who are lost.

This parable is the final one in the beautiful trilogy of parables and completes the entire picture of the work of Christ in saving the lost. In distinction from the two preceding parables, this one assures the Church that God is always ready to receive His wayward children when they come to Him in sorrow of heart.

If it is possible to compare the teachings of the Lord, this parable is surely one of the most beautiful of all those truths which Christ taught His Church. It is beautiful because it so graphically displays the amazing love of God which not only welcomes us back into His house when we return to Him, but which is also the very power by which we are brought back into fellowship with our heavenly Father. The love of God seeks and restores, for it follows us wherever we wander. This is a blessed assurance for the Church. Because of the horror of our sin, the great iniquities which rise to condemn us, we may very well conclude that we will no longer be received by God, for we have sinned to often. But this is never the case. Transgressing God's commandments is a terrible sin; doing it repeatedly is beyond belief; yet God receives us again and again. And being assured of this, we need never fear to return in repentance to the Lord our God and Father.

The Waywardness of the Son

The two sons described in the parable were evidently Jews. As such they are to be construed as children of God, for the father in the parable is God Himself. They were children of God, however, only in the outwardly manifested sense. One was the true son of God, while the other was spiritually no son of God at all. But they were both sons outwardly in that they were both born in the line of the covenant. They were children of Abraham, born in the dispensation of the covenant, privileged outwardly with the privileges of the covenant which God had established with the nation of Israel. They both had received the sign of sonship in the sacrament of circumcision. They both lived in the house of God their Father, for they were both outwardly in the Church and under the dispensation of types and shadows. The comparison, therefore, is between two people born into covenant lines, brought up within the Church, receiving the sign of baptism upon their foreheads, coming under the preaching of the gospel and the administration of the Lord's Supper.

But here the similarity ends. The elder son remained at home working hard in the fields of his father and apparently remaining faithful. In fact, this faithfulness is very much on the mind of the elder son, for he takes pains to call it to his father's attention at the earliest opportunity when he thinks that it has been overlooked. In this he revealed that he was very proud of his diligent labor and that by it he had earned the right of his father's approval. This was a typical picture of the Pharisees of Jesus' day.

It was quite a different story with the other son. He evidently wearied of the place he occupied in his father's house. He no longer wanted to be bound by the rules of the home and disciplined by the requirements placed on him. He was dissatisfied with the comforts and benefits provided him. A wave of independence surged through his soul and the glittering lights of distant countries beckoned him. He decided to strike out on his own and show the world that he could stand on his own two feet. The pleasures of foreign lands seemed to him to be glittering and bright in comparison with the seemingly drab and colorless existence of the house of his father.

He asked for his share of the inheritance, which was one-third of his father's possessions. The elder son, heir to the birthright, would receive the double portion. But with his share of the inheritance the younger son would be able to sever his connections with his father and his father's house, declare his independence, and strike out on his own.

But he was a very foolish young boy. No sooner was he cut off from the watchful and loving eye of his father than he began to live the life that appealed to him. He did not start his own business and attempt to establish himself independently. Rather, he began to squander his gifts and goods in riotous living. He found the pleasures of life and the lusts of the flesh agreeable to him. He became important to a circle of cronies who were all too eager to help him spend his wealth. He lived for himself alone and for the satisfaction of his carnal lust with harlots and drunkards. How narrow and distasteful, how drab and colorless now appeared the house of his father in comparison with the free and easy life that he was living.

This is intended by Jesus to be a picture of the wandering sinner. Born in our Father's house, the gifts we receive from God are many. He gives us our health and life, our wives and children, our earthly possessions and daily needs, our gifts and abilities with which we are called to work. But beyond all these things He gives us also all the blessings which come to those who are born and raised within the Church. But we so often are filled with distaste for the discipline of the calling to serve our God in His Church. The world beckons. And so we take what we have received and use it to enjoy the pleasures of life. We become interested only in ourselves, in the satisfaction of our own desires, in the pursuit of our own ends and goals. We live a life that revolves around our own interests and we use what God has given to us to deny Him rather than to serve Him, to serve ourselves rather than to deny ourselves. We squander what we have received, for what is not laid on the altar of sacrifice to God is wasted in riotous living. The child of God who is conscious of his sin sees himself mirrored in the wayward son.

Nor is this an occasional event in our lives, or a characteristic of comparatively few within the Church. This is true of us all when in our sins we depart from God and seek ourselves. Whenever sin engages our attention and drags us into the byways of evil and self-service, we wander from our Father's house. We stray willfully and with deliberate and conscious choice.

But trouble comes. Step by step it increases. First, the possessions of the younger son were at last gone and he had nothing left of all that he had received. He was sated with lust and pleasure, the lights that formerly attracted him were dimmed, the cup of pleasure was drunk to the full, the carnal lust of life had turned to ashes in his sin-filled heart. The friends, formerly eager to spend his money, are now no longer interested in him. They are "fair-weather friends" who quickly find another "friend" with whom they can spend their time.

Then a famine came into the land so that the boy was stricken with hunger. The land was barren and empty. Its attractiveness had grown pale and its alluring temptations had faded. He could not even eat. In desperation he attached himself to a certain citizen of the country, evidently not even wanted by this citizen, but desperate in his need.

Then came the final degradation. He was sent to feed the hogs. All day in the hot sun under the cloudless skies he could watch the hogs to see that they had enough to eat while he starved for lack of food. Because the pig was prohibited in the land of Canaan, it was also considered the lowest sort of work to guard them, and, in fact, a sin to have anything to do with them. But now the young boy was to be found at the side of the swine trough, trying to still the gnawing pain in his belly that never went away.

Such are always the consequences of sin. Sometimes indeed these consequences appear to a lesser degree of despair and hopelessness than pictured in the parable, but nevertheless they are the consequences for the sinner who strays from God.

The Unchangeable Love of God

But the parable would have us focus our attention elsewhere. It is the love of God that stands on the foreground, a love that is absolutely unchangeable.

This is pictured forcibly by the Lord.

Although the son strayed far from home, the father continued to love him. The father is pictured as a man old before his time as the weight of worry and grief bend his back and make white his hair. He is pictured as looking each day from the window to see if perchance his son should appear on the distant horizon. This foolish and wayward boy is still his son. He may have gone astray where the father cannot follow. He may have wandered far down the road of life where a father's heart can go. But still he is a son. In a foreign country he remains a stranger. The man to whom he had joined himself was a *citizen* of that country, born and raised there and living there throughout his life. But the son was a stranger among strangers, a foreigner in a foreign land, always a son of his father's house.

This is a picture of the unchangeable love of God. God's love is eternal. It is a love that is from eternity to eternity the same. It is a love that is rooted in God's own Being. It is not a love that is dependent on the people whom God loves, for then it would change as they change. But God loves Himself. He loves His own purpose and work. He loves His own Name and the cause which He determined in His counsel to realize. And His love for His people is rooted in Himself and in His own unchangeable purpose to save His people. It is a love that is toward His people even when they are still sinners. It is a love that is absolutely first. For this is love, not that we loved God, but that He loved us (see I John 4:10). It is a love that is not affected or altered by the sins we commit. Often we sing about this: "Though we oft have sinned against Him, still His love and grace abide."

It is because of this love that we remain sons. God has made us sons eternally. He chose us to be His sons before we were born or saw the light of day. He adopted us as sons in His eternal love for us. When we disown our Father and choose rather the pleasures of sin, still He remains our Father. Though we deny our sonship and scorn His Fatherhood, He maintains His promise faithfully and remains our Father through it all.

But God's love is not only unchangeable, it is also absolutely sovereign. Though the proud heresies of Arminius and Pelagius maintain that we turn to God of our own free will and initiate the beginning of our restoration, this is a lie.

It is the love of the Father which follows His son to the distant land. It is the love of God which follows us wherever we wander. First it brings trouble to us. The heavy hand of chastisement comes upon us. And by this we see the utter hopelessness of sin's folly and the inability of the pleasures of life to bring satisfaction and contentment. Often adversity and trouble come to us. Perhaps the heavy hand of suffering and pain is laid on us; perhaps the loss of earthly goods; then again the daily problems of life multiply and grow larger. Sometimes we are reduced to the lowest extremity of want and need when our condition becomes hopeless and filled with despair. But it is always the hand of God's love, for God loves every son whom He chastens. His love follows us down the dark paths of sin. His love is revealed in difficult trials with the purpose of bringing us back.

When by these chastisements we have seen the hopelessness of our life without our Father, our thoughts are brought back again to our Father's house. So it was in the parable. The young man came to his senses. He remembered in the hour of his need the home that he had despised and left. He saw in the thoughts that flashed through his mind the servants of his father with all their needs supplied and their wants cared for. He recalled the pleasures of home which once he had scorned, but which now took on all the luster of peace and happiness. Even the lowest slave in his father's house was far more blessed than he at the side of a pig's trough.

In this way the love of God beckons us again to the joys of our Father's house. When we leave it in our futile and empty pursuit of pleasure it seems drab and monotonous. But in the despairing miseries and hopelessness of sin, God's love reminds us of the blessings which we receive in His house. There, in the house of God, is God's comforting Word—the Word of our Father to speak to us in our needs. There, is true happiness and joy in the fellowship of the saints. In that house is peace and safety, true friends to be found, true joy, true satisfaction for every want. It is the love of God which draws us to our Home.

The Need for the Assurance of God's Love

We stand in great need of the assurance of this love of God. And this, too, is pictured in the parable.

In his desperation the son resolved to return home once again. He resolved to return with a confession of sin on his lips and in his heart. On the one hand, his confession is both beautiful and complete. He confessed to both God and his own father against whom he had sinned. He made no excuse or attempt at self-justification. He did not plead to be forgiven on the basis of his own folly and youth. He did not try to cover up what he had done or hide from his father the awfulness of his plight. He said simply: "Father, I have sinned." That is all.

On the other hand, he came with a sense of his own unworthiness. He knew that he was no longer worthy to be called a son. He knew that he had forfeited every right to sonship in his father's house. Even to be a servant was something which he did not deserve, but which he nevertheless resolved to ask for. To be a doorkeeper in the house of his father was better than to dwell in the tents of wickedness.

But why does he have this assurance that when he returns and confesses his sin, his father will also receive him? Where does the courage come from to return to his father's house after he has so grossly sinned against him? The answer can only be that he knew his father's unchangeable love.

So it is also for us. How wonderful this is! We need never fear that when we return again with confession of sin our Father in heaven will refuse us. Oh, how we need to know this.

In the first place, our sins are so great that we cannot possibly see how they can be forgiven. We are not guilty of little sins and minor transgressions that could perhaps be overlooked. Our sins are great and horrible, especially in the eyes of a Holy God. In the second place, we sin so often. We commit the same sins over and over again. Even when we return for forgiveness, and also experience that forgiveness, we turn right around and commit again the sins of yesterday. Does there not come a time in our long life of sinning when our Father will say: "This is enough. You have sinned over and over again. I cannot forgive you anymore"? Does not the Lord weary of forgiving and come to a point when at last He turns us away? We must know.

In the third place, there is no reason why we should be forgiven. There is no reason in God, for God does not need us for His glory. He is full of glory in Himself. He lives a life that is full and blessed and we cannot add to it in any way. Nor is there any reason in us why we should be forgiven; we never deserve it. Even the fact that we come back to Him is of His grace. We have done nothing to earn forgiveness. We are not even worthy to be His servants, much less His sons. We have daily done nothing but forfeit every right to His favor. Why then should He forgive us? Will He forgive us again?

The child of God needs to know the answers to these questions. If he does not have the answer to them, he will, with fear in his heart, be unable to come again to his Father. Overwhelmed by the consciousness of his sin, he will sink deeper and deeper into the despair and hopelessness of the loss of his Father's favor.

The answer of the parable is, God is always ready to receive His wayward children. Each time He receives them back. He shows them that He will receive them because His love is eternal. By His love He seeks them when they are far from Him. In His love He brings them to confession and to cry to Him in sorrow and repentance. When there arises in their hearts the agonizing cry, "Father, I have sinned," that too is His love working in their hearts. This very love is the assurance that He will receive them.

This willingness to receive us in love is graphically depicted in the parable as the father leaves his home to meet his son when he sees him coming in the distance. The anxious father was watching out the window as he had watched for many days. There far in the distance he saw his son—weary and thin, worn and travel-stained, ragged and dirty. But he recognized him as his son. Now nothing could restrain him. He ran speedily out of the house with tears welling in his eyes and with his heart moved with tender compassion. And before the son had a chance to utter a word, the father threw his arms about him and smothered him with fond kisses of love. The son began his carefully rehearsed confession of sin, but the father interrupted. It is enough that his son is home with sorrow in his heart.

Thus God in love is always ready to receive His wayward children.

Even before we confess our sins to Him the consciousness of His love sweeps our soul. Embraced in our heavenly Father's eternal arms of love, we are borne up into His heart. Already His favor and grace surround us. Already His tender regard and earnest care fill our hearts. When we look at ourselves, stained and worn, crippled and helpless in our sin, this love of our Father is overwhelming. As the words of a heart broken with confession pour from our lips, already the comforting words of our heavenly Father interrupt us and fill us with the assurance of His eternal and unchangeable love.

How is such forgiveness possible?

This forgiveness is rooted in the cross of Christ, for in that cross is the perfect revelation of the love of God. While we were yet sinners Christ died for us. And dying, Christ took away all our sins. Before we were born or had done good or evil, Christ died for and paid for all our sins, as well as the sins of all the people of God. Objectively, before God's face, all of sin for all the elect was destroyed forever. The sins we had not yet committed were paid for already by the suffering and death of the Savior. And so, with a love that flows from the eternal heart of God and catches us up in its mighty stream, the blood of Christ is there to take away every sin. No matter how many they are, and no matter how often we commit them, Christ died for them all. In this is the forgiving love of God rooted and upon the cross of Christ it is based.

Hence, we need never doubt that we are once again received by God. We need never fear to come to Him because we have sinned over and over again. We need never have hesitation in returning to our Father every time anew. We need never wonder whether God's love is enough, Christ's blood sufficient. Every time we return, our Father surely will welcome us back. It is this truth which we must appropriate by faith, and, in faith, return every time with confession in our hearts and on our lips to seek the mercies of our God.

God's Love Revealed in Restoration to Sonship

The parable makes clear that the father not only received again his son, but restored him to the full rights of sonship. When the wandering and lost son returned to the house of his father, the father commanded his servants to fetch the best robe, the family ring, and sandals for the wanderer's feet. These are all signs of sonship. The robe is the robe of sons which they wear in the house. The ring marks the heir in the family. Since slaves were accustomed to going barefoot, the sandals restored the son to his former place. All this stands in sharpest contrast with the rags with which the son returned and his own piteous request to be established once again in the home of his father as a servant and not as a son.

In this way God also restores His people to the full rights of their sonship when they return to Him. This is not to say that God's people do not always remain sons. No matter how far they wander from their Father's house, they remain the sons of God, for God's act of making His people sons is eternal and unchangeable. But when they stray, they lose the *consciousness* of this sonship. Far from home and intent on their own sinful way, denying their Father and their own sonship, they lose the assurance of this sonship. But when they return with confession and humility, this assurance is again theirs. God tells them of His love and His joy at their return. He speaks of the greatness of His love that remained unchangeably rooted in the cross even while they wandered, and they know once again the joy of being the sons of God. He speaks to them the Word of His gospel and sends His Spirit into their hearts. He reveals to them the joy of His love so that they know and see and taste that once again they are taken with open arms into the family of God.

But even this is not all. God in His love prepares for them a banquet. This is a symbol of the joy in heaven of which Jesus speaks—the joy of Christ and His angels at the repentance of one sinner. But it speaks of another banquet also, a banquet that will finally be celebrated in heaven. This is the banquet so often called in Scripture the wedding feast of Christ and His Church. It is a picture of the final and full perfection of God's covenant when His people enter forever into the joy of their Lord. It is perfectly realized when the last repentant sinner is taken from this life—in which he wandered away so often—into his Father's house, there to be safe forever. It is the final joy of heaven's hosts when the history of this world has all been written and when the people of God are presented without spot or wrinkle in the assembly of the elect in life everlasting.

17

The Church's Joy in the Sinner's Repentance

Now his elder son was in the field: and as he came and drew nigh to the house, he heard musick and dancing.

And he called one of the servants, and asked what these things meant.

And he said unto him, Thy brother is come; and thy father hath killed the fatted calf, because he hath received him safe and sound.

And he was angry, and would not go in: therefore came his father out, and intreated him.

And he answering said to his father, Lo, these many years do I serve thee, neither transgressed I at any time thy commandment: and yet thou never gavest me a kid, that I might make merry with my friends:

But as soon as this thy son was come, which hath devoured thy living with harlots, thou hast killed for him the fatted calf.

And he said unto him, Son, thou art ever with me, and all that I have is thine.

It was meet that we should make merry, and be glad: for this thy brother was dead, and is alive again; and was lost, and is found.

—Luke 15:25-32

This passage of Scripture properly belongs to the parable of the lost son. It contains a description of the elder son's reaction to the return of his brother and the joy of the father who received the son back into the fellowship of the home.

But from a certain point of view it stands apart from the parable. It contains the final answer of Jesus to the murmuring of the Pharisees and scribes which was described in verse 2. It is a part of the thought of all the parables recorded in this chapter. Each parable speaks of the joy which is expressed when a sinner returns from the ways of his sin. But it is only in connection with this last parable of the chapter that the Lord expands on this idea.

It is obvious that the Church's joy at a sinner's repentance is expressed here negatively. The elder brother is a picture of the Pharisee. He is not himself one of those whom Jesus received, but is rather found murmuring when Jesus receives sinners. He is outside the kingdom because of his own self-righteousness. Before his consciousness he had no sin, and therefore no need of Christ.

But implied in this negative description is the positive element which Jesus specifically mentioned in the two preceding parables. The shepherd is pictured as rejoicing and as calling his friends and neighbors to join with him in his happiness. The woman who found her lost coin is described in the same way. And in every instance Jesus speaks of the joy in heaven and among the angels when one sinner repents.

In this rejoicing the Church is called to join as well.

The Elder Brother

There is little doubt that Jesus intends the elder brother to be a picture of the Pharisees. There are several points of comparison.

In the first place, the elder brother, according to the parable, was born in his father's house. He was a member of the household; in fact, he was the firstborn. He was brought up under the influences of a pious and godly home. He had received the sign of circumcision and had been subjected to the influences of covenant instruction. He was heir of his father's possessions and could look forward to assuming responsibility for the operation of the farm when his father could no longer manage the work.

This was true in the spiritual sense of the word with the Pharisees. Of course, this was true only outwardly. They were not the true seed of Abraham. Nevertheless, they belonged outwardly to the historical dispensation of the covenant. They had been circumcised and had in this way received the outward sign of the covenant. They had been brought up within the commonwealth of Israel where they had learned all the oracles of God and had been instructed in the truth concerning the promise of the covenant. They knew the law and the prophets and took part in the ceremonies which were an integral part of Israel's ecclesiastical life. They even made the claim that they belonged to that covenant: "We have Abraham for our father."

But they were not the true seed of the covenant, for they were wicked. Their observance of the law was outward, the observance of lip-service. Repeatedly in His ministry the Lord condemned their self-righteousness and warned them that, unless they repented, they had no place in the kingdom of God.

There are always people like this in the Church. This is because, as Paul puts it in Romans 9:6-8: "For they are not all Israel, which are of Israel: Neither, because they are the seed of Abraham, are they all children: but, In Isaac shall thy seed be called. That is, They which are the children of the flesh, these are not the children of God: but the children of the promise are counted for the seed." These people too are born in the historical dispensation of the covenant of God. They are born in Christian homes, receive the mark of baptism, are instructed by godly and pious parents, attend Christian schools, and

come under the preaching of the Word. But they are not the true
seed of the promise.

In the second place, the elder brother had seemingly remained
faithful. He had so conducted himself that outwardly you could not
criticize his work. He had labored hard and diligently in the fields of
his father. When he comments to his father, "Lo, these many years
do I serve thee, neither transgressed I at any time thy commandment," his claim was not contradicted. He had accurately described
his years of faithful toil. He had not run away from home as his
brother had done and squandered his father's possessions. He had
not committed sins of gluttony, drunkenness, adultery. Added to
this, he had always done all that was demanded of him.

The Pharisees were also like this. They too had kept all the law of
God. In fact, they were so zealous in keeping the law that they had
invented innumerable additional laws which they religiously observed so as to avoid even the least transgression of God's commandments. They kept the feasts, paid their tithes, made their
pilgrimages to the temple, observed the code of dress, of eating, of
washing, and so forth. There was no fault to be found in their lives.

When the lives of the Pharisees, from an outward point of view,
were compared with the lives of publicans and sinners, their virtuous conduct stood out all the more sharply.

The elder brother however, revealed his true character when his
brother returned. He was apparently working in the fields until late
in the day. He was unaware of the fact that his younger brother had
returned home and that a feast had been prepared for the prodi-
gal—a feast which was now in progress. And so, upon returning, he
heard the sound of festivities. Evidently suspecting something, and
already jealous that he had not been included, he did not enter the
banquet hall but called a servant to inquire what the rejoicing was all
about. The servant explained with ill-concealed excitement that his
younger brother had come back again and was received by his father
"safe and sound." In celebration of this event, the father had prepared this feast to welcome the son back into the fellowship of the
family.

One would think that this news would fill the elder son with the
same happiness which had prevailed among the rest of the family.
But instead, he was very angry. Sourly he refused to go into the
banquet hall and join the festivities—even when he was admonished
to do this by his father. His anger is evident from the very words he
speaks. He refuses to call his father "father"; and he refuses to call
his brother "brother," contemptuously referring to him as "thy son."
Rather, he is concerned with his own faithful labors and the lack of
any kind of reward for all his diligence. The fact that his brother is
back leaves him unmoved. How grating and harsh is his refusal in
contrast to the merriment in the house. How sour and discordant is
his anger in contrast to the joy of the father and the servants.

The Sin of the Elder Son

The sin of the elder son was manifested in the anger he showed when told of the reason for the festivities. This anger was not so much that he had not received what was coming to him, even though he attempted to leave the impression that this was the case. "Thou never gavest me a kid, that I might make merry with my friends." But the father quickly reminded him: "Thou art ever with me, and all that I have is thine." The son only used this as a rather petty excuse to cover up his real reason for being angry. His sin went much deeper than that.

His sin was the sin of criticism of his father's love. He resented the fact that his father loved his younger brother even though that brother had wandered in the ways of sins. And this criticism of his father's love was rooted in an inability on his part to love either his father or his brother. He hated his brother and was sorry that his brother had returned. And he hated his father for loving his brother.

But all of this was, in turn, due to his own carnal pride in his accomplishments. This became evident in his complaint. He bragged about how he had labored many years with unswerving devotion. He contrasted his faithful work with the evil life of his brother. He insisted that he had earned the right of his father's favor. He was really a liar; for, although he had worked hard, he had never worked out of love for his father. He had worked for his own benefit and reward. He was entirely devoted to himself and his own interests.

What a clear picture this was of the carnal and self-righteous Pharisees! They boasted of their good works and their faithful observance of the law. But their keeping of the law was never an observance of the very heart of the law: "Love God." Instead, their strict conformity to every precept was rooted in self-love. They were proud—proud of their own accomplishments, at the same time despising with scorn and contempt the publicans and sinners who crowded about Jesus. And their pride was rooted in self-righteousness, for self-righteousness and pride go hand in hand. But in a heart filled with pride there is no room for the love of God. And this always leads to contempt for those who fall into sin. But this contempt is hatred—hatred of God and hatred of one's brother.

Jesus is not talking here about a sin which is far removed from our lives. He is talking about a sin which, unless it is strenuously resisted and overcome by the power of grace, is a dominating characteristic of all our thinking. How often do we not pride ourselves in what we have done and boast of our tremendous accomplishments. How often are we not enamored with our faithful labor in the kingdom. But if we give in to this sin, the result is that we become like the proud and haughty Pharisees. And, an inescapable part of such a sin is contempt for the sinner who falls into the snares of the evil one.

Pride in ourselves leads to contempt of others. Only when we recognize the truth that we ourselves are sinners of the gravest sort, can we see with sympathy and understanding the sins of others. If pride conquers us, then we begin to have the utterly wicked idea that we earn God's favor and put our Father under obligation to bless us. When we see ourselves as sinners, then we see that everything we receive is of grace.

And all of this is true because pride blinds one to the cross. The Pharisees had no need of the cross. They were without sin in their own eyes. They needed no suffering Savior to atone for their sins, for they had no sins which needed atonement. And they could not understand the love of God in Christ for publicans and sinners for whom Christ shed His own blood. They hated God's love in Christ for sinners because they hated the cross which is the highest manifestation of that love.

Always pride closes one's eyes to the cross. And, unable to see the cross, one becomes unable to see God's love in Christ through the cross for those who are dead in trespasses and sins.

This was the sin of the elder brother. It is a common sin. For it we must be on our guard.

Joy at Repentance

In contrast to this sour criticism of the elder brother stands the joy of the whole household at the return of the younger brother.

In connection with the other parables, Jesus explains that this is, first of all, the joy of Christ. The Good Shepherd rejoiced when He found His sheep. Because this joy is the joy of Christ, it is first of all the joy of God Himself. God rejoices when His people return to Him in repentance and confess before Him, "Father, I have sinned against heaven and in thy sight. I am no longer worthy. . . ." This joy is rooted in the fact that God's eternal purpose to reveal His great grace and love is accomplished in His own work. God always rejoices in the work of His hand.

It is not hard to understand then why Christ also rejoices. Christ is sent by God to accomplish God's purpose. When sinners are brought to repentance, Christ sees the fruit of His own terrible suffering and death and the fruit of His mighty resurrection. His work bears its fruit as the sinner comes to Him, lays hold on Him by faith, and confesses: "My only comfort is that I belong to Jesus."

In this rejoicing the angels join. They are the ministers of God. They are undoubtedly pictured in the parable as the servants. But they are especially busy with the affairs of the salvation of the elect. And in the repentance of sinners they see what God has accomplished, and they see their own part in this wonderful work of salvation. Heaven rings with their rejoicing.

But the Church is called to participate in this joy. The Church is exactly composed of those who confess their own sins. They are not a congregation of those who need no repentance. They are not a company of men who welcome a few who stray away. The apostle Peter puts it very bluntly when he says: "For ye were as sheep going astray; but are now returned unto the Shepherd and Bishop of your souls" (I Peter 2:25). They who return are exactly the same as they who rejoice. In this respect all the saints are alike. They were all in perilous danger. They all squandered their Father's possessions and devoured His living with harlots. And they rejoice together as one by one they are returned by the Shepherd of their souls.

Hence, there is implied here an admonition. It is indeed true that the elder brother represents the Pharisees. But the sin that the Lord describes in a sin which can easily be in us. We will, if we are not careful (for pride is deep within all of us), take the same attitude as the elder brother. For the power of sinful pride is very strong in us. The admonition is therefore to rejoice as Christ and His angels rejoice. This rejoicing must be wholly unselfish and generous. It must be sincere and from the heart. It must be rooted in a genuine happiness at the recovery of the lost. And it must be a joy that arises in us because the purpose of God in Christ is accomplished.

The Reason for This Joy

The joy which characterizes the Church must, first of all, be rooted in God's work. God leads His children to confession and repentance. God is glorified in the salvation of the lost. If the self-righteous are saved, the glory goes to them because they have earned it. But when sinners are saved, the glory belongs to God alone. Their salvation is the wonder of God's unchanging love and the miracle of His sovereign grace. The salvation of sinners is the victory of the cross of Christ.

In the second place, the reason for rejoicing is found in the personal assurance of salvation. The Church rejoices at the repentance of sinners because the saints know that they too have been saved in that same way. They know that this need for repentance comes each day anew. They know that all the saints together bow before the foot of the cross. And knowing that this is the way they have been saved, they rejoice when others come with them to Calvary to seek, with tears of sorrow, salvation in the cross alone.

Further, each saint knows that he can go to heaven only in the company of all the elect. If one saint is missing, the Church cannot be glorified perfectly; for the cross, at least in part, has failed. But all the saints, without exception, are brought to glory through repentance of the blood of the cross. In the repentance of one sinner is the victory of the whole Church.

And so their joy is expressed in thanks to God alone for the riches of His mercy. In that spirit of thankfulness they welcome the sinner back, speaking together of the power of the cross and the miracle of grace. In that thankfulness, they help the sinner return, for, "Let him know, that he which converteth the sinner from the error of his way, shall save a soul from death, and shall hide a multitude of sins" (James 5:20). And, thankful to God, they fulfill the law of Christ. For, "Brethren, if a man be overtaken in a fault, ye which are spiritual, restore such an one in the spirit of meekness; considering thyself, lest thou also be tempted. Bear ye one another's burdens, and so fulfil the law of Christ" (Gal. 6:1, 2).

18

Making Friends of Unrighteous Mammon

And he said also unto his disciples, There was a certain rich man, which had a steward; and the same was accused unto him that he had wasted his goods.

And he called him, and said unto him, How is it that I hear this of thee? give an account of thy stewardship; for thou mayest be no longer steward.

Then the steward said within himself, What shall I do? for my lord taketh away from me the stewardship: I cannot dig; to beg I am ashamed.

I am resolved what to do, that, when I am put out of the stewardship, they may receive me into their houses.

So he called every one of his lord's debtors unto him, and said unto the first, How much owest thou unto my lord?

And he said, An hundred measures of oil. And he said unto him, Take thy bill, and sit down quickly, and write fifty.

Then said he to another, And how much owest thou? And he said, An hundred measures of wheat. And he said unto him, Take thy bill, and write fourscore.

And the lord commended the unjust steward, because he had done wisely: for the children of this world are in their generation wiser than the children of light.

And I say unto you, Make to yourselves friends of the mammon of unrighteousness; that when ye fail, they may receive you into everlasting habitations.

He that is faithful in that which is least is faithful also in much: and he that is unjust in the least is unjust also in much.

If therefore ye have not been faithful in the unrighteous mammon, who will commit to your trust the true riches?

And if ye have not been faithful in that which is another man's, who shall give you that which is your own?

—Luke 16:1-12

This parable of the Lord is perhaps the most difficult one to understand. There are literally hundreds of interpretations of it;

and, we are told, there is one book which is completely given over to all the interpretations of the parable which have appeared throughout the years. There is even one commentator who shrugs his shoulders and quite frankly gives up trying to understand it.

While it is perhaps true that this parable presents some difficult problems, it is striking that the audience to which Jesus spoke the parable had no difficulty understanding exactly what the Lord meant. This was especially true of the Pharisees. We read in verse 14, "And the Pharisees also, who were covetous, heard all these things: and they derided him." The Pharisees understood precisely what Jesus meant. They understood that He was speaking this parable especially against them. Their consciences were pricked by these words, and the result was that they resorted to mocking Him to escape the accusations of their own hearts. Their understanding of what Jesus was saying was undoubtedly because the figures in the parable were very familiar to them. Nor could they fail to appreciate the rather sharp humor of the parable, even though it was the means Jesus used to expose their own sin.

The difficulty of the parable hinges particularly on the interpretation of verse 9, and especially the phrase: "Make to yourselves friends of the mammon of unrighteousness." This seems to be a statement which stands in flat contradiction to other teachings of the Lord in which He admonishes His disciples to seek the things which are above in distinction from the things which are below. In fact, in the very next statement of the Lord, recorded in verse 13, Jesus says: "No servant can serve two masters: for either he will hate the one, and love the other; or else he will hold to the one, and despise the other. Ye cannot serve God and mammon." The implication of this word of Jesus is: Forsake mammon. Yet, in the parable Jesus says: "Make to yourselves friends of the mammon of unrighteousness." What can He mean?

It is, however, precisely in this verse that the key to the interpretation of the parable lies. The parable is an illustration of our spiritual calling by way of contrast. It is an example of earthly wisdom or prudence. This earthly (and fundamentally wicked) prudence can nevertheless serve as an example to us. Jesus advises us to be prudent also—only our prudence must be with spiritual character.

Thus the admonition is to use this world's goods—the mammon of unrighteousness—with true and heavenly wisdom. We must use these things with single-minded devotion as a means to the end for which we strive. That is, we must use these things to pursue our calling to seek heaven by seeking the kingdom of God.

The Idea of Stewardship

The parable speaks of a steward. A steward was a most important and powerful man. Sometimes he was a slave, sometimes a hired servant. But he was chief of all the slaves of the master and all the servants who worked for the lord. He was given a position of trust and responsibility in the house of his master that goes beyond anything we know today. Joseph was a steward in the house of Potiphar in Egypt. He himself says of his position: "Behold, my master wotteth not what is with me in the house, and he hath committed all that he hath to my hand; There is none greater in this house than I; neither hath he kept back any thing from me but thee, because thou art his wife" (Gen. 39:8,9). Eliezer was the steward in the house of Abraham. And while his name is not mentioned specifically, it was the steward of Abraham's house who was even entrusted with the responsibility of going to another land (Haran) and obtaining a wife for Abraham's only son and heir (see Gen. 24).

To sum up, a steward was given the responsibility for all the affairs of his master. He had authority to act on behalf of his master without consulting him in matters of the home and the business. He collected his master's revenues and debts, paid the bills and the servants, took charge of overseeing the work that had to be done, and took care of the accounts. Even beyond this, he was often responsible for seeing to it that the household ran smoothly, that the food was purchased which was needed for the family, that the children were cared for and provided with education.

But there was one thing which a steward might never forget. Even though he was solely responsible for all his master's possessions, the truth is that the possessions were always those of the master alone. The steward himself never owned a thing. If he was a slave, even his own life and body belonged to his master. He had one calling therefore: to work in his responsible position for the best possible advantage of his lord. If he did not do this, he was expelled from his position and a man more worthy than he was found to take his place.

Scripture uses this earthly position of a steward to describe the relation in which we stand to the things of this world. It is a very forceful and striking figure. There are various elements implied in it.

In the first place, the figure stresses that we live in the house of God. This creation is God's house, over which He is Lord and Master. He has created all things; He continues to uphold all things by the Word of His power. By this very fact, all things are His—even to the cattle on a thousand hills.

In the second place, God has placed man as a steward in His house. God has given man the responsibility of caring for all the things and all the affairs of the house. But the fact is that man himself belongs to God. He is even more the possession of God than a slave was the possession of his master, for God gives to each man, every moment, the air that he breathes, the food that he eats, the life which he so often calls his own. Man has absolutely nothing which is really his. His job, his home, his children, his abilities, his very continued existence—all are given to him each moment. And God retains the prerogative to take it away at any time He sees fit. And there is no possibility of arguing with God over this matter.

In the third place, this very position of stewardship places man in the position where he is obligated to use everything which the Lord has entrusted to him for the benefit and glory of his God. Never, even for a single moment, may he use anything for himself and his own benefit. He must always seek the welfare of his Lord and Master. If he does not do this, he will be removed from his position and put into hell.

The Wisdom of the Steward

The steward whom Jesus describes was a prudent man. Perhaps he can be described as clever. He was, of course, basically unfaithful. The report came to his master of this unfaithfulness. What precisely his sin was is not told us in the parable. He may have used his position of trust and responsibility to further his own interests. Whatever he may have done wrong, there was apparently no question about it. Although the report came via a third paty, the master did not specify investigation, nor did he give his unfaithful steward opportunity for self-defense. He was obviously guilty and had to pay the penalty. He was asked to put all the affairs in order so that the work might be handed over to another; and with that his work for the master was terminated.

But this placed him before a serious problem with which he had to cope. Somehow he had to provide for his future material well-being. Losing his job was a financial disaster. He had no provisions for the future. He considered himself of insufficient strength to engage in any heavy manual labor. And this was the only area of work open to him now that he had been caught in crookedness. He was too proud to beg for a living. What was he to do?

In making these preparations for the future, he decided that the best course of action was to use his position of responsibility as long as he still retained it to put his master's creditors in debt to him. He called each of the lord's debtors (there are two examples given) and excused a large part of each man's debt. He still possessed the authority to do this, and his signature on the agreement would have to be recognized by the master himself. The result of this stroke of genius would be that he would make friends of these debtors so that, when his position was finally taken from him, these friends would remember his kindness and feel an obligation toward him to take him in and provide for his needs.

This he proceeded to do. He made "good" use of the time remaining to him to make sure that he would not be in want. Although surely his lord would never approve of such high-handedness, the lord, when he found out what the steward had done, could not help but admire his prudence and foresight: "And the lord commended the unjust steward, because he had done wisely" (v. 8).

An Example by Way of Contrast

The Lord uses the example of the unfaithful steward as an instance of the foresight and prudence of the children of this world. He says: "The children of this world are in their generation wiser than the children of light."

We must be careful that we understand the example correctly. The unfaithful steward committed a very serious sin. It is not the Lord's purpose to hold up this steward's conduct as an example for the people of God to emulate. If this would be the case then indeed this teaching of the Lord would stand in flat contradiction with many other passages of Scripture. In fact, such a sin is exactly the heart of the sin prohibited in the ninth commandment: "Thou shalt not steal." The Lord speaks of the "children of this world." These are the people of the world who are without grace. They are the totally depraved who are incapable of doing anything pleasing in God's sight. They are corrupt in all their ways. Their sins are surely not set up by Christ as examples for us to follow in our conduct.

The Lord speaks only of the prudence and foresight of the steward. It is this part of his conduct which must be an example to us. But even then, the act itself is not approved by Christ. After all, the steward, in reducing the debts of his lord's creditors, abused his position and stole from his lord. The Lord is not saying here: "The end justifies the means." There is only one point the Lord is making. The steward had a foresight, a cleverness, a devotion, a single-mindedness of purpose which, if correctly used, we do well to imitate. It is true that the prudence of the steward was applied to earthly ends. This we must not do. We must apply it to spiritual ends.

But in this limited sense, there is an example worth emulating. The Lord is clear on this. It is certainly true that in their generation, the children of this world are wiser than God's people. You may often find innumerable examples of this in the world. The wicked have often one goal which they set for themselves as the goal of their life. This goal is a wicked goal. In the broadest sense of the word, it is a goal which aims at heaven here on earth, at utopia apart from God, at man's reign from God's throne. But this goal, along with the lesser goals subservient to this chief one, is the sole object and aim of their life. They are totally dedicated to it. They pursue this goal with a single-mindedness and devotion which is startling. The means they use are as wicked as the goal itself. But their prudence is evident in the fact that they clearly understand the goal and clearly perceive the best and quickest way to attain it. And they show remarkable dedication to attain it. In general, they care for their old, make provision for unemployment, sickness, death, trouble, and catastrophe. They assemble mighty weapons of science and technology, medicine and laboratory gains to serve their purposes. They establish mighty engines of propaganda in the educational institutions of the land and in the means of communication to promote these goals.

To attain them, they are willing to forego pleasure and comfort. They readily make innumerable sacrifices and place themselves in the greatest dangers. They have a loyalty, an astuteness, a foresight which puts the people of God to shame. Communist insurgents are willing to forego family life and the comforts of home to live in sweltering jungles in pursuit of their ends. Men of science are willing to risk life and fortunes to attain their purpose. In their zeal and consecration they are amazing. Jesus says that they shame the children of light.

The Calling of Children of Light

The world, therefore, serves as an example to believers. The latter are called children of light because they are, by grace, through Christ, brought out of the darkness of sin and unbelief into the light of God's Word. They are given the spiritual power to see the true end of life, the true goal for which men must strive. They are enlightened by the Holy Spirit to understand the Scriptures and know from them how these goals must be attained.

But at the same time, these children of light are imperfect. Indeed, there is a great deal of imperfection in their life; for the power of grace has not yet completely cleansed them from all sin. They must struggle daily with their weaknesses.

The result is that the people of God often halt between two opinions. They are often uncertain and hesitant about the goal for which they must strive. This goal is, of course, the glory of their God. But as often as not, they too seek their goals in the world. They set their hearts and minds on the accumulation of riches, on the pleasures of life, and on the world as a permanent dwelling place. They are torn between two goals, and their allegiance seems often to be divided. This necessarily dampens their enthusiasm for the heavenly goals to which they are called, and they lack a certain devotion and consecration, a singleness of purpose in seeking the things of God.

It is within this context that Jesus admonishes the people who would be His disciples: "Make to yourselves friends of the mammon of unrighteousness; that, when ye fail, they may receive you into everlasting habitations. He that is faithful in that which is least is faithful also in much: and he that is unjust in the least is unjust also in much. If therefore ye have not been faithful in the unrighteous mammon, who will commit to your trust the true riches? And if ye have not been faithful in that which is another man's, who shall give you that which is your own?"

The antithesis between the children of the world and the children of light is very sharp. The aim of all of life for the child of light ought to be the kingdom of God and His righteousness. Jesus specifically speaks of this in a somewhat similar context when He says: "But seek ye first the kingdom of God, and his righteousness; and all these [earthly] things shall be added unto you" (Matt. 6:33). This implies that the calling of the child of God is to seek God's glory in all that he does, for he is only a steward in God's house. It implies, further, that he must seek as his eternal destination the kingdom of heaven: for that is the goal and end of his journey. It implies, also, that he must seek the welfare of that kingdom of Christ as that kingdom is manifested here in the world in the cause of the Church, of the preaching of the gospel, of the salvation of the Church, of the cause of Christian missions, of the covenant education of the children of the covenant, and so forth.

However, to attain this goal we must make unrighteous mammon our friend. This does not mean that we ought to serve mammon, for Jesus expressly repudiates this in the verse that follows the parable. If we serve these things—riches, material possessions, and a place and name in the world—we sin. No less does it mean that all these earthly things are ends in themselves to be used for our personal enjoyment. This is the wickedness of the world. That truth is, all things belong to God.

The point is that while the kingdom of Christ is manifested in this present world, it has need of material things. The Church is dependent on finances to carry on its work. We must eat and drink to walk our pilgrim's path. Christian schools cost money to operate. And so on. These material things belong to the mammon of unrighteousness for two reasons: (1) they are precisely the things which the world of unrighteousness makes the goal of their lives; (2) they are part of this world which is under the curse and which is destined to pass away. In themselves they have no abiding value and the mere possession of them is not of worth for the individual.

There is, therefore, the sharpest contrast in the text. Mammon is contrasted with the true riches. The mammon of wealth, money, gold, material possessions fades away and is no more. The true riches of which Jesus speaks are the riches of the kingdom of God: the new creation, the knowledge of God, the blessings of Christ and His cross, the treasures of heaven. These endure forever.

Mammon is of value only as a means to gain other treasures. The treasures of the kingdom of heaven are of value in their own right. Mammon is least; the true riches are very great.

God has placed us as stewards over these lesser things now. They too belong to His house. Presently He will make us not only stewards, but possessors of the true riches. For this reason we must be faithful. We must be faithful in setting our whole life upon the goal of the eternal kingdom of God. We must use all that God has put into our care for the purpose of attaining the true riches. We must do this with complete devotion, unswerving loyalty, true wisdom and dedication and zeal which is unwavering. In this way we prepare genuinely for the future.

This is the way the unfaithful steward operated with uncommon shrewdness and a clever use of the authority of the position he still occupied. Even his lord was surprised at the prudence which the steward showed in providing for his future with the means available. This is the shrewdness which also characterizes the children of this world, even though their goals are wicked and the means they use to attain these goals are contrary to the will of God.

In this way we must emulate them, though our goals are different and the means to attain these goals are keeping the commandments of God. We have nothing for ourselves. Even our own bodies, our own abilities, our own children are not ours, but belong to God. Never may we make use of even one part of these things which are God's alone without seeking the welfare of our heavenly Father's kingdom. If we would follow this path, what could not be done by the Church, by Christian schools, and for the cause of Christ's kingdom? Total devotion to the goal of the kingdom of heaven would move the cause of Christ forward more rapidly into new fields and unto greater callings. We speak of sacrificing for kingdom causes. We do not really know what sacrifice is. And, indeed, if we understood that everything belongs to God, there would be no talk of sacrifice even when we give our all. Truly, the dedication and wisdom of this world is often greater than that of God's people. The children of this world are surely wiser in their generation than the children of light.

The Reward of Grace

In the text Jesus emphatically points out the reward which is given to those who are wise.

In the parable already, the faithless steward was undoubtedly successful in his efforts to gain the friendship of men who would provide for him when his stewardship was ended.

But Jesus adds negatively: "An unjust and unfaithful steward over the lesser things of money will not be entrusted with the greater riches of the kingdom." And, positively: "One faithful now over these earthly things that belong to God will surely be entrusted with the greater things of the kingdom." Hence, faithful stewardship in this life prepares for the future. By faithful stewardship a man lays up treasures in heaven, where moth and rust do not corrupt and where thieves do not break through and steal.

Presently we must die. When we leave this life we cannot take gold and silver or the things of this world with us. All these things shall fail. Our stewardship will have come to an end. The things of this world are only of temporary value. They serve a purpose; they are a means to an end. But when their purpose is served they pass away. The goal is attained when we enter the kingdom and when the kingdom is brought to glory. Then there shall be a new creation where the need for "unrighteous mammon" no longer exists.

So, to him who uses "unrighteous mammon" to lay up treasures in heaven will be entrusted the spiritual and heavenly riches of the kingdom of heaven.

But this does not mean that we earn our salvation. The reward is of grace. Jesus was talking primarily to His disciples, who were citizens of the kingdom by a wonder of grace. They have their devotion to the kingdom recorded for us in the Scriptures. They gained through grace the reward of the kingdom.

So it is with every faithful child of God. The reward is given based on and in proportion to faithfulness. He that is faithful in little shall be rewarded with little. He that is faithful in much shall receive a great reward.

But always it is all of grace. The faithfulness is of grace, and the reward granted to that faithfulness is of grace. Grace gives the strength and the proportionate reward, for it is all of God. The everlasting life of the child of God in the tabernacle of God's covenant is the inheritance of God's people when the wicked perish. Our Belgic Confession puts it very beautifully when it says: "Therefore we do good works, but not to merit by them, (for what can we merit?) nay, we are beholden to God for the good works we do, and not he to us, since it is he that worketh in us both to will and to do of his good pleasure. . . . In the meantime, we do not deny that God rewards our good works, but it is through his grace that he crowns his gifts. . . ."

This reward of grace is the incentive to spur us on, for presently we shall hear the Lord say to us: "Well done, thou good and faithful servant; enter into the joy of thy Lord."

19

"Son, Remember ..."

There was a certain rich man, which was clothed in purple and fine linen, and fared sumptuously every day:
And there was a certain beggar named Lazarus, which was laid at his gate full of sores,
And desiring to be fed with the crumbs which fell from the rich man's table: moreover the dogs came and licked his sores.
And it came to pass, that the beggar died, and was carried by the angels into Abraham's bosom: the rich man also died, and was buried;
And in hell he lift up his eyes, being in torments, and seeth Abraham afar off, and Lazarus in his bosom.
And he cried and said, Father Abraham, have mercy on me, and send Lazarus, that he may dip the tip of his finger in water, and cool my tongue; for I am tormented in this flame.
But Abraham said, Son, remember that thou in thy lifetime receivedst thy good things, and likewise Lazarus evil things: but now he is comforted, and thou art tormented.
And beside all this, between us and you there is a great gulf fixed: so that they which would pass from hence to you cannot; neither can they pass to us, that would come from thence.

—Luke 16:19-26

The parable which occupies our attention in this chapter is somewhat different from the type that Jesus usually spoke. Most generally, there is a definite pattern in the parable and a clear correspondence between the various elements in the parable and their spiritual counterparts. So, for example, in the Parable of the Sower, the sower is the Son of man, the seed is the Word, the field is the world, and so forth. But this is not the case in the parable of the rich man and Lazarus. This parable is more like a story. This fact has led some commentators to conclude that Jesus does not teach a parable here at all, but recites for His hearers something which actually happened in Palestine—something with which all His hearers were familiar. The purpose of Jesus then would be not so much simply to recall to the mind of His followers something they already knew, but to interpret this recent death of two of their acquaintances in the light of eternity. Yet this interpretation is not likely, since the text has a very definite occasion in the preceding verses. Added to this, the text as a whole quite obviously contains elements which make it a parable.

The occasion for this parable is the parable of the unjust steward. The Pharisees, who were covetous, were aware of the fact that Jesus had spoken that parable against them. They were deeply offended at this and began to deride Jesus for His teaching. Jesus responded by telling them that they are the ones who try to justify themselves, but God knows their hearts. John came on the scene, followed by Jesus; and the Pharisees rejected them both. In particular, they rejected them out of an evil heart and out of purely selfish and covetous reasons. Now, in this parable, Jesus describes for them the punishment that shall surely be theirs.

The emphasis of the parable falls therefore on the rich man. His condemnation forms the chief subject. Lazarus is introduced only by way of contrast in order to better heighten the effect of the parable. Nevertheless, there is also a word of comfort here for the people of God. They are the scorned and mocked publicans of Jesus' day; but they are also the saints of all ages who are killed all the day long, counted as sheep for the slaughter, oppressed by the rich and cast out by the world. To them is addressed the comforting assurance that there shall come a day when their cause is vindicated and their righteousness rewarded in Christ Jesus.

There is a natural division in the parable between verses 26 and 27. In fact, a new subject is introduced with verse 27, a subject important enough to be treated separately. The treatment of the last part of this parable must wait therefore until my next chapter.

The Sin of the Rich Man

The scene opens on the life of two men here on earth. There is, first of all, "a certain rich man." It is obvious that this man was a natural child of Abraham. In verse 24, from the depths of hell, he calls to heaven to "Father Abraham"; and Abraham responds, according to verse 25, by calling him "Son." He was born a Jew, outwardly of the seed of Abraham, Isaac, and Jacob. No doubt he could trace his genealogy back through the four hundred years between Malachi and John the Baptist, through the captivity, through the ages of the kings of Judah and the Judges, all the way back to the twelve sons of Jacob. He was proud of his genealogy, for it gave him a privileged place in Palestine, and later—so he thought—in heaven.

He knew well Moses and the prophets. He lived an outwardly upright life. Deliberately Jesus points to no sin which he committed.

There is not added to his name the crimes of Sabbath desecration or blasphemy or murder or adultery or theft. He always kept within the strict limits of the law, faithfully attended church and prayed every day, even on the street corners. He made his sacrifices with monotonous regularity and annually paid his tithes of a tenth of all that he had. In fact, he probably had the mind of a philanthropist, and may have erected a costly synagogue with his fortune, a certain "Dives Memorial Synagogue."

This was possible because God had entrusted to his care an abundance of the things of this world. He was extremely wealthy. His whole life was evidently a life of ease and luxury. He dressed in purple and finest linen. He would not be seen in the work clothes of a common laborer; in his home and on the street he dressed in the attire of princes. Every day was a banquet day at his house. There were many servants to wait on long tables heavy with this earth's bounties. There were delicate foods, the best of imported wines, music, dancing, laughter, rejoicing, merriment. His life was of ease and plenty, a life coveted by many but attained by few.

Nor is the point of the parable that these riches in themselves constituted his sin. It is, of course, true that God does not often make His people rich. And it is also true that it is difficult for a rich man to enter the kingdom. But it is not impossible. Riches in themselves are not wrong. Nevertheless, one gains the impression that this man served mammon. He lived for himself in idleness and luxury. He was interested only in his personal enjoyment. No man, whether rich or poor, has the right to live sumptuously as this rich man did.

Yet this was not his sin. His sin and his true character are revealed only in relation to Lazarus sitting in the gate. In this situation the picture is quite the opposite. Here is something utterly repulsive and wretched. Lazarus is as poor as it is possible to be. He was dumped helplessly at the gate of this rich man, no doubt by men who were only too happy to be rid of the responsibility of caring for him. He was a beggar. He had no means of support, no way of providing himself with the necessities of life other than seeking these necessities from charitable folk who passed his way. He was dressed in rags, dirty and unwashed, disheveled and unkempt, a deplorable sight to all who passed. He was very hungry—not just once in a while, but all the time. The gnawing in his belly could not be stilled. He was satisfied with the few crumbs that fell from the table of the rich man and which were swept out into the street as food for the wild dogs that roamed the streets of Palestine's cities.

Yet even this is not all. For his needs were not limited to a little to eat and a cup of cold water; he was very ill. He was covered with ulcerous sores which were running and filled with pus and which would not heal, for there was no oil to clean them and no medicine to dry them. He lay suffering in the gutter outside the door of the rich man's house, praying for deliverance. He had friends, but the only friends he had were the dogs who came to lick his sores and scavage with him in the filth of the streets for a little to eat.

Yet his poverty was only material. In another way—an important way—he was very rich. Although Jesus does not refer to this except by implication, we may nevertheless deduce this from the parable. For one thing, his name was "Lazarus." And this beautiful name means "whom God helps." This was also his confession. He was a true child of Abraham, wretched and miserable though he appeared to men. The fact that he was carried to Abraham's bosom indicated that he waited on God and trusted in God's promises as they had been made to his father Abraham. He looked for his daily bread from the hand of his Father in heaven. He looked for his salvation to appear from on high. Each time he dug up a few crumbs he prayed, "Lord, we thank Thee for this food; for Jesus' sake, Amen."

It was the presence of Lazarus that served as the immediate occasion for the rich man to reveal his true character.

For one thing, the rich man has no name while Lazarus is given a name by Christ. It was no doubt true that the rich man had a name here on earth, but that name would soon pass away and he would be known no more. His name was not worth remembering. And into eternity he remains the nameless one. But Lazarus has a name which endures because his name is written on the pages of the book of sovereign election—written in the ink of the blood of the Lamb. That name is recorded on the roles of heaven, and shall continue forever.

This is, however, because the sin of the rich man was terrible. He kept the law with earnestness and devotion, but he forgot that the law spoke of the care of the poor. He ignored Lazarus and would have liked to sweep him away if he dared. He lived only for himself and the praise of men. His god was his belly. He ignored what Micah the prophet had once said: "But what doth the Lord require of thee? To do justly, *love mercy* and walk humbly with thy God." With Lazarus at his gate all his selfishness, his covetousness, his mammon worship became evident. The beggar lying in the gate revealed his hatred of the poor, his contempt for God and for the inner demands of God's law, his bitterness for those for whom Christ died.

Yet, in this first scene, all seems utterly inequitable. Dives, the wicked man, seems to be the blessed one. Lazarus, who waits on God, seems to be ignored by heaven and earth. Dives, the fool, has all that his heart desires. Lazarus, who humbly trusts in his God, seems to be deprived of even life's necessities and forgotten by the God he served. Is this the way it is in reality? Often indeed it looks that way. Many times the saints are moved to take up the doleful dirge of Asaph in Psalm 73: "But as for me, my feet were almost gone; my steps had well nigh slipped. For I was envious at the foolish, when I saw the prosperity of the wicked. For there are no bands in their death: but their strength is firm. They are not in trouble as other

men; neither are they plagued like other men. . . . Their eyes stand
out with fatness: they have more than heart could wish. They are
corrupt, and speak wickedly concerning oppression: they speak
loftily. . . . Behold, these are the ungodly, who prosper in the world;
they increase in riches. Verily I have cleansed my heart in vain, and
washed my hands in innocency. For all the day long have I been
plagued, and chastened every morning" (vv. 3-5, 7, 8, 12, 13).

The Rich Man's Condemnation

But wait. The scene changes. Death comes along the street on
which Dives lives. Not surpirsingly, it sweeps the wretched and ill
beggar before it. One morning his body was found outside the gate
cold and stiff. With an almost audible sigh of relief, someone dragged his body to the dump. Unmourned, unwanted, without dignity,
Death sweeps away its first victim.

Yet all men must go the way of death. And so Death comes again,
but this time to knock on the door of the rich man. For Death does
not pay attention to whether a man lives in palaces or gutters,
whether he eats meat or crumbs, whether he wears the robes of
princes or filthy rags.

Only, Dives' death is different. The best physicians in the land
were called to struggle and fight for his life. And when Death
nevertheless had the victory, he died with dignity and surrounded
by friends. His funeral was an elaborate affair. They were many,
many mourners. There were long speeches and beautiful eulogies
recalling for the benefit of his friends his many noble deeds. The
funeral procession seemed to have no end. And at last when the
beautiful and expensive coffin was laid away in the family sepulchre
in a beautiful garden, a large monument was erected in his memory,
so that his deeds might live after him.

But that was all. What else can one do at the side of the grave? He
died; and, emphatically, he was buried.

But there is also something significant about the notice of Lazarus'
death. The obituary column in the *Jerusalem News* carried a long
story about the rich man, but made no mention of the death of a
beggar. Yet, when Jesus pauses to recount his death, He says: "And
it was, with respect to the beggar, that he died." It came to pass that
he died. This is true, of course, of all men. But that it is mentioned in
connection with Lazarus' death is significant. Nothing really simply
"comes to pass." Lazarus died by divine appointment. He was called
according to the timetable of heaven to come home. It was the
passing of the moments of God's eternal counsel that brought
Lazarus to the door of death. And so, while indeed all men die by
divine appointment, heaven takes no notice of the funeral, the
eulogies, the monuments, the mourners of the rich man. But heaven
is vitally interested in the death of the beggar who lay at the gate of
the rich man's palace. When at last the weary head of Lazarus fell

into the gutter in the silence of death, angels hovered about to carry that tortured but released saint to the bosom of Abraham.

We must remember that this is figurative language. That is, we do not know how our souls fly away to God; but Jesus does not mean that we take this literally. Nor is it true that the resting place of Lazarus in Abraham's bosom must be taken literally. But there are important truths conveyed nonetheless.

The scene has changed very rapidly. Death has come. And Jesus takes us for a momentary look beyond death to see what takes place on the other side of the grave. He reminds us that the angels of God are vitally interested in the death of the righteous, and will surely welcome them home when the last call comes to depart this life. And, although heaven is not Abraham's bosom, Lazarus was a true child of Abraham. This now becomes clearly evident. Lazarus was taken home by the angels of heaven and laid to rest in the bosom of Abraham. Abraham is, after all, the father of *believers*. And, as the father of believers, he is also the father of Christ according to the flesh. And so, to be with Abraham is to be with Christ. It is to be covered with Christ's blood, to be clothed with Christ's holiness and righteousness, to be in the house of Christ forever and ever. And this is heaven indeed.

But let us look at the rest of the scene which Jesus opens before our eyes. The rich man awoke in hell—even while the funeral was still being conducted and the eulogies sung on earth. He found himself in a place of everlasting torment. Just as heaven is so glorious that it is beyond what can be seen with the eye or heard with the ear or conceived in the heart of man, so hell is something that cannot be adequately explained while we tarry here on earth. It is a definite place—that is beyond dispute. It is a place of unimaginable torment and suffering. It is total suffering where the fire is never quenched, where the worm never dies, where there is only weeping and gnashing of teeth. And there the rich man was. One can only gain a glimpse of the horror of his suffering. And that glimpse is enough to frighten.

And so it is that beyond the grave the problems and inequities of life are solved. Then it appears that he who was despised here on earth was nevertheless the beloved of God, and that his light afflictions which were but for a moment worked for him an exceedingly great weight of glory. Now it is clearly shown that he who appeared to be blessed here on earth was being put on slippery places and was coasting rapidly the way to destruction. Lazarus—once poor, now rich; once ill, now glorious; once wretched, now supremely happy; once clothed in rags, now wearing garments of white; once hungry, now eating of the tree of life. And all because his name was written on the pages of life and his sins were covered in the blood of the cross; he trusted in God to help him. The rich man —once rich, now poor; once gluttonous, now suffering; once a winebibber, now pleading for a drop of water that is denied him; once richly robed, now stripped naked of purple and linen. And all this because he sought himself and not God, because he trusted in his wealth and not in Christ, because he would not feed the fatherless or show mercy to the downtrodden. God is just indeed.

The Eternal of the Rich Man

The most horrible of all are the words that ring everlastingly in hell: "Son, remember. . . . "

Once again our Lord makes use of figurative language. We must not suppose that Jesus means to teach that hell is visible from heaven or that heaven is visible from hell. Nor is it true that there is always the possibility of conversation between the inhabitants of hell and the inhabitants of heaven. This is not the case. The figurative language is employed in harmony with the nature of the parable.

Nevertheless, once again an important truth is brought to our attention.

The request of Dives is only a further revelation of his wickedness, for it is a very evil request. Indeed, it accents the terrible suffering of hell: one drop! A fleeting moment of respite! That will make hell a little endurable! Even that is denied.

But the wickedness of the request is evident, in the first place, from the fact that Dives tries now to call Abraham his father. On earth, while outwardly boasting of "father Abraham," he refused to have the faith of Abraham. But now he will try to make Abraham his father. Second, he who had scorned Lazarus on earth would now try to make Lazarus his servant and to fetch for him a drop of water. Third, he who never knew of mercy and refused to acknowledge its existence in his selfishness, now begs for mercy from the depth of his punishment.

But the answer comes ringing throughout hell: "Son, remember. . . !"

It should not surprise us that Abraham calls him "son." This is exactly what the rich man had always claimed to be. In this way he is reminded of his life on earth. Was he not indeed a son of Abraham? And does not that mean that he had Moses and the prophets? Does not his very sonship imply that he possessed the oracles of God? that he knew all about the demands of the law and the prophets to feed the fatherless and beggars? to show mercy and walk humbly with God? Indeed it did. But he would not. Let him then remember that he knew better and that therefore his judgment is just. For he had possessed all that life could give. Everything he had asked for, he had received. Everything his heart desired had been given to him. But he had not shared them except for a few crumbs. He had been merciless and cruel. He had oppressed the poor and closed his ears to their sobbing cries. He had ignored their outstretched hands and had not given a cup of water in Jesus' Name.

"Son, remember. . . . " That is hell. It is the memory of life. It is the everlasting remorse of wasted hours and evil days. It is to see in the fires of hell the faces of the poor reflected who cry to him for mercy. But it is to see in the heights of heaven the blessedness which is the portion of those hated on earth.

But this is also the justice of Almighty God. And this sense of justice in hell in indelibly impressed on the consciousness of the wicked. Even in the parable, Dives knew that what he received was justly his. There are some—and I suppose always will be some—who complain that the suffering of the rich man is far greater than he really deserved. But he himself knew better. He dared not complain. And when even his request is refused because no mercy overflows into hell, he knows that this is his just recompense of reward. And though it be forever, his cry is stopped in the agonizing knowledge that all that he suffers is coming to him from God Who punishes sin in wrath and justice. The chasm is fixed. There is no bridge to cross. Eternity is separation. This is justice.

And so it shall be to all who make mammon their god, who serve the idol of their belly, who oppress the poor and suffering.

But for the righteous there is everlasting comfort. This comfort is not rooted in the fact that they have been in this life better than the wicked. They have not earned their way to heaven. Nor is there comfort merely in the fact that they were poor. There are countless poor who never come to Abraham's bosom. But those who come are all named "Lazarus," "he whom God helps." And this means that they are the ones for whom Christ died. They are the purchased with Christ's blood because their names are written on the pages of the book of life. They are those who have fled for refuge to the cross of Christ. They have waited for their God and trusted in Him. And when oppression came and they were ground under the heel of their tormentors, they knew that they suffered for Jesus' sake. They knew that some day their cry would be answered and their cause vindicated. They are surely saved to the end. For truly the day will come that God will justify their cause, punish their tormentors, make all things right—even that which was crooked in this life—and take them home at last into the bosom of Abraham where they shall be comforted forever.

20

The Sufficiency of the Gospel

Then he said, I pray thee therefore, father, that thou wouldest send
him to my father's house:
For I have five brethren; that he may testify unto them, lest they also
come into this place of torment.
Abraham saith unto him, They have Moses and the prophets; let them
hear them.
And he said, Nay, father Abraham: but if one went unto them from
the dead, they will repent.
And he said unto him, If they hear not Moses and the prophets,
neither will they be persuaded, though one rose from the dead.
—Luke 16:27-31

Although this text forms the conclusion of the parable of the rich
man and Lazarus, it deals essentially with a different question. The
parable opened here on earth. There we found the rich man who
was upright in all his walk as far as the outward demands of the law
were concerned but was was inwardly covetous and a servant of
mammon. This inward sin became evident in his scorn for Lazarus,
the poor beggar thrown at his gate. The scene soon changed to
eternity where the rich man is seen lifting up his eyes from hell to
behold Lazarus in Abraham's bosom. Then the point was made that
both the blessedness of Lazarus and the torment of the rich man
were illustrations of the justice of God Who gives to every man as his
works are, Who never judges outward appearance, but Who knows
the heart.

While the first request of the rich man was denied him, he has one
other request to make of "father Abraham." Again, we do well to be
reminded of the fact that in reality there is no possiblity of discussion
between those in heaven and those on earth. The saved and the
damned cannot be in contact with each other, for the blessed rest of
the righteous is forever undisturbed, and the torment of the wicked
is everlastingly uninterrupted. But Jesus is speaking a parable. And

through this request of the rich man a very important truth of Scripture is emphasized.

This important truth is made over against objections that are still raised today against the preaching of the gospel. Although it takes on many forms, the objection basically is that the gospel is really not enough to accomplish the purpose of God and bring about salvation. More is required. If only God would somehow give a special sign from heaven or do something highly unusual, then the wicked would be brought to repentance. Over against this objection, the parable emphatically makes the point that the gospel is sufficient to accomplish all the good pleasure of God, for it is the power of God unto salvation. In that gospel alone, therefore, we must put our trust.

A Seemingly Good Request

At first glance, it might appear as if the request of this rich man was a good request that we should not condemn.

It is important to notice that these brothers evidently lived the same kind of a life as their rich brother who was now in hell. They too were natural children of Abraham who were brought up in the sphere of the covenant. They too were undoubtedly wealthy, highly esteemed by men and praised for their deeds. They received the plaudits of their fellow Jews for their faithful observance of the law and their strict adherence to the precepts of Moses. But within their wicked hearts they also were vain and arrogant, hypocritical and self-righteous, afflicters of the poor and despisers of the humble. Their sin was, no less than their brothers, the sin of covetousness and service of mammon. They were men who made their bellies their gods.

Besides, their lives were closely intertwined with the life of their departed brother. They evidently knew of Lazarus who had been laid at the gate. The request of the rich man in hell seems to presuppose that when Lazarus would return, they would recognize him. They knew the kind of life their brother had lived, and enjoyed that life themselves. They rested in the false and carnal security that their brother had gone on to glory and that they would surely follow.

The request of the rich man seems to be filled with genuine concern for his brothers' well-being. He seems to have accepted his own lot. He does not deny the justice of his being in hell; nor does he trouble Abraham further about a drop of water, once that request was denied. His thoughts seem now to have turned to his brothers. And he seems to want to spare them the fate that has come on him. He sees that they will surely come to hell where he is because they lived the same kind of life that he lived. He does not want them in hell but in heaven if at all possible. He therefore considers the possibility of doing something to warn them of the consequences of their life so that they will repent. The way to do this, he is convinced is to send Lazarus back to them to tell them what lies beyond the grave both in heaven and in hell. He is sure that, should this be done, they will repent of their sins and escape the torment of everlasting fire.

But if we adopt such an interpretation of the request of the rich man, we will also be forced to adopt the conclusion. That conclusion is then that there is good even in hell. Evidently, the fire of hell has a purifying effect. The torments of hell purge a man of sin and bring about in him a degree of holiness. These torments set about correcting a man's faults so that, granted a long enough stay in hell, a man will become good. But this position is impossible to maintain. The wicked in hell are eternally wicked. There is no good in hell. It is true, of course, that in the suffering of everlasting desolation there is no more opportunity to do evil because the hands of the wicked are tied and their mouths are stopped and they are totally absorbed in their dreadful punishment. But this does not mean that they become capable of doing any good. Indeed, if the fires of hell purified the wicked, eventually they would become righteous and reach a point where they would at last be delivered from their just punishment.

The Wickedness of the Rich Man's Request

Rather, if we closely examine this request of Dives, we will be forced to the conclusion that it is very wicked. On the one hand, it was a very selfish request. It was not a feeling of pity for these five brothers that motivated his request; it was a purely selfish concern for himself. This will become evident if we consider the real character of hell. The rich man was himself partly responsible for the wicked walk of his brethren. By his own life he had given them a bad example. He had never condemned their sin, but had rather encouraged their selfishness and covetousness by his own deeds. He had ignored and mocked the poor beggar at his gate in their presence, and suggested that they do likewise. We often quote the familiar proverb, "Misery likes company"; but in hell this is far from true. The presence of his brethren would only have increased his torture. He would have intensified his agony because it would have reminded him of his faithlessness and of his failure to fulfill his responsibilities by pointing out to them the true calling of the law of God. Their presence would have made the fires of hell hotter, the bitter remorse more dreadful, the horror of God's justice more deeply cutting.

This presupposes that beyond the grave we will recognize those we knew on earth. While this is sometimes questioned, it is undoubtedly true nonetheless. The old relationships of husband and wife, parents and children, friend and friend will be no more; for all relationships of this earth will be destroyed. But the memory of them will undoubtedly linger. In heaven this will add to heaven's blessedness. The Church, gathered in the line of generations, will be the organic Church in glory. The believers will be there with their elect children. But this same truth will add to the agonies of hell.

Those whom the wicked have led in evil paths will face them in the fires of destruction. Their accusing voices will rise above the gnashing of teeth. The communal responsibilities of the wicked will make hell even more desolate. From this the rich man was trying to escape.

But that is not all. On the other hand, his request was really a very sly and subtle accusation of God and a very covert attempt at self-justification. He is apologing to Abraham for his brethren. He is saying in effect that his brethren walk the way they do because they have not been sufficiently warned. There is more that could be done for them. And if this more is done for them, they will surely repent. He is more concerned about his brothers than he is about God's justice. He is seemingly more merciful than God is. He is more aware of what his brothers need than God is. And he complains bitterly, but subtly, that God is not doing enough.

But if this is true of his brothers, it is also true of him. He means to say that he did not receive sufficient warning of what his lot was to be. He was not given enough information about the life to come and about his calling in the world to persuade him to forsake his evil way. There are, he says, additional factors that must be taken into consideration when judgment is meted out. There were circumstances in his life beyond his control—circumstances that were forced on him that make his present punishment unjust. God is really to blame because He did not tell him the right way to walk and the terrible consequences of the wrong way. He really ought to be excused, for the fault is not his.

This excuse of the rich man is really not so foreign and is often found even in the Church. When children of the covenant go astray and become delinquent, they are easily persuaded to blame others. They blame their parents who were either too strict or not strict enough. They blame others for doing the things they do and leading them in evil paths. Wayward husbands blame their wives; wayward wives blame their husbands. And oftentimes the Church is blamed. It is said that the preaching is over their heads; it is either too doctrinal or too practical. It is dry and hard to understand and does not hold their interest. It is not their idea of what good preaching ought to be. Or, perhaps, the Church is too small, is too filled with bickering, is not socially minded enough, and the people are not friendly enough. Everyone is to blame but themselves. They only are justified in their conduct. And all these excuses are so many echoes of Adam and Eve in Paradise: "The woman thou gavest me." "The serpent tempted me and I did eat." But, indirectly, the blame is always brought to the feet of God.

Such is the wicked request of the rich man from the depth of his suffering in hell.

The Justice of Abraham's Refusal

Abraham's answer is short and to the point: "They have Moses and the prophets; let them hear them."

As short as this answer may be, it is nevertheless very important. By speaking of Moses and the prophets, Abraham refers to the Old Testament Scriptures. This was the common way of referring to the Old Testament in Jesus' day. The Church of the Old Dispensation had the Word of God as well as the Church of today. This was their Bible as well as it is ours. In these Old Testament Scriptures the law and the promise were revealed. But both the law and the promise pointed ahead to Christ Who was the fulfillment of all the Scriptures. All the sacrifices and ceremonies of the law, as well as all the words of the prophets, were but arrows that pointed ahead to the coming of Christ, the seed of the promise, the redemption of Israel. Moses and the prophets were servants of God who wrote under divine and infallible inspiration. They recorded the words of God Who revealed the salvation He had prepared for His people. Even though this revelation was clothed in types and shadows, it nevertheless clearly pointed to the Christ Who was to come. Through this Word Abraham saw the day of Christ and rejoiced. Because of this Word there were the heroes of faith who died not having received the promises, but having seen them afar off were persuaded of them. They sought a city whose builder and maker is God (see Heb. 11:13-16).

This same Scripture was also the possession of the rich man and his brothers, for they too were brought up in the generations of the covenant. In this Scripture which they possessed, the way of salvation was clearly defined. Christ is that way. And by repentance and faith in Christ God's people are brought to their everlasting salvation.

This implies two fundamental truths—truths that still are in effect today. In the first place, we cannot emphasize strongly enough that God binds Himself to the use of means. Even as the body has need of food for its life, even so—and more—does the soul need heavenly bread for its life. These means, as appointed by God, are the means of His Word. He binds Himself to their use. With the sacraments, they are the way in which God saves His people.

In the second place, these are the only means. It is true that all things are means of grace to God's elect. Indeed, Scripture teaches that all things work together for our good. God uses even suffering and trial to work for the good of His saints. But all these things are always subservient to His Word. It is by His Word that suffering is sanctified to the hearts of the faithful. It is by His Word that affliction and sorrow are made to serve the good of those who are called according to God's purpose. And all this is true because Christ works through His Word to bring His people to conscious faith and salvation. Through the operation of the Spirit that Word is implanted in the hearts of the elect. And by that Word and Spirit the people of God are saved.

And this Word is preached to all to whom God in His good pleasure sends the gospel. Through that preaching of the gospel all men are brought to know that the way of salvation is the way of the cross of Christ, and thus, the way of faith and repentance. On this point the gospel is very clear. There can be no mistake about it. This is the God-ordained way and there is no other way than this. All men are placed before the solemn obligation to turn from their evil way, forsake their own works, and repent of their own deeds. All men are told that Christ is the way and the truth and the life. Faith in Him is the road of salvation. The consequence of ignoring this is always hell. Destruction awaits the rebellious and impenitent. Desolation is the lot of the unbelieving. This is God's solemn word. There is no mistaking it. It is clearly spoken.

But this the rich man denies. "No, father Abraham," he says. He wants something more than the Word of God. He is not satisfied with the God-ordained way. It, in his opinion, is not sufficient. It is not enough to warn and rebuke and save.

He wants Lazarus to return from the dead and witness to his five brothers. He knows that they will remember Lazarus. And if Lazarus would return from the dead and witness of heaven and hell as he has seen them himself, if Lazarus would speak of the consequences of sin and the reward of the righteous as an eye-witness —this, the rich man is convinced, will be enough to bring his brothers to repentance.

In other words, he wants something unusual and startling. He wants something spectacular. God's ordained way is not enough. A voice must come from heaven. An apparition must appear and tell of what he has seen beyond the grave. That is far better than the means which God has determined.

And this request of the rich man is, after all, not so strange. Already the Jews in Jesus' day asked for a sign in proof of the claim that Jesus was the Christ. This perpetual clamoring after a sign continued throughout the life of the Lord. And when at last they nailed Him to the cross, they stood at the foot of it, taunting and reviling: "Come down from the cross if thou be the Christ; then we will believe on thee."

It is this way still today. Men ask for something startling and drastic to happen in the hopes that that will convert the impenitent. They do not think the Word of God is enough. It is too dry and there is no power behind it. It is too inclined to make men careless and profane.

This lack of trust in the Word takes on many different forms. Sometimes it leads men to seek for the assurance of their salvation outside the Word of God in some unusual experience in their lives. And if this unusual experience does not come, then God has not given it to them and they must wait for their assurance until this happens. Then again, men who become dissatisfied with the Word try to alter its contents in the form of the preaching of the Word to bring about more spectacular results. This often happens especially in connection with missionary or evangelistic work. Those who bring the gospel to the unconverted are not happy because in their estimation insufficient converts are made. They quickly blame the Word for this. And the result is that the sharp truths of the Word are toned down and the distinctive doctrines of the Scriptures are altered in the hopes that a watered down gospel will be more appealing to men. Or they substitute for the preaching alterations in liturgy and entertaining programs in the hopes that these will fill the empty pews in today's churches. Sometimes, dissatisfied with the power of the gospel, they seek assurance for the truth of the gospel in unusual happenings. This is particularly characteristic of neo-pentecostalism. It is still the age-old clamoring for a sign. But the clamoring for a sign is rooted in discontent with the Word of God. And so, in their rebellious superstitions, they seek the help of means which God has not ordained. They seek the dramatic and unusual. The Word of God is not enough. A wicked and faithless generation seeketh after a sign. Send Lazarus from the dead. Then we will repent. But there shall no sign be given them. . . .

The Sufficiency of the Gospel

But Abraham's answer is: "The gospel is enough. If they will not believe Moses and the prophets, they will not be persuaded though one should rise from the dead."

There is an interesting and important difference between the request of the rich man and the answer of Abraham. The rich man asks: "Send Lazarus; then they will *repent;* then they will be converted." But Abraham uses a different word in his answer. He says: "Even if one should arise from the dead, they will not be *persuaded.*" The point is that, while the rich man speaks of conversion, Abraham speaks of being persuaded. And the point is that conversion is after all rooted in regeneration. Except a man be born again he cannot even *see* the kingdom of God (see John 3:3). Regeneration is the work of God by which the heart of man is renewed so that his mind is enlightened to see heavenly things, his will is renewed so that instead of being hard and rebellious, it is made soft and pliable; his eyes and ears are opened to see and hear heavenly things. There is no conversion without regeneration. And regeneration is the work of God.

This is a fundamental point. The gospel, the God-ordained way, is always enough. God's Word is sufficient. In God's Word, God speaks of Himself and of His work of salvation. Who can speak better of this or more authoritatively concerning this than God Himself? Can Lazarus? How is that possible? Only God can speak concerning Himself. Only God can speak of the salvation He prepared for His people. And of this, God speaks in His Word. If men will not believe this Word, then they will not believe anything. And if they will not receive this Word, then they will not receive a special sign, a voice from heaven, an apparition which rises from the dead.

But even this in turn is because God always accomplishes all His purpose through the gospel. The gospel is, after all, the *power* of God unto salvation. It surely saves His people. Of this there can be no doubt. But the opposite is also true. The gospel is two-edged. Indeed, through the gospel God places all men before the command to repent and believe. But this same gospel to repent and believe is the sovereignly ordained means in the hand of a sovereign God not only to save the elect from their sins but also to harden the wicked in their sins.

This fact history conclusively proves. Unbelief always will and only can reject the Word of God. So it was already in Jesus' day. John the Baptist came neither eating nor drinking, and the wicked Jews condemned him for this and would not believe him nor repent. Jesus came both eating and drinking; but they would not believe Him either and condemned Him and called Him a gluttonous man and a winebibber, a friend of publicans and sinners. They ask for a sign, but they would not believe the sign of Jonah the prophet. They saw all Jesus' mighty miracles, beautiful signs of the power of the gospel; but they explained them away and claimed that He cast out devils by Beelzebub the prince of the devils. The rich man said he would repent if Lazarus would come forth from the grave; but another Lazarus did come forth from the grave, and they made plans to kill Christ. They wanted someone to rise from the dead; but when the Prince of Glory burst forth from Joseph's grave on resurrection morning, they explained it away and said the disciples stole the body.

And so it is also in our day. Never while the world lasts will men devoid of faith believe God's Word. And because they will not believe God's Word they will not believe any signs that would be given them. They shout and clamor for signs while the signs are all about them. But the signs that are about them they will not see, for they are rebellious and hard of heart. It is not the fault of the gospel or of Christ Who is preached in the gospel that they will not believe. The fault lies with them. They are wicked and obdurate. They are evil and perverse. And even when God sovereignly accomplishes His own purpose through the preaching of the gospel, they are at fault, for they hate God's Word. No, the rich man cannot have what he asks. Nor can the wicked have what they ask. The gospel is enough.

This we must remember. Faith always believes. This is the power of faith which God gives. It believes the Word of God. It believes Moses and the prophets and hears them. It believes God in Christ. It believes the impossible. It believes that God saves His people through the blood of the cross. It believes in such a way that faith brings about repentance and sorrow for sin. It believes that Christ will come again to punish the wicked and take His Church to glory. It believes because God says so. That is enough.

Hence the implied admonition of the text is: trust the gospel. Do no doubt but that it will always accomplish the purpose of God. It is sufficient. We need not add to it. We must not add to it. God will, through the gospel, perfect the good work He has begun.

21
An Incentive Not to Faint

And he spake a parable unto them to this end, that men ought always to pray, and not to faint;
Saying, There was in a city a judge, which feared not God, neither regarded man:
And there was a widow in that city; and she came unto him, saying, Avenge me of mine adversary.
And he would not for a while: but afterward he said within himself, Though I fear not God, nor regard man;
Yet because this widow troubleth me, I will avenge her, lest by her continual coming she weary me.
And the Lord said, Hear what the unjust judge saith.
And shall not God avenge his own elect, which cry day and night unto him, though he bear long with them?
I tell you that he will avenge them speedily. Nevertheless when the Son of man cometh, shall he find faith on the earth?
　　　　　　　　　　　　　　　　　　　　　　—Luke 18:1-8

It is quite probable that this parable was spoken by the Lord in the latter part of His Perean ministry. From the time of the transfiguration, Jesus had set His face steadfastly toward Jerusalem in the consciousness that soon He would face the cross. As the suffering of the cross neared, the Lord's thoughts turned more and more to the climax of His ministry and His atoning death. Along with these thoughts of His death, the Lord's attention also turned to two events which were intimately connected with His cross: the final destruction of Jerusalem and the end of the world. We find, therefore, that the Lord's instruction turned more and more to those truths which were connected with His ascension into heaven and His return again on the clouds of heaven at the end of time. He utilized the days that remained in His earthly ministry to instruct His disciples concerning these things and to urge them to watch unto prayer. This instruction we find in the context of the parable we discuss in this chapter. It is with this truth in mind that the Lord uses this present parable to encourage His disciples and His Church never to grow weary in the battle and to persevere in the prayer: "Come, Lord Jesus; yea, come quickly." Hence the purpose is described by Luke in this way: "And he spake a parable unto them to this end, that men ought always to pray, and not to faint."

The parable speaks of the relationship between God and His people in the midst of the world. On the one hand, it speaks of this relationship by way of comparison. In the parable, the widow is God's Church militant; the widow's adversary is the wicked world with the devil at its head. The widow's request is a picture of the prayers of the Church. The delay which the widow experienced is God's long-suffering. And the final sentence of the judge when justice is meted out is God's final deliverance of His people.

But on the other hand, there is also a contrast in the parable. God's relationship to His people is contrasted to that of the judge's attitude toward the widow who came to him for help. The judge feared not God nor regarded man. He was very wicked, and only finally helped the widow out of the basest of motives. But the Lord loves both Himself and His Church, and delivers them at last. He delivers them out of the purest of motives. Thus the parable means to say: If even the judge finally helps the widow though he be wicked and though he does it for wicked reasons, *how much more* is it not true that God will surely hear the cries of His people and deliver them; for He is holy and just and good.

The Comparisons of the Parable

As I have said, the widow in the parable is a picture of the Church of Christ in the midst of the world. She is deprived of her natural protector and provider and is thrown upon her own weak resources. She, in her loneliness and grief, is required to make her own way in a hostile world with the little strength that she can muster and with the limited means at her disposal. This is a picture of the Church. Jesus Christ is the husband of the Church. But He has gone to heaven and has left His Church alone in the world. It is true that Scripture often speaks of the fact that Christ is present with His Church. He promised His disciples and His Church before His ascension: "Lo, I am with you always, even unto the end of the world." And on the eve of His passion He told His disciples: "I will not leave you comfortless: I will come to you" (John 14:18). It is also true that Scripture tells us that the Church is the bride of Christ who will be brought to her Bridegroom when He comes again at the end of time. Nevertheless, this does not alter the fact that while Christ is in heaven and His people are on earth, the Church resembles a widow. She lives apart from her husband in the midst of hostile men. She is of herself weak and helpless, seemingly easy prey to all who would take advantage of her.

The widow had an adversary, as does also the Church. The law of Moses spoke emphatically of the care that must be bestowed on widows so that they would never be deprived of the necessities of life. But there were in Israel—and are always in the world—base fellows who will, through subtlety and cunning, take advantage of the helpless condition of a widow and seek to enrich themselves at her expense. This widow also had an adversary who was determined to destroy her by taking away from her what was rightfully hers. She had a just cause, and her enemy was determined unjustly to make her possessions his own.

The adversary of the Church is the world of wicked men with the devil at its head. The adversary lives in the same city as the widow. This evidently indicates that the most terrible adversary of the Church lives, not in the faraway lands of heathendom, but within the Church visible. The enemies of the Church who constitute the gravest threat to her welfare are not the enemies without, but the enemies within. The world attempts to take from the Church all that is dear to her. The world seeks the destruction of the Church, for this is the unalterable goal of Satan. To gain this end the wicked try to take away the ministry, the pulpit, the Christian schools, the truth which the Church confesses. They try to do this sometimes with flattery and subtle attempts to persuade the Church to discard her heritage and to compromise her principles with the world. But then again they try to do this by ripping off their masks of friendship and showing their deep-seated hatred for the cause of God. They threaten the Church with contempt and ostracism. They take from the saints their means of livelihood. They come with the sword and shed the blood of those who are not moved by their seductive words. It is always the wicked who attempt to take from the Church her heritage and rob the Church of her dearest possessions. They do this that they may corrupt these precious treasures and prostitute them in the service of sin.

The adversary is very strong. The wicked are great in numbers and in strength. If their forces were marshaled against the saints, they could overrun the Church in a moment. They have power and sheer weight of size on their side. Besides this, they have far more influence than the Church has. They control the means of communication and propaganda, and all news media are in their hands. They are in a position to influence the minds of men. In contrast to this, the Church is, comparatively speaking, very weak and helpless; and its influence is very small.

In the second place, the judge in the parable is, by way of contrast, a picture of our Holy God.

The judge was a very evil man. He feared not God and cared not for God's law nor for truth and justice. He scorned his calling to punish evildoers and to reward the just. He mocked at the thought that he would have to render an account of all that he did before the face of the Most High. Nor did he regard men. He cared for no man's welfare. He ignored justice and popular opinion. He went his own way and sought only what was good for him and did only what would advance his own purposes.

Yet he was the only hope of the widow. She had no one else to whom to turn in her need. She had to have justice from his hand or she would die when her adversary gained his ends.

God is also Judge. He, too, is the only help of His people. They also have no one else to whom they can turn in their need. They are hated by their adversaries and despised by the world. They are killed all the day long and deprived of their rights. They are vastly outnumbered and in imminent danger of being swallowed up. They have only their God to whom they can turn. He must help them or they will surely perish. He is their only hope, their only refuge, their only source of strength and deliverance.

But God is the absolutely righteous and just Judge. He loves Himself and seeks His own glory and honor. He regards His people, for His own sake, with mercy and love and compassion. He will always do what is right and just. As wicked as the earthly judge was, so, by way of contrast, God is holy. In Him is no evil, no darkness, no shadow of turning. He is righteous in all His works and ways. He will render just and righteous judgment.

The Contents of the Prayers of the Church

Accordingly, the saints come to God in prayer. In the light of all this, their prayer can be no other than that God will deliver them from all their adversaries.

This is not to say that this is the only petition which the Church brings to God in prayer. Indeed, all her needs must constantly be brought to the throne of grace. But the parable takes the viewpoint of a very basic and fundamental need of the Church. All her other needs are, in a sense, subservient to this one. She must ask for her daily bread; but this petition is necessary only while the Church tarries in the world. She must seek the forgiveness of sins; but when her final deliverance is accomplished, even this need will vanish away. Basically, the Church, and each individual saint, prays for deliverance from her adversary.

This implies several things. In the first place, the Church prays for the public and final vindication of her cause. She is mocked in the world because the world scorns her cause and speaks of her cause as being evil and foolish and out of date and old-fashioned. In her consciousness of the fact that her cause is ridiculed and that almost all men mock her, she longs for the public testimony that her cause, in distinction from that of the world, is a cause which is just and righteous.

In the second place, the Church prays for protection from all her enemies. It is very easy for the wicked to swallow her up. It is very easy for her to lose completely her place in the world. The wicked are ever attempting to rob her of her place and to destroy her witness. So she prays, in the consciousness of her helplessness and need, that the Lord will protect her and preserve her cause.

In the third place, she prays for the restoration of what is rightfully hers. The wicked take these things away from her, and are seemingly eminently successful in accomplishing their evil goals. It has been this way throughout all history. The pulpit and the ministry belong to the Church. But already in the Old Dispensation wicked men corrupted the priesthood, sat on David's throne, and brought prophecies which were not the Word of God. It has been this was throughout all time. The Christian schools belong to the people of God. But so often the wicked succeed in taking them away from the Church and subverting them to their own evil purposes. These schools, established by Christian parents for the education of covenant seed, become institutions of evil and false religion. They become forums for heresy and corruptions of the truth. This happens to everything that belongs to the Church. Repeatedly the Church is robbed of what is hers. And again and again she is required, through the way of Church reformation, to abandon what she has erected and to begin all over to build her churches and her schools and to reestablish the Christian ministry which is faithful to the Scriptures.

In the fourth place, the Church longs for just punishment on her adversaries. It is not enough that what is rightfully hers is restored. Justice requires that the wicked be punished for their horrible crimes. The blood of the martyrs cries out for vengeance. The slain of Jehovah plead for justice to be accomplished in the punishment of their adversaries.

All of these things are really implied in the one prayer for the speedy return of the Lord. The prayer of the saints is after all: "Come, Lord Jesus; yea, come quickly." The saints long for deliverance. The Church longs to be delivered from her widowhood. The Church longs for the time when the crooked shall be made straight, when the injustice of men shall be righted. And the Church knows that this shall happen only when her Lord Jesus Christ returns in power and in glory.

The Basis for Her Prayer

You may well ask, On what basis do the saints make this prayer? This was a question already in the parable. The widow was pleading for what was right and just. She knew that justice demanded that the judge help her. The Church also prays for what is right and just. But the fact remains that really the saints do not deserve to be delivered. They are themselves weak and sinful, and they daily forfeit all right to God's love and favor. They do not for a moment harbor the thought that they have merited that for which they ask.

The answer to this problem is that the Church pleads for the cause of Christ. Her cause in the midst of the world is not really her own, but is the cause of Jesus Christ her Lord. Christ came also into this world and died on the cross. He made the cause of God His cause by His suffering and death. And He calls His people to represent His cause and to maintain that cause no matter what may be the cost. Thus the saints pray for a cause which is not theirs only, but which is also the cause of Christ and of God. They pray that righteousness may be done, but it is the righteousness of the cross of Calvary and of the kingdom of heaven that the saints want to triumph. The people of God pray for justice, but this justice is the justice of the cross of Christ. In other words, they pray for the final vindication of God's name, God's honor, God's glory, God's majesty—all of which was revealed on Calvary and which will be realized in the kingdom of heaven. This is the basis on which they, undeserving sinners, can ask for all these things.

The Need for Incentive to Pray

Jesus admonishes the Church never to grow weary in prayer. Men ought always to pray and never to faint. The need for this admonition is very great and there are many reasons for this.

One reason surely why this admonition is necessary is because of the weakness of the Church herself. The longing of the Church for the return of Christ is not always the urgent prayer in her consciousness that it ought to be. Sometimes the people of God grow lax in their prayers. They do not always see the need for vengeance on the wicked who have shed the blood of the righteous. Especially in this age of "tolerance," the prayer for vengeance seems so out of keeping with the spirit of the times. The saints do not always long earnestly for the return of Christ. This is because they do not live always in the clear consciousness of their widowhood. Then again, the prayer dies on their lips; not because the world has ceased her attacks, or even because the Church is unusually strong spiritually; but especially in times of peace and economic prosperity, the Church becomes spiritually lethargic and doctrinally sleepy. The Church no longer seeks the return of her husband, but seeks instead a lover in the world. And so she is ready to sacrifice her principles and compromise her heritage for the sake of peace. When a spirit of indifference and lethargy seizes the Church, she grows faint in her prayers for deliverance.

In the second place, the Lord admonishes us to be sure that we do not become weary because we are often afraid of the enemy. This is really no wonder. We know that the enemy is very strong and has great influence. We know that, in comparision with the might of the wicked, the Church is few in number and is lacking in power. We know that Scripture even admonishes the saints that they may not fight back, that they must put their sword back into its sheath, and that they must live lives of quietness and peace which are free from a spirit of revenge. The saints are also aware that the world can do many things to the Church, for they have read of the horrors which appear on the blood-stained pages of history. And they know that the worst is yet to come. No wonder then that they grow fearful and sometimes question whether it is worth it all. They lose courage and grow weary in prayer.

In the third place, the admonition is necessary because the Lord does not seem to answer. This is particularly the point of the parable. The evil judge would not hear the pleadings of the oppressed widow, but turned a deaf ear to her cries. He did not want to be bothered by her. He did not care what happened to her. She came again and again with her anxious pleadings, but it made no difference. It appears this way often to the people of God. They cry loud and long to their Father in heaven. They are described by the Lord as those who cry night and day for deliverance. But often heaven seems closed and the Lord does not come. The wicked continue to oppress and oppose the saints while the Lord tarries. Waters of a full cup are wrung from the saints. They are killed all the day long. Their righteous Judge does not seem to hear their anxious cries. In fact, added to their prayers are the prayers even of the souls under the altar, the saints made perfect: "How long, O Lord, holy and true, dost thou not judge and avenge our blood on them that dwell on the earth?" (Rev. 6:10). But still history pursues its relentless course and the wicked prosper in their way.

All of this might cause the saints to grow weary in prayer. And so the admonition is very urgent. This urgency is further emphasized by a solemn warning of the Lord, with which He concludes His parable: "Nevertheless when the Son of man cometh, shall he find faith on the earth?" In a certain sense, the answer to this question is: "No, He will not." The point is that there will be yet greater apostasy. There will be many who at one time seemed to pray for Christ's return, but now pray no longer. There will be many who seemed to fight in the battle, but who have laid down their weapons and joined the enemy. This great apostasy will increase as time goes on, until the end when indeed there will not be faith left on the earth.

But in another sense, the answer is: "Yes, there always will be faith." There will always be a Noah, and Elijah, a saint here or there who will stand faithfully. But even then, their faith will be silenced so that it will no longer publicly be heard. The meaning of the Lord is, therefore, on the one hand, be warned of the fact that things will get a lot worse than they are now. In fact, so bad will they become that if the days were not shortened, the very elect would perish. And so, on the other hand, we must watch and continue to persevere in prayer.

How important then does this admonition become!

The widow could easily have been discouraged. She came to a very evil judge and he would not hear her. She could just as well have resigned herself to her fate and permitted her adversary to take from her what was rightfully hers. But she did not. She continued to come to him. Though he ignored her, turned coldly away from her, scorned her pleas, she continued to come; for he was her only hope. So also we are urged never to grow weary in the battle. We must not give up praying even though everything seems against us. We must always stand, fight to the last ditch with unswerving patience and loyalty for what we know is right; for it is the cause of Christ our Lord.

In order to do this we must always pray. Jesus does not mean that we must forget our work and our calling in life in order to assume a formal attitude of prayer. It is not the calling of the saints to spend all their time on their knees. This is impossible. But it does mean, in the first place, that we must pray in every circumstance of life. No matter what our way may be or what the circumstances may be in which the Lord places us, we must pray for the Lord's coming. As persecution becomes more severe and the troubles of the Church mount, the saints will be increasingly conscious of their need to pray this prayer. But this does not alter the fact that even in times of prosperity and comparative peace this prayer must arise from their hearts. In suffering or in well-being, in sickness or in health, in wealth or in poverty, in persecution or in prosperity, always the prayer of the saints must be: "Give us strength to be faithful in the battle. Come, Lord Jesus; yea, come quickly."

In the second place, this means that although the saints cannot continuously assume a formal attitude of prayer, they must nevertheless learn to pray without ceasing. They must be constantly aware of their needs and their utter dependence on God. They must never conceive of the possibility that they are strong enough of themselves to stand. They must know that they are weak and help-less. They must in their spiritual attitude, in all the deepest longing of their hearts, live in the consciousness that their only strength is in Christ. In the midst of their families, at their workbench, on the street; in the school, in the church, wherever the way may lead, they must walk with uplifted heads expecting their deliverance from Christ. And so they must assume a position of constant vigilance and watchfulness and seek untiringly the day of the Lord. In this way they pray without ceasing. "Men ought always to pray, and not to faint." This is the calling of the Church.

The Certainty of Our Prayers being Heard

The parable gives us the assurance that we may pray in the full consciousness that we will be heard.

God is contrasted with the judge in the parable. The latter was a very evil man. He finally listened to the widow's plea and did what was right and what she had all along demanded. But he frankly admitted that he did it only for the basest of motives. He admitted that he did not fear God or men, but this woman wearied him. The word which is translated "wearies" in the King James Version is a very expressive word. It means literally: "to give someone a black eye." And although this must not be taken literally, the point is that the judge at last granted the widow what she wanted because she was an intolerable annoyance to him. She drove him frantic with her pestering and clamoring. He could hope to have peace only if he got rid of her by doing what she wanted.

Similarly, the idea is that if even such a wicked judge will at last listen to the righteous claims of the widow whom he wanted to ignore, how much more will not God listen to the prayers of His people? Unlike the wicked judge, God is holy and just. He always does what is right; indeed, He can do nothing else. Will He not then hear their cries? Unlike this judge, God loves His people with a love that never falters nor swerves. How can He do anything but open His ears to their cries? Unlike the judge, God always acts out of the highest and purest motives. He does all things that are in harmony with His own counsel and purpose. And we know that it is His will to save His people.

This assurance, then, is based especially on two things. First, it is based on the fact that those who pray are, according to Jesus' words, the elect. In brief this means that God loves His people with an eternal and unchangeable love, a love that is so great that it can only be measured by the cross and the death of Christ. It means that God has predestinated His people with an eternal purpose and that He leads His people through this life to their everlasting destination. This counsel stands unchangeable. It will surely be accomplished.

Second, this assurance is based on the fact that God is long-suffering. The question still remains: why does God not immediately hear and answer the prayers of His people? This is not because He does not will to hear them, nor because He forgets their anxious cries. It is because He patiently bears with all their suffering and anguish even though their cries pierce His own heart and their suffering is His own. But He bears with all their cries because He knows, although we cannot see it, that this way of suffering and oppression is the best way to bring us to our salvation. It is through fire that we are purified and prepared for our home in glory. Suffering is necessary. It is the only way. It is indeed true that only through affliction can we inherit the kingdom (see Acts 14·22).

Thus Jesus assures us that God will answer us speedily. "Will not God avenge his own elect, which cry day and night unto him, though he bear long with them? I tell you that he will avenge them speedily."

God must accomplish all His purpose. This is essential. He will answer the prayers of His people and send His Son on the clouds of heaven as quickly as possible. Not only that, but the time is short. After all, the Lord is not slack concerning His promise as some men count slackness. But a day is with the Lord as a thousand years, and a thousand years as a day. And so the Lord is long-suffering toward His people, not willing that any of them should perish, but that all should be saved. Only in this way can the whole Church go to glory. We must remember this (see II Peter 3:8, 9). Our light afflictions are but for a moment. But the Lord works for us an eternal and an exceedingly great weight of glory.

When the end comes, then the crooked shall be made straight.

History shall be rewritten so that it may be evident that all things were done according to the counsel of God. The blood of the righteous shall be avenged. The cause of God's people shall be publicly declared as the cause of God and of Christ. And so again, we must never faint but always persevere in prayer.

22

Self-Righteousness and Its Condemnation

*And he spake this parable unto certain which trusted in themselves
that they were righteous, and despised others:*
*Two men went up into the temple to pray; the one a Pharisee, and the
other a publican.*
*The Pharisee stood and prayed thus with himself, God, I thank thee,
that I am not as other men are, extortioners, unjust, adulterers, or
even as this publican.*
I fast twice in the week, I give tithes of all that I possess.
*And the publican, standing afar off, would not lift up so much as his
eyes unto heaven, but smote upon his breast, saying, God be merciful
to me a sinner.*
*I tell you, this man went down to his house justified rather than the
other: for every one that exalteth himself shall be abased; and he that
humbleth himself shall be exalted.*

—Luke 18:9-15

The manifestation of sin in the life of man is always exactly the
opposite of what man's calling before God is. Man was created to
glorify God and to praise his Creator. When man sins he does the
opposite of this. He robs God of His glory and tries to make that
glory his own. He does this because at the root of all sin lies pride,
and in pride a man attempts to gain for himself what is rightfully
God's. The terribleness of sin is then precisely that man denies his
sin and makes himself greater than the God of heaven and earth.

Although this fundamental sin of man comes to many and varied
expressions throughout history, it had its own unique character in
the Pharisees of Jesus' day. Jesus characterizes these Pharisees in the
words of this text as those who put their confidence in themselves
and despise others. Their pride manifested itself in their opinion
that they could earn their salvation through keeping the law. From
this it followed that they despised others who did not keep the law.
These Pharisees represented the chief evil which characterized the
nation of Judah in the days of Christ's sojourn on earth. Judah after

the captivity never fell again into idolatry. Their years in Babylon cured them of this once and for all. Instead they fell into the sins of formalism and lip worship, the sin of pride in their own righteousness.

As the ministry of Jesus neared its end, His words in condemnation of this sin and these sinful men grew sharper. These men were the real enemies of Christ, the real opponents of God and of His works—these men who prided themselves in their own holiness and trusted in themselves that they were righteous. The words with which Jesus condemned them become ever more severe.

But this sin is present in the lives of all of us. Because pride lies at the root of all sin, the evil of which Jesus speaks in this parable is an evil that afflicts us all. It is against this sin that we must fight. And he who thinks he has succeeded in mastering this sin ought to heed the words of the apostle Paul: "Let him that standeth beware lest he fall."

Jesus speaks His words of condemnation in this parable by way of contrast. The contrast is between the self-righteous Pharisee and the sin-stricken publican. The publicans were the most despised people in Jesus' day, hated perhaps more than any other group in Israel. Yet the publican is justified, while the Pharisee is condemned. The point is not that the publican is a better man. Both were equal in the sight of God despite their personal opinion of themselves. The differences lay in their prayers, and in the state of heart and mind which their prayers revealed. The Pharisee denied what was true —that he was a sinner; the publican confessed it. And Jesus means to say, therefore, that even a Pharisee can be condemned, while even a publican can be saved.

A Difference in Attitude

There was not simply a difference in the prayers of these two men, there was a difference in their attitudes.

The Pharisee was a member of a sect which had been founded sometime during the four-hundred-year period between Malachi and John the Baptist. The members of this sect, as their name indicates, separated themselves from the nation of Judah. Judah, during this period, had fallen into laxity of morals, into worldliness and spiritual indifference. The nation had come more and more under the influence of Hellenism while the distinctive spiritual and national traits of the people had gradually disappeared. The Pharisees lifted a protest against this and made an attempt to preserve the nation from spiritual ruin. But, over the years, the Pharisees had fallen into the doctrine of work righteousness: a man could become righteous through the works of the law and be saved from sin by strict adherence to the legislation of Moses. The result was that they began to pay rigid attention to the outward precepts of the law while they cut out the heart of the law. Their lives began to conform to their teaching, as life always does. The result was that they claimed to be able to keep the law, and therefore they claimed to be the only heirs of salvation and of God's promises. Since they had accomplished this themselves, they became proud and haughty.

The Pharisees as a sect were personified in this Pharisee who went up to the temple to pray. It was probably the time for prayer—either the third or the ninth hour of the day. Many people made their way to the temple at this time to lift up their hearts in prayer to God. Among them was this particular Pharisee. His dress, his bearing, his appearance, his actions were all calculated to attract the attention of the people. He walked solemnly and with a pious air into the temple where the people gathered. In the temple he went immediately to the very altar itself which stood in the court and moved confidently into God's presence. Before the altar he raised his eyes and his hands toward heaven where God dwelt to bring his prayers to the Most High.

Even as the Pharisees were most esteemed among the people, the publicans were the most despised. The Romans, conquerors of Palestine and all the known world, were dependent on the taxes they collected in the provinces. They appointed certain chief tax collectors who were responsible for certain districts. Zacchaeus, who is mentioned in Luke 19:1-10, was an example of one of these chief tax collectors. These men in turn hired others to do the actual collecting. The Jews hated the publicans with a passion. And it must be admitted that sometimes there was good reason for this. These publicans had the authority of the law of imperial Rome behind them and used their positions to charge as much as they pleased by was of taxes, with the result that they often became thieves and extortioners who were wealthy at the expense of their fellow countrymen. But mostly they were despised because they consented to work for the hated Romans who were imposters in the land of Canaan. They were therefroe considered traitors to the cause of God and of His people.

This publican also went to the temple to pray, evidently also at the time of prayer. He presents a strong contrast to the Pharisee, for his attitude was quite different. He did not go to the temple in the hopes that people would see him. Despised by his brethren according to the flesh, hated by his fellow countrymen, he could be seen sneaking along in the hopes of attracting little notice. And when he came into the temple, he sought the farthest corner—not only a place where men could not see him, but a place where also God could not see him. He did not dare to come as close to God as the Pharisee. Nor did he dare to look up into heaven where God dwelt. He cast his eyes to the ground. And when the prayer which he had rehearsed was ready to be offered, it fled from his consciousness. He could only beat upon his breast in mortification and alarm, for he knew no longer what to say.

The Contrast of Their Prayers

The great difference in the attitude of these two men became evident also in their prayers.

The Pharisee did not pray to God; but, as Jesus says, he prayed to himself. He did not enter consciously into the sanctuary of prayer and into the presence of God. He was rather filled only with a sense of his own importance and with the consciousness that the eyes of the people were on him.

It is well to pause here a moment and ponder one important truth concerning prayer. Jesus used the illustration of prayer in the parable because a man reveals himself most clearly in his prayers. Prayer carries a man consciously into God's presence. There, in the sanctuary of prayer, a man is aware of the fact that God sees him and knows him and watches him. But at the same time, as he enters the sanctuary of God's presence he is also conscious of God's transcendent glory and infinite majesty, of God's absolute perfection and unblemished holiness. This consciousness will determine the contents of all his prayer.

To this truth the Pharisee paid no attention. He never really entered prayer's hallowed courts. If he had, he would never have prayed as he did. For this reason too his thanksgiving was deceptive and hypocritical. It was really a gloss, for in reality he had nothing to be thankful for, as his prayer revealed. His own goodness concerning which he prated so piously came not from God but from himself.

You will notice that in his prayer he was interested in comparing himself with his fellow man. But all these comparisons came out in favor of himself. This is the case inevitable when men make comparisons between themselves and others. But the error was that he failed to make comparison between himself and God. If he had actually entered into the presence of God he would surely have done this. And if he had done this he would have become lost in a contemplation of his own evil heart as compared with the greatness of the God before Whose face he stood. But now he found that he was far preferable to other men. And happily, he found at hand an illustration of what he meant—the publican who was praying in the far corner.

So his prayer spoke of these things. On the one hand, he spoke negatively of the sins of other men—sins of which he claimed to be free. There was nothing in his life which could possibly be condemned. He found that he stood head and shoulders above all his countrymen, free from their sins and their stains. On the other hand, he not only found that he kept the law, but that he performed far more good works than the law required. The law demanded that a man fast once a year; he fasted twice a week. The law demanded tithes from income; he gave tithes of all that he possessed. Because he excelled the law in his works, he was confident that he had earned the righteousness of the law; for he had done far more than Moses required.

But—and this was fatal—he never mentioned the heart of the law.

The law required that he love God and his neighbor. Of this he made no mention. He cut away the heart of the law.

The prayer of the publican was far different. In fact, he forgot his prayer and did not know what to ask. What finally poured forth from his mouth was a spontaneous and unrehearsed plea that flowed from a heart filled with agony. This man had entered the corridors of prayer and had obtained a glimplse of the Holy God. To him this was so overwhelming that all his carefully rehearsed petitions were forgotten. He not longer knew what to pray.

The publican asked for mercy. The customary word for mercy which is found in the New Testament is not found here, however. The word really means "to make propitiation, to be appeased, to cease being angry." The publican evidently meant to say: "O God, let there be some way in which Thy fierce anger can be turned away from me."

Furthermore, he spoke of the fact that he was a sinner. In fact, the text in the Greek is far more emphatic. He spoke of the fact that he was *the* sinner." By this he meant, no doubt, that in the overwhelming consciousness of his sin he saw himself as the greatest of all sinners. No man in all the world could be as great a sinner as he. While the Pharisee found that he was more holy and more righteous than other men, the publican found that there was no man who had sinned as much as he. Therefore he did not know whether he dared to make his request. Cringing in the corner, he poured out his agony in only this brief cry. There are no works which he can bring to God. There are no deeds of which he can boast. He can find nothing in his life which would in any way be acceptable to God. All he knew was his terrible sin, and somehow he hoped in the depths of his soul that God's just anger could be turned away from him.

A greater contrast in prayer there could not be.

The Contrast of Their Hearts

But behind these two prayers were two hearts—hearts which were as different as the prayers.

The heart of the Pharisee was filled with thoughts of himself and his own goodness. Jesus described him as one who placed his confidence on himself. He trusted in himself that he was righteous. He believed that he was sufficient unto himself; that especially with respect to the matter of salvation he was fully capable of accomplishing all that was necessary to assure him a place in heaven. He was fully persuaded that whatever was lacking in this life to keep man's blessedness from being perfect was earned by him in his rigid adherence to the demands of the law.

If this were true, there would be no objection to the Pharisee saying it. But it was exactly the opposite of the truth. The Pharisee was a sinner no less than anyone else, including the publican far off in the corner. The Pharisee was a sinner as great as all other sinners because he too was born in the generations of Adam. He carried the guilt and pollution of Adam's sin. He was thoroughly corrupted and depraved as well as any other. In fact, his corruption was so complete that he was incapable of doing any good by his own strength and power.

It is obvious that sin becomes manifest in different ways. Some men sin by breaking the commandments of God in a life that even outwardly is in violation of all that God commands. But the Pharisee revealed his sin in a different way. He revealed his sin by denying that he was a sinner depraved and corrupted. He revealed his sin by denying that God had punished Adam's sin with total corruption and depravity of the human nature. He denied that he was a sinner; that was his sin. As paradoxical as this may sound, this is really the most terrible sin possible. It is the sin of pride which comes to expression in man's life in such a way that he denies the awful truth of his own inability to do good.

Of this sin the Pharisee was guilty.

There are several implications of this. In the first place, the Pharisee rushed into God's presence fearlessly in his prayers. There was so much pride in his heart that he never thought of the holiness and glory of God. He rushed through the gates of prayer's sanctuary with boldness and with no thought of God. This is always the terrible fruit of pride.

In the second place, and in close connection with this, he gave no glory to God, even though this was the heart of the law which he professed to keep. He took all the glory for himself. He was fully satisfied with himself. He was interested in the glory that would come to him. He waited in God's presence only for God's thank you to him and for God's commendation of his fine life.

In the third place, because he had no sin, he had no need of the cross of Christ. The hatred of the Pharisees for Christ was rooted not only in the fact that the Messiah was not the kind they had expected, it was rooted in the fact that they wanted no Messiah at all. The law which they professed to keep was a law which specifically and in all its details pointed out that Israel needed atonement for their sin, atonement that could only come through the way of the promised seed. But the Pharisees denied their sin and denied the need of atonement. In their professed observance of the law, therefore, they ignored precisely what the law always said: salvation can come only through the shedding of blood. For this reason they hated Christ, for Christ spoke of the sins of men and of the need for their sins to be taken away through the blood which He would shed. If Christ saved them, then they needed salvation. If the blood of the cross was necessary, then they were hopeless sinners, miserable wretches, detestable and unworthy men in the sight of God. The cross humbles people. And the Pharisees were proud. They hated and despised Christ and His cross.

In the fourth place, they also despised others. This ought not to surprise us. Pride in oneself always leads to the sin of despising others. The two are necessary companions. The one follows with unerring certainty from the other. Does a man love himself? Then he hates others. If a man is proud of himself and of his own ability, he will inevitably despise his fellow man. Any love for one's fellow man and respect for him can arise only out of humility and a sense of one's own unworthiness. This is because of the fundamental principle of the law. If we love God we hate ourselves. If we love ourselves we hate God. If we hate God we hate others. If we love God we love others.

Finally, we ought to notice in this connection that the sin of pride is rooted in the sinful nature of man. Man by nature is so depraved that he is blind to every spiritual truth. Among these spiritual truths to which he is blind is the truth concerning his own sinful and depraved nature. Man, apart from grace, is spiritually incapable of seeing his own sin. Blinded to his own sin, he always has the spiritual opinion of himself that he is good and that he has no sin in his flesh. It is only by the work of grace in the hearts of God's people that the blindness of sin is taken away and that it becomes possible for the sinner to see himself as he really is.

This evil of the Pharisee was contrasted with the prayer of the publican which revealed a very humble heart. All his prayer was rooted in the consciousness of sin. This is evident, in the first place, from the fact that the publican did not speak simply of his deeds, but of his nature. He did not say merely: "I have sinned." Rather, he confessed: "I am a sinner." The importance of this ought not to be overlooked. The publican was, of course, well aware of his sins. But he was also more deeply conscious of the basic reason for his sins: the fact that he was a sinner. This meant that what moved his soul to bitter cries was his awareness of his own depraved nature and his own incapablilty of doing any good. His sin was not merely the external deportment of a man, but it was sin which flowed forth as a stream from the corrupt fountain of his own evil heart. That sin was deeply rooted in the depths of his being. This filled him with fear and alarm. He knew what it meant to pray with David in Psalm 51:5: "Behold, I was shapen in iniquity; and in sin did my mother conceive me." And for this corrupt nature which was the source of all his sin he was also responsible before God.

In the second place, he was deeply impressed with the fact that he deserved only the most terrible punishment. He knew that he had sinned against God. He came, not seeking favor and blessing but knowing that he deserved the punishment of a righteous and holy God against Whom he had transgressed. The only thing to expect with any justice was damnation. In this consciousness he cried for forgiveness. He cast himself on God's mercy. When he entered prayer's hallowed courts his heart was filled with the consciousness of God's shining holiness and God's unalterable hatred of sin. He knew that he had sinned against God Who demands perfection. And he knew that God could only be angry with him. And so he was afraid. He dared not lift up his eyes toward heaven nor appear in the presence of men.

Nevertheless, he considered the possibility of there being some way to be restored. But this way was only the way of the satisfaction of God's justice. It had to be a way in which God was appeased of His anger by some propitiation for sin. This was the sacrifice for sin toward which all the sacrifices of the Old Dispensation pointed. He needed—and he knew it—the cross of Christ.

How sharp was the distinction between these two! The Pharisee was utterly fearless and without awe as he marched into God's presence; in terror and alarm the publican cringed in the far corner, knowing that it would be a wonder beyond comprehension if God would take him into His presence. The Pharisee had many things to say; the publican was speechless with consternation. The Pharisee demanded God's approval for his fine life; the publican knew only his undeserving sin. He made no comparison with other men, but was entirely absorbed in his own unrighteousness. The Pharisee was wholly self-satisfied; the publican cried out for mercy. The Pharisee glorified himself in the sight of God, in his own consciousness, and in the eyes of those who watched; the publican had no glory, only shame. The glory was God's alone.

This is the way it always is with those who seek their salvation in whole or in part in their own works. This is exactly the terrible sin of all Pelagianism and Arminianism that has reared its ugly head in the theology of the Church over the years. Arminianism always claims salvation by the works of men. It claims salvation which is dependent on man's choice for God and for His Christ. It claims that man takes the initiative in salvation. It claims that man puts God under obligation by works which man has succeeded in performing. And as such, it always places the man who is Arminian in heart and confession alongside the Pharisee in the temple who stood before the altar and boasted of his goodness.

If you who read this had been in the temple on that memorial day recorded on the pages of sacred Scripture, what would your reaction to these two men have been? Would you have joined with the crowd to give your plaudits to the Pharisee while you sneered at the anxious sobs of the publican? Or would you have gone to publican to comfort him in the sight of all and take on yourself the condemning stares of your fellow men? Do not forget that you would have joined the side of the one whose prayer most closely resembles your own. The prayer for the forgiveness of sin, with all that it implies, is the most difficult prayer to make; for it runs contrary to the pride of sin in our flesh.

The Contrast of Reward

Yet it was the prayer of the publican which brought peace.

The Pharisee went back to his home unchanged. Oh, he went back satisfied with the ringing praises of men which had sounded in his ears. But he was the same man on the way home that he was on the way to the temple. Prayer had left him unchanged. He had been in God's house, but he had never been in God's presence. He had made a pretense of praying, but he had never entered the gates of prayer. He had lifted his eyes and hands toward heaven, but had not seen God Whom the heaven of heavens cannot contain. He had come in his pride and left in his pride.

He was also condemned. God must receive all the glory. When men steal this glory from God, they do so to their own condemnation. God cannot give His glory to the creature. Nor will He permit the creature to sin against Him with impunity. The pride of man lies at the root of all sin. It must be punished. The proud must be abased.

When God punishes the sinner, whether that punishment be in this life or in the life to come, then God receives the glory that is justly His. The glory must be God's. God will receive it even if He receives it in the punishment of those who exalt themselves before Him. He is God alone. He is exalted in the heavens. He is the just Judge of proud man. He abases those who haughtily boast of their own goodness and power.

But the publican went to his home justified.

Jesus refers particularly to the consciousness of justification. God's elect are eternally justified. They are the elect whom God justifies from before the foundations of the world. They are righteous in Christ; they are righteous forever. This decree of God is unalterable. This justification is accomplished through the death and resurrection of Jesus Christ. The cross and the resurrection are the grounds of the justification of God's people.

But the parable speaks of the consciousness of this blessing of justification. It is the personal and experiential assurance of justification which is the blessed gift of the people of God. It is the assurance of the forgiveness of sins; the consciousness of peace with God; the awareness of God's favor and love. The publican returned to his home with his tears wiped away, with his sobs stilled within him, with peace flooding his soul, with joy and thanksgiving welling up in his heart. He could sing with the Psalmist: "Blessed is he whose transgression is forgiven, whose sin is covered. Blessed is the man unto whom the Lord imputeth not iniquity, and in whose spirit there is no guile" (Ps. 32:1, 2).

This gift of justification is the most basic, the most fundamental, the most blessed of the gifts of the cross of Christ. If we have this we have everything; if we lack this we have nothing. On it rests all the blessings which we receive in this life and in the life to come. It is the pulse beat of Christian experience, the heart of assurance, the basis for all we need and seek. If our sins are forgiven and we have peace with God, we have all things. The lack of this robs us of everything.

This blessed gift comes to us through faith in Christ. The righteousness which we need is not in ourselves, it is in Christ. Christ merited it all on the cross. This righteousness becomes ours only through faith in Him. Faith is the bond that places us in abiding contact with Christ. By faith we put our confidence not in ourselves and in our works, but in the work of Christ. On that work alone we rely.

But the way of faith in Christ is the way of despising ourselves and confessing that we are wretched sinners. When we know that we have nothing of ourselves, only then will we go to Christ. We can come to Christ only empty-handed. If we boast in ourselves or reserve to ourselves any goodness at all, then we cannot come to Christ and to His cross. Clothed in filthy rags of our own righteousnesses, only in bitterness of heart and agony of spirit over our works, only with nothing that our hands have done, can we come to Him Who is the fulness of all blessedness.

And then also the glory belongs to God alone. It belongs to God because Christ belongs God and the righteousness of the cross is the righteousness of God which He prepares for His people. This implies that all our sorrow for sin and the faith that carries us to Calvary is given as God's gift to us through the cross. Nothing is of us. All is of God Who saves us.

This is our confession. We know we have nothing. We know we have not even the power to confess our sins and to cling to Christ by faith. We must receive it all. We then give glory to God alone. "All that I am I owe to Thee." *Soli Deo Gloria.* This is the everlasting song of the saints saved by the mercy of God Almighty.

23

The Reward of Sovereign Grace

For the kingdom of heaven is like unto a man that is an householder, which went out early in the morning to hire labourers into his vineyard.

And when he had agreed with the labourers for a penny a day, he sent them into his vineyard.

And he went out about the third hour, and saw others standing idle in the marketplace,

And said unto them; Go ye also into the vineyard, and whatsoever is right I will give you. And they went their way.

Again he went out about the sixth and ninth hour, and did likewise.

And about the eleventh hour he went out, and found others standing idle, and saith unto them, Why stand ye here all the day idle?

They say unto him, Because no man hath hired us. He saith unto them, Go ye also into the vineyard; and whatsoever is right, that shall ye receive.

So when even was come, the lord of the vineyard saith unto his steward, Call the labourers, and give them their hire, beginning from the last unto the first.

And when they came that were hired about the eleventh hour, they received every man a penny.

But when the first came, they supposed that they should have received more; and they likewise received every man a penny.

And when they had received it, they murmured against the goodman of the house,

Saying, These last have wrought but one hour, and thou hast made them equal unto us, which have borne the burden and heat of the day.

But he answered one of them, and said, Friend, I do thee no wrong: didst not thou agree with me for a penny?

Take that thine is, and go thy way: I will give unto this last, even as unto thee.

Is it not lawful for me to do what I will with mine own? Is thine eye evil, because I am good?

So the last shall be first, and the first last: for many be called, but few chosen.

—Matthew 20:1-16

Generally speaking, the parables of Jesus may be divided into three main groups. The first group was spoken during Jesus' Galilean ministry and contain descriptions of the character of the kingdom of heaven. The second group was spoken predominantly during Jesus' Perean ministry and deals with spiritual relationships within the kingdom and between the kingdom's citizens. The third group was spoken to the people during the week of Jesus' passion, probably on Wednesday when He taught the people for the last time. This latter group is introduced by the parable which forms the basis for this chapter. In these last parables Jesus speaks predominantly of judgment. The lengthening shadows of the cross are cast more darkly over Jesus' life. More and more heavily does the darkness of His "hour" weigh upon the Lord. It is not at all strange therefore that Christ's thoughts turned more anxiously toward the glory which was laid away for Him, a glory which would be finally perfected when He would come again at the end of the age to establish finally and everlastingly His own kingdom. But with this coming would also come judgment—judgment on the nation of Israel which crucified her Messiah, but also judgment on all the world which despises Christ and crucifies afresh the Lord of glory. At the same time, this coming means the final salvation and redemption of the Church, the final glory of the body of Christ that our Lord had come to save.

To these weighty matters the Lord addresses His attention in these last parables.

This parable also had its occasion. A rich man had come to the Lord desiring to know the way to eternal life. The Lord had pointed him to the law; but evidently the man thought Jesus was referring only to the outward precepts of the law, and claimed, no doubt rightly, that he had fulfilled all these commandments. And so the Lord pointed him to the deepest principle of the law: "love God"; but particularly as that principle touched on his own life. He was very rich; he must now go and sell all that he had and give his possessions to the poor.

After Jesus had explained the difficulty of the rich man entering the kingdom, Peter was prompted to ask the Lord what he reward of the disciples would be, inasmuch as they had left all and followed Him. Although this question might have sounded boastful and presumptuous on Peter's part—as, no doubt, to a certain degree it was—the Lord assured the disciples that they would indeed be rewarded for their faithful life. They would sit on twelve thrones judging the twelve tribes of Israel.

But immediately the Lord added to this assurance a note of urgent warning. It is so easy for us to have the wholly mistaken notion that this reward would be something we merited. This was not only the sin of the Pharisees, but is a sin as old as the pride of man, a sin which always arises in the hearts of men. And so on the one hand, Jesus warns that many who are first here on earth will be last in the judgment day; therefore we must be careful that we do not judge according to outward appearances. But on the other hand, Jesus tells us that no matter what the reward may be, it is always of grace alone.

The Elements in the Parable

The general lines of the parable are comparatively clear. God is the householder, for He is the sovereign Owner of the vineyard. Christ Jesus is the Steward Who, in the vineyard, does all the will of God and accomplishes His Father's purpose. The vineyard itself is the kingdom of heaven viewed in the parable from the viewpoint of its earthly and historical manifestation. It is the Church visible here on earth, the Church in its broadest scope and widest manifestation. This visible manifestation of the kingdom will come to its end at the end of the age when the kingdom is perfected and glorified on the return of the Son of man. The laborers are those who are called to work in the Church visible—those who without exception find some place and station in the Church and perform some work in the kingdom, whether they be good or whether they be evil.

When we address ourselves to the question of what is meant by the wages each laborer receives, we find many interpretations and many problems. As such, the wages were, for each laborer, a penny. This penny or denarius was an average day's wage in Jesus' time and equal to about 17ᶜ in our money. Although we will have occasion to return to this and discuss some interpretations and their objections, suffice it to say for the present that Jesus means by these wages the proper recompense which each laborer in the kingdom receives. It is a recompense reckoned according to the work of each man, whether it be good or bad, but not according to the length of labor. The recompense may be either condemnation or glorious salvation.

It is immediately evident that the Lord places considerable emphasis in the parable on the call that goes out to gain laborers for the vineyard. The marketplace from which these laborers are called is evidently intended to refer to the world. While it was customary in Jesus' day for men to go to the marketplaces of the towns and cities and there wait for someone to come and hire them, here obviously Jesus means to say that those who labor in His vineyard are called to labor from the world in which they live. This is a critical part of the parable, for when the householder says to some of those He hired, "Why stand ye here all the day idle?", the Lord emphasizes that any work which is done that is not devoted exclusively to the cause of the vineyard of God is empty and vain. No matter what great accomplishments may come forth from the hands of men, if these are not consecrated in the service of the kingdom of God they are foolish and empty, vain and useless. So is all the labor of every man outside God's vineyard.

The Call of God

This call of God to labor in the vineyard is emphatically God's call. So often it is forgotten in our day and the idea is spread abroad that men call or that preachers of the gospel bring into the kingdom. It is true that God is pleased to use mere men when He calls through the ministry of the Word as a means of grace to those who are without. But the word of men is always powerless and useless unless God Himself calls by His Spirit in the hearts of His own. It must never be forgotten that when God calls, His call is always sovereign and efficacious. God's Word which God speaks and by means of which God calls into service in His vineyard is the call which always accomplishes sovereignly all the will of God. That Word contains the entire sum of the promises of Scripture to the elect as well as the entire sum of the curses and condemnation of God's wrath on the wicked. And that Word is sovereignly executed.

There is, therefore, according to the will of God, always a twofold effect of the call of the gospel. God calls His people and says to them: "I love you. You are mine. It is my purpose to bless you with all spiritual blessings." And while that Word as it is objectively proclaimed does not specifically mention the names of God's people, nevertheless the Spirit applies that Word to the hearts of God's people in such a way that they hear the voice of their Shepherd call them by name and they know they are His. That Word of promise and comfort sovereignly converts and saves. But God never says this to the wicked. He never tells the wicked that He loves them. He speaks of wrath and displeasure against sin. And the fruit of this Word is that the wicked are, through the way of their unbelief, sovereignly hardened and condemned. This is according to the purpose of Almighty God.

Here the fruit of the call of God is that many more than are saved are called to work in the vineyard. "Many are called, but few are chosen." Jesus refers here to the general call of the gospel. This does not mean that the call of God is a general *offer* of salvation which proceeds from a general love of God to all men. Nor does this mean that Christ speaks here of a general promise to all that hear the gospel and which expresses a general desire on God's part to save all men. Rather, the meaning is that the call comes to many to repent and believe. It never comes to all, for God sends the gospel only to those whom He in His good pleasure is pleased to send it. But it does come to many more than the elect. And in this call God places all these men before the command to repent of their sins and believe. This is their solemn obligation before God, for no man has a right to continue to live in sin. Whether because of his sin he can hearken to this call or not makes no difference; he is solemnly commanded to forsake sin and love God with all his heart.

The result is that the call produces laborers for the vineyard. Some are called by the sovereign operations of grace and the Spirit of God. They come into the vineyard as believers to labor for God. Others hear the call as it sounds within the historical realization of the kingdom, and belong for a time only to this outward and visible manifestation of the Church. They show that they understand the Word of God even though with their heart they never believe it. But they too seem outwardly to labor in the vineyard.

The Different "Times" of the Call

But now also the Lord points to the fact that those who are called are called at different times. The reckoning of the parable is according to Jewish time. The day was reckoned from sunrise to sunset and divided into numbered hours. The third hour corresponds approximately to 9 o'clock in the morning; the sixth hour to noon; the ninth hour to 3 o'clock; and the eleventh hour to 5 o'clock in the afternoon, just before the working day is over.

There are various interpretations of this point of the parable. Some say that the meaning is that the history of the world is divided into various hours: the hour before the flood; the hour of the Old Dispensation of Israel; the hour of the New Dispensation; the hour of the end. Then the meaning is that God calls His people throughout the world's history from the dawn of creation to the end of time. Some are called later on the clock of God than others. But this interpretation cannot be the meaning here. While it is true in itself that God calls men throughout the ages to work in His vineyard, here the Lord teaches that all the laborers labor to the end of the day. This is not true in this world's history.

Others interpret this to mean that God calls some to many years of labor in His kingdom while others labor a comparatively short time. There are the young who die in infancy or in the prime of their life, and there are the old who accumulate gray hair in the long and hard "burden of the day." There are those who are converted in the infancy of their lives; there are also those who, as the thief on the cross, are converted at the "eleventh hour." There is an element of truth to this interpretation, but it is not the whole meaning of Jesus' words.

Evidently the Lord refers to the fact that there are in the kingdom degrees of labor as well as different stations and callings. And there is considerable variation between these manifold stations. There are some very important people in the Church who hold high positions and exalted callings. There are those who are in critical positions in the Church and who have considerable influence. There are those who are very busy in the cause of God and who spend night and day in the work of the Church. There are ministers, elders, deacons, teachers, and those who are entrusted with important responsibilities. There are many who suffer intense persecution and give their bodies to be burned. There are others who literally forsake all and give of all their gifts to the poor. They bear the heat and burden of the day and toil with unremitting effort for God's covenant.

But there are also others of considerably less importance. They never seen to accomplish significant tasks. Nothing much seems to be required of them. They work in the cool of the day without ever bringing any sweat to their brow for the Church and the kingdom. They are never called to suffer intensely or bear heavy burdens. Perhaps the reason for this is that they are the poor and the despised; the sick and suffering; the shut-ins and invalids. Seldom, if ever, does their name appear on nominations for elder or deacon. Or perhaps they may be mothers in the home, who are so busily engaged in the responsibilities of caring for their family that they are scarcely noticed in the Church of Christ. For these and other reasons their station is relatively lowly.

Now we are very much inclined to form our judgment about these things. We would usually conclude that the great men with important positions must have a great place in the kingdom. They surely earned a great reward and are worthy of high honors. But the insignificant and unimportant are not nearly as worthy and will surely receive a much smaller reward, if any at all. It is precisely this judgment that Jesus warns against, for it is a judgment that is rooted in pride. There were the Pharisees of Jesus' day who insisted that they had carried the burden and the heat of the day and were therefore worthy of special honors. But there were also the poor and despised, the publicans and sinners, the adulterers and adulteresses, the thieves on the cross; surely their reward is very small. But this is the judgment of carnal pride, a pride which lingers in our hearts and which expresses itself in the opinion that we somehow and in some way earn the reward that is coming to us.

"But many that are first shall be last; and the last shall be first."

The Meaning of the Wage

The steward in the parable is commanded, at the end of the day, to give to each laborer his wages. By this point in the story Jesus alludes to the day of judgment when He Himself shall sit upon the throne of God and reward every man according to his works. What then will happen?

According to the parable, very strange and unpredictable things happen. In the first place, the steward is commanded to begin with those that were hired last and to pay them first. Then proceeding from these, he is to pay those that were hired first at the very end.

But that is not all. When the wages are passed out, it soon becomes apparent that these wages are paid in a manner quite different from the way other employers pays their wages. Indeed, the ones who worked all day in the boiling sun and are now ready to return home exhausted are given their penny. This is what they earned. This is a fair day's wage. This is what, in fact, they agreed upon. But all the others are given an equal amount. Even those who came at the very end of the day as the sun was already sinking in the west, who worked in the cool shadows of the evening and spent only a brief hour in the field are also given a penny for their wages. This we would surely not expect. That the ones who received a penny received a just wage is understandable. But then we would expect, as they did, that those who worked less hours would receive proportionately less pay. And if the householder was pleased to pass out any special rewards, these rewards should really be given to those who labored hard throughout the whole day.

But this is not the way of God.

What does this mean? The interpretation hinges on the meaning that Jesus attaches to the penny. And here also there are various explanations given, of which a few are worth our consideration.

There are those who say that this penny refers to eternal life, which all God's people receive equally. Then the meaning is that all the laborers are at last taken to heaven and there receive the reward of eternal life from God. Now this is, in itself, true. But there are objections against its interpretation here. On the one hand, it is evident that not all the laborers are elect people of God. Some are wicked. This is clear from the fact that they murmur and grumble and are not satisfied with their wage. Besides, Jesus sends them away with the curse-words: "Friend, I do thee no wrong: didst not thou agree with me for a penny? Take that is thine, and go thy way: I will give unto this last, even as unto thee. Is it not lawful for me to do what I will with mine own? Is thine eye *evil*, because I am good?" Besides, this matter is clinched by Jesus Himself when He solemnly assures us: "Many are called, but few are chosen." On the other hand, the emphasis of the parable is not on the mere fact that all receive an equal amount of money. This is really, in itself, incidental. The emphasis is rather on the fact that there is a reward given to different amounts of work. In the parable these different amounts of work would not necessarily have to be recompensed with an equal reward.

There are others who maintain that this parable is proof of the fact that Scripture teaches that we will all be equal in glory. But again, this is not true. Scripture everywhere emphasizes that there are indeed degrees of glory. Paul tells us in I Corinthians 15 that the glory of one star is greater than that of another. So will it be in the resurrection from the dead. And Jesus, in the immediately preceding context, emphasizes the same truth. In answer to Peter's question, the Lord replies: "Verily I say unto you, that ye which have followed me, in the regeneration when the Son of man shall sit in the throne of his glory, ye also shall sit upon twelve thrones, judging the twelve tribes of Israel." In the parable itself Jesus emphasizes that all will not be equal. "Many that are first shall be last; and the last shall be first." This is the teaching of the whole of Scripture.

It is evident, then, that the penny simply refers to the final proper reward which all receive. There is even, in a certain sense, a reward for the wicked, though it be the reward of condemnation. In the parable these men received exactly what they had coming. They received their hire—that which they agreed to. And the point is that they received directly proportionate to their works. But they have no place in the kingdom.

But the others received their reward, not according to their works, but according to grace. This is the fundamental difference emphasized in the parable.

Jesus does not mean to say by this that we do not have to work. Nor is this a denial of the fact that the reward which the people of God is in direct proportion to their work of faith. There are indeed various degrees of glory in heaven. The apostles alone will sit on twelve thrones judging the twelve tribes of Israel. Some will have more glory in heaven than others, although all will be full of glory according to their own capacity. This very truth is even an incentive to press on to more faithful labor in the vineyard of God. We see ahead of us the reward which shines brightly beyond the horizon of history. And caught up in the glory of this reward, we press on with renewed earnestness to complete our tasks.

But the reward is not earned. It is of grace alone. We never receive according to the measure of *our* work. We receive according to the measure of grace. And if you ask how this can be, then you must remember that all the work which we do is also of grace. Our works which we do of our own strength are nothing and can never meet the approval of God. That work which is pleasing in His sight and which is rewarded is the work which He performed within our hearts and through us.

Thus the first shall be last, and the last first. Jesus does not say that this is true of all, but only of many. *Many* that are first shall be last, and the last shall be first.

There are those who are first in this life. They have high positions of importance and influence. Outwardly they seem to bear the heat of the day and the burden of labor under the sun. But some of them build their life on their own works. They are concerned only about what *they* do and what *they* accomplish by *their* power in *their* work for God. The Pharisees were a striking illustration of this. But nevertheless there is something of this in all of us. Each one has his station and calling in the vineyard. Some have important places. But even in these important places that which is *our* work which we do by our strength means nothing.

So there are many that are first who shall be last. There are many who build only on their own works who will never enter into the kingdom. Their reward is the reward of their works, and this is eternal condemnation. There are others who will enter the kingdom, but when the Judge of heaven and earth weighs their labor, it will be seen that even in their positions of importance much of their work was their own. They will be last in that kingdom, for every work of man must be destroyed. No works of man can ever enter into the kingdom of God.

And so there are many who are last here on earth who will be first

in the kingdom. They always appeared to be the least here on earth.
They had no high and exalted position. Their influence seemed to
be small and insignificant. They brought forth the quiet and almost
unnoticed fruits of the Spirit. They led a quiet and godly life in all
modesty and temperance. They performed their tasks in the small
corner of the kingdom assigned them without murmuring and
grumbling. But the work which they did was not their own. It was the
work of God shining brightly through them. They will receive the
greater reward. For even as the first shall be last, so shall the last be
first.

The Sovereign Reason for This

You may well ask the reason for this. In order to find the reason,
you must go far back to the eternal and unchangeable good pleasure
of God and the decree of sovereign election.

It is well to note in passing that this doctrine is not very popular in
our day. There are many who openly deny it and rail at those who
maintain it. But there are also many, even in Reformed circles, who
profess to believe it. But, while professing to believe it, they never
mention it in their conversation and preaching. They claim that the
doctrine of election belongs to the hidden things of God's counsel
and that we have nothing to do with it. Or they take the position that
the doctrine of election does not belong in the preaching because it
tends to frighten sinners away and make men careless and profane.
They emphasize those texts in Scripture which make no mention of
election and interpret them to teach the Arminian doctrine of the
free will of man. And when they come to those texts which do teach
the truth of election, they are strangely silent about this truth and
leave the doctrine out of their exposition. In this way they show that
really they hate the truth of election and want nothing to do with it.

But Jesus brings this truth emphatically to the foreground in the
parable. He concludes His parable with the striking words, "Many
are called, but few are chosen." We may not in passing that although
some translations of the Bible omit this last part of verse 16, the fact
remains that it most probably belongs in the text. Furthermore, this
is not the only place in the Gospels where this idea is found. It is,
therefore, a thought in Jesus' teaching which is not foreign to the
Scriptures.

The meaning of this is clear. There are many who are called
outwardly by the preaching of the gospel. They hear the gospel and
even understand it to a considerable extent. They know what the
truth is and what it teaches. The result may even be that they begin to
labor in the vineyard of God. You will find this especially in the
revival preaching of well-known evangelists. The audience sees a
glimpse of the truth and hears the outward call and begins to labor in
the work of the vineyard. They may even gain important and in-
fluential positions in the Church. But they always build their hope
on their own work. They bring forth only the sham fruits of repen-

tance and sorrow for sin, the fruits of unstable emotions. But the further they drift from the truth of Scripture, the more they build on their own works. In their work is all their salvation. And when they are rewarded exactly according to these works, then they grumble; for their works are nothing other than the works of condemnation.

But, while many are called, only a few are chosen. This was historically true also because only a remnant was ever saved by God. But the point is that the most basic reason why some receive the reward of grace is the sovereign election of God. It is, as Jesus says, entirely just that God does with His own as it seems good to Him. He wills to give His people His grace. And who has the right to complain about the goodness of God? Those that do, only show that their own eye is evil. If God wills to reveal His own goodness in the choosing of His elect and in giving them the reward of grace, those that grumble about this only show that they are evil and cannot understand the infinite depths of the goodness of God. Election is the sovereign cause of salvation. And the reward of grace which the people of God receive is a reward that is rooted in the eternal decree of election.

So, the conclusion of the matter is clear.

Indeed our works shall be rewarded whether they be good or bad. We, too, must ask ourselves the all-important question: have we forsaken all to follow Christ as Peter and the other apostles did? And then we also may ask: what then shall we have? When the Lord assures us that this shall be surely rewarded in the life to come, then we have our peace and a comfort and joy that passes understanding.

But we must surely be reminded of the truth that it is then not our labors that are being rewarded, but God's work in our hearts. It is all of grace. God chooses us in sovereign election, not on the basis of works, but in grace. God gives us a place in His Church; but this too, is of grace. In God's Church we have work to do. But this work is the privilege of grace. And if we, in a measure, faithfully carry out this work, that too is of grace. When at last we arrive at our heavenly home and our work is rewarded, then even the reward is of grace alone. It is always what we have not deserved, but what our God has graciously given to us.

Paul expresses it in this way: "For by grace are ye saved through faith; and that not of yourselves: it is the gift of God: not of works, lest any man should boast" (Eph. 2:8, 9). And our fathers, catching the wonder of this truth, incorporated it into our confessions. They said in one place: "There are not various decrees of election, but one and the same decree respecting those, who shall be saved, both under the Old and New Testament: since the Scripture declares the good pleasure, purpose and counsel and the divine will be one, according to which He hath chosen us to eternity, both to grace and glory, to salvation and the way of salvation, which He hath ordained that we should walk therein" (Canons I, 8). Or again they say: "In the meantime, we do not deny that God rewards our good works, but it is through His grace that He crowns His gifts" (Conf. of Faith, Art. 24). In truth, all the glory belongs to God alone, now and to eternity.

24

Our Calling While the Lord Tarries

And as they heard these things, he added and spake a parable, because he was nigh to Jerusalem, and because they thought that the kingdom of God should immediately appear.

He said therefore, A certain nobleman went into a far country to receive for himself a kingdom, and to return.

And he called his ten servants, and delivered them ten pounds, and said unto them, Occupy till I come.

But his citizens hated him, and sent a message after him, saying, We will not have this man to reign over us.

And it came to pass, that when he was returned, having received the kingdom, then he commanded these servants to be called unto him, to whom he had given the money, that he might know how much every man had gained by trading.

Then came the first, saying, Lord, thy pound hath gained ten pounds.

And he said unto him, Well, thou good servant: because thou hast been faithful in a very little, have thou authority over ten cities.

And the second came, saying, Lord, thy pound hath gained five pounds.

And he said likewise to him, Be thou also over five cities.

And another came, saying, Lord behold here is thy pound, which I have kept laid up in a napkin:

For I feared thee, because thou art an austere man: thou takest up that thou layedst not down, and reapest that thou didst not sow.

And he saith unto him, Out of thine own mouth will I judge thee, thou wicked servant. Thou knewest that I was an austere man, taking up that I laid not down, and reaping that I did not sow:

Wherefore then gavest not thou my money into the bank, that at my coming I might have required mine own with usury?

And he said unto them that stood by, Take from him the pound, and give it to him that hath ten pounds.

(And they said unto him, Lord, he hath ten pounds.)

For I say unto you, That unto every one which hath shall be given; and from him that hath not, even that he hath shall be taken away from him.

*But those mine enemies, which would not that I should reign over
them, bring hither, and slay them before me.*

—Luke 19:11–27

Although there are many who find, with considerable justification, enough similarities between this parable and the parable of the
talents (Matt. 25:14-30) to treat the two together, it nevertheless
remains a fact that the circumstances and content of each are so
markedly different that they warrant separate treatment. While the
parable of the talents was spoken by Christ probably on Wednesday
of Passion Week, this parable was spoken in the doorway of the
house of Zacchaeus in Jericho. At least in part, the parable finds its
occasion in the events which are recorded in the first part of this
chapter. The Jews, as always, were complaining that Jesus chose to
stay with Zacchaeus, who was so obviously a sinner. The parable,
which was "added" to what Jesus said in explanation of His stay with
Zacchaeus, speaks consequently of the judgment that was sure to
come on the wicked house of Judah which constantly murmured
against Christ as He went about His work "to seek and to save those
that are lost." In this respect, this parable, while having the same
occasion as the parables of the lost sheep, the lost coin, and the lost
son (Luke 15), nevertheless differs in important points. In the parables recorded in Luke 15 the Lord explained His work as the Christ.
Now, since the Jews gave no indication that they had changed their
opinion of Him, Jesus speaks of judgment that shall come, beginning with Jerusalem.

Nevertheless, Luke points out a more specific occasion for this
parable. "He . . . spake a parable, because he was nigh to Jerusalem,
and because they thought that the kingdom of God should immediately appear." Jesus and His disciples were nearing Jerusalem.
There was a growing expectancy and excitement among Jesus' disciples and among the crowds that followed Him as Jesus neared the
holy city. This was due on the one hand to the sermons Jesus had
preached, which had increasingly emphasized important events that
were to transpire shortly in Jerusalem. But this excitement was due
on the other hand to the knowledge of the crowds that the leaders of
the Jews were determined to kill Christ at any cost. Things could not
go on any longer the way they were; a crisis was approaching.
Something had to happen; and it was very possible that this would
happen at the time of the feast, which was just a few days off.

So the disciples—and many of the people with them—thought
that now certainly Jesus would establish His kingdom. He could not
afford to wait anymore. It was, so to speak, now or never. It was
imperative that if Christ was to become king He had to ascent Mount
Zion now, throw off the Roman yoke, and seize the throne of David
which so long had remained vacant.

It is this erroneous idea which the Lord corrects in this parable. It is
true that He was going to Jerusalem to enter His kingdom. That is

why He presently also rides into Jerusalem in triumph. But He is not going to enter an earthly kingdom. He is going to enter the kingdom of heaven. And the way to this heavenly kingdom is a way that leads Him to a distant country for a long time. It is a way that leads, first of all, far distant to hell where He suffered its torments on His cross. But it is also a way that leads far distant to heaven until the time comes to receive the kingdom. This is why, although Jesus rides triumphantly into Jerusalem, He rides upon the colt of an ass.

But because the Lord will tarry before He returns, He gives to His disciples and to His Church a very serious calling. The calling is to be faithful. It is to be faithful in representing His cause and kingdom; it is to be faithful to His Word of promise. For when He comes again, He comes quickly; and His reward is with Him to give to every man as his works shall be.

Why the Lord Tarries

The broad lines of the parable are rather generally agreed upon. Jesus is the nobleman. This is true because Jesus was of royal blood, of the royal line of David. David's blood flowed in His veins and He was destined to sit on David's throne. In this respect the people who thought He had come to establish His kingdom at that moment were correct. But although Christ was David's royal son, as the nobleman in the parable had royal blood in his veins, Christ had not received the kingdom as yet. He had not received the kingdom because He had to enter the kingdom through the way of His own cross and the shedding of His blood.

But Jesus is the nobleman in a far greater sense of the word, for Jesus is the eternal Son of God. Although He came into our flesh and although His glory was hidden behind the veil of our flesh which He bore, nevertheless He remained the sovereign God Who rules over all. He is thus infinitely greater than any earthly nobleman can ever be.

In the parable the nobleman journeyed to a far country. This was necessary to receive a kingdom. This figure, if Josephus is correct, was a very familiar figure to the Jews. Some time before this, Herod the Great had died and left his kingdom to Archelaus his son. But Archelaus had traveled to far-off Rome to receive the kingdom for himself from Augustus Caesar and had then returned. In fact, according to Josephus, the Jews had also sent an ambassage to Augustus to try to persuade him not to give the kingdom to Archelaus because the Jews did not want him to be their king.

But Jesus applies the story here to Himself. He is not now going to Jerusalem to lead an army against the legions of Rome and to establish for Himself the earthly throne of David. Neither the disciples nor the people must expect this. Rather, He is going to a far country. Only there will He receive the kingdom—not here on earth. Only when He receives that kingdom, will He also come again. But that day of His coming is very far in the future.

But the question arises: why could not Jesus establish His kingdom in earthly Jersualem on earthly Mount Zion? This question is important for more than one reason. For one thing, the answer to this question will determine to a considerable extent the entire meaning and significance of the parable. For another thing, the disciples and the people who followed the Lord were really the first pre-millennialists. They made the same error that so many make today. The fact of the matter is that Jesus not only did not *want* to establish His kingdom in earthly Jerusalem, He *could* not. The very nature of His kingdom prevented it.

The disciples expected an earthly kingdom. But this could never be. This had once been possible under Adam. But Adam had fallen and sin had come into the world. Any earthly kingdom, therefore, which belongs to this present dispensation of things is necessarily a sinful kingdom in which the principle of sin remains a fundamental principle of its operation. But the kingdom which Jesus had come to establish was a kingdom of righteousness and truth. It was to be a kingdom in which the glory of the perfections of God would shine.

But this kingdom also had to be a heavenly and spiritual kingdom which would be built on the ashes of the kingdoms of this world. In order to establish such a kingdom it was necessary that Christ go far away—far away from this earth and even far away from God. He had to go all the long and tortuous way to hell itself, there to bear the full fury of God's wrath against sin so that God's justice might be satisfied. He had to go to hell to overcome sin and destroy the power of Satan and his mighty armies. Yet even this was not enough. It was not enough that Christ merely go to hell and then return to this earth to establish an earthly kingdom. He had to enter into death. And from death He had to go forth in power, not on this side of the grave but on heaven's side. He had to go away from us to heaven, for only there could He receive the kingdom. And then it would be a very long time before He would come back again.

But yet the question persists: why is it necessary for Christ to go to heaven in order to receive His kingdom? The disciples could imagine nothing more blessed than that their Lord remain with them; and nothing more terrible than that their Lord would leave them. Yet they had to learn that in the mere earthly presence of the Lord there could be no blessings. The choicest blessings, the blessings that counted, could only come to them if their Lord would go away from them for a while.

The nature of the kingdom of Christ demanded this. In the first place, His kingdom is a kingdom that includes all God's elect. Christ rules over all the elect of God by His grace and Spirit. He redeemed these elect from sin and death to make them His own people. He takes them into His kingdom and makes them His loyal subjects so that they do His will and bow before Him as their Sovereign and Lord. Within that kingdom He blesses His citizens with all the treasures of the kingdom, all the spiritual and heavenly blessings of salvation.

In the second place, Christ rules over the wicked also. We may not conclude from this that the wicked constitute part of His kingdom. Nevertheless, His sovereign rule extends over them. When Christ ascended into heaven, there was no more need for Him to fight to overcome the devil and the wicked who oppose Him. Christ is sovereign also over the wicked. He had crushed their power by the victory of His cross. The wicked only do what is His will that they do. In all their opposition to Christ and to His kingdom they only accomplish the will of God. Christ is the Lord of lords, and the King of kings. He uses the evil intents and godless strivings of wicked men to fulfill His purpose. They too, even in their rebellion, must serve to establish His kingdom. But in this way they also fill the cup of iniquity. Their wickedness and rebellion grow worse and worse. They become more and more opposed to Christ, and in their sin they become ripe for judgment. When punishment comes on them, it comes because they have filled the cup of iniquity to overflowing.

Thus Christ must go to heaven to receive His kingdom and tarry there. On the one hand it is in heaven that Christ received the promise of the Holy Spirit. This Spirit Christ poured out on His Church. Through that Spirit the elect of God are taken into the kingdom, for they are through the power of the Spirit translated from the kingdom of darkness into the kingdom of God's dear Son. Within that kingdom and through the same Spirit the citizens of the kingdom are blessed with all the spiritual treasures of the kingdom of heaven.

But through this same Spirit Christ rules sovereignly over all the works of God. He rules over all, for His authority has no limitations and His sovereign scepter is swayed over every part of God's domain. But this is possible when Christ goes to heaven because He is exalted at His Father's right hand. From heaven His true kingdom is established, not from earth. He *must* leave us for a time.

On the other hand, He tarries in heaven and does not come back immediately because He cannot return until all is in readiness. All the elect must be born and converted. They must all inherit the kingdom. Besides, all the purpose of God must be accomplished. Everything must be in readiness. All the wicked counsels of evil men must be fully exposed. Only when this is done can Christ come to execute final and righteous judgment. Only when this final and righteous judgment is at last executed can the kingdom of Christ be fully established. This shall come at the end of the age; then Christ shall return to inherit the kingdom prepared for Him from before the foundations of the world.

Our Calling in the Absence of Our Lord

The emphasis of the parable falls on the fact that the citizens of

Christ's kingdom have a very particular calling while their Lord is absent from them. This calling is first of all defined negatively by way of contrast with the wicked who corrupt their calling.

It is evident from the parable that there are, in the historical manifestation of the kingdom, two kinds of wicked men. The parable speaks of citizens of the kingdom who send an ambassage after the nobleman to express that they do not want this nobleman to reign over them. It also speaks of servants who receive a pound, but one of whom is unfaithful and is punished for his wickedness.

All these citizens and servants are therefore those who belong to the kingdom as it is historically manifested here on earth. The reference is not to the kingdom as it will finally be perfected, for there no wickedness shall ever enter in. But while the kingdom is manifested here below, there remain many wicked within that kingdom. They labor in one way or another within that kingdom. We noticed this already in our discussion of the last parable.

But as far as the wicked within that kingdom are concerned, there is a difference between the citizens and the wicked servant. All the citizens are without distinction wicked. They agree on the one point that they do not want Christ to rule over them. This evidently refers to the people who are outwardly part of the kingdom, who belong to the kingdom because they were born within the generations of the citizens of that kingdom, yet who become, in the process of time, the false church. In the days of Jesus they were the Jews who were the children of Abraham, but who, through the years and in the generations of history, apostatized from the truth of God and departed from the true principles of the Church of Chrsit. Their apostasy was total. These Jews had become apostate Israel and they were on the verge of crucifying their King. But they represent those who are always present within the historical development of the kingdom and who, while outwardly professing to be members of that kingdom, nevertheless go the way of apostasy and become the false church.

The sin of these wicked citizens is therefore also very dreadful. In the parable they repudiate the nobleman and flatly refuse to acknowledge him as their king. This expresses vividly the truth concerning the Jews of Jesus' day. As far as the leaders were concerned, they had repudiated Christ long ago. But this was also true of the crowds who followed the Lord. They were the ones who at the moment Christ spoke this parable were looking forward eagerly to Christ's return to Jerusalem. It was but the next day and these crowds were shouting their hosannas as they threw their palm branches before the Christ and welcomed Him into the royal city. But this was only because they anticipated an earthly kingdom in which their earthly and carnal desires would be satisfied. They wanted a Christ who would make bread in the wilderness so that they would not have to work. They looked for a Christ who would lead their armies against Rome and deliver them from the yoke of

Caesar. But when it became evident that Christ would never be this kind of king, they hated Him. Only a few days after their hosannas rent the air they would fill the streets of the holy city with their cries: "Away with him; crucify him: we have no king but Caesar; we will not have this man to reign over us."

It is no doubt for this reason that the apostate church always turns to a social gospel. As the church which walks the way of apostasy repudiates the truth of the Scriptures, it still outwardly professes to represent the cause of the kingdom of Christ. But in fact that church denies Him, denies His divinity, His blood of atonement, the salvation He brings through the sovereign operation of His Spirit. The false church crucifies to itself the Son of God afresh. And instead of speaking of the kingdom which is in heaven, the false church speaks of a kingdom here on earth. It looks for the realization of the kingdom in social renewal and reform. It looks for the realization of a kingdom which is purely earthly and which will be the means to satisfy their own carnal desires. These are the ones who make Antichrist their king and worship him. These are the ones who set up a kingdom which is directly opposed to Christ and who seek to destroy the kingdom Christ establishes.

But there is also the sin of the wicked servant who wrapped his pound in a napkin. His sin was also very great, but it was a sin of a different kind. He did not openly repudiate Christ as the citizens did. He continued to claim to be a servant, and he attempted to justify his conduct as if what he did was the proper thing to do.

The interpretation of this part of the parable hinges on our interpretation of the pound.

There are some who interpret this pound in the same way that they interpret the talent in the parable of the talents. But this is probably a mistake. A pound was worth approximately eighteen dollars in our money, while a talent was worth far more. But the real reason why the pound cannot mean the same thing as the talent is to be found in the fact that the servants received different amounts of talents. To one servant was given five talents; to another, two; to another, one. And the limiting clause was significantly added: "To every man according to his several ability."

But in this parable each servant received exactly the same: one pound. It is evident then that the pound refers to something which each one the the Church receives equally with the other members, something that they all have in common. What is this one thing that all the members have equally and in common? The answer to this would seem to be that the pound must refer to the Word of God. Although in the last parable it was pointed out that the place which each one occupies within the kingdom is different, and although in the parable of the talents the truth is emphasized that those within the kingdom receive greater or lesser ability, all the citizens of the kingdom share equally and in common the Word of God. This is in fact true of the wicked as well as of God's people. Outwardly at least all receive God's Word. From this it follows that the command of the Lord to trade with the pound and to gain for Him by trading refers to the calling to be faithful to that Word while the Lord tarries in heaven. The fact that one servant's pound earns ten pounds and another five pounds refers to degrees of faithfulness to the Word of God which are found within the various citizens of the kingdom and the various servants of Christ.

It is true, of course, that one is either faithful or unfaithful. And we could well ask the question how it is possible to have degrees of faithfulness. But the answer to the question lies in the fact that we are still wicked while we live on this earth and while our Lord is in heaven; that, therefore, we are not always faithful to God's Word. Everyone is very much inclined to deny the Lord and to forget His calling of faithfulness in some part of his life.

But then the calling of the parable is very clear. When our Lord goes to heaven to receive the kingdom He gives to His people His Word. This Word is the Word which is incorporated infallibly into the Scriptures. It is the Word which when it is preached is the means by which Christ gathers His Church and establishes His kingdom. By this Word He calls the citizens of the kingdom out of darkness into light. By this same Word He preserves His people in the way of His truth, comforts them in their sorrow because their Lord has left them, instructs them and their children in the way of His kingdom, and assures them of His blessed promises that He will presently come again to take them to Himself. It is, as it were, that this Nobleman leaves with His servants a letter which He writes to them, in which they are to find instruction concerning the truth of the kingdom; in which they are encouraged to carry on in the defense of His kingdom; in which they are comforted while they wait the return of their Lord. By this Word Christ assures His people that He is with them always even to the end of the world.

This Word is put in the parable under the figure of a pound because the citizens of the kingdom are called to take that Word and make use of it within the kingdom. They are to use it in the spread of the gospel and in the witness they are called to make of the truth. They are to use it in the instruction of the seed of the covenant. Every servant has this pound. And in his use of the pound he is to apply the truth of that Word to his own particular place and calling in life. He is to take that Word into his family and into his work. He is to follow that Word's direction in his walk and conduct. He is to take that Word with him into the schools he builds to teach his children. He is to make that Word the guiding principle of all his life. And to accomplish this he is under the solemn obligation to remain faithful to that Word in all his ways.

It is precisely this which the unfaithful servant did not do. The citizens rejected that Word altogether. They rejected Christ Who is King. Openly, bluntly, without equivocation, they simply rebelled and refused to submit themselves to the rule of Christ. But the sin of the servant was quite different. He did not as such repudiate that Word. He took the Word and professed to love it. In fact his profession of love for that Word was part of his defense when he was called to give account. But he wrapped that Word carefully in a napkin so that it would not be spoiled. He did not use it. That was his sin.

When the nobleman required an accounting of the use of the pound which his servants made, the defense of this unfaithful servant is very striking. He appealed to the fact very significantly that he knew that his master was a very hard man. Evidently he meant to say that he knew that the punishment which comes upon those who misuse the Word of God is very severe. And in this he was correct. But he reasons from this that it was far safer to hide that Word where there was no possibility of his ever using it improperly. He was like people who dare not use the Word of God because they claim that they are afraid of misusing it and of incurring severe punishment on themselves for that sin.

But he had also a second excuse. He said: "Thou takest up that thou layedst not down, and reapest that thou didst not sow." He evidently meant by this that the nobleman could have anything he wanted. Was not he sovereign in his kingdom? He did not need the feeble efforts of his servants to enhance his glory and make his kingdom richer. All the kingdom is his anyway. Or, to apply this to the reality, the meaning of the objection of the servant was that Christ is supreme in His own kingdom. All authority and power is His. He can have and do whatever He wills. He does not need the efforts of men to fulfill His counsels.

And, of course, this is true. Christ Himself says so: "Thou knewest that I was an austere man, taking up that I laid not down, and reaping that I did not sow." But this does not alter the calling. In reality, the objection of this servant was intended to accuse his master of laying on him a greater responsibility than he could carry. He charged him with asking too much of him and with requiring faithfulness in too difficult circumstances.

This sin is not at all uncommon. How often is it not true that we insist that the Lord requires too much of us? Faithfulness requires the payment of a great price. The way of faithfulness is a difficult way to walk. The road is very steep. The night is very dark. To make use of the Word of God in every part of our life is something which requires hardship and struggle and pain; because of that Word we must endure the hatred and contempt of the world. But with the servant, excuses of this sort are simply attempts at self-justification. The servant attempted to cover up his refusal to obey Christ with a few pious platitudes. He was trying to shift the blame of his sloth on the Lord. He really despised the Word of God and hated the calling that had been given him. He would not take that Word and use it. It is true that the calling to take God's Word and be faithful to it and use it in all our life in the kingdom is a very difficult calling. It is filled with danger and requires suffering and trial. But one who is deeply impressed with the seriousness of his calling labors in the consciousness that Christ will be his constant support and help. The work is not his own but it is the work which Christ has given him to do. Christ will enable him to be steadfast also. This is our calling. From it we may never depart.

Nevertheless, it seems as if those who have a place in the kingdom have their excuses why faithlessness to the Word can be justified. Many who belong to churches that walk the road to apostasy refuse to separate themselves from such churches for one reason or another, though they know that continued membership in such a church requires unfaithfulness to the Word. Many, often for economic reasons, refuse to give their children instruction in the truth of the Scriptures; and, though they knew this is unfaithfulness to the Word, they continue to do it and find various reasons to justify their faithlessness. When there is in the midst of life a lack of spiritual ability to apply the abiding and eternal principles of the Word to the specifics of our life and calling in the home and in the shop and in our relationships to others, this failure to be faithful is justified by ready excuses which come to our lips. It is of such faithlessness that the Lord speaks in His condemnation of this wicked servant.

The Reward which Christ at His Return Gives

At the proper time the nobleman returned, having received his kingdom. So also does Christ return when the time comes for Him to realize His kingdom in all its fulness in glory. There is a fixed time, fixed by the immutable counsel of God, when Christ returns. It is the time when the purpose of God is accomplished, when all is in readiness for Christ to inherit the kingdom prepared for Him. Then the kingdom is ready to be taken to glory. At that time Christ will come again riding on the clouds of heaven to bring an end to this present age. Then the everlasting kingdom that shall never be destroyed will be established in the new heavens and the new earth.

But Christ will come with His reward.

The citizens who refused to have Christ reign over them are taken and slain. Evidently that they are slain before the face of the Lord refers to the fact that their punishment is according to strictest justice. They committed terrible sins. They are sentenced to everlasting destruction. But in their punishment the cause of Christ is vindicated. While they were on earth they denounced this cause of Christ and mocked His kingdom. But now in their punishment the kingdom of Christ is publicly shown to be the true and abiding kingdom that can never end.

In reality, the unfaithful servant receives his reward. He hated the Word of Christ and would not use it. And so his pound is taken from him. Even his outward place in the kingdom is taken away. The

Word which came to him while he lived on earth is gone, silenced in the doom of hell. He has nothing left. His judgment is righteous and just.

But the faithful also receive their reward. First, the reward is the word of our Lord: "Well done, thou good and faithful servant." What could be more blessed as one stands before the glorious judgment seat of Christ the King than to hear these words? To hear these words echo over the throng gathered there, to hear them directed to you and to me—this is blessedness beyond compare.

Second, the reward also consists in this that each is given rule over certain cities. The meaning is evidently that God's people who served Christ here on earth are made kings with Christ in the new kingdom of heaven. These people shall always remain subjects, citizens, servants, those who bow before the Lord of glory. But they shall also be kings with Christ to rule in His Name over that new and glorious kingdom which Christ has inherited for them.

Notice that the reward is in proportion to faithfulness. Once again, this does not mean that the citizens of the kingdom earn this reward. The reward is of grace alone, even as the work and the faithfulness of their lives is of grace. But this does not alter the fact that each man receives as his work has been. He whose pound earned ten pounds receives the rule over ten cities. He whose pound earned five pounds receives the rule over five cities. The measure of faithfulness here below is proportionately rewarded above. The diligence with which we labor in the kingdom, the earnestness with which we make use of the Word of God, the single-heartedness of purpose with which we pursue our heavenly calling—all will be proportionately blessed.

This is our incentive to spur us on. Faithfulness is a difficult calling while the Lord is gone from us. It is the way of self-denial, of hardship, of trouble. It can never bring a life of ease and pleasure according to the standards of the flesh. But such a great reward beckons us and urges us on. It is the encouragement that presses on us faithfulness to death.

Be faithful then to that Word, faithful in its use. The reward will certainly be ours.

25

The Exaltation of the Cornerstone

Hear another parable: There was a certain householder, which planted a vineyard, and hedged it round about, and digged a winepress in it, and built a tower, and let it out to husbandmen, and went into a far country:

And when the time of the fruit drew near, he sent his servants to the husbandmen, that they might receive the fruits of it.

And the husbandmen took his servants, and beat one, and killed another, and stoned another.

Again, he sent other servants more than the first: and they did unto them likewise.

But last of all he sent unto them his son, saying, They will reverence my son.

But when the husbandmen saw the son, they said among themselves, This is the heir; come, let us kill him, and let us seize on his inheritance.

And they caught him, and cast him out of the vineyard, and slew him. When the lord therefore of the vineyard cometh, what will he do unto those husbandmen?

They say unto him, He will miserably destroy those wicked men, and will let out his vineyard unto other husbandmen, which shall render him the fruits in their seasons.

Jesus saith unto them, Did ye never read in the scriptures, The stone which the builders rejected, the same is become the head of the corner: this is the Lord's doing, and it is marvellous in our eyes?

Therefore say I unto you, The kingdom of God shall be taken from you, and given to a nation bringing forth the fruits thereof.

And whosoever shall fall on this stone shall be broken: but on whomsoever it shall fall, it will grind him to powder.

—Matthew 21:33-44.

This parable was taught by the Lord during the last week of His life on earth. Sunday He had come riding triumphantly into Jerusalem, and all the people had shouted their hosannas to the Son of David. In the city of Jerusalem Jesus had taught the people, had performed many wonderful miracles of healing, and had thrown out of the temple those who made His Father's house a den of thieves.

All these things only increased the fear and hatred of Jesus in the hearts of the leaders of Israel. They saw that more and more there were only two alternatives: either they had to repent of their sin and believe on Christ, or they had to defend their coveted position as Israel's leaders and get rid of Christ. There was no room anymore in Palestine for both them and Christ. But they refused to repent and believe. So the alternative was to find some reason, no matter how small, on the basis of which they could condemn Christ to death.

And so the day after Jesus cleansed the temple they came to Him with a question concerning His right to do this: "By what authority doest thou these things? And who gave thee this authority?" At first blush they seemed to be interested only in learning more about the nature of Jesus' calling and ministry. But this was a hypocritical mask for a deep-seated hatred. Jesus answered with a counterquestion, not because He had any desire to evade their question—it was easily answered—but because Jesus knew full well that they had not the slightest concern for any authority whatsoever because they hated the authority of God. Jesus and John were, after all, one; and if they despised the authority of John, what point was there in speaking of and explaining His own authority?

But to show their sin in all its terrible rebellion, Jesus told two parables. In the first He likened the leaders of the Jews to a hypocritical son, pointing out that they were, even in their positions of leadership, inferior to publicans and harlots. In the second parable Jesus emphatically and sharply condemned their terrible crimes. He showed them that they were as evil as their fathers who always rejected the authority of God by killing the prophets; that they filled the cup of iniquity by killing God's Son; and that, while Jesus used their sin to exalt the cornerstone of the Church, judgment on them and on all that reject the cornerstone is swift and terrible.

Jesus brings this truth of Himself as the Cornerstone to the foreground in the conclusion of the parable; and, although the figure changes, this is the main idea.

God's Care of His Vineyard

The figure of the vineyard is not foreign to Scripture, and we have met it before in our discussion of the parables. In Psalm 80, a Psalm to which Jesus may have had reference in this parable, the Psalmist sings: "Thou hast brought a vine out of Egypt: thou hast cast out the heathen and planted it. Thou preparedst room before it, and didst cause it to take deep root, and it filled the land. . . . Why hast thou then broken down her hedges, so that all they which pass by the way do pluck her?" (vv. 8, 9, 12).

Again, the care which the householder bestows on the vineyard is described in the song of the vineyard in Isaiah 5: "Now will I sing to my well beloved a song of my beloved touching his vineyard. My well beloved hath a vineyard in a very fruitful hill: and he fenced it, and gathered out the stones thereof, and planted it with the choicest vine, and built a tower in the midst of it, and also made a winepress therein: and he looked that it should bring forth grapes, and it brought forth wild grapes. . . . What could have been done more to my vineyard that I have not done in it?" (vv. 1, 2, 4a).

While the reference of the parable is primarily to the Old Dispensation because it speaks of the wickedness of the Jews, the meaning is no less applicable to the history of the Church in the New Dispensation; for, contrary to the position of the premillennialists, the two Testaments are essentially one and the Church is one throughout all ages. So once again, the vineyard refers to the historical and visible manifestation of the kingdom of heaven, the temporal and outward aspect of the kingdom of God. This was in type and shadow during the years of the Old Dispensation. It is part of the visible church, nominal Christendom, in the dispensation of the coming of Christ.

With respect to the husbandmen, there are some who maintain that they are the leaders of the Jews: the Priests and Levites, the Scribes and Pharisees of Jesus' day. Now there is no doubt that this is true. Immediately after Jesus' application of the parable we read: "And when the chief priests and Pharisees had heard his parables, they perceived that he spake of them" (Matt. 21:45). But this cannot be the entire meaning, for Jesus also speaks of the fact that the kingdom will not simply be taken away from the leaders and given to other leaders, but that the kingdom will be taken away from the nation and given to another nation. Naturally, the leaders are directly referred to by Jesus since, in their position of leadership, with its greater responsibility and trust, their accountability remains the greater. But this does not alter the fact that Jesus refers to the entire nation when He speaks of husbandmen in the parable. To all the people of the nation was entrusted the keeping of the vineyard. Upon all of them lay the obligation to bring forth the fruit of the vineyard for the welfare of the householder who is God, the sovereign Lord of heaven and earth.

Nevertheless, two things must be borne in mind. In the first place, the husbandmen do not refer to all the members of the commonwealth of Israel, to all the natural Jews. The husbandmen are wicked. They constitute the outward shell of the nation, the reprobate in Israel who, although they are Israel, are not of Israel. They are the majority of the nation; in fact, organically speaking, they are the nation. But they are the reprobate in the nation. There is also the elect kernel that persists by the grace of God throughout the ages and which will enter the kingdom of heaven even when it is taken away from the others.

In the second place, throughout the parable the husbandmen are pictured as being the same men. They depict, however, the generations of Israelites from Moses to Christ, generations that covered many centuries of history and included many different men. That

Jesus speaks of the same men in the parable is not a point incidental to the main thought, however. By it Jesus means to say that throughout these generations, for many centuries of history, from Moses to Christ, these people were always really the same. They acted the same, did the same things, and committed the same sins. Stephen later expressed this when he said: "As your fathers did, so do ye."

Now the Lord had bestowed much care on this vineyard. He had done, in the words of Isaiah, all that was necessary to have a vineyard that would bring forth abundant fruit. Although Jesus may not perhaps refer to specific incidents in Israel's life when He speaks in the parable of the wall, the tower, and the winepress, nevertheless these things emphasize the care bestowed on the nation. God had "let out" his vineyard to husbandmen when He had called Israel out of the bondage of Egypt and brought them with a strong arm and with mighty signs and wonders through the wilderness into the land of Canaan, a land flowing with milk and honey. God had "fenced about" His people when at Sinai He had delivered to them the law and the whole body of legislation which marked Israel as a separate people distinct from all the nations of the earth. God had given to them His own oracles through the ceremonies and sacrifices of the tabernacle and temple, through the land in which they dwelt, through the wonders which He performed before their eyes.

In all these things God had revealed His promises and covenant He had made with His own. So to speak, He had been Israel's "tower," their refuge to Whom they might flee in times of trouble. God had fought for them against their enemies, caused the skies to rain down fire and hail on those who warred against Israel, ordered the angel of death to smite the armies of the heathen. God had sheltered and protected Israel in a land of promise from the nations which daily threatened its existence. Israel was but few in number and it had not strength of its own. The nation was easy prey to all those who were gathered about it. But God had been their refuge and strength. And, as long as they walked in the ways of the Lord, no enemy could hurt them.

This vineyard God had entrusted to the care of the nation. This does not mean, as some are accustomed to express it, that God was doing all in His power to save Israel because it was His earnest desire and intense longing to make the whole nation head for head His own. It does not mean that God's purpose was frustrated by the wicked in Israel. As the parable goes on to make clear, the rejection of the cornerstone by the nation was exactly according to God's purpose that through this rejection the cornerstone might be exalted into a position of highest glory. Hence this Arminian conception is not the viewpoint of the parable, nor is it the teaching of Scripture. Rather, the emphasis must be placed on the fact that God did everything that was necessary so that Israel might know what her calling was. He had given the nation every means to bring forth the fruit that He required. But His purpose was to reveal the terrible sin of the nation as a whole.

Nevertheless, fruits would normally be expected of the nation. Would not you expect of your children or friends gratitude if you had bestowed so many things on them? These fruits were not the outward fruits of the law. There were often plenty of these fruits in Israel and especially in Jesus' day. In fact, Scripture contains many loud complaints that all of Israel's sacrifices were a stink in the nostrils of the Most High. But the law and all that God had given to Israel revealed the promises of God in Christ. The land of Canaan, the laws—civil and ceremonial, all the wonders which God performed were but fingers pointing Israel to Christ Who was the fulfillment of God's promise. And therefore the fruits which were expected were the fruits of faith in God's promise and in Christ first of all. This faith in God's promise which is Christ leads to the works of repentance and sorrow for sin. And this in turn leads to works of the righteousness of the kingdom, that those who walk in that kingdom may walk in the way of the precepts of the kingdom of heaven.

This is no less true in the New Testament than it was in the Old. Now too we speak of a Church visible. Within that Church are many people, elect and reprobate alike. By far the majority of the people are reprobate, for they outnumber the remnant according to the election of grace. Nevertheless within the Church all the members have many privileges. There is in that kingdom centrally the ministry of the Word of the gospel. From this ministry of the Word come many more things: the sacraments of baptism and the Lord's Supper, the Christian education of the seed of the covenant, the communion of the saints in the fellowship of the Church, and so forth. Everything is there in the kingdom that is necessary for those who are in it to know what their calling is and what fruits they are to bring forth in the Name of God.

This is the purpose of God. He wills it to be this way. He wills that there are many men within the outward and visible kingdom. He wills that in all the institutions, forms, and structures of the visible kingdom, the vineyard is entrusted to their care in order that they may use it for God's benefit. In this way God accomplishes His own sovereign purpose.

The Sin of the Husbandmen

Did Israel bring forth the fruits that were required of them? They did exactly the opposite.

Indeed they used the things of the kingdom in which they had been placed. They used the law, the temple, the burnt offerings, and the feast days. In fact, in Jesus' day this was preeminently true. But they always used the vineyard of God to sin. They despised God's promises and trampled under foot His covenant. They mocked with holy things and played with the precious heritage that had been committed to them. They served other gods and committed all the abominations of the heathen whom God had delivered into their hand. They rebelled against God and did all they could to advance their own personal gain and acquire praise and honor of men.

To them God sent His servants rising up early and bringing to them the unchangeable Word of God. Thses servants were the prophets that had come to Israel from Moses to John the Baptist. Each in his own time, in the unique circumstances of his own calling, had appeared on the stage of Israel's history to gather the fruit from the vineyard. But although these servants were primarily the prophets, they included also the faithful kings and priests that Israel had had throughout her years, and even the remnant according to God's purpose of election, the seven thousand who had never bowed the knee to Baal. These servants warned and threatened when they saw all the sins of the nation. They were filled with grief and sorrow over the rape of God's heritage. They called Israel again and again to repentance, to bring forth the fruits of God's vineyard. They never wearied in all their life in coming "to seek for fruit."

This continues throughout the entire New Dispensation. The servants whom God sends are the faithful in His Church who come into the vineyard to seek fruit for God. These bring the witness of the Church—the witness not primarily outside the Church to the heathen, but the witness within the visible Church to the unfaithful. This witness will remain on the earth until the end—that is, until Antichrist himself finally silences that witness with the sword. So now too the call goes out to the wicked husbandmen in God's vineyard to repent of their sins, produce the fruits of truth and righteousness, and walk according to the precepts of the kingdom of heaven.

The result of this is that sin develops with the kingdom. This development is particularly emphasized in the parable. On the one hand, the Lord speaks of the fact that more servants are sent with greater power and authority. As time progressed, there were Isaiahs and Jeremiahs and Daniels. And finally there was the greatest of all the prophets, John the Baptist. On the other hand, there was development also in the sin which the husbandmen committed. They beat with whips. But then they committed the sin of murder. And finally they stoned those whom God had sent.

So, in proportion to the increase in the power and authority of the servants of Jehovah which He sends, so did the sin of the husbandmen also increase.

In explaining this sin of the husbandmen, Jesus suddenly changed the picture in the parable to the figure of a stone. This was done precisely in order that the Jews might see that the truth which He taught in the parable was the fulfillment of their own prophecies in which they claimed to believe. The Scriptures had said they would reject the cornerstone (see Ps. 118:22). The Jews on their part claimed to be building the house of God in their work in the vineyard. This was their proud boast and their continuous claim. But when they came to the cornerstone, the only stone on which the house of God could be built, they looked at it, considered it, and threw it away as unfit for use.

They did this throughout the entire history of their nation. For Christ, the Cornerstone of God, was already in the prophets of the Old Dispensation. But always they rejected this Cornerstone. Think only of some of the brief glimpses of this which Scripture gives us: how Ahab and Jezebel sought the life of Elijah; how Josiah killed the prophet Zachariah the son of Jehoida the priest; how Jeremiah rotted in the dungeon because he brought the Word of God. We are told, if tradition is correct, that Isaiah was sawn in pieces with a wooden saw by the command of Manasseh who made Jerusalem run red with the blood of the saints. Jeremiah never had a happy moment and was stoned at last in Egypt far from God's heritage. John the Baptist was put in prison by godless Herod, and, without a protest from the Jews, was beheaded.

Israel's history is written with the blood of God's martyrs. "And the Lord God of their fathers said to them by his messengers, rising up betimes, and sending; because he had compassion on his people, and on his dwelling place: But they mocked the messengers of God, and despised his words, and misused his prophets, until the wrath of the Lord arose against his people, till there was no remedy." This is the sad complaint of the chronicler of Judah's history (see I Chron. 36:15, 16).

Jesus Himself expressed it in these words: "Woe unto you, scribes and Pharisees, hypocrites! because ye build the tombs of the prophets, and garnish the sepulchres of the righteous, And say, If we had been in the days of our fathers, we would not have been partakers with them in the blood of the prophets. Wherefore ye be witnesses unto yourselves, that ye are the children of them which killed the prophets. . . . Wherefore, behold, I send unto you prophets, and wise men, and scribes; and some of them ye shall kill and crucify, and some of them shall ye scourge in your synagogues, and persecute them from city to city: that upon you may come all the righteous blood shed upon the earth, from the blood of righteous Abel unto the blood of Zacharias son of Barachias, whom ye slew between the temple and the altar. . . . O Jerusalem, Jerusalem, thou that killest the prophets and stonest them which are sent unto thee . . ." (Matt. 23:29-31, 34, 35, 37).

Stephen expressed this same sentiment in his powerful speech before the Sanhedrin when he concluded with the words: "Ye stiffnecked and uncircumcised in heart and ears, ye do always resist the Holy Ghost: as your fathers did so do ye. Which of the prophets have not your fathers persecuted? and they have slain them which shewed before of the coming of the Just One; of whom ye have been now the betrayers and murderers" (Acts 7:51, 52).

The slaughter of the prophets was principally the murder of Christ, for Christ was in the prophets speaking through them. No wonder then that the sin of the nation culminated in the murder of God's Son. "But last of all he sent unto them his son, saying, They will reverence my son." This does not mean that God did not know what the wicked Jews would do with Christ. But the point is that this emphasizes the greatness of their monstrous crimes. Mark puts it this way: "Having yet therefore one son, his well-beloved, he sent him also last unto them, saying, They will reverence my son." Anyone would expect that even though they were very wicked they would not dare to kill the son or have the courage to commit such an unspeakable crime.

How literally the parable was fulfilled only a few days later! The coming of Christ indeed exposed their sin for what it really was. They had tried to make a pretense of piety and leave the impression they were building the house of God. But now that the son is come, all pretense is gone. "This is the heir; come, let us kill him, and the inheritance shall be ours." Their mask of piety is ripped away. Their evil designs are fully exposed. They are shown now for what they really were. They have every intention of stealing the vineyard from God and making it their own possession.

Literally was this prophecy fulfilled. Only a few days later the Jews dragged Christ outside the holy city and crucified Him without the gate. Christ had also come demanding fruit. He preached obedience and repentance. He spoke of the householder, His Father in heaven. He revealed the glories and promises of the kingdom, and all the evil consequences of disobedience. Did they hearken unto Him? Did they bring forth fruit? Far from it. In the evil of their hearts and with deliberate and conscious sin they cast Him out of the vineyard and called His blood upon themselves and their children.

But this was the climax of centuries of sin. Sin always develops organically in the line of generations. The wicked Jews of Jesus' day were responsible for all the sins of their fathers. This was true because they approved of those sins and showed their approval by killing Christ. All the guilt of all time came crashing on them because they, by killing Christ, really killed all the prophets.

But so it is throughout the ages. Even after Christ ascended into heaven, the apostate church—those who are laborers in the vineyard—killed the servants of Christ. They kill the people of God who speak to them the truth of Scripture. And by doing this they call down the blood of Christ upon their heads, for they kill Christ again and again when they cast out the testimony of Christ.

This sin too develops organically in the line of generations, till it reaches its climax in the end of time when the witness of the Church is finally silenced and the Christ is wholly cast out of His own vineyard. How red the hands of the false church are with the blood of the saints! Never can the waters of a thousand oceans wash that blood from their hands. And as the generations of men progress,

that guilt accumulates; for except they repent, they bear all the guilt
of their fathers before them by approving of their acts. And it must
culminate in the final crime of the ages when the witness of God's
servants shall at last be silenced on this earth.

The Fulfillment of God's Purpose

But Jesus tells us that this is the fulfillment of the prophecy of
Psalm 118: the stone which the builders despised is become the head
of the corner. But this is the Lord's doing!

Indeed, the people of Israel claimed to be building the house of
God. But this was their hypocrisy and their sin. When they came to
the cornerstone they rejected it because they would not use it. They
rejected the cornerstone by nailing Christ to the cross. But this very
rejection of the cornerstone was according to the determinate counsel and foreknowledge of God. God used their wicked designs for
His own sovereign purpose. He brought Christ to the cross and sent
Him to the suffering of the cross to establish through the blood of
the cross the kingdom of righteousness and truth.

And so God raised Christ from the grave and exalted Him in the
highest heavens at the right hand of the Majesty on High. There
Christ became the head of the corner. He became the cornerstone
upon which the entire glorious temple of the Church of God is built.
Upon Christ and His blood that Church rests. From Christ and His
righteousness that Church receives her all. Rejected and despised of
men, Christ is now raised to the highest position of glory and power
in the heavens.

Thus the sovereign purpose of God is accomplished through it all.
God had His purpose in putting husbandmen in His vineyard and
giving that vineyard to their care. And when it was all over two things
appear. One: the husbandmen were desperately wicked and capable
of monstrous crimes, for they threw out the Son of God. Two: God
raised the Stone rejected and despised to the position of Cornerstone, for Christ is God's elect and precious.

Thus judgment is swift and inevitable. These wicked themselves
see the justice of it. When the question was put point blank to them:
"When the lord therefore of the vineyard cometh, what will he do
unto those husbandmen?" they have the answer ready, for anyone
can see that that alone is justice: "He will miserably destroy those
wicked men, and will let out his vineyard unto other husbandmen,
which shall render him the fruits in their seasons." This is exactly
correct. Their own mouths have condemned them.

So the kingdom shall be taken away from them and given to
another nation. This happened at Pentecost and finally at the destruction of Jerusalem. But the complete fulfillment of this will take
place at the end of time when all they have and ever had in the
vineyard will be taken away forever and ever. Then destruction
sudden and swift comes upon them. They fall over the stone because
that stone remains. Nothing can now destroy it. They do not see it;

they reject and despise it and throw it away. But the stone remains and it shall surely come rolling with crushing force on all the workers of iniquity to make them as the chaff of the threshing floor. The apostle Peter puts it this way in his first epistle: "Ye also, as living stones, are built up a spiritual house, an holy priesthood, to offer up spiritual sacrifices acceptable to God by Jesus Christ. Wherefore also it is contained in the scripture, Behold I lay in Sion a chief corner stone, elect, precious: and he that believeth on him shall not be confounded. Unto you therefore which believe he is precious: but unto them which be disobedient, the stone which the builders disallowed, the same is made the head of the corner, And a stone of stumbling, and a rock of offence, even to them which stumble at the word, being disobedient: whereunto also they were appointed" (2:5-8).

The kingdom is given to another nation. This nation is not the nation of national Israel. It is the nation of the whole number of God's elect, Jew and Gentile, gathered from all nations that dwell on the face of the earth. It is the nation of the true temple of God. Christ is the cornerstone and upon Him that temple is built. The apostle Paul describes this very thing in Ephesians 2:19-22: "Now therefore ye are no more strangers and foreigners, but fellowcitizens with the saints, and of the household of God; And are built upon the foundation of the apostles and prophets, Jesus Christ himself being the chief corner stone; In whom all the building fitly framed together groweth unto an holy temple in the Lord; In whom ye also are builded together for an habitation of God through the Spirit." In that kingdom they bring forth the fruits of the kingdom. And that kingdom they finally inherit forever and ever.

What then is the conclusion of the matter?

In the first place, it is well to remember that sin always develops organically in the lines of generations when the guilt of preceding generations is heaped on the heads of those that follow in the way of sin.

In the second place, it is a terrible thing to be in the kingdom and not bring forth the fruits of righteousness and truth. These will be beaten with double stripes. Sodom and Gomorrah will rise up in judgment and condemn them. And we who stand must beware lest we boast in ourselves and fall.

Finally, God will establish His kingdom even through the wicked; for the cornerstone stands forever as the foundation of the Church. Against it all the enemies of the Church are dashed to pieces. Upon it the Church shall abide firm and immovable, world without end.

26

The Victory of the Gospel

And Jesus answered and spake unto them again by parables, and said,
The kingdom of heaven is like unto a certain king, which made a marriage for his son,
And sent forth his servants to call them that were bidden to the wedding: and they would not come.
Again, he sent forth other servants, saying, Tell them which are bidden, Behold, I have prepared my dinner: my oxen and my fatlings are killed, and all things are ready: come unto the marriage.
But they made light of it, and went their ways, one to his farm, another to his merchandise:
And the remnant took his servants, and entreated them spitefully, and slew them.
But when the king heard thereof, he was wroth: and he sent forth his armies, and destroyed those murderers, and burned up their city.
Then saith he to his servants, The wedding is ready, but they which were bidden were not worthy.
Go ye therefore into the highways, and as many as ye shall find, bid to the marriage.
So those servants went out into the highways, and gathered together all as many as they found, both bad and good: and the wedding was furnished with guests.

—Matthew 22:1-10

Many commentators, including John Calvin, have treated this parable as being only a different form of the parable of the great supper which is recorded in Luke 14:16-24. And it is true that there are striking similarities. Nevertheless the differences are of sufficient importance that a separate treatment of this parable is warranted. The differences between the two parables are the following.

In the first place, the occasions of the two parables are different. In the parable of the great supper Jesus was answering the question, who would eat bread in the kingdom of God. And the answer was then given that these would not be the ones whom the Jews expected. In this parable the occasion is the attempt of the Jews to find some reason to condemn Jesus by questioning Him concerning His authority. They were eager to kill Him; only the people restrained their hands. Second, although this is not an essential point, the parable recorded in Luke speaks only of a great supper, while this parable emphatically speaks of a wedding feast, and that for the son of the king. Third, in the final application of the parable of the great supper the Lord makes the point that the house is at last filled with guests. While this is evidently implied in verse 10 of Matthew 22, here the emphasis falls on the fact that the servants were sent out twice to call to the supper. And the application is finally made in verse 14: "many are called, but few are chosen." Fourth, in keeping with this different emphasis, Luke simply speaks in his parable of those that were bidden as excusing themselves; Matthew speaks of the terrible rebellion on the part of those that were bidden. Finally, there is appended to this parable an additional section which deals with the man without a wedding garment. This section of the parable is of sufficient importance that I will treat it separately in the following chapter.

No doubt the main point of this parable can well be said to be an answer to the question the apostle Paul later asks in Romans 9:6: "Since the nation of Israel is rejected, is the Word of God then of none effect?" It could very well be that this question arose in the minds of the disciples. It seemed as if Christ never did accomplish very much in His ministry in Palestine. Rather than rallying the Jews to His banner, He had only succeeded in antagonizing them to the point where they were determined to kill Him. Now the rejection of the nation of Israel is about to be completed, and Christ is ready to be crucified. Has the Word of God failed to accomplish its purpose?

The answer is given by Jesus in this parable. The foregoing is precisely not the case. Even though the nation of the Jews and the majority of those who hear the Word of God reject it, nevertheless the gospel is always victorious in accomplishing the purpose of God and saving the elect. For, although many are called, only very few are chosen. But those who are chosen are surely saved.

The Meaning of the Elements of the Parable

There can be no question concerning the meaning of the different elements in the parable.

God is the King. He is the sovereign Ruler of all the creation He has made with His own hands. He is the One Who prepares the final banquet of the everlasting kingdom of heaven. He and He alone calls to the wedding feast, for He is the One Who preaches the gospel by which His chosen are called.

Christ is the King's Son; He is the eternal Son of God. That He came into our flesh and became the Christ, the Messiah, does not alter the fact that He remains in the unity of His human and divine nature the eternal Son of God. As the Son of God in our flesh He is the King's Son, the Prince, Who is destined to reign over the everlasting kingdom of God.

The ones who are first bidden are, no doubt, the Jews of the Old Dispensation. The emphasis is definitely on the fact that these people had been bidden to come to the feast for a long time. By the use of the perfect tense, Jesus makes clear that the summons to the feast had gone out a long time ago, and all knew that very shortly the wedding feast would be ready. Finally all the preparations are made, and the servants go out to inform them that were bidden that all is now in readiness and that now they must come to the feast. The time is come for the great celebration. Those who knew all along that the feast was coming are now informed that the time is here. That is, the Jews of the Old Dispensation were told repeatedly by God that the wedding feast of His Son was coming. God told them through the types and shadows and ceremonies of the law. He told them through the prophets He had sent to them. But in the fulness of time Jesus came. While all through the Old Dispensation the preparations were in progress, when the fulness of time was come, God sent forth His Son. Now Jesus stood at the very point of His final suffering and death, and He could confidently say: "The oxen and fatlings are killed and *all things are ready.*"

This was true because the wedding feast could come only through the suffering and death and resurrection of Jesus Christ. For Christ to go to His kingdom and to make the final preparations for the wedding feast, it was necessary that He die and rise again. There are several reasons for this. In the first place, the wedding feast was also to be the establishment of His kingdom. This was true because, although this element is not mentioned in the parable, the establishment of the kingdom of Christ is identical with the wedding feast: "The kingdom of heaven is like unto a certain king, which made a marriage feast for his son." Now the only way in which that kingdom could possibly be established was through the blood of the cross. Into that kingdom the people of God had to enter. They are the guests at the feast. But they can enter only through the blood of the cross, for they have no righteousness of their own. The way for Christ therefore was the way of the cross.

In the second place, the only way for Christ to go to His kingdom was through the cross because through His death and resurrection He becomes the Son of God. This is not to say that He is not the eternal Son of God. But as *Christ,* as the Son of God in *our flesh,* He becomes the Son of God only through the resurrection. This is plain from Scripture. In Psalm 2 we read that God says: "Yet have I set my king upon my holy hill of Zion. I will declare the decree: the Lord hath said unto me, Thou art my Son; this day have I begotten thee." According to Scripture this was not actually fulfilled until the time that Jesus rose from the dead. Thus we read in Paul's speech in Antioch of Pisidia: "God hath fulfilled the same unto us their children, in that he hath raised up Jesus again; as it is also written in the second Psalm, Thou art my Son, this day have I begotten thee" (Acts 13:33). Through the resurrection from the dead Christ Jesus becomes the Son of God, the Prince Who sits on an everlasting throne in the kingdom of heaven.

The wedding feast is therefore a picture of the final triumph of that kingdom of God.

The wedding feast for the Son is evidently the marriage of Christ and His Church. That the relationship between Christ and His Church is described in terms of a marriage is an idea not foreign to the Scriptures. The relation between Christ and His people is often pictured in this way. We read, for example, in Ephesians 5:23-33 that the relation between a husband and his wife is an earthly picture of the heavenly relation between Christ and His people; that even inasmuch as husband and wife become one flesh, they picture the union of Christ and His elect. This figure is used in Scripture because marriage is the most intimate of all relationships. Christ enters into that most intimate relationship of spiritual marriage with His people. Together they become one in the mystical body of Christ. They are one in the most intimate and personal sense of the word. This unity is a unity of life and love, a unity of mind and will. But the principle of this unity is only in Christ. The life of the Church is the life of Christ. The love which is shed abroad in the hearts of the people of God is a love which Christ first held for them. The mind and the will of the Church is the mind and will of Christ. That unity is most blessed communion of deepest friendship and fellowship which endures forever.

Yet the figure of the parable is not only the figure of a marriage, but of a marriage feast. Thus the figure is double: the people of God are both bride and guests. This is not surprising, for the people of God are guests at the marriage because in themselves they deserve no place at the wedding feast but are there by the gracious mercies of their Lord and Savior. But neither is this figure foreign to Holy Writ. The final perfection of the saints in glory is often likened to a wedding feast. Both these figures are used, for example, in Revelation 19:7-9: "Let us be glad and rejoice, and give honor to him: for the marriage of the Lamb is come, and his wife hath made herself ready. And to her was granted that she should be arrayed in fine linen, clean and white: for the fine linen is the righteousness of saints. And he saith unto me, Write, Blessed are they which are called unto the marriage supper of the Lamb."

Christ and His bride enter into marriage together, but they also sit down together at the marriage feast with the bride as the guests. This idea of a feast depicts not only the intimate relationship of marriage, but the fellowship and communion and joy and happiness of a banquet. A table is where friends eat and drink together, and it is always an earthly picture of fellowship. But the emphasis falls on the joy and happiness of this marriage. Eating and drinking, feasting and banqueting are signs of rejoicing. The marriage of Christ and His people will be so wonderful because it will be the everlasting joy which pervades the kingdom of heaven.

You may well ask the question, When do these things actually take place? The answer to this question, in the first place, is that these realities take place already in the New Dispensation. From Pentecost to the end of the age these things are principally realized by Christ. Through the cross He pours His Spirit to abide with them. His Spirit and His Word are always present with His bride, so that in this life the Church of Christ enter principally into the joys of that heavenly and mysterious marriage. Already that Church enjoys the blessedness and happiness of banqueting with Christ.

Nevertheless, this can never come in its full perfection in this life. It awaits the fulfillment and perfect realization of the kingdom of heaven. Although Christ is with His Church by His Word and Spirit, nevertheless He is also, in a very real sense, absent from His bride. They are in the world and He is in heaven. Not only that, but the marriage cannot be perfectly consummated nor the joy of the banquet full because the people of God still walk in many sins and imperfections. They still are sometimes guilty of spiritual adultery. They seek the communion of a wicked world and forsake Christ their bridegroom. And in the measure that they do this, they also lose the joys of fellowship with Christ.

And so these things can only be true in principle here on earth. We must look for the day to dawn when our bridegroom will come again to deliver us from all our sin, to clothe us in the white garments of His righteousness, and to take us to Himself into His own house where we will eat and drink with Him in the kingdom of our Father. This is the hope and glorious anticipation of the Church.

The Negative Effect of the Call to the Banquet

The parable speaks of many who reject the call to come to the wedding feast. This call to which Jesus refers by the words "many are called" is the external call of the gospel. This is not always admitted by interpreters of this parable. There are many who make the main point of this parable to be the display of the patience of God. They would have us believe that on the foreground is a picture of God Who could justly destroy these men who refuse to come, but Who continually gives to the wicked another chance in the hope that they will still change their minds and come to the wedding feast. As far as God is concerned, He loves them all and longs to see them all come to salvation. There is, it is true, a certain limit to this patience of God: presently it will be too late. But for the time being God eagerly and longingly seeks to persuade them to change their minds and come to Him.

Others admit that the call of the gospel referred to here is the external call, but they insist that this external call is an offer of salvation. Much like the other interpreters, they teach that God loves all men through a cross that is for all men and an atonement that covers the sin of all men. Based on the universality of the love of God and the universality of the atonement of the cross, God offers the salvation of the cross to all men and gives them all an opportunity to accept this offer and heed the invitation to come to the wedding feast of the Son.

We have noted before that this error is the age-old error of Pelagius and Arminius which makes God a helpless beggar dependent on the will of man. It is an error that has been condemned again and again by the Church. But it is an error which, sad to say, has laid its paralyzing grip on much of the Church world of today.

The external call of the gospel is quite different from this. In the first place, the external call of the gospel comes to all who hear the preaching of the gospel. These are not all men in the world, for all men in the world do not hear this external call of the gospel. But they are many more men than are actually saved. "Many are called. . . . " The conclusion of this parable makes a distinction between the "many" who are called and God's "few" who are chosen.

In the second place, the external call of the gospel is the call to repentance and faith in Christ. This does not mean that God invites men to come to Him. A king never invites, at least not in the sense in which we use the word today. Even an earthly king never *invites* his subjects to come to the palace. They are summoned and commanded to come by the sovereign prerogative which the king possesses. The choice of whether they are going to come or whether they will refrain from coming is not left up to them. They refuse to come at their own peril. How much more is it not true that the sovereign Lord of all never invites to the wedding feast. He calls and commands to come, and He thus places men before the obligation to come.

In the third place, this call of the gospel is principally the demand of God to all men that they love Him. This was the demand which God placed on Adam in Paradise. This demand God maintains. The fact that man has sinned against Him and has by his sin fallen into total depravity, does not alter the fact that the demand remains. But because man sinned against God, this demand becomes the demand to love God in the way of repentance and in the way of turning from sin to faith in Christ. To all who hear the gospel this demand comes.

In the fourth place, God has His own purpose in this external call of the gospel. On the one hand, it is necessary to maintain the demands of God's law which are unchangeable. God still insists that men love Him. He constantly brings to their attention that this is their calling. God must maintain His law and must insist on men meeting the requirements of His command. On the other hand, when men continue to refuse to obey and to hear the external call, the basis is laid for their just condemnation. When at last God sends them to everlasting destruction, they themselves and all the world must admit that their judgment is righteous and just and that God is vindicated in His work of destroying them.

But to this external call there is only a negative reaction. The external call is never enough to save, nor is it intended to be enough to save. The reason for this is obvious. Man is a sinner. He is totally unable to do any good. He is bound in the shackles of sin and guilt and has lost the ability to do anything pleasing in God's sight. Totally depraved, he cannot even will to do the good. He cannot by his own power repent and believe and love God. If a man is to hear the gospel and respond to it with faith and repentance, his heart must be changed by a power which is outside himself. His heart must be regenerated and restored by God. It must be prepared as good soil is prepared for the sowing of the seed before the seed of the Word can take root within him. But the external call of the gospel alone can never effect this. It leaves man's heart spiritually unchanged. And so, because of the sin of man, the external call of the gospel can never bring one person to the wedding feast of the king's son.

But this does not mean that the external call of the gospel leaves man wholly untouched. This is not the case. Rather, the gospel always stirs up the evil heart of man so that his sin is fully exposed. This is also the teaching of the parable. The sin of the refusal of the guests who were bidden stands against the background of the glorious reality of the wedding feast. What could be more wonderful and blessed than to sit down with Christ in this heavenly banquet? No earthly experience can compare with it. It is the only true happiness. It is the everlasting fellowship of man with God. If an earthly king would promise to make his citizens most blessed forever, and would promise to make them happy by giving all that their hearts desire, no man would refuse to come. But when God calls to the infinitely more glorious wedding feast of His Son, men will not come. This is precisely the horror of their sin. They are so filled with inquity and guilt that they will not come. They hate God and Christ with such burning hatred that they refuse to enter into the blessed heavenly banquet. It is the folly of sin, the furious hatred of sin, the terrible power of man's depravity.

It is for this reason that there are different reactions to this call to the wedding feast. There are, in the first place, those who simply flatly refuse. "And they would not come." They have no excuse. They do not hedge. They simply and flatly say no! There are those in this life who do this. They are totally indifferent. They cannot be bothered by it. They do not even want to hear about the matter. They simply say with utter finality: no!

In the second place, there are those who mock the whole matter and simply go their own way. They are too wrapped up in their farms and merchandise. They are engrossed in the pleasures and treasurers of life. They love the life here below and hate the things of the kingdom. And so, when the call comes to enter into the wedding feast, they laugh off the whole thing as a big joke. They say that it cannot possibly be a serious matter for them to consider. It is only a farce and they will have nothing to do with it.

In the third place, there are also those who are aroused to hatred and fury. The more they hear the external call of the gospel, the more their hearts are stirred to anger against God and against those who bring this external call. All their anger and bitter hatred is poured out against God's people. They abuse God's servants and murder those whom God sends. They cannot rest until the witness of the gospel is utterly silenced and they are permitted to go their own ways without their consciences being pricked by the call to the wedding feast. They fill the cup of iniquity and become ripe for judgment.

In all these ways the purpose of God is accomplished.

The Power of the Gospel to Gather the Elect

Does this mean then that the purpose of God is not accomplished? Is the Word of God of none effect? This was the question which puzzled and worried the disciples. But Jesus assured them that this is far from the truth, for the people of God are gathered and the banquet is furnished with guests. These guests are described in a threefold way in the parable.

In the first place, they are described as being worthy. This is stated in the parable only by implication. The others were unworthy; these are worthy. Only we must hasten to add that their worthiness does not lie in themselves. This is evident from the remainder of their description in the parable.

In the second place, they are those who are gathered from the highways. Literally this refers to those who are gathered from the places where the roads which come out of the country converge on the road that leads through the gates of the city. Here were gathered the poor and the despised, the beggars and bums and tramps, the tax collectors and the little merchants. They represent the despised throughout the world's history. The apostle Paul speaks of these when he writes in I Corinthians 1:26: "For ye see your calling, brethren, how that not many wise men after the flesh, not many mighty, not many noble, are called."

In the third place, they are described as the good and the bad. These two words must not be taken in the absolute sense of the word, as if they refer to morally and spiritually good or bad before the face of God. There are none that are good. All men are gone astray and become corrupted in their sin. But the meaning is rather that they are all taken without distinction. There are all kinds of people gathered by God as guests at the wedding feast. There is no regard for their persons, for God takes whom He will.

Thus the meaning, that the Jews as a nation are rejected because they rejected Christ. They are the ones who would not come to the banquet feast when called by the external call. Rather, God gathers His Church from both the Jews and Gentiles throughout all time but especially in the New Dispensation. These are gathered not according to any choice which men would make, but by the choice of the sovereign good pleasure of God. In comparison with the many who are called, they are only few in number. They are the remnant. It is sometimes claimed that this sovereign choice is an arbitrary choice. And it often appears this way to us. We can never imagine why God should choose this one and not that one; why God should choose us and not others. There is no reason in us at all. But from God's point of view there is no arbitrariness about His choice. God chooses whom He will in sovereign wisdom and according to His good pleasure. He chooses the weak and despised because "God hath chosen the foolish things of the world to confound the wise; and God hath chosen the weak things of the world to confound the things which are mighty; and base things of the world, and things which are despised, hath God chosen, yea, and things which are not; to bring to nought things that are: that no flesh should glory in his presence" (I Cor. 1:27-29). But always the reason lies in God's sovereign good pleasure.

There are gathered by the internal call of the gospel.

Notice the change in the description in the parable. The first are bidden and then called and then called again. But the last are simply found by the servants and gathered. It is true, of course, that they too are called; but the parable emphasizes that they are *gathered*. This refers to the fact that while the others are called merely by the external call, these are gathered to the wedding feast by the power of the internal call. This internal call always stands in connection with and is brought by the external call of the gospel. But it is specifically by the operation of the Spirit in the hearts of men which applies the words of the external call to God's people. The Spirit calls within. The Spirit calls sovereignly, efficaciously, irresistibly. The Spirit calls by changing the hearts, by translating out of darkness into light and out of death into life. The Spirit calls to faith and summons irresistibly into the kingdom. This call gathers the Church and brings guests into the marriage supper of the King's Son. When these hear the call of the gospel by the Spirit within them, they come to repentance and sorrow for sin; with joy and thankfulness they enter the kingdom of heaven. In fact, they take the kingdom by force (see Matt. 11:12).

This is the sovereign work of God, a work rooted in election. "Many are called, but few are chosen." The decree of election stands behind it all. Jesus emphatically calls our attention to this. We might be inclined to overlook this important fact. But this is nevertheless the case. The decree of election determines who will participate in the wedding feast of the King's Son. The internal call of the gospel is rooted in and bound by and limited to the decree of election. Those who are elect are called. "For whom he did foreknow, he also did predestinate to be conformed to the image of his son, that he might be the firstborn among many brethren. Moreover whom he did predestinate, them he also called: and whom he called, them he also justified: and whom he justified, them he also glorified" (Rom. 8:29, 30).

This inward call accomplishes all the purpose of God. It brings faith and repentance into the hearts and lives of God's people. It brings these elect through life into the final glory and perfection of the marriage of Christ and His Church. And this is the victory of the gospel. We may be inclined to wonder sometimes whether God actually accomplishes His purpose or whether the Word of God fails to accomplish what it is intended to accomplish. The Church becomes smaller and smaller, and there are increasingly large numbers who reject the gospel. Is the Word of God of none effect? Do the wickedness of men and the evil plots of Satan frustrate the work of God? Such can never be the case. Always the gospel is victorious. It has the final victory. It marches on throughout all time from one victory to the next. The elect are called. The gospel overcomes sin and guilt. It destroys the power of death. It gathers the Church irresistibly. It brings the full number of the wedding guests to the glorious wedding supper of eternity.

In this we may find our hope and comfort. On the one hand, you need never fear that anyone God has chosen to be His own might not be gathered into the kingdom of heaven. Not one will ever be lost. And on the other hand, we may have every confidence for ourselves in our own life that the gospel will be our victory. It will lead us safely through life to final salvation and glory.

27

The Wedding Robe of Righteousness

And when the king came in to see the guests, he saw there a man which had not on a wedding garment:
And he saith unto him, Friend, how camest thou in hither not having a wedding garment? And he was speechless.
Then said the king to the servants, Bind him hand and foot, and take him away, and cast him into outer darkness; there shall be weeping and gnashing of teeth.
For many are called, but few are chosen.

—Matthew 22:11-14

As I mentioned in connection with the discussion of the last parable, there is sufficient difference between the last verses of the parable of the wedding feast and the first verses of the same parable to warrant a separate discussion. This does not mean that there is not a close relationship. The entire section forms one teaching of Jesus. These verses also speak of this great wedding supper which the elect of God shall everlastingly enjoy. In fact, this is really the climax of the entire parable. But there is an important distinction. The first part of the parable speaks of those whom God calls into the joy of this wedding feast. The second part of the parable discusses the reason why those who are called are able to have a place at the feast. That is, the point of these last verses is really: who is worthy to come to the supper of the great king? While in the first verses many refuse to come, in these verses we find a man who actually does try to come but who is cast out because he is found to be unworthy to sit with the guests at this heavenly banquet.

It is for this reason that the concluding words of Jesus in verse 14, "many are called, but few are chosen," are applicable to the entire parable. This man without a wedding garment is among the called; he belongs to those who are called with the external call of the gospel. He does not refuse that call, at least outwardly. He comes. His sin does not therefore lie in a rejection of the call, but in the fact that he insisted on coming on his own terms. He wanted to come but he thought he was worthy to come because of his own good works. He would not put on the wedding garment that was provided for him—the wedding garment of the righteousness of Christ. Without that robe washed in the blood of the cross he cannot come to the heavenly banquet. If we would want to express this idea in a little different way, we could say that the first part of this parable is an illustration of the truth which Paul describes in Romans 8:30a: "Whom he did predestinate, them he also called." The second part of the parable, however, is an illustration of the truth in Romans 8:30b: "Whom he called, them he also justified: and whom he justified, them he also glorified." Not only is the internal call of the gospel rooted in and determined by the decree of election, but also the gift of justification is rooted in election. And only those whom God justifies does He bring to final salvation and glory.

What the Wedding Robe Is

In the previous chapter we noticed that the wedding supper which is described in this parable is the spiritual reality of God's everlasting covenant into which God's people are taken through Christ. This figure has a twofold significance. The wedding itself is the heavenly and spiritual marriage of Christ and His Church. But it is also a wedding feast. And this wedding feast is an earthly picture of the heavenly joy and supreme happiness which is the portion of God's people in fellowship with Him.

It was emphasized in the preceding chapter that this is the portion of God's people already here on earth. The reality of this wedding and wedding feast is principally accomplished in the New Dispensation through the Spirit of the exalted Christ when the Church becomes the bride of Christ and begins to experience the heavenly joy of salvation. But all this will not finally be the portion of the Church until the end of the age when all things are made new upon the return of our Lord and Savior.

Now this part of the parable applies equally to the reality as it is principally experienced here on earth but also as the kingdom will be fully realized in the day of Christ. When the guests came to the wedding feast and the king entered the banquet hall to look at his guests, he was filled with astonishment because he saw a man without a wedding garment. The meaning of this portion of the parable therefore hinges on the meaning of the wedding garment.

We are told that it was customary in those days for hosts —especially the rich and the rulers—to provide the robes which their banquet guests were intended to wear. There is some dispute about this among commentators, but it seems to be more than probable that this was actually the case. And this is certainly the figure of the parable. In the text the passive voice is used to convey the impression that the garment was furnished to the guests and that this man did not have a garment because he had refused it. The rich man or the ruler who invited guests to his house whould have, hanging in his vestibule closet, a large number of robes. His servants would be stationed in the vestibule, to hand out robes to the guests as they arrived one by one at the banquet.

The fact that the king provided these robes for his guests is of crucial importance. It means that these garments were made by the king himself, that they were for the express purpose of clothing those who came to the feast, that they had to be worn by the guests, and that a refusal to wear them was the grossest insult and the crassest display of arrogance. Only these robes made the wearer of them worthy to come to the feast and enjoy communion and fellowship with the king.

We must emphasize the sin of this man who came in his own clothes. The parable does not mean to teach that this man momentarily at least succeeds in entering heaven. It does not mean to say that there is a moment when the man is actually in the wedding and enjoys the blessedness of this wedding. The point is that he only tries. He makes an effort to sneak into the wedding feast under false pretenses. But he is discovered and cast out. Nor is the point, as some interpreters have said, that this man is a picture of Judas, or Antichrist, or for that matter of any one definite individual. He stands in the parable as a representative of a certain class of people who commit the same sin he commits.

Perhaps this man knew that the servants were distributing garments at the front door, and so he came sneaking in the back door of the banquet hall. He went undetected as quietly he made his way into the presence of the guests. He deliberately avoided the obligation to wear the robes which were provided by the king. It was not that he was ignorant of the customs of the day or that he was unaware of what constituted proper clothing or that he was too poor to buy his own robe. He wickedly insisted on coming in his own clothes. He was convinced these clothes were good enough and that he did not need the robe of the king. He refused the wedding garment provided.

The question is: what is meant by this robe?

Without entering into a lengthy and unnecessary discussion of what these robes have been interpreted to mean, we may safely conclude that they are a picture of the righteousness which is in Christ. It is this righteousness alone which makes one worthy to enter the presence of the Holy God. That this is the meaning is evident from several considerations.

In the first place, this is a very common figure in Scripture. It is only necessary to point out a few examples. In a comparable passage in which the wedding of Christ and His Church is also pictured, we read: "Let us be glad and rejoice, and give honor to him: for the marriage of the Lamb is come, and his wife hath made herself ready. And to her was granted that she should be arrayed in fine linen, clean and white: for the fine linen is the righteousness of saints. And he saith unto me, Write, Blessed are they which are called into the marriage supper of the Lamb" (Rev. 19:7-9). In Psalm 132:9 we read: "Let thy priests be clothed with righteousness; and let thy saints shout for joy."

In the second place, this garment of righteousness is a garment which is characteristic of all the saints. Whatever their personal differences may be and whatever their own individual place in the kingdom of God, there is one robe which all must wear—the robe of the righteousness of Christ.

In the third place, it is this righteousness alone which makes it possible for anyone to come into the presence of God. Apart from this robe a man is altogether unworthy to enter into God's presence and has no right to participate in the heavenly banquet. But with this robe, than which there is none other, he can stand before God and enter into fellowship with the Most High.

The righteousness of which the robe is a picture is the righteousness of God, first of all. It belongs to God alone and is an absolute attribute of His perfection. It is that attribute according to which in the final and absolute sense God determines what is good and right because that which is good and right is in conformity with His own Being. God is supremely righteous.

This righteousness was part of the image with which man was endowed at his creation. But it was also part of the image which man lost when he fell. Because of his fall and his loss of righteousness he is totatlly unworthy to stand in God's presence. He has no right to be there. It is not a question of whether he *can* stand before God, whether his moral being makes it possible; it is a question of whether he *may*—whether apart from his moral character he has the right. The fact is that he does not.

The righteousness which is spoken of in the parable is therefore the righteousness of Christ. God revealed His righteousness through Christ. Christ took all the sins and the guilt of all His people on Himself. By the shedding of His blood He took away their sins and earned for them the right to enter the heaven of God. He earned their righteousness. He made garments of righteousness for them which He washed in His own blood so that they are spotlessly holy and without any of the defilement of sin. But this righteousness which Christ earned for His people is the righteousness of God Himself revealed through and accomplished in Jesus Christ.

This righteousness is the righteousness of the kingdom of heaven. The kingdom is found upon the righteousness of the blood of the cross. It is a kingdom that is antithetical to all the kingdoms of the world. It is a kingdom which is God's commonwealth and which is filled with God's righteousness as its chief characteristic. Only they who possess this righteousness have a place in that kingdom.

This righteousness is therefore first of all juridical. It is a righteousness which is given through imputation. God imputes to His people the righteousness of Christ whereby they become worthy to enter the kingdom and find a place in the assembly of the elect. But, in the second place, this righteousness is also moral and ethical. This too Scripture often speaks of. It is a righteousness that actually destroys sin and makes the people of God conformed to God's will. With this robe of righteousness upon them all their sins are covered and gone. They stand before God as without any sin in perfect holiness.

This righteousness is the portion of God's people by faith. We may say that we put on this robe by faith. It must be remembered that even faith is a gift of God, and that therefore we can put on the righteousness of Christ by a faith which only God works within our hearts. This faith is the only way to put on the robe. It is faith which places us in abiding communion with Christ our righteousness. It is by faith that we become members of His body, bone of His bone and flesh of His flesh. It is by faith that we are engrafted into Him so that the righteousness which He earned becomes ours. This same faith is the power by which we reach out and lay hold on Christ our right-eousness. By faith we reside in Christ, live out of Him, and stand in unbroken connection to Him. It is by faith that we cling to His cross and embrace Christ our Redeemer as our own. It is by faith that we adorn ourselves in the robes which are washed in the blood of the Lamb.

The Necessity of Wearing These Robes

The man who tried to come in to the feast without a wedding garment was therefore a man who tried to get in only by his own works. He would not take the garments provided by the king. He came in his own clothes, the clothes in which he walked in the street and in his home. He normally wore these clothes and insisted that they were adequate.

There are always people like this. There are many who try to wear their own robes into God's wedding feast. This was true of the Pharisees of Jesus' day against whom this parable is specifically spoken. This is also true of the Roman Catholic Church, for their theology is based in large measure on the idea of work righteous-ness. But it is very common to find this situation in the world. If you would speak to the ordinary man on the street and ask him whether he expected to go to heaven, he would most likely answer that this was indeed his expectation. If you would pursue the questioning a little further and ask him how he expected to gain entrance into heaven, he would more than likely answer that he would do this by living a good life, by doing the best he could, and therefore by earning his right to heaven by a good and law-abiding life. Perhaps he would add that he intended to sneak into heaven the last minute by the back door, but he would be persuaded that his own works were sufficient to bring him where he wanted to go. There are all kinds of people in the world who live lives which are outwardly above reproach and are encouraged to do this by the idea that in this way they will gain entrance into heaven.

It may surprise you to know that this is an idea which persists in our own hearts and minds. It is a very subtle sin that often crops up in our thinking and in our attitude toward God and heaven. We confess that we are saved by grace alone, but we do not always live this way. We do good works not out of the motive of gratitude to God, but because we are convinced that in this way we earn God's blessing. Does this sound strange to you? Think about it. We often insist that God gives us the things we want because we have done what is right. When we become ill we think God owes it to us to make us better. When we are poor we consider seriously the possibility that God is under an obligation to give us wealth because we have usually done what is right. When we are in trouble we expect deliverance because we have done very little wrong in God's sight. Always we want to put God under obligation to us to reward us for works which we think we have performed.

Yet this is impossible. And there are many reasons why this is true. In the first place, we cannot do good works. We are totally unable to do anything that is pleasing in the sight of God. Our robes which we wear are robes which are unbelievably ugly. We may think that they look very nice because we may live under the impression that the garments of our works are attractive and beautiful in the sight of God. But this is a mistaken notion. Isaiah reminds us that all our righteousnesses are as filthy rags. The best of our works are corrupted and polluted with sin. We wear the tattered, soiled, torn and stinking garments of our works. And these garments make us always unworthy.

In the second place, even if we could do good works (which we cannot), this would never be enough to give us a place in that glorious banquet of the wedding feast of the Lamb. We can never earn anything with God. We can never put God under obligation to us. We can never bring any merit of our own into God's presence. When we have done *all* that is required of us we are still unprofitable servants and have no right to life everlasting.

In the third place, the good works which we do and which we must do are never the reason why we go to glory. We do good works —even though imperfect—only as the fruit of the work of grace. These works are not works which in themselves make us worthy to be blessed. We are worthy before we ever do good works. And when it is our calling (as it surely is) to do good works, this is not because by them we earn or buy our way into heaven. The sole motive is and must be the motive of gratitude to God.

Therefore this man committed a terrible sin. He knew this when the king finally came to quiz him. When the king said to him: "Sir, how camest thou in hither not having a wedding garment?" he was speechless. He had no answer. When he stood face to face with the king and was made to see his own garments in the light of the splendor of the king, he saw also that his own garments were entirely inadequate. For this reason his sin was very great. In his sin of coming in his own garments with his own works, he showed that he wanted nothing of the righteousness of Christ and that he despised

the righteousness of the cross. And he did this because the righteousness of the cross always makes man nothing. He arrogantly
exalted himself above God.In pride he insisted that he had plenty of
good works which placed God under the obligation to bless him. He
insisted that if this blessing was denied, he would be dealt a grave
injustice.

But this is always the terrible sin that lies beneath our claim that
our good works make us worthy before God. We refuse the cross
because the cross makes us nothing. We exalt ourselves in pride and
boast of what we do and are capable of doing. And in this way we
attempt to put God under obligation to us.

The righteousness of the cross of Christ is altogether different.
This is the garment which is washed in the' blood of the cross, the
precious blood of the bleeding Lamb of Calvary. This garment alone
will ensure us a place in the heavenly kingdom. It is a garment that is
put on by faith alone.

To put on this garment by faith means, first of all, that we confess
that our works are filthy rags. This is hard for us to do because we
are proud. Nevertheless, it is true. All our works, every work we ever
do, every deed, every thought, every desire, every imagination,
every word, every step in life—all is worthless. All are filthy rags
which can never cover our nakedness. It is faith which confesses this.

Faith means, second, that we confess that our righteousness is only
Christ. In Christ we are worthy. In Christ we have new robes to wear.
In Christ we have the right to appear before God. But this is only *in
Christ.* We have nothing else or no one else. The cross is our only
glory and our only boasting. If Christ had not died, we would die. If
Christ had not gone to hell for us, our eternal destination would be
hell, with all our works pushing us deeper into the fire of eternal
torment. If Christ had not borne the wrath of God, it would surely be
our punishment. Faith confesses also this.

Only the righteousness of Christ can make us worthy to enter into
God's presence. Do not eve try anything else. Will you tell God that
you go to church every Sunday? But what about the many sins we
commit even while we are in church? Shall we boast of our prayers?
But we better remember the terrible hypocrisy of so many of them.
Are we going to plead our own faithful life in the world? We better
be careful. What the world does in its life, we do in our hearts and
minds. And God knows the heart.

No, let us leave all our works behind. Let us leave them as the
burden of our sin at the foot of the cross. There are our works will be
taken away. And be thankful that this is so, because they are very
terrible. Only at the cross can we lay aside our filthy rags. And only at
the cross can we put on the beautiful and spotlessly white robes of
the righteousness of Christ. How beautiful they are! They are whiter
than any cleaner on earth can make them. They sparkle and glisten
as the sun. They are glorious and majestic. For they are the robes of
the righteousness of God in Christ. They are the only proper wed-

ding garments in the eternal covenant of God's grace. Without them we cannot possibly have a place in the kingdom. With them we are everlastingly worthy.

The Punishment of the Unworthy Guest

Because the sin of this man was so terrible, his punishment is likewise great.

There are those who are inclined toward the view that the punishment meted out is much too severe for the sin committed. But we must remember that behind this sin lies the sin of despising the cross of Christ and of exalting one self in arrogance and pride above God and His Son. There is no punishment too great for this sin.

But the point is nevertheless that this is what *our* works merit. There is a terrible punishment described here from which we recoil in horror. But this is in reality what we deserve. If all we have is our own works, then we have nothing by which to escape this punishment.

In keeping with the parable, figurative language is employed to describe this, but also because we cannot in earthly language describe the sufferings of hell. Hell is called outer darkness because it is a place very far from God where there is only wrath. It is a place of unending weeping because it is a place of eternal remorse. No laughter is to be found there, no joy, no happiness, only despair and remorse. It is a place of gnashing of teeth because it is a place of indescribable pain and torment. Pain that is all but intolerable is the daily meat and drink of those who come to this place. And all this is true because it is the place of the just and righteous punishment of Almighty God Who will vindicate His own honor and glorify His own Name.

But as terrible as hell is, so infinitely wonderful is heaven. It is the place where righteousness dwells. Those who are clothed in the righteousness of Christ enter this place. They enter into the everlasting fellowship of God through Jesus Christ in the marriage of the covenant of grace. And they enter into unending joy in the presence of God and His angels.

Even here election stands on the foreground. We must return to the question we asked at the very beginning: "What makes these guests worthy?" The answer is, the righteousness of Christ. But Jesus leads us back farther and says: "God makes us worthy according to His sovereign and eternal good pleasure." We are not in glory because of ourselves. We are there by the sovereign choice of the Almighty. Election is not only the limitation and power of the internal call, but it is also the fountain of our righteousness. And it is the fountain of our faith. We must not, as it were, at the last moment make faith a work by which we after all earn our righteousness. Faith is God's gift. And faith flows from the fountain of election. "Whom he did predestinate, them he also called: and whom he called, them he also justified: and whom he justified, them he also glorified." To Him be praise forever!

28

Watching unto Christ's Coming

Then shall the kingdom of heaven be likened unto ten virgins, which took their lamps, and went forth to meet the bridegroom.
And five of them were wise, and five were foolish.
They that were foolish took their lamps, and took no oil with them:
But the wise took oil in their vessels with their lamps.
While the bridegroom tarried, they all slumbered and slept.
And at midnight there was a cry made, Behold, the bridegroom cometh; go ye out to meet him.
Then all those virgins arose, and trimmed their lamps.
And the foolish said unto the wise, Give us of your oil; for our lamps are gone out.
But the wise answered, saying, Not so; lest there be not enough for us and you: but go ye rather to them that sell, and buy for yourselves.
And while they went to buy, the bridegroom came; and they that were ready went in with him to the marriage: and the door was shut.
Afterward came also the other virgins, saying, Lord, Lord, open to us.
But he answered and said, Verily I say unto you, I know you not.
Watch therefore, for ye know neither the day nor the hour wherein the Son of man cometh.
—Matthew 25:1-13

This parable forms a part of the Lord's discourse concerning the signs of His coming which is recorded for us in Matthew 24. It was the last day of Jesus' public ministry on earth. This public ministry in the temple He finished by pronouncing a series of judgments on the wicked house of Israel and by speaking the awful words: "Behold, your house is left unto you desolate" (Matt. 23:38). The disciples were astounded by this and interpreted Jesus' words to refer to the temple in Jerusalem. Hence we read that as they were departing from the temple, Jesus' disciples came to Him to show Him the buildings of the temple (see Matt. 24:1). Their implied question was: "Do you mean that all these buildings of the temple will be left desolate?" Jesus assured them that this was indeed to be the case. He said: "Verily I say unto you, there shall not be left here one stone upon another, that shall not be thrown down" (Matt. 24:2).

In their astonishment at this statement of the Lord, the disciples could conceive of these things happening only at the end of time. And so, when they were alone with the Lord, they came to Him privately with the questions: "Tell us, when shall these things be? And what shall be the sign of thy coming, and of the end of the world?" (v. 3). It is striking to notice that the first of these questions Jesus does not.answer except to tell them: "But of that day and hour knoweth no man, no, not the angels of heaven, but my Father only" (Matt. 24:36). But in answer to the second and third questions, the Lord gives to His disciples many signs which mark His coming again. These signs, however, are not discussed from an abstract and objective viewpoint, but are given from the very practical viewpoint of urging upon the disciples and the Church the calling to watch. This practical application of the discussion is found throughout Jesus' discourse, but is emphasized especially in the last part of chapter 24. It was in connection with the practical application of this discourse that Jesus taught the parable of the ten virgins.

Jesus was about to go by way of His cross and resurrection to glory. In heaven Christ would work all things so that He could come again to take His Church unto Himself. And so Jesus addressed Himself to the needs of His Church whom He loves with an abiding and divine love. When He goes to glory, His Church will have to remain in the world. There they will be called to live as these virgins of the parable while they wait the coming of their husband. And the Lord knows that it will seem to them sometimes as if He tarries long. It will seem to them that perhaps their lord is never coming back. And the danger is that, should they begin to think this, they will be in peril of falling asleep. The night grows darker and the hours slip rapidly away, and still the lord does not return. At last the heads of the virgins begin to nod and they become very sleepy.

For this reason the Lord admonishes the Church to watch for His coming. They must keep their lamps trimmed and their hope burning brightly. For He shall surely come again, and blessed are they who are waiting when He returns.

The Figure of a Wedding

The figure of the parable is taken from the customs of Jesus' time which were observed in connection with wedding festivities. Although there is some difference of opinion among commentators about the details, and although indeed these details may have differed from city to city in Palestine, the main course of events seems to be along these lines. After a man had been betrothed to a girl, the date of the wedding festivities was set. On that day, in the morning, the bridegroom would retreat with his friends to a secluded spot where they could celebrate the coming event. Also during the day, the bride would go to the house of her husband-to-be and begin to make herself ready for the evening celebration and ceremony. Then, as the day began to die, around supper time, the groom would return with his companions in a procession of singing and dancing men whose way was lit with flaming torches. As they neared his house where his bride waited for him, the cry would go up from those who were watching for him: "Behold, the bridegroom cometh." That would be the signal for the bride to make last-minute preparations and proceed in the company of her maidens to meet the bridegroom. These maidens too would carry lamps to light the way. Then, when the two groups met, they would return together with singing and rejoicing to the house, where the festivities would go on sometimes for as long as a week. This customary way of celebrating a wedding is adapted to a great spiritual truth in the parable.

The Meaning of the Virgins

First of all, there can be little question about it that the virgins of the parable refer to the Church visible which is here on earth. Jesus used the number ten (ten virgins) not only because that was a favorite number with the Jews, but also because ten bears special meaning in the symbolism of the kingdom of heaven. While the number twelve is the number of the Church from the viewpoint of election, the number ten signifies the fulness of anything with respect to the purpose of God. There are ten commandments because the Decalogue is the full expression of God's moral will. There were ten plagues rained upon Egypt because these plagues were the fullness of judgment and wrath which destroyed this wicked nation. Here the ten virgins express and are symbolic of the full Church at any given time in history as God Himself places that Church in the midst of the world.

In the second place, these women are called "virgins." This is a beautiful figure. In the days of Jesus, an engagement was not a loose and relatively meaningless bond as it is today. In those days when two people became engaged they were to all intents married, and it required a legal divorce to break the engagement. But a bride who was engaged remained a virgin until the marriage was solemnized and finally consummated. So it is in the relation between Christ and His Church. Now already Christ and His Church are engaged. And this is principally already marriage. But while the Church remains in the world she is a virgin, for her lover is far away from her and she, while she waits, keeps herself unspotted from the world. Presently, when her lover comes again, the marriage will finally be consummated and its perfect joy realized.

Here in the parable the emphasis really falls upon the bridegroom. This is usually not the case in our country with wedding ceremonies. And that is no doubt due to the fact that the Church has become more worldly and the figure of the relation between Christ and His Church has gradually been taken out of the marriage. Now the bride is the center of attraction. In fact it seems sometimes as if the groom is present only as a necessary evil. It is the bride's wedding, the bride's wedding dress, the bride's march, the bride's big day, and so forth. Nevertheless, the bridegroom is of central importance in a wedding where there is a figure of Christ and His people.

The virgins of the parable very obviously picture the Church here on earth as that Church comes to visible manifestation in the midst of the world. For five of the virgins are wise and five and foolish.

The Meaning of Wisdom and Foolishness

The meaning of wisdom and foolishness is important to the understanding of the parable. Wisdom and foolishness are not relative concepts, relative in the sense that they depict earthly virtue or lack of virtue. The two are antithetically opposed to each other. They are without any relationship whatsoever, for wisdom is a heavenly gift of grace which is wrought in the hearts of God's people through the Spirit of Christ, while foolishness is sin and comes from the natural and depraved heart of man.

There is always a practical aspect to wisdom. In brief, wisdom is the ability to adapt one's life to the realities of the world. It includes various elements. In the first place, the true reality of things is the Scriptural truth that this world will not last forever, but that the day is coming when it will be destroyed. In the second place, wisdom is the application of this truth concerning the realities of life and concerning the principles which the Word of God teaches to the specific problems of our walk here below. One not only knows these truths, but he lives a life in which these truths are adapted to his own peculiar calling. In the third place, wisdom implies that one prepares for what he knows is coming in the future. With regard to the present parable, wisdom means that one lives all his life in the consciousness that Christ is coming again to destroy the world and to save the Church.

Foolishness is just the opposite. A foolish man also knows the truth. In this case he knows the truth that Christ is coming again. And he knows therefore that he ought to pay attention to this truth, that he ought to adjust his life so that it is in conformity to this truth, and that he ought to make preparation for the future. But he pays no attention. He ignores the truth and acts as if he doesn't care. He lives as if Christ shall never come and as if this world shall go on forever. Foolishness is always principally rooted in unbelief.

The Meaning of the Lamps and the Oil

So the wise virgins took oil in their lamps because they knew the bridegroom was coming. The foolish virgins had lamps which were empty.

The question which arises is: what is meant by the oil and the lamps?

To this question many different answers have been given. There are some who say that the lamp is each individual person, the wick of the lamp is a person's heart, and the oil is the Holy Spirit. Others, with a slight variation on this theme, speak of the bowl of the lamp as the heart, the lamp itself as one's outward confession, and the oil as the grace which makes the lamp burn. Still others would prefer to dispute the question on the basis of a discussion of the merits of works and faith. Some make the lamp faith and the oil good works. Others prefer to change this around and make the oil good works and the fire faith. But in general, these further interpretations are too speculative and really miss the main point of the parable altogether. It remains a question whether Jesus really intended anything specific by these, except to point out in general that the oil in the lamp is a sign of preparedness. Those without oil were not prepared for the coming of Christ and never entered into the wedding hall. Those with oil were the ones who were ready for His coming and were taken into the heavenly wedding banquet with the Bridegroom.

This preparedness is basically the watchfulness of the Church as she is called to live in daily anticipation of the coming of Christ. It is true that five of the virgins were only virgins outwardly. They represent those who belong to the Church only in an outward sense. They claim to carry with them the Word of God and leave the impression that they confess that Word. They even speak of the hope that Christ will some day come again to deliver His Church. For these reasons they belong to the visible manifestation of the Church on earth. But the irony of the matter is that it is precisely this Word which tells of the coming of Christ in judgment and to redeem the Church. However, they paid no attention to that Word.

If the oil in the lamps is a sign of preparedness, then it ought also to be evident that this preparedness is particularly expressed in the Christian's hope. The child of God, the bride in the world, hopes with longing, expectation and eagerness for the coming of the Bridegroom. This hope expresses itself in the prayer for the coming of Christ. And it becomes, for the Christian, a whole way of life according to which he walks while he waits for the Lord to return.

The Need for Exhortation

The main point of the parable is the admonition to watch for the Lord to come. There are especially two reasons why the admonition is so urgent.

The first reason, according to the parable, is that the bridegroom tarries. This is very aptly and dramatically pictured in the parable. Usually, according to the custom of the day, the groom would come around supper time, since this was the time when the festivities were about to begin. But six o'clock came and went, and the groom did not appear. Not only that, but hour by hour the time slipped away. The night grew darker. Presently the houses across the street became dark, for the people had gone to bed. Work ceased. Play came to a halt. The streets were quiet and empty. And still the bridegroom did not come. It was not until the very hollow of the night that at last the groom is seen coming up the road in the distance. But it was only at such a time when one had really given up all hope that he would ever appear.

Now this is also a reality of life.

It is not true of course that Christ tarries from God's point of view. Really Christ never lingers or tarries. He comes at exactly the right moment, a moment which is fixed by God eternally. He cannot possibly come before that moment because then He would appear before all things are ready. Nor can He come after that moment. In fact, not only does Christ not linger or tarry on the way, but always He comes quickly. He Himself assured the Church: "Behold, I come quickly."

But the parable looks at the coming of Christ from our point of view. And from our point of view the Lord seems to tarry.

The Church has always lived in the consciousness that the return of Christ was imminent. This was true already of the early Church, which expected Christ to return before the era of the apostles was ended. And their conviction that the Lord could not wait very long was heightened by the severe persecution under Nero and other Roman emperors. But this anticipation of Christ's coming has always been more or less strong throughout the history of the Church. It was strong at the time of the Reformation when all the might of Rome was hurled in fiery persecution against the Church of Christ. And now again, we often hear the word spoken: "It cannot be very long before Christ returns."

Now it is not our intention to smile a little at these "foolish notions of the Church" as if those poor people did not know what they were talking about. Would to God there was a little more anticipation today for the coming of Christ, a little more of what that Church gone by possessed. But the point is, in spite of all this, the Lord still tarries. Almost two thousand years have elapsed since His ascension. Who would ever have thought it would take that long? And how long will it yet take? The hours and days and years speed by with alarming rapidity. The night of sin and death grows darker and darker. The world is steeped in iniquity and swallowed up on evil. The child of God wonders how long things can go on this way when wickedness abound. Does not the Lord see how terribly wicked men have become? Yet He tarries.

And almost inevitably the thoughts begin to steal into our souls: "Will the Lord ever return? Will He come back? Is it maybe true after all that this world will be on forever? Was it all silliness and foolishness that we expected Him to return? Is the Lord slack concerning His promise?"

This is the first reason why the Lord so urgently presses upon His Church the admonition to watch.

But there is a second reason why this admonition is so urgent. This reason is closely connected to the first one and is the fruit of it. The second reason is that there is grave danger that while we wait, we go to sleep. This is what happened to the virgins. Notice, it happened to all of them. The text however seems to suggest that there were differences. Apparently, some of the virgins fell into a deep sleep while others were only nodding and dozing. But the picutre is plain. As the night grows darker and a hush settles over the city, as the shouting and the laughter and the noise of the day are silenced by the deepening shadows of the night, the waiting virgins begin to feel sleepy. Some of them begin to nod a bit. Perhaps they fight off sleep and doze only intermittently. Others drop off to sleep completely, unable to stay awake in the wee hours of the night.

But this is also a means of expressing a very real spiritual truth. Before He returns, the Lord says that the whole Church will be overcome by lethargy and sleepiness. This will be true even of the people of God. In the preceding chapter (Matt. 24) the Lord spoke of the fact that the very days would be shortened for the elect's sake. And in other places the Lord speaks of the possibility of not finding faith on the earth when He returns. This drowsiness and sleepiness points to the spiritual lethargy which steals over the Church. The members become indifferent to the coming of Christ and fall into the drowsiness of carnality and worldliness. They are, so to speak, drugged with pleasure and become lethargic with the carnal pursuit of earthly happiness.

What a true picture of the Church of our day this presents. We do well to examine ourselves. Much of the Church world is like the foolish virgins who are without oil, and who fall soundly asleep. They are those who profess to hold to the Word of God. They even speak as if they believe that Word and as if they are sure that Christ is coming again. But in their life and conduct they live as if that day will never come. Spiritually they go to sleep. They are worldly and evil. They walk in the pleasures of life. They live and speak as if this creation will never pass away. They are indifferent to the coming of their Lord.

But this is true even of the faithful virgins. God's people find themselves drowsy and nodding. Sometimes it seems as if the deadening stupor of pleasure has all but closed the eyes of the faithful to the coming of Christ. And when we think of that coming, it is often in the hope that it will be many years away—only after we have enjoyed the life of pleasure to the full.

It is striking that before the Lord Himself returns there is the announcement of His coming. In the parable we read: "And at midnight there was a cry made, Behold, the bridegroom cometh; go ye out to meet him." Evidently this must be distinguished from the coming itself. This cry is apparently intended to arouse those who are waiting to make final preparation for His return. In actual fact the Church has need of this. In their inclination to become sleepy, they need the cry to arouse them. This must be associated with the signs which Christ sends of His return. Really these signs are present throughout the entire New Dispensation. And they must be there also in order to remind the Church to watch and wait for the coming of Christ. But especially as the end nears—in fact, just before the end comes—these signs increase sharply in intensity. They shake the Church of Christ awake so that she is aroused to fulfill her calling and to look for Christ. This is the very real effect. In times such as these, when the signs are not too evident, the Church becomes sleepy. But when horrible persecutions come and Antichrist rules in the world, then the Church also looks to the coming of her Bridegroom Who will redeem her from her sin.

But no one knows the hour of Christ's coming. This does not mean, as the premillennialists contend, that Christ may come at any moment—perhaps even today—in some sort of rapture. There are, according to Scripture, very definite things that must take place before He can come again. The signs point to the nearness of the hour. But these signs speak only to those who have the grace to watch.

Nevertheless, the Lord makes the point that we cannot tell the time of His return. That is hidden in the purpose and counsel of God. The point is therefore that the Lord seems to us to tarry precisely because we do not know the time when He will come back. In fact, He does not return until all things seem to say that He will never come. It was this way already in the Old Dispensation. For many years and even centuries the Church looked for the coming of the promise. And it was only when from every human point of view it seemed that Christ would not come and could not come, that at last He did. The night must be its darkest. It must appear that Christ cannot come according to human reckoning. When, humanly speaking, all hope of His return is passed, then and then only does He come again.

The Meaning of the Calling to Watch

So we must watch. What a rich and important admonition this is! It implies, in the first place, that hope is the main principle of our life. This hope reaches out in eagerness and longing for Christ, even as a bride eagerly awaits the coming of her bridegroom.

In the second place, the admonition implies that our lives must always be the lives of pilgrims and strangers in the earth. This is wisdom. This is the oil of preparedness. We have here no abiding city. Our eternal destination is the house of our Father, and to this destination we press forward.

In the third place, the admonition implies a constant prayer. It implies the prayer: "Come Lord Jesus, yea, come quickly." The Church which longs for Christ's return also prays for this day to come. Unceasingly, with great longing and earnest tears and sighs, the Church lifts up her petitions to the throne of grace for the return of her Savior.

And finally, the firmer this hope lives in the hearts of the people of

God, the stronger does the Church make herself ready for the appearance of Him Who loved her unto death.

The Punishment of the Foolish Virgins

There are those who make a show of wanting the return of Christ. But they do not really prepare themselves, nor do they live in this hope of Christ's coming. It soon becomes evident that they care not at all for the return of Christ. Oh, they try to make their hypocrisy plausible to the very end. When the cry goes out they still speak of wanting Christ to come. And they hasten away to try the last minute to make themselves ready. You can probably hear them recite the litany: "Have we not prophesied in thy name and in thy name done many mighty works?" But the fact that they do not watch is clear enough indication that they wanted Christ to stay away. They were fools. They lived as if He would never come.

In the parable the foolish virgins had no oil for their lamps, even though they knew very well they were going to need it. And now that the bridegroom is on the way they are without what they need. They could not borrow from the others, for this is an oil that cannot be borrowed. They cannot buy in the stores, for the hour is midnight and the stores are closed.

This aspect of the parable depicts foolish people who know that Christ is coming, but who live as if He will not come. They make the world their home. Spiritually they are sound asleep. They are caught up in the pleasures of the age and in the stupor of worldly carnality. This is indicative of their fundamental hatred of Christ and His return. They are satisfied with this world of sin and would just as soon see wicked men reign in it forever.

Thus they show that they belonged to the Church only outwardly. In their hearts they were never members. They piously claimed (and you can hear it still today) that they wanted Christ to come, but they pushed this coming off so far into the future that it was gone from their consciousness. And so they cannot enter in. They come with deep pathos knocking on the door. But they are not ready. Now they have no place in that glorious wedding feast.

But even this is the purpose of Christ. Christ Himself once again places election on the foreground. He says to them most emphatically: "I never knew you. You were never My own. I never made you My betrothed. I never loved you. I never died for you. I never intended that you should be My wife." There is no more terrible thing than to hear in the judgment those words: "I never knew you."

The Blessedness of the Faithful

But the certainty of the blessedness of the people of God is strongly emphasized. This is based on the certainty that Christ will indeed come again. Nothing can stop His coming. He comes at the stroke of God's clock, God's midnight. God has appointed the hour of His return; then everything is ready for Christ to come. His coming is not an arbitrary moment, but it is fixed in the immutable purpose of God. Then the elect are all saved and the bride of Christ is ready to be brought to her heavenly mansion. Then the empires of the wicked are crumbling into chaos and disarray, for the cup of iniquity is full. Then all God's counsel is fulfilled and Christ will have to come. He cannot delay another moment.

The certainty of His coming is based on the certainty of the counsel of God. And rooted in that counsel is the victory of the cross and the resurrection. If Christ does not come again, then He never died to defeat the enemy; then He never rose again triumphant over those who opposed Him. Then Christ never ruled in heaven. Then God is not sovereign above all.

But come He will. And the certainty of His coming is the certainty of our blessedness. For as surely as He comes, does He take His bride to Himself. The marriage with Christ will be fully consummated. The eternal joy of that heavenly banquet will be the portion of God's people forever.

Watch therefore. It may be the night is growing darker. Indeed it is. The world of sin increases in its iniquity. The Lord seems to delay His coming. But watch!

Have you become sleepy with the cares and pleasures of life? Have you begun to wonder whether the Lord will ever return? Watch! Watch in hope, in longing, in certainty. Watch unto the end. The victory is sure to be ours.

29

Faithful Labor in the Kingdom

For the kingdom of heaven is as a man travelling into a far country, who called his own servants, and delivered unto them his goods.

And unto one he gave five talents, to another two, and to another one; to every man according to his several ability; and straightway took his journey.

Then he that had received the five talents went and traded with the same, and made them other five talents.

And likewise he that had received two, he also gained other two.

But he that had received one went and digged in the earth, and hid his lord's money.

After a long time the lord of those servants cometh, and reckoneth with them.

And so he that had received five talents came and brought other five talents, saying, Lord, thou deliveredst unto me five talents: behold, I have gained beside them five talents more.

His lord said unto him, Well done, thou good and faithful servant: thou hast been faithful over a few things, I will make thee ruler over many things: enter thou into the joy of thy lord.

He also that had received two talents came and said, Lord, thou deliveredst unto me two talents: behold, I have gained two other talents beside them.

His lord said unto him, Well done, good and faithful servant; thou hast been faithful over a few things, I will make thee ruler over many things: enter thou into the joy of thy lord.

Then he which had received the one talent came and said, Lord, I knew thee that thou art an hard man, reaping where thou hast not sown, and gathering where thou hast not strawed:

And I was afraid, and went and hid thy talent in the earth: lo, there thou has that is thine.

His lord answered and said unto him, Thou wicked and slothful servant, thou knewest that I reap where I sowed not, and gather where I have not strawed;

Thou oughtest therefore to have put my money to the exchangers, and then at my coming I should have received mine own with usury.

*Take therefore the talent from him, and give it unto him which hath
ten talents.*

*For unto every one that hath shall be given, and he shall have
abundance: but from him that hath not shall be taken away even that
which he hath.*

*And cast ye the unprofitable servant into outer darkness: there shall
be weeping and gnashing of teeth.*

—Matthew 25:14-30

This parable is closely connected with the preceding one and
therefore with the discourse of the Lord concerning the signs of His
coming which is given to us in Matthew 24. You will recall that Jesus
had spoken privately to His disciples of the end of the world and the
day of the Lord's coming and of the signs which would precede His
coming. The admonition which the Lord had impressed on the
disciples and the Church was that it was their calling to watch
faithfully unto the end. This admonition Christ had enforced with
the parable of the ten virgins.

In the parable which we are now discussing Christ more completely defines what He means by watching. To watch for the coming of Christ does not mean that the saints cease their work and wait
on some distant mountain top with their eyes scanning the heavens
in anticipation of the Lord's return. Rather, to watch means that the
saints work—work hard and faithfully in their station and calling in
life, but work for the cause of the kingdom of Christ.

It is to be regretted that this parable is usually misnamed, and
consequently misinterpreted. This parable is often called the parable of the talents. The talents are then claimed to be the main point
of the parable. And these talents are interpreted to mean the natural
and perhaps spiritual *gifts* we have received, each one in varying
measure. The result has been that the word "talents" has even
entered into our language so that we speak often of the *talents* of a
man. It is very difficult to dispose of this idea when the idea has
entered into the language itself. In our minds talents are associated
with gifts, and any other idea is hard to overcome.

Nevertheless, not the talents, but the servants stand on the foreground. And, in connection with the talents, it is true that the
natural gifts of a man are presupposed in the parable; but the
emphasis falls on the fact that the saints have a calling to labor
faithfully in the kingdom until the day of the coming of Christ. The
talents then are the concrete responsibilities and opportunities in
the kingdom to serve Christ. The faithful servants are those who are
true servants of Christ and who labor for the coming of the kingdom. The unfaithful servants are those who refuse to work in the
kingdom, who hide their talents in the ground where they are of no
use for the kingdom and its cause.

The Elements in the Parable

The man of the parable is pictured as a rich man. This is a
reference to Christ. The emphasis falls on the fact that Christ is the

Son of Man. His human nature stands on the foreground because it was as a man that Christ suffered and died on the cross and entered into His kingdom. It is in this same human nature that He will come again at the end of this age to judge the living and the dead. Nevertheless, Christ is rich, both from the viewpoint of the fact that He remains the eternal Son of God Who possesses all the virtues of the Godhead, and from the viewpoint of the fact that He is now in heaven where He is made most blessed and is given His kingdom.

The man's journey abroad to a far country where he tarried for a long time refers to the ascension of Christ to heaven, where Christ remains for many years. The return of the man in the parable and his asking an account of his servants is the coming of Christ in judgment to render to every man according to his deeds.

The servants are emphatically servants. They are not the kind of servants who work for wages, but are literally slaves who belong to their master. This is the relationship between Christ and His people. This relation is so rich and varied that Scripture uses many different means of describing it. Sometimes the Church is pictured as the bride of Christ. Then again the Church is described in terms of guests at a heavenly banquet of Christ. Here the picture is one of master and slaves. Indeed the people of God are the slaves of Christ. The apostle Paul even boasts of this on more than one occasion. These slaves belong to Christ entirely. They belong to their Master with body and with soul, with mind and will and heart. They belong to Him because they are purchased by Him with the price of His own precious blood which was spilled on Calvary. And as slaves they are given the calling to serve their Lord and Master in all that they do.

Nevertheless, once again the Lord speaks of His kingdom in terms of the Church visible. The kingdom is referred to as it comes to manifestation in time because also wicked servants find a place in that kingdom. They are not the true slaves of Christ for they do not belong to Christ, nor do they have a claim to the blood of the cross. But they possess an outward place in that kingdom. They bear the name of saints in the world. They have been baptized in the sphere of that kingdom and have received covenant instruction. They are also given a talent with which to labor; that is, they are given a place in that kingdom which entails certain responsibilities and obligations, certain opportunities to serve Christ. But they shall never be found in the final perfection of that kingdom. They are only a part of that kingdom in an outward sense, and they use their place and their responsibilities to sin.

The Meaning of the Talents

It ought to be evident that the entire interpretation of the parable hinges on the interpretation of the talents. This is of central importance.

Usually these talents are defined as being general gifts—gifts with which every man is endowed. These are usually said to be of two kinds: natural gifts and spiritual gifts. In that case they refer to the abilities which every man possesses and which every man is called to employ in his station in life. These can be no question about it that these gifts are indeed implied in the parable. They are in fact referred to when Jesus speaks of every man's "several ability." But they are not the talents themselves. A consideration of the matter will soon show that this is impossible.

In the first place, these talents cannot refer to spiritual gifts because the wicked servant receives one talent as well as the faithful servants; and the wicked are never indowed with spiritual gifts.

In the second place, the Lord makes a point of it that these talents are a share of the household goods. He delivered unto his servants his goods: to one five talents, to another two talents, to another one talent. But if these talents are the household goods, they are not anything inherent in the servants themselves.

In the third place, the parable emphatically states that each servant received talents according to his several abilities. Thus the parable makes a distinction between the talents and the abilities. If a man received talents according to his abilities, the talents obviously cannot be the abilities themselves.

In the fourth place, the servants who are faithful double their talents. This cannot possible be said of the abilities that a man possesses. His natural abilities are already determined at the moment of birth. His spiritual gifts are given to him by the Spirit of Christ. For truly, it lies without the scope of his ability to double his own gifts.

Finally the one talent is taken away from the unfaithful servant and is given to him that had ten talents. Once again, this cannot be said of gifts and abilities with which men are endowed. These abilities and gifts cannot be taken away from one nor given to another.

Thus these talents refer to concrete responsibilities and obligations within the kingdom of heaven. As the parable makes clear, they presuppose the presence of gifts. There are differences of natural gifts among the citizens of the kingdom. There are many of these natural gifts which God bestows on His people—and for that matter, on all men. Some have gifts of intellect: gifts like intelligence, memory, reasoning, perception. Some have gifts of speaking. Others of music, of learning, of teaching, of ruling. And these gifts vary greatly from one individual to another. They vary on the one hand as to kind. Some people have gifts that others do not have. But they vary also as to amount. There are some people with the same gift, but one may have more of that same gift than another.

But these talents are not the gifts themselves. Rather, the talents refer to the fact that God assigns to each man a place in His kingdom where this man has certain responsibilities in a certain calling which is unique to him. In this calling he has obligations and opportunities to be busy in the service of Christ.

Now there are several points about these talents which the parable makes and which will aid us in understanding what the Lord is referring to in this parable.

In the first place, the Lord Himself sovereignly determines the whole matter. He determines, with a prerogative which belongs to Him alone, what gifts each man will receive. No one may criticize this sovereign determination. It belongs to His divine right. Besides, and in connection with this, the Lord also sovereignly determines each man's place in the kingdom. To this place he is called; in this place he is set; to work in this place is his assignment. He does not enter that place by himself, by his own efforts and choice. He is put there, just as each servant is given talents as determined by the lord in the parable.

In the second place, each man receives these talents in different proportion. On the one hand, *each man* receives them. There is no servant in the kingdom who does not receive some talents. These may vary, as indeed they do. But each does have a talent. On the other hand, these talents differ greatly from one saint to the next. Some saints receive a place in the kingdom as office bearers in the Church. This constitutes their talents. Some receive a place as teachers in the Christian schools. This then is their talents. And there are many other such places. Mothers receive an assignment in their homes with their covenant children. There are the talents of maintaining the cause of God in the home, in the shop, in the office, in the whole arena of life. There are the responsibilities that all saints have to instruct others in the truth of God's Word, to confess the truth with their mouths. All have opportunities to serve Christ and obligations to fulfill in such ways as comforting the sorrowing, helping the weak, giving to the poor. There are talents for fighting the battle of faith, for suffering sickness and affliction with patience, and for walking faithfully in the world. These are all the talents to which Christ refers. They are places in the kingdom assigned to us.

In the third place, the parable emphasizes that these talents are assigned to each man according to his abilities. Each man's calling fits his abilities. Christ sovereignly gives both. He calls to these places in many different ways and with varied means. But Christ always calls to the right place. It may not always appear to us as if that is the case. We may think that the place and the abilities are wrongly matched. But this is an attitude of mind which is precisely condemned in the parable. Christ never makes any mistakes. He gives an assignment in the kingdom that is exactly right according to the abilities which He knows a man possesses.

And finally, the parable speaks of this as a very noble calling. It speaks of a rich man who divides to slaves his possessions. He is going away to a foreign land. And, mind you, he entrusts all his possessions to mere slaves so that they will take care of what belongs to him in his absence. The slaves of Christ are given a noble calling in the Church, no matter what that calling may be. Christ owns everything. He owns us. He owns His kingdom. He owns our abilities. He owns our place in that kingdom. But He entrusts responsibilities in that kingdom to us in His absence, so that we have the high and wonderful calling to use what belongs alone to Him. With the nobility of this calling we must be impressed.

The Sin of the Unfaithful Servant

What did the unfaithful servant do with the talent which was given to him?

You will notice that the Lord refers to one particular sin in the parable. This does not mean to imply that there are not other sins which a man can commit with the talent or talents entrusted to him. It is possible, for example, to labor hard in one's station in life, but to do all his work for the sake of personal gain, to be seen of men, and to reap to oneself a harvest of the praise of men. Or again, it is possible for a man to leave his place in the kingdom altogether and devote his efforts to purely sinful pursuits, to aid the cause of sin and the establishment of the kingdom of darkness.

But this one sin to which the Lord refers is of sufficient importance and is general enough in the Church to devote an entire parable to it.

This sin is the sin of refusing to labor in one's place and calling in the kingdom. The unfaithful servant in the parable, after having received his talent, immediately went somewhere and dug in the earth and buried his talent. This does not mean that he refused to employ his natural gifts, although this may be somewhat implied. But it rather refers to the fact that willfully and deliberately he refused to do any work in his place in the kingdom. He refused to assume the responsibilities of his position and calling. Was his place one of confessing the truth by a godly life in his daily work? He did not do it. Was he called to comfort someone who was stricken with sorrow? He refused. Was he given the opportunity to serve Christ by instructing his children in the Word of God? He let his talent lie useless. Did Christ call him to suffer affliction with patience and courage and contentment? He was rather rebellious and grumpy and dissatisfied. Whatever that place in the kingdom may have been, he refused to perform the assignment which had been given him by his master.

There must have been some reason in his own heart why he refused to use the talent which had been given him. What was this reason? The true reason only comes out in the judgment day. It is doubtful whether the Lord means to say that in the judgment day before the great white throne, wicked men will have opportunity to complain and criticize and will attempt to defend themselves as this man does. It seems more likely that in that terrible day they will have to be silent. But the point of the Lord is that in the judgment day the real motives of the wicked servant are laid bare. Perhaps in this life he had all kinds of excuses by means of which he tried to defend his conduct. He perhaps complained that he was called to do too much; that he did not possess the gifts to do what was required of him; that he was too busy and had not the time to accomplish what was asked of him. But in the judgment day the real motives of his heart are laid bare.

It becomes evident that his refusal to use his talents was because pride was in his heart. Jesus says that the sin of pride lies at the root of it all. He despised his talent. He was not satisfied with what had been given him. He complained about the lowliness of his assignment in life. He coveted a greater place.

The kingdom of heaven here on earth can be compared with the building of a house. In the building of this house all kinds of men are needed with all kinds of skills. Each man is given a task to do in harmony with his skills. There are men skilled in the use of saws and hammers. To them is assigned the carpentry work. There are men who are assigned the electrical work, the plumbing, all according to their skills. There are bricklayers, plasterers, cabinet makers, and so forth. There are also men who mix the cement, who carry the bricks who wheel the dirt. This man with one talent, even though his task was to wheel the dirt, was also needed. Without him the work could not go on. Nevertheless, he rebelled against his work. He refused to do it—not because he could not, although he may have used that as an excuse, but because he wanted to be superintendent. And unless he could have the task he wanted, he refused to do anything at all.

So it is in the kingdom. There are those who refuse to do the work assigned to them by Christ because they covet a higher place in the kingdom. They are proud. They have the devil in their hearts. The devil too was not satisfied with his place in glory. He aspired to the throne of God. But this terrible sin of pride is to be found in the hearts of men as well. They must have their way or they will not labor at all. They are not satisfied with their calling, and so they refuse to do anything.

Now, this was true in an absolute sense of the word of the wicked servant, for he was not a true citizen of the kingdom by grace. But it ought not to be forgotten that the Lord means this as a warning to us all. Within the heart of each man lurks this sin of pride, a devilish thing which comes from the pit of hell. Each one in the kingdom thinks at some time that if he cannot stand in a higher place, then he will not work at all. It is the sin which the apostle John condemns so sharply in his third epistle: "I wrote unto the church: but Diotrephes, *who loveth to have the preeminence among them*, receiveth us not" (v. 9). This is the sin of pride, and it is an abomination in the sight of God because God assigns sovereignly to each man his place and does that in harmony with the abilities with which He has endowed man. God fits the man to his place and gives the place to the man. Whatever that place may be and wherever the man is called to labor, it is a very wonderful place because it is a place in the kingdom given by grace. It is in the consciousness of this that the Psalmist sings: "For a day in thy courts is better than a thousand. I had rather be a doorkeeper in the house of my God, than to dwell in the tents of wickedness" (Ps. 84:10). It is therefore a sin that must be rooted out of our lives whenever it raises its ugly head.

The Labor of the Faithful Servants

In contrast to the sin of this wicked servant, the faithful servants labor diligently.

Notice, in the first place, that none of the faithful servants is placed over very much. It is true that one is given five talents and the other is given two talents. But the lord himself says to each: "Thou hast been faithful over a *few* things . . . " (vv. 21, 23). None of us has a very great place in the kingdom of heaven. None of us is indispensable. The Lord can easily do without any of us, and His kingodm will not be harmed in the least. We are all given only a very small place, only a few talents.

Yet these places are not alike. One receives five talents and another two. One receives a relatively large measure of responsibility, and the other not quite so much. One has comparatively large opportunities to serve Christ, another smaller opportunities. And yet each is equally important to the well-being of the whole. The kingdom needs each man's place and each man's calling. The man with two talents did not complain or rebel that he was being unjustly treated. The man with five talents did not boast of his superior position.

In the second place, each one of the faithful servants labored according to his ability. The one who was given five talents earned another five. The one who was given two talents earned another two. Each man did the very best he could with the ability given him in the place that God called him to serve.

In the third place, each labored with what belonged to his master for the benefit and advantage of his lord. These faithful servants labored in the cause of Christ that that cause might be maintained and advanced and that the kingdom might be benefited. They were not ashamed of their place or position. They were not of the opinion that their abilities went beyond their calling. They worked in whatever place they were given to work. Was their talent to stand for the cause of the truth in their shop or office? They did this with faithfulness and thanksgiving. Was their calling nothing more than to care for the needs of their children? wash their clothes and cook their meals? It seemed such a small place, but it was their calling, and they did it cheerfully and with gratitude. Was their assignment to come to society once a week and study God's Word with God's people? Was their calling to teach Sunday school? to play the organ? to comfort someone who was ill and afraid? to teach their children the truth of prayer? to visit the fatherless and widows in their afflictions?

A faithful servant does not refuse to do his calling because it seems to him to be too humble for his abilities. Rather he willingly and faithfully performs his work. And he does it knowing that all the callings in the kingdom of heaven are important for the cause of Christ. There are no great and small callings. Nor does his Lord weigh on the scales of human values. But in a wonder of grace the Lord uses the weak and humble means of His servants to bring about His kingdom and to bring nearer the day of the Lord's return.

And finally, a faithful servant fulfills his calling by grace. Those servants who labor in their assignments, labor with all kinds of sins and shortcomings. They work with a host of imperfections that cleave to them. But they confess all their sins to God and plead for forgiveness. Christ, their Master in heaven, sustains them by His grace, enables them to do their calling, gives them strength for the day, courage for the moment, grace for the trial of the hour. And above all else, Christ forgives their many sins and uses their labors in wondrous wisdom and grace to bring His kingdom to perfection.

The Punishment of the Wicked Servant

Christ's kingdom does come.

How terrible in that day is the judgment of the wicked and slothful servant! He is presented in the parable as blaming the lord for his sloth and wickedness. He said: "Lord, I knew thee that thou art an hard man, reaping where thou hast not sown, and gathering where thou hast not strawed. And I was afraid, and went and hid thy talent in the earth: lo, there thou hast that is thine."

He meant by this that the lord did not give him a good and worthwhile place in the kingdom. He really had nothing to do and it was the lord's fault. What is the use of bothering with one talent? After all, the lord reaps where he does not sow, and gathers where he does not straw. The lord can have what he wants without the efforts of his servants. And so it is the lord's fault that he did not use the talent. From this his sin of miserable pride is manifested and he showed his dissatisfaction with the place that the Lord had given him.

But now in judgment the lord also took him at his word. The servant had claimed that he really never had anything to labor with or any place of sufficient importance to occupy his attention. Now even that place is taken away from him. Now, no doubt, he would give anything if he could have even that humble and lowly place back again. But he committed a terrible sin. He rebelled against his master. He refused to fulfill his calling. And now he received his just punishment. This must serve as a very solemn warning to us that pride is an abomination in the sight of God.

The Reward for Faithful Labor

But for the faithful labor of the faithful servants there is a glorious reward. Notice that each servant receives an identical reward. There is no difference in this parable between the rewards as there was in the parable of the pounds. This is not to deny that in heaven, as the parable of the pounds taught, each man's reward will be different and will be in proportion to his faithful labor. But that is not the point here. In this case each man labored as best he could in his calling and station. And regardless of how high or low his station may have appeared to him, he received nonetheless an equal reward. It makes no difference to Christ in what station a man is placed. It only makes a difference whether he is faithful or slothful, whether that be a high or a lowly station or calling in life.

The reward of these faithful servants is, in the first place, that they are given the place which was assigned to the wicked servant. This is the place that that slothful man occupied here on earth, but he was an indolent and wicked man. Now his place is taken away and given to the faithful. The idea is that the faithful are given all the kingdom as their reward. The new heavens and the new earth are their possession. They are given the care of that new and glorious and heavenly creation, for in it and into all eternity they have their assignment and work. There they will labor diligently and faithfully in their calling before the face of God in perfection. There they will labor forever for the glory of God and the praise and honor of Jesus Christ their Master and Lord.

Hence, they enter into the joy of their Lord. This joy is the complete cup of gladness and happiness that is a full compensation for all their tears and griefs and sorrows which were their earthly lot in their difficult labors. It is a joy unsurpassed and beyond description. What a blessed comfort it is to look forward to that joy and to the sentence of Christ: "Well done, good and faithful servant; thou hast been faithful over few things, I will make thee ruler over many things: enter into the joy of thy Lord!"

30

The Final Judgment

*When the Son of man shall come in his glory, and all the holy angels
with him, then shall he sit upon the throne of his glory:*

*And before him shall be gathered all nations: and he shall separate
them one from another, as a shepherd divideth his sheep from the
goats:*

And he shall set the sheep on his right hand, but the goats on the left.

*Then shall the King say unto them on his right hand, Come, ye
blessed of my Father, inherit the kingdom prepared for you from the
foundation of the world:*

*For I was an hungred, and ye gave me meat: I was thirsty, and ye
gave me drink: I was a stranger, and ye took me in:*

*Naked, and ye clothed me: I was sick, and ye visited me: I was in
prison, and ye came unto me.*

*Then shall the righteous answer him, saying, Lord, when saw we thee
an hungred, and fed thee? or thirsty, and gave thee drink?*

*When saw we thee a stranger, and took thee in? or naked and clothed
thee?*

Or when saw we thee sick, or in prison, and came unto thee?

*And the King shall answer and say unto them, Verily I say unto you,
Inasmuch as ye have done it unto one of the least of these my brethren,
ye have done it unto me.*

*Then shall he say also unto them on the left hand, Depart from me, ye
cursed, into everlasting fire, prepared for the devil and his angels:*

*For I was an hungred, and ye gave me no meat: I was thirsty, and ye
gave me no drink:*

*I was a stranger, and ye took me not in: naked, and ye clothed me not:
sick, and in prison, and ye visited me not.*

*Then shall they also answer him, saying, Lord, when saw we thee an
hungred, or a thirst, or a stranger, or naked, or sick, or in prison, and
did not minister unto thee?*

*Then shall he answer them, saying, Verily I say unto you, Inasmuch
as ye did it not to one of the least of these, ye did it not to me.*

*And these shall go away into everlasting punishment; but the right-
eous into life eternal.*

—Matthew 25:31-46

This section is often referred to as the parable of the sheep and the goats. It is, however, evidently not a parable in the strictest sense of the word. It is not a happening taken from everyday life which is used to picture for us some spiritual reality of the kingdom of heaven. It is rather a vivid and dramatic picture of the final judgment, combined with a passing metaphor in which the separation that takes place before the great white throne is compared with the separation of sheep from goats by a shepherd.

Nevertheless, it is a fitting conclusion to the parables and especially to the last group of parables. In a sense all of Jesus' parables pointed toward the judgment. They were all pictures of the kingdom of heaven. That kingdom will finally be realized only when Christ comes again on the clouds of heaven to judge the living and the dead. But the last group of parables which Jesus spoke during the last days of His life on earth were especially concerned with the judgment day, when sentence will be executed on all men. This central theme reaches its climax in the text.

In this description of the final judgment a twofold purpose is implies. On the one hand, there is implied a warning to the wicked that they shall surely be rewarded according to their sins, even though it seems that they can sin with impunity in this life. But on the other hand, there is implied an incentive to the faithful to persevere to the end, because they are assured that their reward is certain and they need not fear the coming judgment when their cause shall be fully vindicated. The cause which they represented on earth was hated and despised; for it they suffered and died. But it was the cause of Christ, and in the day of judgment that cause shall triumph.

The General Character of the Judgment

Jesus is the Judge. He is called in the text the Son of man. This name is closely associated with His authority to judge in the Name of the Father. It was a name Jesus was especially fond of in His life on earth. The name is taken from Daniel 7:13, 14: "I saw in the night visions, and, behold, one like the Son of man came with the clouds of heaven, and came to the Ancient of days, and they brought him near before him. And there was given him dominion, and glory, and a kingdom, that all people, nations, and languages, should serve him: his dominion is an everlasting dominion, which shall not pass away, and his kingdom that which shall not be destroyed." The name therefore implies in the first place that Jesus Christ came into our flesh. He was truly the Son of man. He is the One Who dwelt among us and was like us in all things. He was born in the likeness of sinful flesh. He was not however as we are, *a* son of man; but He was, through His incarnation, *the* Son of man. He was God with us. He came into our flesh to bear the sins of all His people. He was like us in all things, sin excepted.

Yet at the same time this name is closely associated with Christ's exaltation. Because He came into our flesh and bore the sins of all

His people, He went also to the cross to suffer the full measure of the wrath of God against sin. Bearing this sin on the cross, He bore it to death. But the perfect obedience of Christ in the way of the shame and death of the cross was also the ground of His own exaltation. He was taken, through His resurrection and ascension, into the glory of heaven. There He was given a seat at the Father's right hand, where all power and authority was committed to Him. In this glorious authority He comes again to judge the living and the dead in the Name of the Father.

This is as it should be. Part of Christ's exaltation is that all judgment was given Him by the Father so that He can judge all men in the Father's Name. This is not to say that God Himself is not the Judge of all. But this judgment is accomplished through Jesus Christ Who rules and judges in His Father's Name. The exaltation of Christ will not be complete until His kingdom in heaven is finally and perfectly established, until His elect are brought into that kingdom, and until all things by His power are made new to the glory of God. But the way to this kingdom and the the final perfection of the saints is the way of judgment. The basis for this judgment is always the fundamental question: "What think ye of the Christ?"

So Christ comes again to judge in His glorified human nature. He comes as the Son of man Who was led to the throne of the Ancient of days and Who received there the authority to do all the Father's purpose. He comes, as Jesus Himself says, in the glory of the Father. This glory of the Father is the full glory of God which shines through Him. God is Himself infinitely glorious. His glory is a light unto which no man can approach. He is the infinitely perfect and holy God Whose glory is unique and transcendent above all. All this glory of the holiness of God shines in Jesus Christ. It is a glory that exposes the sin of man and lays bare his inner heart and deepest thoughts. It is a glory that puts men to shame and fills them with utter contempt for themselves. It is a glory that puts sin in its proper perspective, as sin against the Most High Majesty of God. It is a glory that tears away the mask of hypocrisy and penetrates beneath the surface of seemingly external goodness—a goodness which is only a veneer to cover the corruption that lives in the hearts of men.

This glory is also the glory of God's absolute sovereign right to judge all men. God is God. He possesses as the eternal One the sovereign and exclusive right to pass judgment on all His creatures. God is the last court, the final bar of justice, the end of all judgment beyond whose sentence there is no appeal. His judgment is always righteous judgment. No man can question it. No man can appeal higher. No man can deny the truth of God's right to judge nor God's righteous judgment. All this glory radiates through the human nature of Jesus Christ.

The text also speaks of the fact that Christ will sit on the throne of His judgment, the throne of His glory. With Him will be the angels. While it is true that both the good angels and the bad will be judged,

they are also the ministering servants of Christ. They will also be
there in the judgment. They will in some way participate in the
judgment and serve the Judge Who sits upon the great white throne.
From this throne will issue the sentence of God. And Christ on this
throne will be revealed as King over all. It may be that on earth
wicked men denied this. It is surely true that they made man their
king and denied the Lord of glory. But in the judgment there will be
no more question. Christ is King—the King of kings and the Lord of
lords. As sovereign King over all the works of God He judges.
Finally, irrevocably, unappealably, in strictest conformity to the
highest principles of judgment, He will pass the sentence of the
Father.

What a great and terrible day that will be! About that throne will
be gathered all nations. This does not deny the fact that all men as
individuals will be present there. All men who ever lived will be
gathered before Christ's throne. Young and old, infants and gray-
haired patriarchs, men and women, angels and devils, black and
white, from every land, from every dispensation, from all time
—they will all be there. Before the judgment seat of Christ all men
must appear. But Christ Himself emphatically speaks of all nations.
And this is important. Not only will individuals be judged, but
nations will be judged, nations in their organic unity. A man will
surely be judged according to his own works. But his own works will
be judged and weighed in his organic connection with the nation of
which he was a part. In unity with his nation, in the line of continued
generations, in the circumstances of his life and the place that God
gave him in the world, in connection with his own tribe or tongue, in
this way will judgment come to him.

On the one hand, by the time Christ will return to judgment, the
gospel will have been preached to all nations. That is why in the
judgment day the question will have to be answered: "What did you
do with Christ?" Nevertheless, many nations in years gone by never
heard the gospel. This does not mean that they will not be judged,
that there is no ground of judgment, that they are without excuse;
but it does mean that they will be judged as nations. Nor does this
mean that all nations hear the gospel to the same extent. Some
nations are Christianized through the influences of the gospel.
Other nations only receive the gospel on their periphery. The gospel
strikes at the edge, so the speak, while the nation as a whole remains
in paganism. But the nations will then also be judged. All men will be
without excuse. But because of this, Tyre and Sidon will rise up in
judgment against the Jews of Jesus' day. Ninevah will arise and
condemn Capernaum and Bethsaida. This is because *nations* are
judged.

The Separation of the Wicked and the Righteous

Jesus speaks of the fact that these nations will be divided before
Him. In this connection, He refers to the figure of a shepherd and

his flocks. During the day, while the flocks are out in the pasture, the sheep and the goats are together, feed together, and are watered together. So it is with the people who are gathered before Christ's throne. In this life saints and sinners live together. In fact, they not only share life together, they share also the sunshine and rain, the good things of God's creation. They even share together in the preaching of the gospel, in the various administrations of the Church. Whatever their personal attitude toward these things may be, they share in them together. But at night, when the flocks are returned to the corrals and barns, the shepherd separates the sheep from the goats.

So it is also in the day of judgment. Before sentence is actually pronounced, the saints and the sinners are separated before the judgment seat of Christ. The righteous are put on the right hand of Christ, the wicked on His left. It is possible that this may literally happen in the judgment. But the whole scene has symbolic significance. Christ was exalted to the Father's right hand. The right hand of God is a *position* of authority, in which position Christ is given the authority to rule. The fact that the saints are placed at Christ's right hand is therefore significant. The meaning is that in the perfected kingdom of Christ, the elect are not only given the kingdom as their inheritance but are destined to rule with Christ as princes. The wicked are placed at Christ's left hand and are destined not to rule with Christ at all.

This separation takes place in actual fact. Already the separation was principally realized in time. While it is true that the wicked and the righteous share together in the good things of life and are mixed together here below, the fact remains that separation is already spiritually accomplished. Scripture tells us that even now in life the curse of the Lord is in the house of the wicked, while He blesses the habitation of the just. Although the wicked and the righteous have all the things of this creation in common, there is one thing they do not share: the grace of God.

In the second place, this separation becomes physical at the moment of death. When the wicked and the righteous die, physical separation takes place, even before Christ comes back in judgment. The wicked go immediately to the place of everlasting torment, while the righteous go to Abraham's bosom. This takes place even while their bodies go to the grave. And this separation must already be interpreted as an act of judgment.

In the third place, there is also separation before Christ's throne. The judgment takes place after the resurrection. But the resurrection of the bodies of all men is also an expression of judgment. The bodies of all men carry in them in the resurrection the sentence of Christ. The wicked are raised in bodies that are adapted to live in everlasting fire. But the righteous are raised with bodies which are immortal, incorruptible, glorified, and perfectly adapted to live in heaven. And so, before the sentence of Christ sounds, there is already judgment expressed by God. The sheep are separated from the goats.

God's Good Pleasure the Basis of Judgment

While the text speaks of the fact that judgment is meted out on the basis of works, we must not be left with the impression that works are the final criterion of judgment. There are some who quote this text in proof of the contention that the good works of the righteous merit heaven. But nothing could be further from the truth. The text emphasizes very strongly and in more ways than one that in the final analysis judgment is rooted in God's sovereign good pleasure. With respect to the saints there are many elements which speak of this.

In the first place, the saints are called "sheep." This term is very common in Scripture in both the Old and New Testaments. But the term is always a word which refers to the fact that the saints are God's elect. The saints were not once goats and changed somehow into sheep; they are sheep eternally. They are God's sheep because Christ is the Shepherd and He gives His life for the sheep. They are eternally chosen by God as sheep, and are, before God's loving eyes, the sheep of His pasture. In time these sheep are brought into the sheepfold of Christ through the preaching of the gospel. But they were sheep before they were called. Jesus Himself speaks of this when He says, according to the apostle John: "Other sheep I have which are not of this fold . . . " (John 10:16).

In the second place, the saints are called "the blessed of the Father." This is, after all, the fundamental basis for judgment. They are the ones whom God has chosen to bless. Was it because they were better than others? Certainly not. The saints themselves humbly confess this in the judgment. The reason is to be found only in the good pleasure of God. God sovereignly and in amazing grace chose to bless them.

In the third place they are called the righteous. Now this righteousness is certainly also the basis for their judgment. But is this righteousness their own? Is it a righteousness which they earned for themselves by their good works? Once again, the saints themselves deny it. This righteousness with which they are clothed is the righteousness of Christ Jesus their Lord. It is the righteousness of God's eternal mercy; the righteousness of Christ's perfect obedience. It is a righteousness which is the clothing of the saints—not by works but by faith in Jesus Christ. This righteousness which is freely given to them is the basis for all their blessedness.

Finally, the text speaks of the fact that the inheritance of the kingdom of heaven is one which is prepared for the saints from before the foundations of the world. God prepared this glorious inheritance even before they were born and before they had done good or evil. He prepared this inheritance for them from the world's beginning. He prepared this inheritance *for them.* It was before they could earn it that this inheritance was made ready because they were not as yet living in God's world.

All these things clearly teach that Jesus means to emphasize that the sentence which makes the saints blessed is a sentence which is rooted in God's eternal good pleasure.

The same thing is true of the wicked. It is true that they are judged on the basis of their works. But this does not alter the fact that judgment for them is rooted in God.

In the first place, they are called goats. Surely this does not mean that once they were sheep, but that they changed into goats. This is impossible. They were always goats. And the meaning is obviously that they are the reprobate, distinguished from the sheep by the eternal will of a sovereign God.

In the second place, they are called "the cursed" in the text. Surely it is true that this curse of God comes on them in the way of their sin. But it nevertheless remains a fact that God did not once bless them, and then change His blessing into a curse. They were cursed in God's eternal decree. They were cursed throughout all their life. They are cursed in the day of judgment. They are judged therefore as the sovereign execution of God's decree and as the accomplishment of God's purpose.

The Just Basis of Judgment

Nevertheless, there is also just basis for the sentence of Christ. And this just basis is to be found, according to the text, in the works which each man performs.

This does not mean that works have merit; but it does mean that when the final sentence of Christ is pronounced in that great day of days, there is a perfect display of the righteous justice of God. The wicked are sentenced to hell in strictest justice. They go to hell, not because they are reprobate but because they deserve hell by their sins. They were terribly wicked. They deserved the severe penalty inflicted on them. God accomplishes the decree of reprobation and His own sovereign purpose with the wicked in the way of their sin. No man can say in the judgment that he receives what he did not deserve. God must be and will be fully justified. And this justification of Almighty God is manifested because their judgment is on the basis of their sin.

The righteous, on the other hand, are revealed in time as God's people. God's love toward them was shed abroad in their hearts. They lived in the world as those who belonged to the party of God's covenant. They had the grace of God within them, and by the power of this grace they manifested good works in life. This does not mean that they were perfect. But it does mean that they repented of their sins and confessed the Name of their God in the midst of a world of sin and darkness.

So, in the text, a very fundamental work of grace is described.
The most basic question in the judgment is always: "What did you
do with Christ?" This is the sole question. On the basis of the answer
to this question all men are judged. But, of course, Christ was in
heaven for all but a very few brief years. And so the question is:
"What did you do with Christ's saints?" This is a very beautiful idea.
Christ and His saints are one body. They are united together in
perfect union. What is done to the saints therefore is done to Christ
Himself.

We must be careful that we emphasize this. It is not uncommon
for this passage of Scripture to be quoted in support of a certain kind
of social gospel. Men claim that his gospel enjoins upon us the
obligation to do good to all men. They claim that the gospel teaches
that the essence of the Christian life is to put forth strenuous effort
to solve the social problems of the day. They interpret this passage to
mean therefore that the Christian has social obligations and a social
calling. But they overlook the fact that very emphatically and point-
edly in the text Jesus is talking about what both the righteous and the
wicked do to His saints. In verse 40 we read: "And the king shall
answer and say unto them, Verily I say unto you, Inasmuch as ye
have done it unto one of the least of these *my brethren*, ye have done it
unto me." While therefore it is true that the people of God have the
calling in life to love their neighbor as themselves, this must never be
interpreted in any way in terms of a general social calling. And this
passage with which the Lord concluded His ministry has nothing to
do with the social gospel which is so popular in the pulpits of the land
today.

Thus the people of God showed that they loved Christ. When He
was hungry they fed Him. When He was thirsty they gave Him a
drink of cold water. When He was a stranger they took Him into
their homes and made Him part of their family. When He was naked
they clothed Him with their clothing. When He was sick and in
prison they came to Him and visited Him and comforted Him. They
did this to Christ because they did this to the least of Christ's
brethren.

This implies several important truths. In the first place, this is the
highest possible manifestation of grace in the hearts of the people of
God. These are good works par excellence. These works are far and
away more important then the mighty deeds of which men boast.
The righteous do not often perform works of earth-shaking significance. They do not move nations and set the world upside down.
They do not do the mighty deeds of which men boast in the
conquest of time and space. Rather, they feed and clothe and comfort the saints. And truly, this is far more important.

In the second place, these good works are not the superficial
works of external piety. They are deeply and profoundly rooted in a
heart filled with love. The saints love God and love Christ. And this
love of God is revealed in their love for Christ's brethren.

In the third place, this work of the saints is a direct fulfillment of the command of Christ. Christ warned His disciples that they could not be His friends unless they learned that the highest of Christian duty is to serve one another. Only a few days after Jesus spoke these words He washed the feet of His disciples at the last supper and told them: "Know ye what I have done to you? Ye call me Master and Lord: and ye say well; for so I am. If I then, your Lord and Master, have washed your feet; ye also ought to wash one another's feet. For I have given you an example, that ye should do as I have done to you. Verily, verily, I say unto you, The servant is not greater than his Lord; neither he that is sent greater than he that sent him. If ye know these things, happy are ye if ye do them" (John 13:12b-17).

This is so important because when we learn to be servants to our fellow saints we have learned the fundamental lesson of grace: that each of us is the least of all the saints because we are unworthy sinners, saved by grace alone.

In the fourth place, this is a manifestation of a love which we have not for the world, but for God's kingdom and cause. It is a love that is unflinching in the day of danger, courageous in the day of temptation, unyielding in the hour of suffering. It is a love that endures to the very end.

For all these reasons, it is really no wonder that the righteous deny having done these things. There are probably two reasons for this. On the one hand, when they stand before the holiness of God, all they are conscious of is the awfulness of their own sins. They immediately respond and say, "We never did this. We only sinned throughout our life. We never helped Christ. We never showed any love for Him." The people of God are amazed that Christ could say this of them. But they are assured by a voice of unspeakably tender love that this was the fruit of grace in them, and that indeed they did these things. They are called to gaze on the mercy and love of their Father Who worked these things in them.

On the other hand, this denial of the saints is probably indicative of the fact that the saints—though they did these things—were not conscious of them because a good work which is genuinely a good work is done with complete self-forgetfulness. Those works which are good are only those done to the glory of God. If the child of God does works for himself or for this own glory, they cease to be good. Those works therefore which are genuinely good in the sight of God are works of which the child of God himself is not even conscious.

But the very opposite is true of the wicked. They never fed and clothed Christ. They never made Him a member of their family when He was homeless. They never showed any compassion toward Him nor did they visit Him and comfort Him. They hated Christ with a deep and implacable hatred. They nailed Him to the cross when He was on earth. And when He was beyond their reach in heaven, they shook their fists in His face and denied His truth and crucified Him afresh. They would have killed Him again even after

He had risen from the dead if only they could have put their hands
on Him once again. They did all they could to oppose Him and His
cause and His kingdom.

Nevertheless they tried to justify themselves. They do not mean to
say in their reply that they did actually help Christ. They know full
well that they did not. But they try to cover their sin with their own
hypocrisies. This they did already on earth. While they lived on
earth they tried to cover up their sins with a semblance of good
works. They tried to cover up the evils in their hearts with a veneer
of being pleasing in God's sight. That is why you will hear them say in
the judgment day: "Lord, have we not prophesied in thy name? and
in thy name have cast out devils? and in thy name done many
wonderful works?" (Matt. 7:22).

Nevertheless the viewpoint is somewhat different here. They
know that they never did the things which Christ commanded. And
they know too that they cannot lie before Christ as He sits upon His
throne. It is for this reason that they try to justify themselves by
saying that they never had opportunity to help Christ. This is the
force of their argument: "When saw we thee an hungred, or athirst,
or a stranger, or naked, or sick, or in prison, and did not minister
unto thee?" Perhaps they did not do what Christ said, but they
argued that they never had the chance. They never saw Christ. They
never were given the occasion to do anything which Christ says they
should have done. They try to blame Christ for it all. And, although
they do not dare to say it in so many words, they nevertheless mean
to say that Christ does not really know what they would have done.

But none of this is true. Christ's saints were on earth. And these
saints belonged to Christ Himself. The wicked showed their deepest
attitude toward Christ by their attitude toward His people. They had
the opportunity to help the saints. This they never did. In fact, they
did quite the contrary. The saints came with the gospel of Jesus
Christ. But they hated the saints, caused them endless suffering and
grief, killed them all the day long and took their place away in the
world, tried to blot out their name from under heaven, and silenced
the gospel which they preached. This was their terrible crime, for in
doing this to the saints they did this to Christ Himself Who was
always with the saints and in them. They could not conceal their
attitude toward the Christ of glory when they came into the presence
of God's people. They revealed their hatred and filled the cup on
iniquity.

The Punishment of the Goats

And so the punishment of the wicked is just. They are driven from
the face of Christ and from the presence of God. Their punishment
is the punishment of everlasting fire. There they will remain
forever. This fire is the fire prepared for the devil and his angels.
While the wicked were in the world, they allied themselves with the
devil in opposition to God. They refused to serve God or to enter the

kingdom. They persistently joined with the devil in trying to defeat Christ's kingdom. And now their lot is with the devil and his angels whom they serve. This is just and in keeping with their own sinful choice.

But God is justified. While they were on the earth they seemed to succeed in destroying the kingdom of Christ. But now in the judgment it is manifest that they failed utterly. The sovereign God Who hates sin and loves righteousness, Who delights only in holiness, is fully justified in sending them to perdition. This is their just reward. And this just punishment is universally manifested and must be universally acknowledged. They are condemned before all the world. And they themselves, be it from the depths of hell, have to admit that they have coming to them only what they justly deserve.

The Blessing of the Righteous

But the righteous are supremely blessed. They are called into the fellowship of God. "Come ye blessed of my Father. . . . " No sweeter words will ever sound in all history than these. No words will more greatly thrill the hearts of those saints who appear before the judgment seat of Christ than the words of their Savior calling them to the everlasting fellowship of the Father.

Their reward is the inheritance of the kingdom. They are given that kingdom as their possession; and in it they will rule with Christ forever and ever. They were hated on the earth. The world was not worthy of them. The things of the world were taken from them. They were slandered and maligned, killed all the day long. They were despised and mocked—all because they mentioned the Name of the Lord their God. Their cause seemed to go down to defeat time and time again. The wicked seemed to triumph over them and to gain victories by means of their crimes. But now the righteous inherit the kingdom. All their strife and warfare is over. Their heads rest forever in the bosom of the Father. Their swords are laid aside, for a reed of victory is given to them. The helmets which they wore in the battle for the faith are now useless, for to them is given the crown of life. The shouts of the battlefield are silenced, and the songs of Moses and the Lamb come forth from their hearts.

But in this also God is justified. God gave them His cause to confess. God called them to represent His Name and kingdom. And God gave them the grace to do this with meekness and fear. Now that they are gathered into His kingdom, they are impressed with nothing so much as the fact that it was all of their God. They deserved nothing. To God alone belongs the glory.

What is then the conclusion of the matter?

Help the saints, even the least of them; for in so doing you serve the Lord Christ.

Be faithful in the kingdom, even in its most bitter struggles; presently the kingdom will be yours.

Look forward to the day of judgment, not with fear and trembling

but with eagerness and hope. You shall not be put to shame. Your
cause—which is the cause of Christ—shall be vindicated before all
the world.